ireland
in crisis

a study in
capitalist colonial
undevelopment

raymond crotty

BRANDON

First published in 1986
Brandon Book Publishers Ltd.
Dingle, Co. Kerry, Ireland
and 51 Washington Street,
Dover, New Hampshire 03820, U.S.A.

Crotty, Raymond
  Ireland in crisis: a study in capitalist
  colonial undevelopment.
  1. Ireland — Economic conditions
  I. Title
  330.9415'07   HC260.5

  ISBN 0-86322-083-5

Cover design by Brendan Foreman
Typeset by Printset and Design Ltd., Dublin
Printed by The Leinster Leader, Naas.

Contents

Ireland in Crisis: List of Tables, Diagrams and Maps

Preface

This book has been written for the plain people of Ireland. It tries to explain why for so long so many of us have been denied a livelihood in Ireland. Millions who could not get a livelihood starved to death in the early nineteenth century. Then the Irish learned to emigrate and, for more than a century, almost half those born here did so. Now with emigration on this scale no longer possible, those denied a livelihood back up in an ever-growing and hopeless mass of unemployment.

My first perception of these problems came many years ago when farming in Kilkenny. There an awareness grew of the sharp conflict that exists between the interests of the individual operator of Irish land and the interests of Irish society: the individual benefits from minimizing inputs into the land while society requires output to be maximised. I tried to analyze that conflict and to show how it could be reconciled in *Irish Agricultural Production: Its Volume and Structure,* published 20 years ago.

But — to paraphrase slightly — what does he of Ireland know who only Ireland knows? I had opportunity over the following decade to observe conditions in a score of countries in the Caribbean, South America, Africa and South and Southeast Asia. In all of these there was the same failure to mobilize resources that is so obvious in Ireland. It became clear that the failure of the Irish to get a livelihood in their own country is part of a much larger problem. It is part of the heritage of capitalist colonialism; or of the vast, spreading and worsening poverty of all the countries of the Third World which, like Ireland, are former colonies of the capitalist system. Some of these — the countries of South America — have been independent for 160 years. I endeavoured to explain how this colonial heritage has precluded effective use of a major Third World resource — its grazing land and the animals on it — in *Cattle, Economics and Development.*

It now seems timely to draw together the lessons of several years farming in Ireland, of working as a consultant/advisor in a score of Third World countries and of considerable research and cogitation on these matters in an attempt to explain to my fellow Irish why so many of us have been, and continue to be, denied a livelihood in Ireland. But if that were all, this would be merely another academic exercise. Whatever merit the work has lies in its identification of means of ending Ireland's heritage of capitalist colonialism and of providing a livelihood for all the Irish in Ireland. These means, it is right to say, do not involve more of the effort and sacrifice so regularly called for, so freely given, and so fruitlessly and appallingly wasted. The only sacrifice this book suggests is the critical examination — and preferably the discarding — of habits of thought that have been ingrained by centuries of colonialism.

The problem itself, the readership addressed and the shortcomings of the author have determined the book's structure. The body of the book comprises eight chapters, the first six of which analyze the problem with the last two suggesting and discussing means of resolving it. Some may wish to go no further. But it is the writer's conviction that an adequate understanding of the denial of a livelihood to so many of the Irish can only be understood in the context of the much broader problem of Third World undevelopment, of which that denial is an integral part. That context is sketched in three lengthy appendices.

I very gratefully acknowledge financial assistance from Emmet O'Connell which has made publication possible. I thank my colleagues, Myra O'Regan, Elaine and David McColl, Alan Kelly and Gabriel Mathews, of the Statistics and Operations Research Laboratory in Trinity College for teaching this old dog new tricks of word processing that greatly facilitated the production of successive drafts. I also thank Pauline Kelly, who found time from her onerous duties as a departmental secretary to give much help in producing those drafts.

Raymond Crotty

Systems Development Programme,
Trinity College,
Dublin.

*Felix qui potuit est
rerum cognoscere causam.*

Virgil

I

Ireland in Crisis

Measuring Achievement

Average Irish[1] incomes rank 27th among the 126 countries with populations in excess of one million recorded by the World Bank.[2] Irish incomes have almost doubled in real terms during the past 30 years.[3] Ireland also scores well by most non-monetary criteria of well-being. Income inequalities are less in Ireland than in most countries; levels of literacy, nutrition and health are high, as is life expectancy. The incidence of disease and of child and infant mortality is low.[4] The 26 Counties area that comprises the Republic of Ireland, which is the main concern of this work, has not experienced a major war on its territory for 300 years, and it has been free from serious civil strife for 60 years.

These conditions, which by world-wide standards are not disagreeable for its residents, are not the most appropriate criteria for assessing the performance of the Irish polity. Irish living standards have been determined, to a unique extent among countries now listed as independent, by factors beyond the control of the polity. In fact, they have been determined almost entirely, for some 140 years, by living standards in neighbouring Britain and in other English-speaking countries, and by the outward mobility of the Irish to those countries. The appropriate criterion for the performance of the Irish polity under these circumstances is the degree to which it has provided a livelihood for its people at living standards determined by those obtainable elsewhere and by the ability and willingness of the Irish to emigrate in order to obtain those living standards.

No more than half those born in Ireland (26 Counties) since 1821 and surviving childhood have got a living there. For the first 30 years of this 160-year period, before the channels of emigration were open and clear, very many of those who failed to get a living in Ireland starved to death. Many did so during the chronic famine conditions of the 1820s and 1830s. A million people, or one eight of the island's total population, perished by famine or famine-related diseases in the 1840s.[5] With the opening up of the channels of emigration, few Irish remained to starve after 1851. Almost half those born and surviving childhood have emigrated from Ireland since 1871, when registration of births and deaths became compulsory.[6] The rate at which people have emigrated has hardly changed since the country became independent in 1922. Net emigration between 1911, the last pre-independence census year, and 1961 was 45% of the number of births registered.[7]

A comparison of the workforces now and in the past, in Ireland and in neighbouring Britain, provides another measure of Ireland's failure. The country's workforce was 38% of Britain's in 1841. It has since declined by more than half while Britain's has more than trebled, so that the Republic's workforce is now only 7% of its neighbour's. The number at work in the Republic has continued to decline since 1911, while that of Northern Ireland has increased. The 26 Counties' share of the number getting a livelihood in Ireland has declined from 77% in 1841 to 66% now (see Table 1.1). It is, in effect, less than at any time during the past 250 years.[8] This is a period during which the world's population has increased sixfold.[9]

Responsibility for this loss of livelihood could be attributed to the colonial British power for 100 of the last 160-odd years. But Ireland has been politically independent for over 60 years and, as noted above, the failure of people to secure a livelihood has been almost as pronounced in post-independence as in pre-independence years.

Table 1.1
The Workforces of Britain and Ireland: 1841, 1911 and the 1970s

Period	Britain	Ireland			26 Counties as % of	
		26 Cos.	6 Cos.	Total	Britain	Ireland
1841	7,094	2,715	797	3,512	38.3	77.3
1911	17,758	1,274	543	1,817	7.2	70.1
1970-80 Total workforce	25,235	1,156	602	1,758	7.0	65.8
Employed workforce	24,254	1,079	555	1,634	6.7	66.0

Note: Figures in thousands. Data for 1970-80 are annual averages over the period.
Source: BPP 1843 (433) XXIV; BPP 1844 (587) XXVII; BPP 1912-13 (Cd 6663) CXVIII; BPP 1913 (Cd 6896) LXXX; BPP 1913 (Cd 7018) LXXVIII; UK, *Annual Abstract of Statistics,* 1982; Central Bank of Ireland, *Annual Reports,* 1972-82.

Table 1.2
Public Sector Borrowing and the Irish Economy, 1953-1982

Average Annual	National Income (£ mn.)	Balance of Payments Deficits (£ mn.)	Public Authority Borrowing (£ mn.)	Cost of Servicing Outstanding Debt (£ mn.)	Servicing Debt as % Nat. Inc. (Col. 5 ÷ Col. 2) %	Balance of Pays. as % Nat. Inc. (Col. 3 ÷ Col. 2) %
(1)	(2)	(3)	(4)	(5)	(6)	(7)
1953-7	451.2	10.6	34.1	18.3	4.06	2.35
1958-62	557.9	4.5	34.2	25.1	4.50	0.81
1963-7	808.1	19.2	57.3	41.1	5.09	2.38
1968-72	1,341.5	54.0	108.8	83.3	6.21	4.03
1973-7	3,109.6	150.7	527.5	312.1	10.04	4.85
1978-82	7,185.8	1,046.1	1,829.2	1,035.7	14.41	14.56

Source: Ireland, *National Income and Expenditure*, various years 1960-81; Central Bank of Ireland, *Annual Report*, 1983.

Public Debt

The nature and extent of the debt. National debt expansion has been the keystone of Irish economic policy since 1948. The creation of public debt makes possible a greater level of government activity and of government demand than would be sustained by taxation or by the sale of government services. Borrowing makes possible a level of government expenditure relative to Gross National Product (GNP) that is much higher in Ireland than in most countries. This, in Ireland's case, has prevented a decline in the workforce since the late 1950s. However, over the long run, the accumulation of debt also causes the growth of public debt service charges. In Ireland these now absorb a higher proportion of GNP than in any other country.

For decades the conventional wisdom in Ireland was that public debt, held for the most part internally, was economically unimportant. Now, however, the public debt is recognized as of extreme economic importance. Nevertheless, much obfuscation persists about its nature. It is, in particular, suggested that government indebtedness on a serious scale is of recent origin in Ireland; that Irish public indebtedness, particularly to foreigners, is less than that of major Third World borrowers; and that foreign indebtedness relative to export earnings is lower in Ireland than in other major debtor countries. These points need clarification.

Table 1.2 shows the role of public sector (i.e. government and local authority) borrowing by five year periods since 1953, when the official series, *National Income and Expenditure,* began. Public authority borrowing has been on a large scale relative to national income throughout (Cols. 4 and 2). The balance of payments deficit, as a proportion of national income, grew closely in line with the cost of debt service (Cols. 7 and 6), except in the period 1958-62. The initial impact of the policy changes introduced by the *Programme for Economic Expansion* (Pr. 4796), which redirected public expenditure away from houses, schools and hospitals and towards hotels, offices and factories, was a temporary improvement in the balance of payments in 1958-62. This policy impact was, of its nature, shortlived (see below, Chapter 5).

Irish government expenditure is exceptionally high relative to Gross Domestic Product (GDP). This is made possible only by a correspondingly high level of government borrowing (Table 1.3).

Few governments borrow as high a proportion of their funds as Ireland's does. This heavy borrowing, over a protracted period, accounts for the exorbitant cost of servicing public debt in Ireland (Table 1.4).

Ireland chooses to categorize itself as an 'industrialized' country. It is therefore not included by the International Monetary Fund (IMF) in the 20 major non-oil, Third World debtor countries, the foreign borrowings of which are the cause of present (1986) international instability and concern

Table 1.3
Overall Deficit in Central Government Operations, as a Percentage of GDP for Certain Countries* in 1979

World	2.95	Ireland	12.32
Industrial countries	2.97	Liberia	13.98
USA	1.56	Mauritius	14.21
United Kingdom	5.45	Tanzania	15.41
Argentina	2.59	Egypt	15.75
Brazil	0.23	Guyana	17.68
Mexico	3.32	Panama	12.97

(*includes all countries where the deficit is relatively greater than in Ireland).

Source: International Monetary Fund, *Government Finance Statistics Yearbook,* Vol. VI, 1982, pp. 52-3.

Table 1.4
National Debt Interest Payments as a Percentage of Total Central Government Expenditure and of GDP, 1979

	1974	1979[a]	Government Expenditure as % GDP	National Debt Interest Payments as % GDP (Col. 2 and Col. 3)
	(1)	(2)	(3)	(4)
World	5.49	7.21	38.15	2.75
Asia	6.93	8.28	25.57	2.12
USA	5.64	7.07	33.74	2.39
United Kingdom	7.88	10.52	45.68	4.81
Ireland	8.53	13.01	58.83	7.65
Brazil	5.39	19.75	29.96	5.92
Singapore	7.03	14.46	22.77	3.29
Ghana	8.67	12.23	n.a.	n.a.
Argentina	1.96	10.10	29.00	2.93
Mexico	8.34	9.70	19.57	1.90

Note (a): The most recent year for which the data for Ireland were available on an internationally comparable basis.

Source: IMF *Government Finance Statistics Yearbook* Vol. VI, 1982, pp. 49-51; Vol. VII, 1983, p. 51.

(Table 1.5). Ireland's external debt, which is 1.84% of that of the 20 major Third World borrowers, is relatively greater than its GNP, which is only 1.57% of the combined GNPs of the major borrowers. Reflecting Ireland's relatively larger external indebtedness and the fact that most of it has been incurred in the recent years of high interest rates, the proportion of total product paid abroad to service foreign held debts, 2.21% in 1981, is also higher in Ireland than in the major Third World borrowing countries. Moreover, while factor income paid abroad has been growing also in the major Third World borrowing countries, Ireland has traditionally had a net inward factor income flow and only in 1976 began, like the major Third World debtors, to incur a net outflow.

Table 1.5
Particulars of the 20 Largest Third World Borrowing Countries and of Ireland (data for 1981 unless otherwise stated)

	Twenty Major Borrowers	Ireland	Ireland as % of Major Borrowers
	(US$ mn.)	(US$ mn.)	%
GNP	1,012,137	15,877	1.57
Exports	189,743	8,711	4.59
Balance of payments deficit	46,699	2,387	5.11
Cumulated balance of payments deficits:			
1973-7	155,100	1,561	1.01
1978-82	395,800	7,636	1.93
Net factor income paid abroad	24,341	537	2.21
Total external debt	447,000	8,234	1.84
Population (millions)	625.59	3.44	0.55

Note: The 20 countries were: Mexico, Brazil, Argentina, Chile, Peru, Ecuador, Colombia, Korea, Philippines, Thailand, Malaysia, Greece, Morocco, Egypt, Yugoslavia, Israel, Turkey, Portugal, Romania and Hungary.

Source: IMF, *Annual Report, 1983*; IMF, *International Finance Statistical Yearbook, 1983*; Ireland, *National Income and Expenditure,* various years; Central Bank of Ireland, *Annual Report, 1983.*

It is sometimes soporifically suggested that the most appropriate criterion of the economic significance of Ireland's large and rapidly growing foreign debt is the size of the foreign debt relative to the value of current exports.

Thus, Dr Noel Whelan, former Secretary of the Department of Economic Planning and Development and current Vice President of the European Investment Bank, was reported as saying in Dublin: 'On the criteria which count, export earnings relative to debt interest, foreign exchange earnings, foreign debt profile, Ireland ranks very strongly vis-a-vis many other countries'.[10] This is as misleading as the 1960s and 1970s orthodoxy that internally held public debt was unimportant. It overlooks the extent to which the value of Ireland's major indigenous exports, meat and dairy produce, is determined politically by the EEC, with little relevance to market conditions. It also overlooks the extent to which the value of exports by new enclave industries is overstated, through the practice of transfer pricing, in order to minimize the tax liabilities of the multinational companies that operate those industries (below, Chapter 6). Finally, this interpretation assumes that the export earnings of foreign-owned enclave industries are available, if necessary, to service foreign debt. In fact, these cannot even be taxed. Any attempt to appropriate them to service foreign debt would result in these highly mobile industries disappearing even more rapidly than they first appeared.

Ireland's foreign debt was less than the value of its exports in 1981, while the combined foreign debts of the 20 major Third World debtor countries was more than twice as great as the combined value of their exports (Table 1.5). This, however, reflects Ireland's greater dependence, as a small economy, on foreign trade, rather than the scale of its foreign indebtedness or its ability to service that indebtedness. Ireland's GNP in 1981 was less than one-third of the average GNP of the 20 major borrowers. Its exports were 55% of its GNP while the major borrowers' exports were, on average, only 19% of their's. Given Ireland's much larger balance of payments deficits and the more rapid growth of those deficits, Ireland's foreign indebtedness relative to export earnings will, in a short time, be as large as those of the 20 major Third World debtor countries. By 1984, the government's foreign debt was 20% greater than the value of Irish exports. When, like that of the 20 major Third World borrowers, Ireland's foreign debt becomes equal to twice the annual value of its exports, then its foreign indebtedness relative to its GNP will be three times greater than that of those debtor countries. Its financial position is already, in all other respects, considerably worse than theirs. Per head of population, Irish foreign debt is already three times greater than that of the major borrowers.

Irish academic economists, in the 1950s, 1960s and 1970s, myopically propounded the view that the service of public debt had no adverse economic consequences as long as the debt was held internally. They argued that taxation to service internally held debt was merely a transfer of resources within the country and involved no loss to the economy. This simplistic view overlooked the serious deterrent effect on producers of taxes to service debt held by rentiers. If taxes are used to service rentier-held debt rather

7

than to pay for public services, producers seek to compensate by raising their prices. If they cannot raise prices, they may cease production. In the one case, taxes drive up prices; in the other, they depress output. In either case, taxes to service accumulating public debt exacerbate the underlying structural inefficiency and uncompetitiveness of the Irish economy, and cause the balance of payments deficits to increase in line with service charges.[11]

The exhaustion of credit. Sustained government borrowing inevitably accelerates. This is partly because the economy becomes increasingly dependent on the stimulus injected by government expenditure in excess of what the government removes in taxation. It is also because of the need to borrow funds to cover the expanding cost of servicing the accumulated debt. That cost in Ireland increased 3.6 times relative to national income between 1953-57 and 1978-82. With equal inevitability, sustained public borrowing spills over into balance of payments deficits and into accelerated foreign borrowing to finance those deficits. These large, accelerating balance of payments deficits are due to the sustained borrowing of Irish governments since 1948. According to T.K. Whitaker, Chancellor of the National University of Ireland, sometime Governor of the Central Bank and sometime Secretary of the Department of Finance (in which last two capacities he was more responsible than any other person for Ireland's unique public indebtedness) these deficits have 'misused and almost exhausted our foreign borrowing potential'.[12]

The doubt now cast on the state's ability to continue to borrow abroad on a large and expanding scale has changed fundamentally the economic role of government. Irish governments, since 1948, have first determined the amount they wished to spend, and then the amount they were prepared to raise by taxation. The public sector borrowing requirement (PSBR) emerged as a residual. Now, however, the PSBR is determined more and more by reference to the continued willingness of foreign creditors — in a world atmosphere of increasing financial uncertainty — to lend to the Irish state.

The compelling need to borrow more, either at home or abroad, reduces the willingness of foreign creditors to lend. This occurs in a world situation where, in any case, foreign creditors are becoming increasingly sceptical of the wisdom of lending to governments with an insatiable need for funds and a limitless capacity to use them unproductively. Without the backing of foreign credits which, unlike domestic credits, can be witheld at any time, Irish government promises to pay will literally be worth no more than the paper on which they are printed. Irish governments will be able to acquire only those goods and services and to make those transfer payments that they can pay for with a fixed money supply; which implies balancing government expenditure with government revenue from taxes and the sale of goods and services. Without the backing of foreign credits, attempts by government to continue to pay with promissory notes would lead to hyperinflation; with prices doubling annually, weekly or even hourly. The inevitable need to 'balance the books' will cause an initial reduction in domestic demand of about 26%.[13] That large drop in demand will subsequently have a multiplier effect as non-government firms and households are forced to cut back their expenditure in response to the reduction in incomes from government. The ultimate outcome will be drastic: demand and the level of economic activity could easily drop to half the present level; if, that is, the economy and the polity manage to survive the trauma in any form recognizably similar to the present.

The Political Context

The crisis associated with Ireland's exploding public debt develops within a fundamentally changing political context. The sources of political change are, firstly, demography and secondly, Northern Ireland.

Population growth. An increase in Ireland's extraordinarily low marriage rate from 4 per 1,000 at the end of the nineteenth century to 6.8 per 1,000 in 1971-79 has been an aspect of the raising of living standards under those exogenous influences already noted.[14] This increase in marriage rates has offset the decline in births per family so that the Irish crude birth rate has been well maintained, giving a continuing and even rising population growth rate.[15]

All of Ireland's natural population growth was in the past removed by emigration. This is no longer the case. Consequently, the population is now growing for the first time since the 1840s. It is growing faster than the population of any other European country; and even more rapidly than it did in the pre-Great Famine decades.[16]

The sudden, dramatic termination of emigration, with the consequent increase in population, has not been a matter of choice for Irish people. Emigration on a demographically significant scale is no longer possible. The world's empty spaces are filled. The empire that Irish emigrants served, either in its widespread territories or in the factories, offices and shops of metropolitan Britain, no longer exists. With those outlets now closed, Irish living standards will be determined by what happens in Ireland now. Given a rapidly growing population and the decline in economic activity caused by the exhaustion of the government's ability to borrow, they are likely to plummet.

Northern Ireland. The failure of the Republic's economy and the desperate state of its public finances confirm for the Protestants of Northern Ireland that they were right not to join the rest of Ireland in seceding from the United Kingdom of Great Britain and Ireland in 1922. Northern Ireland has provided for more of its people than has the Republic. The number in the workforce of Northern Ireland increased between 1911, the year of the last census prior to the Republic becoming independent, and the 1970s (see Table 1.1). It has done so at living standards that are higher than those of the Republic (Table 1.6).

Table 1.6
Average Incomes, Northern Ireland and the Republic, 1980

	N. Ireland	Republic
Total incomes (I£ mns)	4,932.3	6,957.4
Population (000's)	1,547.3	3,408.0
Income per person (I£)	3,188	2,042

Note: Northern Ireland incomes are derived using the official rate of exchange for 1980, which was I£1 = £0.8862 stg. That this overvalues the I£ is demonstrated by (a) its subsequent devaluation to around I£1 = £0.8 stg; and (b) the large flow of people from the Republic to shop in Northern Ireland. This accounted for a large part of the otherwise 'balance unaccounted for' in the Republic's external payments deficit in 1983.

Source: Northern Ireland, *Annual Abstract of Statistics, 1980;* Republic of Ireland, *National Income and Expenditure, 1981; Statistical Abstract of Ireland, 1980;* Central Bank, *Quarterly Report,* Summer, 1983.

The intransigence of northern Protestants, caused by the economic failure of the Republic, is matched by an increasing impatience on the part of the Catholic minority in Northern Ireland with Protestant privilege and the corresponding Catholic disability.[17] That that disability has not prevented a larger proportion of Catholics from attaining in Northern Ireland higher living standards than those secured by a smaller proportion of their southern co-religionists accentuates rather than attenuates the impatience. The vigorousness of Northern Ireland protest, in accordance with a universal pattern, measures better the economic strength of the protesters than the degree of injustice that they suffer.

It is understandable that Catholic protest should spill over into the Republic. The Republic's politicians have fuelled that protest in two ways. Firstly, their failure to use 60 years of independence to secure a livelihood for more of their people confirms northern Protestants of the wisdom of remaining aloof from a state in which their livelihoods would be threatened. The Republic's politicians have fuelled northern Catholic protest, secondly, by repeated intervention in Northern Ireland affairs. This is the common ploy of politicians of seeking, by foreign adventurism, to deflect attention from domestic failure. The Anglo-Irish Intergovernmental Conference on Northern Ireland is a recent typical example of that intervention.

No Ordinary Crisis

The crisis that confronts Ireland in the 1980s is no ordinary crisis such as confronts every society occasionally and such as has confronted Ireland from time to time in the past. It is not, as repeatedly suggested by politicians and others, the result of some recent and transient maladjustment of the public finances, to be set right by appropriate fiscal adjustment. Nor can it plausibly be attributed to a general, world-wide recession. The disarray of the public finances and particularly the critical dependence on foreign borrowing, which have only recently come under public scrutiny as matters of serious concern, are, in fact, the inevitable and predictable outcome[18] of policies that have been followed consistently in Ireland for 40 years. The slowing down of exceptionally rapid world economic growth, like the levelling off of a downward gradient, merely highlights the impossible defects of the Irish economic vehicle.

Undevelopment: a Third-World Phenomenon

Ireland's failure to provide a livelihood for its people is best understood as part of a much more widespread failure. It is to be seen as part of the Third World's failure to develop. Development, in relation to societies, is here defined as a situation where (a) more people are better off than formerly and (b) fewer people are as badly off. If both of these conditions were not specified, it could have been said that Ireland developed in the 1840s, at the end of which, thanks to the Great Famine, there were certainly fewer people who were as badly off as formerly: because they had starved to death or had fled from famine. The corollary of these two conditions for development is that the opposite, undevelopment, obtains when either of these conditions is absent. That is, there is undevelopment when there are (a) fewer people who are as well off as formerly; or (b) more people who are as badly off as formerly. Ireland fulfills the first of the conditions that equate with undevelopment: there are fewer people who are as well off as formerly. Less than half as many people get a livelihood in the Republic now as did so 140 years ago; fewer get a livelihood there now than when the country became independent (Table 1.1).[19] Throughout the Third World, the second condition that defines undevelopment obtains: more people are worse off than formerly.

Several million Indians now have incomes comparable to those of Europe.[20] To that extent, India may be said to have developed: it now has

11

more people than ever before with high incomes. But India does not fulfill the second condition specified for development; it does not have fewer people who are as badly off as formerly. On the contrary; India certainly has tens of millions, and perhaps hundreds of millions, of people subsisting at lower real incomes, at lower levels of nutrition, than ever did so in the past. India, in that very real sense, undevelops. And in that it mirrors the rest of the Third World.

More poor people. The total population of what is commonly referred to as the Third World was an estimated 2,098 millions,or about half the world's population,in 1978.[21] It had increased by 23% in the period 1970-78. Average per caput income in the Third World was the equivalent of US $661. (Average Irish incomes in 1980 were I£2,042, or US $4,208: Table 1.6 above). Average Third World incomes had also increased by 23% in the period; or, in constant 1978 prices, from US $536 in 1970.[22] Even if the increase in incomes had been the same for all income categories in the Third World, it would not follow that there were fewer very poor people in these countries in 1978 than there had been in 1970. Taking people with half or less than half the average Third World income, or US $268, as 'very poor', it is conceivable that while per caput incomes increased by 23% by 1978, because of the simultaneous 23% increase in the total population, there may have been as many or more people in 1978 than there were in 1970 with incomes of US $268 or less.

National income divided by population, which gives average per caput income, can be a very misleading measure of the degree of poverty. This is because of the uneven distribution of incomes, which is pronouncedly more so in poor than in wealthier countries. The Gini coefficient is an accepted measure of this uneveness of income distribution. It ranges from zero, when incomes are perfectly evenly distributed, to 1 when all incomes accrue to a single person/household and all others have none. The Gini coefficient of income distribution to households in the wealthy countries in the early 1970s was 0.382 and for the Third World it was 0.490. It was highest, 0.539 in Africa and the Middle East, where average incomes were also lowest.[23] There is considerable evidence that in poor countries, as average incomes increase, more of the increase goes to the wealthy and less of it to the poor. Thus, while per caput incomes of all the countries of the Third World taken together increased on average by 23% in 1970-78, average per caput incomes of the poorest countries increased only by 5%.[24] Just as between countries, the improvement in the incomes of the poorest countries was least, so within countries between income groups, the incomes of the poorest are also likely to have increased least, if at all. There is evidence of this in the form of Gini coefficients rising over time in many countries.[25]

While the incomes of the very poor arc likely to increase at less than the average rate of income growth, the natural growth in the population of the very poor is likely to be higher than average. In 1978, which is the latest year for which the necessary data are available, the annual rate of population growth in the poorest countries was 2.7%, while that of middle income Third World countries was 2.4%. The higher population growth of the poorest countries was the net result of higher death rates and much higher birth rates.[26]

Given the double probability of a less than average (i.e. 23%) increase in incomes during 1970-78 for the very poor countries, and of a more than average (i.e.23%) population growth, it is probable that there were more people in the world with average incomes equivalent to US $268, of constant 1970 purchasing power, in 1978 than there had been in 1970. Only a substantial increase in the number of the very poor, caused by a pronounced skewness in the distribution of the increase in incomes, with most or all of the increase in output going to the wealthy and little if any going to the poor, could account for the very small average increase in agricultural output per person, from US $118 to US $119, between 1970 and 1978 in the Third World as a whole. That position was much worse in the poorest countries where,as already noted, average incomes increased by 5% but where agricultural output per person is reported to have declined by 10% in the 1970s.[27] A decline in average output per person in agriculture — which is mainly food production — in poor countries, strongly suggests an absolute decline in the real incomes of the majority, with all of the total gain in output going to the better off; or being lost as factor income paid abroad. Again, assuming that the statistics are not hopelessly incorrect, an increase in average agricultural output per person from US $118 to US $119, while gross domestic product per person increased from US $536 to US $661 is only likely to have occurred if most of the increased income went to the wealthy or was paid abroad as factor income, with, in either case, little or none of the increase reaching the poor majority of the Third World's population.

It is hardly disputable that more people exist now in the Third World at lower incomes than formerly. That was stated to be the case by the Director General to a council meeting of the United Nations Food and Agriculture Organization: 'The overall situation of the Third World countries is worse than it was a generation ago, despite an increase in global food production'.[28] Nor are prospects better. 'With US $300 (1976) per head as the threshold of poverty', Godet and Ruyssen predict that the number living in poverty, below that threshold, will increase from 1,280 millions in 1976 to 1,650 millions by the year 2000.[29] Moreover, the extent to which the relative prosperity of the higher income Third World countries is dependent on foreign borrowing has become clearer recently (see Table 1.5). The difficulty of continuing to borrow abroad and the cost of servicing existing debt will impede future growth in these countries, heighten further political tensions in them (see Appendix C), and will cause more of their people to experience worse poverty.

Illiteracy and poverty are closely correlated. Data on illiteracy therefore adds to information on poverty. It has been suggested that 'between 1975 and 2000 the number of functional illiterates will double from about one to two billions'.[30] That trend in illiteracy is consistent with, and confirms other evidence pointing to, an increase in the scale and severity of world poverty. While half the world develops the other half undevelops.

It would be misleading to suggest that this undevelopment is a recent phenomenon. In Java, the principal capitalist colony of Southeast Asia, 'the quality of peasant diet deteriorated, with an apparent decline in calorie intake. Per capita rice consumption in Java and Madura seems to have started its long decline shortly after 1850 and, if the figures are to be trusted, average annual consumption per head in the late 1930s was only four-fifths of that seven decades earlier.'[31]

In India, the most populous of the former capitalist colonies, 'the frequency of famine dramatically increased under the British Raj. There have probably been 90 famines in that country in the last 2,000 years; but 66% occurred since 1701.'[32] It was estimated that around 1918 India had available about 20 ounces of food grain per day per head of population. 'By 1945...the average daily quantity of food grain available per capita had fallen to about 15 ounces, and per capita food supply diminished substantially between 1945 and 1952.'[33] Myrdal made the same point a little earlier: 'The average standard of living of humanity as a whole is still below the level of 1900.'[34]

Development Studies

The principal concern of the father of the intellectual discipline of economics and author of *The Wealth of Nations,* Adam Smith, and of his successors for 150 years, was to explain the wealth of some societies. More recently, and especially since the Second World War, economists have directed much of their attention to the failure of some societies to develop, or *The Poverty of Nations.*[35] This branch of economics, known as development studies, has amassed a large body of data and many insights; although clearly, in view of the persistence of undevelopment in countries that together contain almost half the world's population, the data and insights have been of limited effectiveness. Notwithstanding this limited effectiveness of development studies, it nevertheless appears to be the appropriate context for studying Ireland's undevelopment, as this was defined above. Much that is otherwise inexplicable about the Irish economy appears less so when viewed in the light of the body of insights acquired relating to the undevelopment of the Third World. Moreover, Ireland's inclusion within the discipline's purview can itself contribute substantially to development studies. It can do so partly because of the much better documentation of the Irish scene in relation both to past and present than that of any other undeveloping country. Ireland's inclusion can also contribute by proving, in the sense of testing the validity of, many important generalizations pertaining to development and undevelopment. For example: the emphasis given by development studies to education seems question-begging in view of Ireland's having one of the first national education systems in the world, introduced in 1831.[36] Ireland's experience in such matters as saving, where the proportion of income saved is very high; in land reform, where it had one of the earliest and most thorough; or in marketing agricultural produce, where prices have consistently been among the highest in the world: the Irish experience in these matters challenges some of the central generalizations of development studies. The Irish case also challenges the somewhat more profound suggestion of Myrdal that warm climates cause undevelopment: '[The undevelopment of the tropics] cannot be entirely an accident of history, but must have to do with some special handicaps, directly or indirectly related to climate, faced by countries in the tropical and subtropical zones.'[37] That suggestion was echoed by Mahatir bin Mohammed, with the double authority of being Prime Minister of Malaysia and a physician, who suggests that the Malay people have been made physiologically incapable of strenuous effort by a debilitating, equatorial climate.[38] The undevelopment of the Caucasian Irish in a climate that is as harsh, if not more harsh, than that of Myrdal's native Sweden, challenges theories of undevelopment that are based on the physiological consequences of climate or race.

The greater undevelopment of the Catholic Republic than of Protestant Northern Ireland (Tables 1.1 and 1.6) would seem, on the other hand, to lend credence to the 'Protestant ethic' as an explanation of material progress. This quasi-racial explanation has been favoured by Black to account for industry's better progress in Northern Ireland: 'Why Ulster has so much industrial growth when the rest of Ireland had so little...it seems to me in most instances personal initiative overcame comparative lack of natural advantage.'[39] The greater achievements of the 'personal initiative' of Ulster Protestants can, however, be readily traced to critical initial advantages enjoyed by the Northern Ireland Protestant garrison class over the garrisoned Catholic majority of the island (below, Chapter 4). The question remains though: why did Protestants garrison Catholics rather than Catholics garrison Protestants? This point is pursued below.

Capitalist Colonialism

Probably the single most valuable insight derived from recognizing Ireland as an undeveloping country is the emphasis this gives to the role of capitalist

15

colonialism in economic undevelopment. The one thing that Ireland shares with all the countries of the undeveloping Third World in the Caribbean, Latin America, Africa and Asia is their colonization by metropolitan capitalist powers.

There are some 138 of these former capitalist colonies; the number is augmented from time to time as another tiny colony becomes independent. They had, in 1975, a combined population of 1,699 million, or about 45% of the world's population in that year.[40] The average size of their populations is around 15 millions; but populations vary in size from India's, which is over 600 millions, to less than 100,000 for tiny political entities like Dominica in the Caribbean. Their combined populations are growing at over 2% annually, or by almost 30% per decade. The value of their annual output per person, in 1975, was around US $280, no more than one-eight of the value per person in Ireland in that year.[41]

An alien, individualistic, capitalist culture was, in every case of capitalist colonization, superimposed forcefully on an indigenous, collectivist, non-capitalist society of food producers. 'The concomitant of cultural contact is social strain.'[42] That social strain, foisted on the Third World by capitalist colonialism, manifests itself in every case in the persistent undevelopment of these former capitalist colonies.

There is however development in the western European heartland of individualistic capitalism. There is development in those regions of the New World where Europeans encountered hunting-gathering indigenes, whom they exterminated or pushed aside and did not allow to influence settlement growth: America north of the Rio Grande, South Africa as far as the Limpopo river and the Drakensberg mountains, and Australia and New Zealand. There is development, if slower, in Russia, the marchland between Europe and the Asian steppes that has belonged to both of these worlds. Living within these two different worlds 'is a spiritual ordeal... [which] in the nineteenth century... evoked a literature that was not surpassed anywhere in the world in that age.'[43] Russia, for a thousand years or more, has been deeply influenced by Europe (see below, Appendix A); but it was never colonized by metropolitan Europe.

There is very rapid economic development in those east Asian countries, Japan, Korea and Taiwan, which, like Russia, never had western individualistic capitalism forcefully superimposed on their indigenous cultures by the process of capitalist colonialism. These countries were left largely free to borrow eclectically from the West (see below, Appendix C). There is also rapid development in the city states of Hong Kong and Singapore where, as in North America, South Africa and Oceania, the handful of indigenous islanders did not influence the course of settlement. There is finally China, with almost a quarter of the world's population; which has experienced far deeper penetration by the metropolitan western powers than Japan, Korea or Taiwan; but far less than Ireland or the other former capitalist colonies of the Third World. Its struggles to develop, while so far not crowned with anything like Japan's phenomenal success, do appear more hopeful than those of almost equally vast India; or than those of Latin America or Africa. China, for example, is one of the few non-western countries where population is growing at less than two per cent annually.[44]

The evident failure of Ireland's economy must be viewed in the context of Third World undevelopment. Ireland, though geographically part of the West, alone of European countries shares the profound historical experience of having had superimposed on its own indigenous, tribal pastoralism, an alien, individualistic capitalism (see Chapter 4). And alone of European countries it undevelops: and does so in company with every one of the 138 or so countries that were colonies of the capitalist system.

This imposed undevelopment has been affected not at all by political independence. It has proceeded in the post-colonial era both under western, liberal regimes, as in Ireland's case; and under Russian Marxist regimes, as in the cases of Cuba, Peru or Tanzania. Capitalist colonization is analogous to infection with a disease against which the infected body is unable to build up antibodies. No former capitalist colony has developed. Even 160 years after Latin America secured independence from the Iberian colonizing powers, the debilitating, undeveloping consequences of capitalist colonialism persist in every country of the region. The odds against Ireland, or any other former capitalist colony, breaking out of that invariant mould must, therefore, be regarded as slim.

II

The Evolution of Individualistic Capitalism: Regional Variations

Introduction

Underdevelopment is perceived as the invariable, peculiar and enduring consequence of the interaction of western, individualistic capitalism with non-individualistic, non-capitalist, indigenous societies through the process of capitalist colonialism. It is necessary, in order to understand why this should be, to recognize and to appreciate the significance of relevant aspects of western, individualistic capitalism. It is also necessary to acknowledge and understand different, relevant aspects of the non-western, non-individualistic cultures upon which individualistic capitalism was imposed. In order to do this, it is necessary first to consider the different cultures before they commenced to interact, which in Ireland's case was 500 years ago.

A recent important contribution, *The Miracle of Europe,*[1] seeks answers to the question of why, of the four major cultures of 500 years ago (Ottoman, Moghul India, China and Europe) the last progressed to dominate the others and the world. Most valuable as the exercise is,[2] it does not carry the inquiry much further than such observations as that Europeans, uniquely, preferred material wealth to children.[3] If they did, why did they? More fundamentally: the last five centuries of world political and economic history have been largely an extrapolation of the history of the preceding three millenia or so. The slow, hesitant, uncertain, but gradually accelerating development of Europe from a cold, bleak forest fastness during those millenia contrasted with the static character of other societies and made almost inevitable Europe's global dominance during the most recent 500 years.

19

If the disparate characters of western and non-western cultures are to be understood, it is essential to carry the inquiry much further back than 500 years ago, when Europe was about to discover China, and not China to discover Europe; when Europeans already preferred wealth to children; when Luther was articulating 'the Protestant ethic'; when, in a word, western, individualistic capitalism was already formed and was about to interact with the other very different cultures of the world. Much more can be understood by returning to the very beginning of the formation of those different cultures, which was the beginning of civilization itself. Then man progressed from being a hunter and gatherer of food to being a food producer; and, as a food producer, adapted his environment rather than moved on to a different one.

The significance of the individual, the rule of law and the institution of property are here perceived as the key, distinctive characteristics of western culture. Other cultures are not without these characteristics; but nowhere are they such critical features of society as in the West. They evolved in Europe under ecological and historical circumstances that were unique. Those circumstances, which caused a society of this distinctive nature to evolve when and where it did, are considered below (Appendix A).

Regional Variations

Europe, though the smallest of the continents, has pronounced regional ecological variations. These gave rise to regional differences in the pattern of cultural evolution, which are considered in more detail in Appendix A. Interaction within this regional complex of evolution became itself an important factor in shaping the manner of overall, individualistic, capitalist evolution in Europe. Its consequences are especially germane to the capitalist colonization of Ireland and its subsequent undevelopment.

Continental Europe. Bloch has identified a heartland that, from early on, can be most clearly associated with Europe's distinctive, capital-based production. North of the river Loire and the Burgundian plain 'was the classical area of the *seigneurie*, the one in which it was oldest and most solidly established'.[4] This region is referred to here as Central Western Europe and is perceived as having been the heartland of western, individualistic capitalism.

Southwards, in a less rigorous climate, had occurred the precocious growth of the individualistic Ancient Mediterranean culture, followed by its collapse when its slave labour supply failed (Appendix A). But though the social order might change, the climate and other ecological characteristics did not. Yields in the warmer south continued higher than in the colder north. As the south's development had come earlier, so its recovery was quicker in the early Middle Ages, after the *völkerwanderung* that marked the end of the Roman empire in western Europe. The very ease and speed of southern Europe's recovery obviated the need for radical change. The region became an exporter of capital to the north, either in the form of credits by Italian bankers given to northern rulers and traders; or in the form of plunder taken by northern conquerors.[5] But without the need or the opportunity for radical institutional adaptation, the south, over the long run, developed more slowly, and the population of the previously sparsely populated north surpassed that of the south by around 800 A D.[6]

Climatic conditions for crop-growing were much less favourable in the Scandinavian peninsula than in mainland Central Western Europe. They were probably too difficult ever to permit the spontaneous, indigenous emergence of the sort of capital-based, crop-growing economy that emerged in Central Western Europe (see Appendix A). But there were offsetting compensations. Further to the north of the Indo-European Scandinavians were the Lapps. These, under the influence of European pastoralism, had partly domesticated the reindeer, unlike their racial cousins, the Eskimos, across the Bering Straits, who continued to hunt the caribou.[7] The partly pastoral, partly hunting Lapps offered no threat to the rear of the agricultural Scandinavians; but they did produce enough from their reindeer to trade beneficially with the Scandinavians. With a secure and lucrative rear, the Scandinavians were strategically well placed to tap, by plunder and trade, the wealth of Europe as it pulled itself together and progressed at a perceptibly more rapid pace following the shock and instability of the period of *völkerwanderung*. The Scandinavians, in exploiting the opportunities afforded by their location, circumnavigated Europe, along the great rivers of Russia, by the Atlantic ocean and through the Mediterranean sea.[8]

The Scandinavians evolved their institutions in ways particularly favourable to individual endeavour. For example: Vikings, often thousands of miles from home and alternatively oarsmen at sea and swordsmen on land, could be led by accepted leaders but could not be driven by despots, as — by contrast — were the massed land armies of the great riverine states (Appendix A). With wealth secured from outside and with institutions especially favourable to individual effort, Scandinavians, after a late and slow start, developed more rapidly than the rest of Europe and now have Europe's and the world's highest living standards.

The eastern marches. Eastwards, beyond the deciduous forests, Russia had the climatic difficulties, without the strategic advantages, of Scandinavia. The open, tree-less country was exposed to the mounted pastoral hordes from the east. Ancient Kievan Russia was devasted by the Mongols in 1237, 1240 (when the capital Kiev was sacked) and again in 1395. Russia's rulers thereafter moved northwards to Moscow. The pinewoods there gave shelter from the Golden Hordes; but the climate,

21

unlike that in the deciduous forest areas of Central Western Europe, was too severe for crop-growing. As recently as the nineteenth century one grain sown in Northern Russia yielded only 2.4 grains when harvested.[9]

Russia, a marchland between the capital-based, crop-growing civilization of the West and the pastoral barbarism of the East (Appendix A), depended absolutely on trade with the West. In exchange for its own crude, hunted, gathered and pastoral products, it secured the manufactured and other processed goods of the West.[10] Russia's rulers, with these western products, were able to beat off, and eventually to subdue, the Mongolian invaders.

Russia's trade with the West had to flow northwards or southwards along a few major river arteries and thence the Baltic and Black seas. It was, therefore, easily controlled.[11] That control of trade, in turn, gave to Russia's rulers a monopoly of western technology. This enabled them not only to provide an essential defence service, but to exercise autocratic power over their subjects. Russian autocracy, for a millenium under the tsars and more recently under the communist party, has precluded the emergence of individualism, law or property, which are the distinctive characteristics of the culture of Central Western Europe.[12]

Offshore northwest. Conditions were also unfavourable for the emergence of these characteristics in Europe's north-western fringe. Ireland remained uninhabited until after the last Ice Age and until around the time, some eight millenia or so ago, of the emergence of the first civilization in Mesopotamia.[13] Percolating through Europe's forests, the lactose tolerant, Indo-European Celts did not reach this western fringe until the first millenium BC (see Appendix A). 'Warriors with lavishly decorated weapons and jewellery came into Ireland from Celtic Europe in the centuries immediately preceding the birth of Christ.'[14] Again: 'The period stretching from the late seventh century BC, may even have been the time that Celtic settlement took place.'[15] They eliminated, with little other than archaeological trace, their less well adapted, lactose malabsorbent, non-milk-drinking predecessors, for whom 'cattle primarily served as beef producing animals and [for whom] secondary uses such as milk or traction were of less importance.'[16]

Ireland's insular climate — its rainfall substantially higher than continental Europe's and its summer temperatures lower, but its winter temperatures higher than on the continent — favoured grass and cattle against woodland. The predominant original woodland was birch and hazel, species favoured by cold, wet conditions.[17] In extensive areas, when the original woodland was removed by early farmers, it was not regenerated but was replaced by slowly growing blanket peat bogs.[18] This was especially so when the Celts reached Ireland and cleared the woodlands more extensively. The woodland recovered less quickly in Ireland than elsewhere in Europe, where grass grew less well and where too the winter constraint on cattle-keeping was more severe (Appendix A). The enduring sparsity of Irish woodland is illustrated by the map of part of County Carlow in the year 1580 that is reproduced by McCracken.[19] It persists today.[20]

The clearance of the woodlands resulted in a more open terrain, which facilitated transhumance, or 'boolying' in Gaelic. This mobility, combined with milder winters, made the need for winter fodder for livestock less pressing in Ireland than in continental Europe. The reduced need for winter fodder weakened one of the major incentives to grow crops in Central Western Europe (Appendix A). At the same time, Ireland's combination of coldness and wetness makes grain production exceptionally difficult.[21] There was, therefore, less need for crops and greater difficulty in growing them in Ireland than in continental Europe.

A predominance of grassland favoured the preservation, or possibly even the restoration, among the Celts in Ireland of the tribal pastoralism that was also characteristic of the Eurasian steppes and of Africa. In Celtic Ireland, where most of the land was cleared of woods and where there was little crop-growing, cattle relied principally on transhumance to survive winters that were milder than on the continent. Understandably then, the cows of the Irish Celts appear to have had the *Bos indicus* characteristic of refusing to let their milk down without the presence of their live calves.[22] With much of the land deforested, cattle in Ireland, unlike Central Western Europe, were held in the open and cattle-raiding — or *creaghs* in Gaelic — was, as in Africa, a central feature of life.[23] Significantly too perhaps, as in Africa, 'the Irish law of marriage countenanced plurality of wives'.[24] Finally, in Ireland the diet up to a few centuries ago had more in common with Africa's tribal pastoralists than with the diet of the capital-based crop-growers of contemporary Central Western Europe. The Irish diet was predominantly milk and its products, blood drawn from the veins of live animals, and meat: 'When they are almost starved, yet they will not kill a cow, except it be old and yield no milk. Yet will they upon hunger in time of war open a vein of the cow and drink the blood, but in no case kill or much weaken it. A man would think them near to be Scythians, who let their horses bleed under the ears and for nourishment drink their blood...They swallow lumps of butter mixed with oatmeal and often let their cows bleed, eating the congealed blood with butter and love no meat more than sour milk curdled.'[25] In neighbouring Britain people had adopted a predominantly crop-based diet by the time of the Norman conquest in the eleventh century.[26]

The cold, wet climate and the related woodland clearances militated against the emergence of the sort of capital-based crop-growing that evolved in Central Western Europe (Appendix A). The crop-growing Romans 'dismissed Ireland as not worthy of invasion'.[27] The Normans, also crop-growers, easily conquered Ireland, but could not so easily retain it. They were not driven out by a Gaelic revival in the fourteenth century, as suggested by Dolley.[28] They were washed out by Irish rain. The castle-dwelling, crop-growing Normans were forced either to revert to pastoral tribalism and become *Hiberniores ipsos Hibernos,* or to retreat to the dryest, warmest south eastern part of the island, within the 'Pale'.

Law in Ireland was the customary law of the *breathamh:* a statement of of accepted norms of conduct, but lacking the powerful sanction that the economic significance of the individual and of the individual's property gave to law in Central Western Europe (see Appendix A). 'There was no public authority in Ireland to execute the law, but the sureties as well as the kin, played an important part in securing a man's rights.'[29] 'Property' was based on the strength of the holder, rather than on a social recognition of, and willingness to defend, rights. The traditional view was: 'The Gaelic Irish first won the land by conquest, and ever since have adhered to the principle of swordland as the basis of title.'[30] A fifteenth century ode to O'Reilly of Cavan on the subject goes: 'The broad spear in the hand, the weapon from Vulcan's smithy, the sword, this is our charter.'[31]

Whether an indigenous, individualistic capitalism might have evolved in time had Ireland not been capitalist-colonized is a historical 'might-have-been' that can be dismissed with more than usual confidence. The more deforested the island became, the more likely was tribal pastoralism to dominate and the less likely was it that people would, or could, have saved to invest in the means to grow crops and to establish a more advanced civilization. The inchoate crop-growing and urbanization of Gaelic Ireland were more likely, in the absence of the Norman invasion, to have regressed further to tribal pastoralism, as in Africa, than to have evolved into individualistic capitalism, as in Central Western Europe. The all-important ecological conditions for the spontaneous evolution of individualistic capitalism, did not extend beyond Central Western Europe to Ireland (see Appendix A).

III

The Evolution of English Capitalism

Introduction

Ireland lay beyond the margin of ancient, capital-based crop-growing. England lay on that margin. It has, over the centuries, shifted between crop-growing and pasture — 'up corn, down horn' — according to the circumstances of the time. The crop-growing Romans were established there for centuries and supported themselves on locally grown crops,[1] before the *Völkerwanderung* tribes of Central Western Europe occupied the island and caused a reversion to pastoralism.

But even before the Normans came, crop-growing had been well and widely re-established, though it was capital-based rather than slave-based as under the Romans. Domesday Book recorded 71,785 plough teams, each team capable of cultivating around 120 acres.[2] But it was only after the Norman conquest that the English changed from a predominately pastoral to a predominately crop-based diet. It was only then that 'the edge to edge bite gave way among Anglo-Saxons to the overbite, which was the ultimate consequence of a shift to more starch and carbohydrates'.[3] But because England was marginal for crop-growing (with Ireland located beyond that margin), the disruption caused there to established crop-growing by the Black Death of the 1340s was particularly severe.

The Black Death

Capitalist growth, from the start, had an inherently peristaltic character (Appendix A). A cycle may be perceived as commencing from a base of low population and large capital; from high incomes, and from high rates of saving, capital formation and output growth. Because of high incomes

25

and good nutritional levels, death rates were below average and population growth was above average. Population growth, always able to outstrip capital formation and growth of production, caused declines in incomes, savings, capital formation, rate of growth of production and nutritional levels. Population growth proceeded to a point of collapse, when an impoverished and malnourished people, living under climatically more difficult conditions than those experienced by any other major centre of population, were devastated. Meanwhile the capital stock survived, largely unimpaired (Appendix A).

The Black Death of the 1340s is the best known and was perhaps the most severe of these calamities which marked the peristaltic progress of capitalist growth. Titow documents for the Winchester estates in England the failing capital formation and the approaching crisis of the Black Death.[4]

The latter half of the fourteenth century and the fifteenth century were something of a golden age for the surviving people of Central Western Europe. The population having been almost halved by the Black Death, the stock of capital — principally in the form of cleared and manured land, draught and milch cattle, stocks of fodder and seed, ploughs and other implements, houses and barns — per survivor had almost doubled. This made possible also a virtual doubling of incomes. The transformation was perhaps most clearly marked by changes in three sets of prices that were particularly critical in England. By comparison with prices in 1350, the price of wheat was reduced by a quarter, the price of wool went up by half, and the cost of labour also went up by half by the end of the century.[5] As peoples' incomes increased (reflected in the rise in wages), their demand for clothes and wool rose (reflected in the rise in the wool price) relative to their demand for bread (reflected in the fall in the price of wheat). This price transformation created a particularly powerful incentive in England, which at best was marginal for crop-growing, to shift from labour-intensive crop-growing to the production of wool, which was now high priced and which required little labour. It was very much a case of 'up horn, down corn'.

The military possibilities of moving from grain to sheep were also particularly favourable in England at the time. The Plantagenet and Lancastrian monarchs, in the course of the Hundred Years War with France, had been forced to abandon all their French territories except Calais. England's defences then became the 'wooden walls' of its navy. Paradoxically, sheep could 'man' these wooden walls better than a numerous peasantry. In Central Western Europe a numerous peasantry was to remain, until the twentieth century, a vital factor both for mounting attacks against neighbouring territories and for defending the home territory against invasion. In island Britain, however, stripped of its continental territories, profits, which were originally derived from wool, were more important than people. With these profits, it was possible to construct a navy, provision it, and man it with experienced sailors.

From Lordship to Proprietorship

A transformation of feudal relationships was a precondition for realising the potential profits to be made uniquely from sheep in post Black Death England. The pastoral chieftains of the Eurasian steppes had evolved into the feudal lords who occupied the castles that were the focal points of the 'islands of population' in crop-growing Central Western Europe (Appendix A). The lords defended the peasants and the peasants fed the lords in a symbiosis between rulers and ruled that was unique to this region. Excessive exactions by lords could easily exhaust the meagre capital of their serfs; or more frequently, cause them to shift, with their vital capital, elsewhere in the 'sea of forest' to seek the protection of a less predatory lord (Appendix A). The feudal relationship between lord and peasant, which survived in continental Europe until 1789, was as much political and jurisdictional as it was economic: 'it involved rights of jurisdiction over people as well as rights over the land itself'.[6] It involved the rendering by the occupant to the lord of fees and services that were fixed by custom rather than subject to the vagaries of an increasingly unstable market.

Europe's unique feudal relationship, which made possible the slow accumulation of the stock of capital necessary to grow crops in this agronomically unfavourable region (Appendix A), precluded the realization of the potential profits from wool-producing pastureland in post Black Death England. It was necessary, in order to realise those profits, to transform lordship into proprictorship. Thus, the erstwhile feudal lord, who had evolved from the tribal chief, was in turn metamorphosed into that quintessentially English phenomenon: the landed proprietor. The landed proprietor replaced feudal relationships with economic ones. In place of the feudal peasant providing material sustenance for the lord, who in turn rendered justice and protection to the peasant, landed proprietorship reduced the relationship to payment of a rent that was determined by the most profitable available use of the land. Sheep grazing, as already noted, was English land's most profitable use.[7]

The power of the erstwhile feudal lord, transformed into a landed proprietor, to exact payment for the use of land depended on titles of property in land. These titles could be granted and maintained only by a superior authority. The price that England's feudal lords paid to be transformed from an obsolete and unprofitable feudal lordship into a profitable landed proprietorship was the creation of an absolute Tudor monarchy.

Squabbling over the succession had cost the lives of one-third of the monarchs and their immediate families in the Norman, Plantagenet and Lancastrian dynasties. It killed four English kings in the fifteenth century alone, before the accession of the Tudors in 1485.[8] Yet, during 120 years of Tudor rule, a usurping king, a syphilitic king, a boy king and two queens regnant — of whom one, Elizabeth, was of doubtful legitimacy — reigned more effectively in England than any earlier dynasty had done; reigned more effectively than any rulers in contemporary Europe did; and they died natural deaths.

England's Tudor monarchy anticipated by nearly two centuries the absolute monarchies of continental Europe. Its absolute power was necessary to transform England's feudal lords into a new class, previously unknown in the world: the class of landed proprietors. The Tudor monarchy, at the same time as it created a class of landed proprietors, deprived all others of the right that every people everywhere previously had, of equal access to land. The Tudor dynasty first dichotomized society into the landed and the landless.

The Reformation

If the right of some to exclude all others from access to land was to be absolute, then the power of the bestower of that right had to be absolute. The security of the newly created property in English land could be ensured only if the sovereignty of 'the king (or queen regnant) in parliament' was absolute. That sovereignty was not to be qualified by any higher authority on earth, including that of God's vicar, the pope in Rome. The property titles bestowed by the monarch would have been less absolute and might have been subject to papal approval, without the English Reformation (Appendix A).

But profits from wool from English land provided further powerful motives for reformation of the Church in England. The security of novel, questionable and questioned titles to the proprietorship of land, which yielded great profits but resulted in a situation where, as Sir Thomas Moore observed, 'sheep do eat up men', demanded secure and certain succession to the throne. But Henry VIII had only one child, a daughter by his wife, Catherine of Aragon. Henry desired to divorce Catherine and to remarry in order to produce a male heir and so secure the succession. The erstwhile feudal lords, transformed into landed proprietors, supported Henry in this move which promised to make more secure their novel and precarious titles to land. They were prepared to support Henry in his divorce even if that course meant a confrontation and a break with Rome.

A third important consideration singled out England, which had been a peripheral, European backwater, to lead the Protestant Reformation. Up to a third of English land was in the possession of the Church,[9] a fact which in itself was perhaps an indication of English backwardness. Yet nowhere else in sixteenth century Europe did land offer such prospects of profit as it did in England where, if not already in pasture, it could easily be put to grass to graze profitable sheep. The confiscated Church lands made possible immediate rewards of land grants to the supporters of Tudor absolutism; and they provided the means over the longer run for the absolute Tudor monarchs to 'live off their own', as traditional feudal kings did, without encroaching by taxation on the property rights in land they had created, sustained and legitimized.[10]

To summarize with regards to the Reformation: England's revolutionary and unique transformation of feudal lords into landed proprietors and the resulting simple dichotomy of society into landed and landless (Appendix A) made it peculiarly important for its ruling class to break with Rome. That break ensured the 'sovereignty of the king in Parliament' and the absoluteness of the property titles that he bestowed. The break made possible the king's divorce and the enhanced prospects that offered of a son to secure the peaceful and orderly succession to the throne, and therefore the security of land titles, which stemmed from the throne. Finally in England, where land was valuable centuries before elsewhere, the Church's extensive lands were a far richer loot than was available in continental European countries. These attractions of the Reformation for England's ruling class explain what Macauley found so puzzling:

> The History of the Reformation in England is full of strange problems. The most prominent and extraordinary phenomenon which it presents to us is the gigantic strength of the government compared with the feebleness of the religious parties...There was nothing in England like the fierce and bloody opposition which, in France, each of the religious factions in turn offered to government...Neither Protestant nor Catholic engaged in any great and well organized scheme of resistance.[11]

The Property Owners' State

The painfully slow accumulation of capital over the millenia in Central Western Europe's bleak woodlands changed first the tribalism of the pastoral steppes into the feudalism of capital-based European crop-growing (Appendix A). But the continued and intrinsicly accelerating growth of capital over time shifted the balance of political, as well as economic, power away from the feudal military caste and towards the proprietors of the capital that was the basis of Central Western European production (Appendix A). The fall of the Bastile on 14 July, 1789, symbolically marked the final acquisition, from the 'nobles of the sword', of political power by the owners of Europe's capital.

That appropriation of power by the property owners was initiated in England some centuries earlier. While a three-cornered contest continued in continental Europe for centuries more between the emerging power of the state (personified by the monarch), the waning power of the feudal lords, and the ascendant power of the property owners (Appendix A), the issue had been reduced to one between the state and property in Tudor England. But even there, new concepts, relationships and political institutions could not easily emerge. 'The idea that property and income counted for more than rights of lordship was only finally established by the cataclysm of civil war in the seventeenth century, and the extinction of the castle as a form of local defence.'[12] The English Civil War of the 1640s, followed by the Glorious Revolution of 1688, gave to England's property owners the control of the state that their peers in continental Europe did not acquire until more than a century later. This English political precociousness, which stemmed from an insular location on the pastoral margin of cropgrowing Europe, thrust a backward country into the forefront of European political, military, commercial and economic development.

The social cost of dichotomizing England into landed and landless was great. Real wages were forced below their fifteenth century level and remained so until the nineteenth century.[13] Forced off the land to make way for sheep, English people were less well able to marry; and England's population growth, which had been higher than continental Europe's, dropped behind and remained there until the eighteenth century.[14] The appropriation of English land as private property caused the common people, for centuries, to be less well fed and to be less well bedded.

Capitalist Colonialism

The Tudor revolution was one element of the general, multi-faceted acceleration of development which was the European Renaissance. That accelerated development can be traced to the Black Death of the 1340s. By halving the population, the Black Death doubled per person the stock of that capital which had been the sole constraint on production (Appendix A). This doubling of the stock of capital per person raised living standards for the surviving half of the population. That, as well as increasing the demand for wool, made possible larger savings, more capital formation and the accelerated development that has since become known as the Renaissance. Economic, political and intellectual development was driving Europeans beyond familiar shores and seas, and led to the discovery of the sea route to the east, and of America in the west. The discoveries were to lead, during the following centuries, to the spread of European influence and of European culture world-wide, through the process of colonization by European powers of most of the non-European world.

England, which lay on the margin of medieval European crop-growing, was the most advanced European country when Europe commenced its world-wide expansion in the sixteenth century. Ireland, which lay beyond the crop-growing margin, was the least advanced country in Europe. But Europe's expansion, coupled with internal events in England, conferred a new significance on the English crown's desultory lordship of Ireland. England, in a maritime age, became threatened as much from the west as it had always been from across the Channel. This new source of danger was expressed by the Tudor quip: 'He who would England win, let him in Ireland first begin'. The defence of England, as a maritime power in a maritime age, required control of Ireland, which lay on England's exposed western flank.

Another consideration, peculiar to England, called for the advancement of the English crown's largely nominal lordship of Gaelic Ireland towards full, formal colonization. Unlike in Central Western Europe land had become scarce, valuable and profitable in Tudor England, and this situation continued for several centuries. As a result, enterprising Englishmen looked to neighbouring Ireland for profitable land. Later the same consideration caused other English people to move into the wilderness of North America, and later again to move to Australia and New Zealand. In all these cases they sought, as peasants had done for millenia in the 'sea of forest' that was Central Western Europe, for land, which was no longer free in England (Appendix A).

Land, by contrast, remained abundant, effectively limitless and free in continental Europe (Appendix A). Why this should have been the case becomes clearer from a comparison of continental French and of insular English farming. The French, in a different ecological environment, engaged in the enormously time-consuming (i.e. capital-consuming) enterprise of wine production. The resources it takes to clear, to plant and to tend an acre of vines until they yield a vintage; the further time that elapses before that is consumable: these resources, over the same eight to ten years maturation period, would bring about 200 acres into sheep production.[15]

Many misconceptions exist, particularly among economic historians, about the distinctive character of English agriculture. English agriculture is normally presented as capital intensive, whereas French and continental European agriculture is deemed to be labour intensive. Thus: 'Wine was to French agriculture what wool was to English agriculture and society....Viniculture...was what economists call a labour intensive variety of agriculture requiring large amounts of fairly skilled peasant labour and relatively small amounts of capital.'[16] Wallerstein makes a similar point:

> To make a sensible comparison of development in English and French land tenure in this period, we must bear in mind that they each had two major modes of utilizing the land, but that they had only one in common — cereals. The second mode in England was animal husbandry, which lent itself more to economies of scale than did wine

31

production, the second mode in France; and animal husbandry required more capital investment. This simple economic fact may explain more about the differences in land tenure development than is explained by laws, traditions, attitudes, prior class structure, or the presumed heritage of 'feudal' rights.[17]

Many others make the same error about English agriculture being capital-intensive and Central Western European agriculture being labour-intensive. But, as suggested, approximately the same amount of capital is required to bring an acre of vines or 200 acres of sheepland into production. An acre of vines and 200 acres of sheepland produce about the same value of annual output, of mature wine in the case of the vines and of wool and meat in the case of the sheepland. Both enterprises have approximately the same current labour inputs. Thus, output per person or per unit of capital was not very different from French vines and English sheep grazing. The great difference was (is) that for a given output 200 times more land was required for English sheep-farming as for French vinegrowing. The distinctive and critically important, but generally unrecognized, characteristic of English agriculture was its land intensiveness: it required about 200 times as much land for a given value of output as Central Western European agriculture. That land intensiveness of English sheep-farming transformed the resource endowment situation. It caused land to be scarce and capital to be relatively abundant in England, while land continued to be abundant and capital continued to be critically scarce in continental Europe (Appendix A). This transformation of the resource input relationship conferred power and wealth in the modern era on the English successors of the feudal lords who acquired control of a resource that, uniquely in England, was scarce in western society. This happened at the same time as their peers in Central Western Europe, where land was effectively limitless and valueless, saw their power ebbing away to the ascendant property owners and to the emerging absolute monarchs. This transformation in input relationships, which occurred in marginal, insular England alone (and precisely because it occurred in England alone) is the neglected key to understanding England's enormously important world role since the Tudors dichotomized the English into landed and landless.

Capital and not land, on the other hand, remained the limiting factor for the French and other continental European peoples (Appendix A). There was little regard for the wastelands, either of Europe or of the new territories made available as a result of the Great Discoveries. It was understandable then that, at the Peace of Paris in 1763, when the French were given the choice between Canada, with a billion hectares of land, and Guadaloupe, with 178,000 hectares, they should choose the tropical island with its possibilities for the slave-based production of sugar that could not then be produced in temperate Central Western Europe, even with its limitless land resources.

IV

Irish Capitalist Colonialism

A Superimposition of Cultures

It was conceivable that the Chinese would have 'discovered' Europe. Their influence did spread to the east coast of Africa.[1] It was inevitable, given the dynamic character of western, individualistic capitalism, that Europe, one way or another, would 'discover' China, the rest of the non-European world and, now, the universe.

The spread of individualistic, capitalist influences beyond the Central Western European heartland of capitalism has been a major factor in the last 500 years of European and world history. It has shaped every aspect of life in the non-European world during that period. The spread of individualistic capitalism to tribal, pastoral Ireland 500 years ago has likewise determined the entire course of subsequent Irish history. The topic is vast. The present concern is to secure a sufficient understanding of the phenomenon of the colonial spread of European individualistic, capitalist influences for an appreciation of the consequences of that spread, firstly for the colonizers and secondly, and more importantly, for the colonized.

The more general aspects of the matter are studied by tracing a number of disparate threads through the convoluted skein of world-wide European colonialism (Appendix B). Eight such threads in the pattern are considered: (1) motivation; (2) sequence and timing; (3) interaction with the indigenes; (4) land appropriation; (5) race and ascendancy; (6) the nature and role of property in the colonies; (7) the consequences of colonialism; and (8) the ending of European colonialism. The extent to which the Irish experience was consistent with, or deviated from, the general pattern woven by these threads is examined here. In addition two specifically Irish aspects of colonialism are examined. First, in relation to the nature and role of property in the colonies, the difference between landed property in Ireland and in England are identified. Second, as part of the consequences of colonialism in Ireland, four remarkable nineteenth century Irish successes are examined.

Ireland, with some important reservations, fitted into the broad, world wide pattern of European colonialism, and more specifically, of capitalist colonialism. Capitalist colonialism here refers to those situations where the indigenous societies were agricultural, to be "'squeezed" after conquest, to provide labour, or commodities or tribute'.[2] It is used particularly to distinguish this type of situation from the settler colonies of North America, South Africa and Oceania, where the indigenes were hunter-gatherers, where the land was appropriated and settled by migrating Europeans (especially British), and where there was little prospect of profit for home-based, metropolitan interests (Appendix B).

Motivation. None of the first three motivations that are identified for the spread of European colonialism from the fifteenth century onwards — looting precious metals, the salvation of souls, or profit (Appendix B) — caused the Tudors to assert their lordship over Ireland. The English, after three centuries of desultory involvement in Ireland, were well aware that precious metals were as rare in Ireland as in most parts of the world. They also knew that, beyond some salmon and some cattle hides, which were then virtually the country's only exports,[3] there was no prospect of profit from trade with Ireland as there was from trade with the East for its exotic produce. Nor did the English evince towards the Irish any of the deep concern for the salvation of souls that the Iberians indubitably had for the souls of the unfortunate inhabitants of the lands that they colonized, and which in metropolitan Spain found expression in the Inquisition. Ireland was colonised for more practical purposes: for strategic considerations and to acquire land (see Chapter 3). It was an unusual combination of motives. Possibly the closest parallel to it was the Dutch settlement of the Cape of Good Hope in 1617. Originally settled as a staging post on the long voyage from Rotterdam to Batavia in the Dutch East Indies, the Cape in time attracted Dutch/Boer settlers, whose influences subsequently spread far into southern Africa.[4]

Timing. Ireland's twelfth century Norman conquest was part of a Central Western European process of spreading into, and settling, the forest wilderness (Appendix A). Each Norman lord with his followers sought to hack out and to secure with a castle an area of mixed crop and pasture land, and to subsist in feudal isolation on that fief, neither expecting nor getting support from any sovereign power. Winning Irish territory was easy; retaining it was more difficult. The Tudor Henry VII, hereditary Lord of Ireland, had himself declared King of Ireland, thus asserting the sovereignty of the monarchy over Ireland no less than over England. Henceforth Irish land would be held in fief from an English king in Parliament, the proprietor's title being supported by the full force of the centralized Tudor state and its successors. It was consistent with the overall timetable of capitalist Europe's spread that Ireland should have been conquered and colonized by the Tudors at the commencement of that process, when colonizing activities were concentrated in the Atlantic basin (Appendix B).

The capitalist colonization of Ireland by the Tudors meant that the island was a colony of the capitalist system for longer than any other territory. From its commencement in the reign of Henry VII to its ending with the Anglo-Irish treaty of 1922, the colonization of Ireland lasted a century longer than that of the next longest lasting, the Barbados, a colony from 1627 to 1966 and also an island in the Atlantic.

Interaction with the indigenes. The record of the relationship between the English capitalist colonists and the indigenous Irish was also consistent with the world-wide experience of European colonialism (Appendix B). Irish society was agricultural and therefore could be 'squeezed after conquest to provide labour, or commodities or tribute'.[5] That retention and integration of indigenous agriculturists into the imposed capitalist colonial system differed fundamentally from the procedure where the indigenes were hunter-gatherers. In all such cases — North America, Oceania and South Africa — which are referred to here as 'settler colonies', the indigenes were either obliterated or driven into reserves. Settler colonies were thus established on a *tabula rasa* from which the indigenous culture had effectively been erased. Capitalist colonies, by contrast, were established by superimposing individualistic, capitalist culture on top of the non-individualistic and non-capitalist, indigenous food-producing cultures.

It was consistent with contemporary capitalist colonial experience elsewhere, in Latin America and in the Caribbean, that the 'squeezing' of Ireland's indigenous agricultural population in the seventeenth century should have threatened its existence (Appendix B). The Elizabethan conquest and the Cromwellian reconquest almost exterminated the Irish. It was fortuitous that the country was not converted into a sparsely populated cattle walk, as was proposed by William Petty.[6]

Land appropriation. The record in relation to the appropriation of Irish land does deviate importantly from the general practice of capitalist colonialism (Appendix B). European colonists normally only seized land in the settler colonies, from hunter-gatherers. They did not usually appropriate land from the agricultural indigenes of Africa or of South and Southeast Asia. The colonists, for the most part, were content to seize the 'commanding heights' of the economies of the capitalist colonies, leaving the land to the indigenes to operate it with profit to the colonial system. The appropriation of the land from the agricultural people of Latin America was an important exception to that general pattern for which two factors would appear to be accountable. First, the Americans did not have domesticated ruminants, which seemed to have made them less martial than the denizens of the Old World with their horses, herds and flocks (Appendix A). The buccaneers, Cortez and Pizarro, each with a handful of followers, were able to conquer respectively the Aztec and Inca empires, which together contained one of the contemporary world's major concentrations of populations. Second, Latin America's stores of gold and silver together with its mineral reserves offered a far greater incentive to conquer, to hold and to exploit the region than existed anywhere else in the world. Exceptional ease of conquest combined with exceptional profit from conquest would together seem to account adequately for the expropriation of land from Latin America's agricultural indigenes, which ran counter to the general practice in other capitalist colonies (Appendix B).

The situation in Ireland differed from that of Latin America in that, like the rest of the Old World, the Irish had their flocks and herds; and they were sufficiently martial to cost their English Tudor conquerors much of the loot they had confiscated from the English Church on the suppression of the monasteries. 'The cost of conquering Ireland was enormous; more than any other single factor, the cost of Elizabeth's Irish campaigns set parliament and crown on the course which culminated in civil war in the 1640s.'[7] And when Ireland was conquered, there was precious little gold or silver to recompense its conquerors for their costly outlay. The explanation for this remarkable deviation in Ireland from the general practice of capitalist colonists with respect to land appropriation lay in the unique combination of motives for colonizing Ireland. These, as already noted, were strategic and to acquire land. Given England's strategic interest in Ireland, it was understandable that it should have become sufficiently involved to establish and to maintain the titles of its local agents to the lands of the Irish. These agents, in many cases, were the same Englishmen to whom were ascribed, by the English crown, proprietary rights to land in the North American colonies.[8] But there, the metropolitan English power had no economic interest, as Spain had in the gold and silver of its Latin American empire; nor strategic interest, as England had in Ireland. Without metropolitan involvement, it was impossible to enforce the titles to American land that English monarchs and parliament accorded.[9]

One aspect of Ireland's experience in relation to land expropriation was even more exceptional than the appropriation of land from agriculturists, which occurred also throughout Latin America. That exceptional aspect was the situation where, as a result of the Plantation of Ulster under King James I, the land was not merely expropriated from the indigenous farming people, as happened also in the rest of Ireland and throughout Latin America: but the expropriated land was subsequently operated by settler farmers, who in some cases employed as labourers the Irish who had previously farmed the land.

There appear to have been only four similar cases in the entire record of European colonialism where land was expropriated from indigenous farmers and then operated by settler farmers of metropolitan origin, usually employing the expropriated indigenes as farm labourers. The other four cases were all in Africa and occurred some centuries later than the Plantation of Ulster. The four cases were (1) the expropriation of Algerian land and its operation by French *colons* after the conquest of Algeria by France in the 1830s; (2) the settlement and farming of the 'white highlands' of Kenya by Britons, mainly after the First World War; (3) the invasion of what was to be known first as Rhodesia and subsequently as Zimbabwe by the British South African Company in the 1890s, and the appropriation of half of the territory's land to be worked by white settler farmers; and (4) the appropriation by the Boers in the nineteenth century of Bantu land in the Transvaal and Natal (Appendix B).

The expropriation of land from Ireland's indigenous farmers was neither easy nor profitable for the crown of England, unlike the similar and more or less contemporaneous expropriations in Latin America, which were both easy and profitable for the crowns of Castile and Aragon. The explanation for the exceptional expropriation by capitalist colonists of Irish land, and the explanation for the even more exceptional operation of the Ulster part of that land by British farmers, lie again in the unique combination of motives for the colonization of Ireland: the prospect of profit from land ownership and the need to secure Ireland against maritime powers hostile to England.

Race and ascendancy. The essence of capitalist colonialism was the securing of distant territories for the benefit of metropolitan interests. A garrison, or ascendancy, class was necessary in every case to secure the colony and to ensure its government in a manner conducive to metropolitan interests (Appendix B). The persons of mainly English origin who, under the Elizabethan policy of 'surrender and regrant' and under successive Cromwellian and Restoration settlements, had acquired the land, which had previously belonged to the Gaelic clans, were the garrison or ascendancy class in Ireland. They upheld metropolitan English interests in Ireland, and in turn were sustained by England. 'Did insurrection break forth in Ireland? The aristocracy of the country never stirred; it was English artillery that subdued the insurgents; and when everything was restored to order, the aristocracy continued to receive the revenue of its land as before.'[10]

Race distinguished the European garrison from the non-European garrisoned. White Europeans could be relied upon, especially in crises, to support and defend a capitalist colonial regime which the black or brown majority could be expected to undermine, oppose or assault. Ireland diverged from this otherwise universal pattern of racial distinction in the capitalist colonies. Colonizers and colonized in Ireland were distinguished instead by their religions. The former were Protestant; the latter were Catholic. These fine theological distinctions have proved more durable than the sharpest racial contrasts. The inevitable miscegenation between white colonizers and black or brown colonized produced sub-classes of mestizos, mulattos and Eurasians, who occupied the middle ground and eroded in time the sharp distinctions between black/brown and white. But successive generations born in Ireland, whether of mixed parentage or not, were Catholics or Protestants, with no diminution over the centuries of the fine theological distinctions between them.

Converts from Catholicism, whose motives might be suspect, were not immediately accepted into the privileged garrison class. Like the Irish felons shipped to the West Indies, converts were regarded as potential enemies within the camp at a time of crisis (Appendix B). Only the children or grandchildren of the converts could aspire to the privileges of the garrison. Meanwhile, 'such as conform and go to the state church are derided and oppressed by the multitude.'[11] The prospect, of being rejected by the class aspired to and anathematised by the class from which escape was sought, was an investment on behalf of children or grandchildren which impoverished people could not contemplate. It was a measure only to be contemplated by persons of substance, for whom the adoption of Protestantism helped to secure their property, which property in turn insulated them against Protestant rejection and Catholic hostility. Understandably, therefore, 'the eighteenth century had seen a steady stream of defections to the Established Church from the ranks of the Catholic gentry and middle class. But among other sections of the population, in the absence of any serious missionary effort from a lax, worldly Church of Ireland, the number of losses through conformity had been negligible.'[12] The majority of the Irish, *faute de mieux,* adhered to the old religion.

There are very few parallels in history for the incompatability between the religions of the rulers and of the ruled in colonial Ireland.[13] The normal role of religion has been to sustain the temporal power, which frequently has been perceived as the terrestrial manifestation of society's spirit world. It may please the Irish to attribute their stubborn adherence to the Roman Church to their religious constancy, which caused Ireland to be the only part of western Europe where, after the Peace of Augsburg in 1555, the pragmatic principle *cuius regio eius religio* did not apply. A more plausible explanation is the fact that Ireland was the only country in Europe within which a new social order — that of individualistic capitalism — had been superimposed on, and ruled uneasily over, an older order of tribal pastoralism. In the resistence of the indigenous culture against the superimposed culture, Catholicism has been to Irish nationalism what race has been to nationalism in other capitalist colonies.

There is no parallel in capitalist colonialism for the differentiation along religious lines between colonizers and colonized, of substantially similar racial type which occurred in Ireland. Parallels do, however, exist in other, non-capitalist colonial situations, where, as in Ireland, colonizers sought to retain and to 'squeeze' indigenous agriculturists who were of similar racial type to themselves. One such case was the pastoral Aryan invaders of India. These were able to have a wide range of relationships, including sexual, with the indigenous crop-growers, without being swamped by the much larger indigenous population (as the erstwhile ruling whites of the West Indies have been in large measure by the more numerous blacks). This was because the progeny of alliances between persons of different castes never attained the caste of the upper caste parent.[14] A similar caste-like arrangement existed between the Nilo-Hamitic pastoralists and the crop-growing Bantus of interlacustrine Africa. It obtained especially between the Tutsi pastoralists and the Hutu crop-growers of Rwanda.[15]

Property. The quintessentially European institution of property is the sixth of those topics that have been chosen here to throw light on the nature of capitalist colonialism. Property was the nexus that bound the garrison class and their local fellow-travellers in the colonies to the metropolitan power. The metropolitan European powers accorded the garrison rights of property and protected those rights against assault by the indigenes. The garrison, for its part, served the metropolitan interests, which created and protected their property rights.

Property in Europe (with the exception of England from Tudor times onwards) and in the settler colonies was, for the most part, in people (or slaves) and in things (Appendix A). Property in people and in things emerged spontaneously, under particular circumstances, in Europe and in the settler colonies (Appendix A). Property in the capitalist colonies, as it was in post-Tudor England, was invariably and overwhelmingly in land (Appendix B). Property in land uniquely evolved spontaneously in England under altogether exceptional circumstances (Chapter 3). Property in land in the settler colonies has invariably been imposed on those colonies by the metropolitan powers in pursuit of metropolitan interests. Property in Irish land, though *de lege* similar to property in land in the neighbouring island, was, therefore, *de facto* very different (see also below). Property in Irish land, as in land in all the capitalist colonies, was a metropolitan superimposition, designed to serve metropolitan interests regardless of the needs or interests of the colony. There are powerful conflicts of interest inherent in property in land which, because of the peculiar circumstances attaching to the spontaneous evolution of landed property in England, never became dominant there (Chapter 3). These conflicts did manifest themselves in Ireland as in all the other capitalist colonies (Appendix C). They have been principally responsible for the grievous consequences for the colonies of capitalist colonialism. The consequences are the seventh aspect of capitalist colonialism that help to reveal its character. And, singularly, the consequences for Irish society of the creation of property in land are especially revealing of the character of Irish capitalist colonialism.

The consequences (part 1). The appropriation of the clan lands as private property, following the Elizabethan conquest and the implementation of the policy of 'surrender and regrant',[16] opened for the first time the possibility of deriving profit, as distinct from a livelihood, from Irish land. That profit was to be made by shipping livestock to England and thereby sharing in the profits that accrued to English land, and to English land alone, in the sixteenth and seventeenth centuries (Chapter 3). Ireland, which had previously exported little except hunted, gathered and crude pastoral products,[17] developed under the early Stuarts an export trade in cattle and sheep that almost certainly exceeded any similar trade in the world at that time. Given that the trade only commenced after the Elizabethan conquest, which was completed by the battle of Kinsale in 1601; and given that England's population at the time was about one-tenth its present size with average real incomes about one-tenth the present level,[18] annual exports of around 45,000 cattle and a similar number of sheep achieved by 1640[19] were a remarkable testimony to the efficacy of capitalist colonialism in mobilizing resources for profit.

Sir William Petty, with the perspicacity of 'one of the most original social engineers who ever lived'[20] and who had himself nefariously acquired the extensive Irish lands on which the House of Landsdowne was founded, drew the logical conclusion from the fact of ownership of Irish land by metropolitan interests. Petty, in *A Treatise of Ireland,* written in 1687, recommended that most of the disaffected Irish be removed to England, to work there as labourers and tradespeople; that the country be converted into a cattlewalk, supporting six million cattle; these cattle to be tended by 200,000 people left in Ireland; and the cattle's produce to be shipped to England.[21] Petty argued that the island, by the removal thus of most of the disaffected population, could be most easily secured by England against foreign enemies; and could in this way also be made to yield the greatest profit to its new proprietors. Had Petty's recommendations been implemented, there would have been no 'Irish question' any more than there has been a North American, New Zealand or Australian 'question'.

Perspicacious though he was, Petty was blind to the political realities of a trade in livestock from Ireland to England in the seventeenth century. The rapidly growing livestock trade of early Stuart Ireland impinged critically on the equally rapidly evolving constitutional situation in England. The Stuart kings collected as a right custom duties on livestock imported into England.[22] They could also, through the determined efforts of an able Lord Lieutenant like Sir William Wentworth, share in the profits to be made from property in Irish land that were realized by the livestock trade. The Stuart kings were able to share in those profits through votes of taxation passed by a pliant Dublin parliament, which was concerned to protect the newly created and very uncertain rights of its members to property in the confiscated lands of Ireland.[23] The crown, in both ways, acquired resources that were outside the control of the Westminster parliament. There the heirs and assignees of those who had been made the proprietors of England's land by the Tudor dynasty were engaged in a struggle with the Stuart dynasty, from which would emerge in England the first property owners' state of modern times.[24] Moreover, the rapid growth of what, in relation to contemporary demand, must have been a very large supply of imported cattle and sheep, cannot but have depressed the profits of England's landed proprietors. This point was put, with only a little hyperbole, by a speaker in the Westminster House of Lords: ' The infinite number of Foreign Cattle that were daily imported did glut our markets and bring down the price of both our home-bred cattle and our land.'[25]

Understandably, therefore, the Restoration parliament, where England's landed proprietors were unquestionably dominant, quickly directed its attention to terminating an Anglo-Irish livestock trade that gave resources to the crown that were beyond parliament's control and that simultaneously depressed the profits from English land. The Cattle Acts of 1663-6 excluded from England virtually all Irish livestock and livestock products, except wool. The Acts precluded what would otherwise have been the logical way to maximize profits from Irish land, first recognized by Petty in 1687 and rediscovered by Irish government economic planners in 1962:[26] that was, to maximize the number of cattle and to minimize the number of people on the land.

Barred from mercantile England, Ireland's temperate zone produce had to find other markets if profits were to be made from Irish land. Markets were unavailable in Europe, where continued capital formation created a chronic agricultural surplus.[27] An outlet was secured in the West Indies and in provisioning the ships that served or protected that trade. Irish exports of provisions to feed the slaves of the British West Indies plantations increased eightfold between 1682/83 and 1773/74.[28] Williams observed that, even in the case of the French West Indies colonies, 'beef was generally obtained from Ireland, the Nantes traders making a profit estimated at 43%.'[29] The proceeds from the sale of Irish temperate produce, which was unwanted in Europe, were used to buy the tropical products that the West Indies slaves grew and for which, with growing populations and incomes, England and Central Western Europe had a strong demand. Ireland's agricultural resources, mobilized with a typical capitalist colonial ruthlessness, thus, through an indirect triangular trade, earned the profits that were the sole function of individually appropriated land. The efficient mobilization of agricultural land resources meant that, throughout most of the eighteenth century, Irish provisions for feeding the West Indies slaves were second in importance only to those of the North American colonies, which were much closer to the Caribbean market and where land was far more abundant and the climate more congenial for agriculture. 'Ireland exported large quantities of beef and pork to the West Indies. It was cheaper and better than the North American article.'[30]

The potato, which by tradition was introduced into Ireland by Sir Walter Raleigh, was the key to profit from Irish land once the Cattle Acts precluded a livestock trade to England. Originating in the Andean highlands, the potato produced in Ireland's cold, wet climate, more than enough food for the maintenance and reproduction of persons using hoe or spade cultivation. The exotic potato thus created in Ireland the agronomic conditions in which a coolie class could subsist by cultivating land without capital, other than a spade and a basket of seed potatoes. The potato made possible in Ireland the existence of a coolie class 20 degrees of latitude further from the equator than any other coolie class in the world (Appendix A). The Irish coolies provided the cheap labour on which was built an Irish economy that between 1660 and 1820 grew more rapidly than any other in Europe.[31] The rent roll from Irish land increased tenfold, from an estimated £800,000, or one-fifth of the national income, in 1670, to £8 millions in 1800.[32]

The Irish coolie class was created by a specific, unique combination of circumstances. These were, first, agricultural production conditions in Ireland's cold, wet climate; second, capitalist colonial institutional conditions that allowed no prescriptive rights of the indigenous people to impede the pursuit of profit by the proprietors of Irish lands; and third, a particular set of agricultural commodity price relationships. Market conditions particularly favoured the growth of an Irish coolie class during the reign of George III, from 1760 to 1820; and the coolies, who had hardly existed at its commencement, expanded to become the largest class in the land by the end of the reign.[33]

A combination of production and of capitalist colonial institutional conditions — that were peculiar to Ireland among European countries — made Ireland's population extraordinarily responsive to the market-determined demand for labour. The best available proxy for measuring that demand for Irish labour at that time is the level of exports of pigs.[34] Ireland's population, between 1712 and 1831, increased or decreased almost precisely by 6.88 persons (or, say, one family) for every increase or decrease of one pig exported. The survival and reproduction of the Irish was almost entirely determined by their ability to produce and export pigs.

Those metropolitan conditions referred to as 'the Industrial Revolution'

Table 4.1
Pig Exports and Population: Ireland 1712-1831

Year	Pig Exports	Estimated Population (000s) A. Connell	B. Regression
1712	10,723	2791	2945
1718	17,118	2894	2989
1725	19,566	3042	3006
1726	20,042	3031	3009
1732	24,506	3018	3040
1754	52,653	3191	3233
1767	88,682	3480	3481
1772	104,158	3584	3587
1777	152,178	3740	3918
1781	190,472	4048	4181
1785	179,739	4019	4107
1788	199,140	4389	4241
1790	221,223	4591	4393
1791	232,265	4753	4468
1821	519,575	6802	6444
1831	760,058	7767	8098

Note: Regression equation: $Y = 2871 + .00688X$, where Y is population in thousands and X is the number of pigs exported. The correlation is almost perfect: $r^2 = 0.984$.

Source: Pig Exports: R. Crotty, Irish Agricultural Production, p.277. Population: K.H. Connell The Population of Ireland, 1750-1845, p.25.

affected powerfully the market conditions that, together with climate and institutional conditions, created Ireland's coolie population. Demand in the metropolises shifted from energy-rich bread and butter to protein-rich beef and mutton; or from labour-intensive grain and milk to labour-extensive sheep and cattle. That shift in demand, which marked too a shift from mercantile, to factory, capitalist colonialism, was reflected in the long run (i.e. 1820 -1970) rise in the price of cattle fivefold relative to the price of wheat and threefold relative to the price of butter.[35] The Cattle Acts having been earlier repealed, it at last became possible to implement the logic of property in Irish land, as perceived by Petty in 1687. 'The landlords of Ireland are at length deeply convinced that, though a stock of cattle or sheep will afford profit, a stock of mere human creatures, unemployed, will afford none,' was how a landlord expressed the point to a parliamentary commission of inquiry in 1825.[36]

People were replaced by more profitable livestock. 'You have stated the rent to be for tillage thirty shillings per acre; what would you say was the rent of the same quality of land for grazing?,' asked a Devon commissioner. The reply: 'Higher, from thirty shillings to forty.'[37] The value of output was greater on cropped land than on grassland;[38] nevertheless profits could be increased by switching from crop-growing to pasture. This was because, although output declined when land was changed from tillage to grass, it was possible to reduce even more the cost of inputs, especially labour. Cattle exports, which had not changed for the preceding 160 years, increased sixfold between 1820-25 and 1866-70; or from 76,000 to 451,000 annually. Annual exports of sheep, 'the poor man's cattle' which require less capital but more labour, increased thirteenfold, from 50,000 to 681,000.[39] The number of people getting a livelihood in Irish agriculture declined meanwhile from 1.7 million in 1841 to 1.1 million in 1871.[40]

Industrial expansion was not an answer to agricultural decline. As agricultural output and the number getting a livelihood in agriculture declined, so too did the output of, and the numbers employed in, non-agricultural industries. During a century of exceptionally rapid, world wide urbanization, population declined in 87 out of the 100 Irish towns that, in 1926, had populations of 1,500 or over. Only Dublin and its environs, together with a handful of garrison and seaside towns, registered population growth. The Republic's total urban population declined from 979,000 in 1841 to 944,000 in 1926.[41] In 1871, the first census year for which the necessary data are available, the number in the Twenty-six Counties engaged in agriculture was 828,000 and the number in manufacturing industry was 328,000.[42] By 1926 these numbers had declined to 672,000 and 187,000 respectively.[43] While the agricultural population declined by 19%, the manufacturing population declined by 43%.

The decline in the proportion of the Irish population producing non-agricultural goods was part of a colonialwide process that occurred during the first century of factory capitalist colonialism (Appendix B). Ireland was distinguished from other capitalist colonies only by the fact that while the other colonies supplied more crop and other primary products to the metropolises and their agricultural populations expanded, Ireland's agriculture was redirected into cattle and sheep production which required less labour. As Ireland's agricultural population declined, the number producing non-agricultural goods and services declined both absolutely and relatively.

The size of the market determines success in the age of factory capitalism. England, as a result of that long sequence of events commencing with the Black Death of the 1340s and the country's native genius and considerable natural wealth, provided within its boundaries, in the early nineteenth century, the largest, richest market in the world. England had the genius and capacity to exploit the possibilities offered by that situation. In colonial

Ireland, by contrast, the domestic market was being wiped out along with the coolie population. Reduction in real industrial wages ('incomes policy') was no answer to this loss of a local market. This was partly because such reductions were double-edged: while improving the competitiveness of the firm or industry immediately concerned, they reduced still further the domestic market for other firms and industries. It was also because reductions in wages below a critical level caused the industrial workers' starvation. This was common in Ireland in the 1840s.

Transport improvements were not neutral as between metropolitan and colonial economies. Better sea and land transport made it easier in particular to ship livestock from the Irish hinterland to English urban consuming centres, thereby enhancing the relative profitability of the land-intensive and labour-extensive cattle and sheep production. Better transport also made it easier to distribute English manufactured products into the Irish hinterland, to compete there with the products of local cottage and craft industries. If industries in the Irish hinterland were to fight back successfully they would have had to attain the same scale as that of metropolitan industry. Given their own depleted market, to sustain such a scale of production they would have had to export most of their product. Meanwhile their English competitors, with a large market on their doorstep, only had to export a small fraction of their total product to achieve the lowest cost, large scale level of output. Except in special cases, a metropolitan location had major advantages over a colonial one for manufacturing in the age of factory capitalism.

Denmark illustrates the critical importance of a domestic market in this era. Located in continental Europe and therefore having summers a little warmer and drier, and winters that were colder — and therefore also being uncolonized — its economic history was very different from Ireland's in the nineteenth century. Danish agriculture and the Danish land tenure system were such that the same English industrial revolution and the same English market for food that caused the obliteration of the Irish coolies and caused Irish agricultural output at best to stagnate, caused Danish agricultural output to expand rapidly.[44] An expanding agriculture provided the buoyant domestic market to support even more rapidly growing secondary and tertiary industries.

Property in land: England and Ireland. Consideration of the manner and the circumstances in which the institution of property in land was applied in England, on the one hand, and in Ireland as well as in other capitalist colonies on the other, helps to make clear the fundamental difference in this institution as it was applied in the metropolis and in the colonies. First, property in land was a novel concept in Tudor England and was implemented tentatively, with due regard to circumstances, from time to time and from place to place. The Tudor state, for all the absoluteness of the monarchy, was weak administratively and perpetually concerned with the maintenance of a fragile internal peace:

Tudor policy was quite tender to vested interests.... The idea that a whole industry should be wiped out because the same goods could be produced elsewhere made no sense to the Tudors; and if their economics were crude, their knowledge of the cost of suppressing the riots and rebellions of men thrown out of work, being founded on experience, was most precise. The vast mass of Tudor legislation on economic activities rests solidly on three principles — privilege, regulation and supervision. The purpose was to prevent the unchecked greed and ambition of any group — middle class or other — from dislocating social order.[45]

Three centuries not merely legitimized property in land, but sanctified it as a divine right emanating from the Creator. England's colonial administration in nineteenth century Ireland was one of the most competent and powerful in the world at the time. It was ready and able to enforce property rights that were deemed legitimate, regardless of the social and political consequences in the colony.

Second, the institution of property in land was applied in England under very different transport conditions. Profits from English land in the Tudor age resulted from exporting wool and woollen cloth to Europe. The wool and the cloth were taken to the ports for export by pack-horse, which was the principal means of transport in an age when transport facilities were poorer than they had been 1,500 years previously. Then there had been the well-constructed and maintained Roman roads; but these had meanwhile broken up and had been largely abandoned through centuries of neglect and decay. Only items of high value, like cloth and wool, could bear the cost of long distance overland transport. Those who owned and those who tended the sheep, as well as those who spun and wove the wool from them, had all to be fed from the produce of English land. Notwithstanding the profits from the wool trade, England remained not merely self-sufficient, but a net exporter of grain in most years, up to the beginning of George III's reign in 1760.[46]

Demographic momentum maintained earlier trends in Ireland for some decades after 1820, when external demand changed fundamentally. Population, and grain and pig production for export, all continued to expand and reached a peak in the early 1840s.[47] All changed at the turning point of the Great Famine, 1845-48. Population commenced its long term decline; pig and milk production stabilized; and Ireland, from being a major grain exporter in the 1840s, became a major grain importer by the 1920s when annual grain, meal and flour imports to the Twenty-six Counties alone were almost a million tons.[48] Vastly improved transport facilities, which included much larger, steam-propelled, iron ships, canals and railways made possible and profitable a far more complete switch to pasture in nineteenth century Ireland than had been possible in sixteenth century England.

The third major difference between the institution of property in land as applied in England and in Ireland derived from the difference in the role of profit in both cases. A substantial part of capitalist Europe's small total surplus was channelled towards England's landed proprietors in the sixteenth and seventeenth centuries. These profits, at a time when there were few profits anywhere, made England's landed proprietors the most powerful property owners of the age:

> The great landowners...alone had the capital to set up works, the ready cash to pay for the high overhead costs, and the woods to supply the necessary fuel....In this expansion (of iron production) the nobility and the leading gentry played the decisive part, the bulk of English production at any time being in the hands of the great county families. Nearly every technological innovation in the smelting and further processing of iron and steel was financed and operated in the first instance, not by City merchants or *nouveau riche* gentry, but by established aristocratic families.[49]

Profits from land also played an important part in initiating England's overseas expansion: 'Elizabethan maritime ventures sprang from the initiative and financial backing of two very restricted social groups: the great merchants of London (and to a small extent of the west country) and the peers and leading courtiers.'[50] The wealth of English landowners, unequalled by that of any coherent, contemporary social class elsewhere, enabled them to force through the constitutional change of replacing an absolute monarch, who claimed to rule by divine authority, with a state governed by property owners in the interests of property. That constitutional change, effected much earlier than anywhere else in Europe, together with the continued enjoyment of profits from land were central to the emergence of England as the leading world power through the eighteenth and nineteenth centuries.

Profits, which comprised an exceptionally high proportion of the small total output from Irish grassland, were, in contrast to the profits from English landed property, used for the most part in ways that reduced rather than increased Irish national product. Much of the profits were ploughed back in order to expand livestock numbers in response to changing market demand. Because of the lower output, but higher profit, from land grazed with cattle or sheep, savings invested in this way tended to reduce agricultural output.

The rest of the profits from Irish grass farming were transferred to London; as rent to absentee landowners, as payments on mortgages on Irish land, or as the savings of Irish grazier farmers. These savings, first deposited with the burgeoning Irish branch-banking system of the nineteenth century, were drawn to London as lesser bodies are attracted by gravity to larger ones. In London, the Irish funds were used to help the financing of English factory capitalism, which was playing havoc with Irish cottage and craft industries. These had already been grievously weakened by agriculture's switch from milk and crops to sheep and cattle, which lost them their markets and, in the case of the staple provision trade, their raw materials as well.

The process of transferring Irish savings to London gave rise to one of the few 'successes' in the Irish economy since the emergence of factory capitalism in England around 1820.[51] A list of the hundred oldest, and therefore by definition most successful, banks in the world in 1962 showed that the USA had the most, 35; Britain was next with 15; and Ireland came third with six banks, including the banks now incorporated into the Bank of Ireland group and the Allied Irish Banks.[52] The foundations of this grotesquely disproportionate banking prosperity were set in the safe and lucrative task of transferring to the London money market the proceeds of 'rackrenting slum landlords... [of] grinding exploitation of workers, [of] petty swindling of customers, [of] learning how to

"fumble in a greasy till
and add the halfpence to the pence
and prayer to shivering prayer.'"[53]

There was no profitable outlet for these savings in undeveloping Ireland and they were used instead by the London money market to help finance the industrial growth in Britain that was destroying Irish manufacturing.

These then were the major *de facto* differences in the *de lege* similar institutions of property in land in metropolitan England and in colonial Ireland. First, property in land evolved spontaneously in England in response to unique circumstances there and as befited such a radically new concept, it was applied tentatively, pragmatically and with a keen consciousness of local economic, social and political consequences. By contrast, in nineteenth century Ireland it was applied doctrinarily, as an indisputable, fundamental element in a social order, to which colonial Irish society was forced by metropolitan power to adjust as best it could. Second, because of the vast improvements in transport that had occurred during the three centuries that intervened between the reigns of Elizabeth I and Victoria of England, the adjustments required to maximize profits from Irish land were far greater than those required in Tudor England. Third, the profits from property in English land, secured at a time when there was little profit or property anywhere, were a key factor in triggering economic, commercial and constitutional development, which resulted in England being the foremost world power of the Victorian age. Profits from property in Irish land, by contrast, were used either to finance the replacement of more people by livestock, which produced less but made more profit; or they were attracted, as by gravity, to the vastly greater store of English capital, adding to that capital's capacity to undermine and destroy Ireland's already weakened industrial capital.

48

The successes of the nineteenth century. There emerged out of that destruction four outstanding 'successes', which tower dramatically above the socio-economic decay upon which they flourished. Consideration of their successful, fungus-like growth on the putrifying mass of Irish society throws light on their role in the process of social decay. Reference has already been made to one of these 'successes', the Irish branch-banking system. The others were Guinness's brewery in Dublin, which emerged as the largest brewery in the world in 1900; Harland and Wolfe's shipyard in Belfast, which again was the largest in the world in 1900; and the Catholic Church.

Guinness's success owed little to any exceptional ability of the Guinness family, contrary to Lynch and Vaizey's sycophantic theme.[54] According to them, Guinness's success was due to the family's ability which, had it been more common in Ireland, could have saved the country much of the disaster it experienced in the nineteenth century. Guinness, in fact, owed its success in the first instance to being brewers at a time when a ruined people sought oblivion in alcohol, which was thus one of the very few commodities for which demand was growing in nineteenth century Ireland. Even then, Guinness could not have survived in competition with English brewers had it not, like other Irish brewers, swindled the excise of malt taxes.[55] Thereafter it was mainly a matter of retaining the position acquired by Arthur Guinness when, in 1759 with a gift from the Protestant archbishop of Cashel to his mother, who was the archbishop's housekeeper, he bought Dublin's largest brewery. As Catholic, Gaelic Ireland retrogressed, Dublin, the navel that joined the colony to the metropolis, became exceptionally predominant. Dublin brewed 53% of Ireland's beer while London brewed only 22% of Britain's beer in the 1850s.[56]

Guinness, like the other Irish brewers, gained enormously from the consolidation of the Irish and British spirit duties between 1852 and 1862, which doubled the cost of whiskey in Ireland.[57] That unification of the duties only became possible when the colonial administration had acquired a sufficiently firm control to suppress illicit distilling and the associated shebeens which were regarded as hotbeds of sedition.

Being a brewer in a country that sought solace in alcohol; having survived by swindling the excise; being the largest brewer in a Dublin that dominated a ruined hinterland; and experiencing an upsurge in sales when a sharply increased duty on spirits doubled the price of whiskey: Guinness was ideally placed to benefit from the next twist of fortune. This was the introduction, in 1869, of legislation to curb drinking by Britain's working class. The legislation, which applied throughout the United Kingdom, tightened the issuing of licenses to premises for the sale of intoxicating liquor. Getting these licenses had, up to then, been a formality; thereafter, new licenses became virtually unavailable.[58] Local British brewers availed of the new legislation to buy up licensed premises in their localities and to 'tie' these to their own beer, excluding the national brewers' product. The latter, in order to expand nationally, had to divert the bulk of their resources away from brewing, into real estate, by buying the now limited and therefore costly houses licensed to sell alcohol.

The legislation had a different effect in Ireland. There, because of the halving of the population in the preceding decades and its continuing decline, there was a chronic surplus of licensed public houses. Irish local brewers could not use the defensive tactic that saved their counterparts in Britain. While the British national brewers were stymied by having to divert their resources from brewing and marketing beer into real estate acquisition, Guinness, free from such hindrances, was able to continue its expansion in Ireland; and, on the basis of its exceptional dominance of the Irish market, to win an increasing share of the British market.

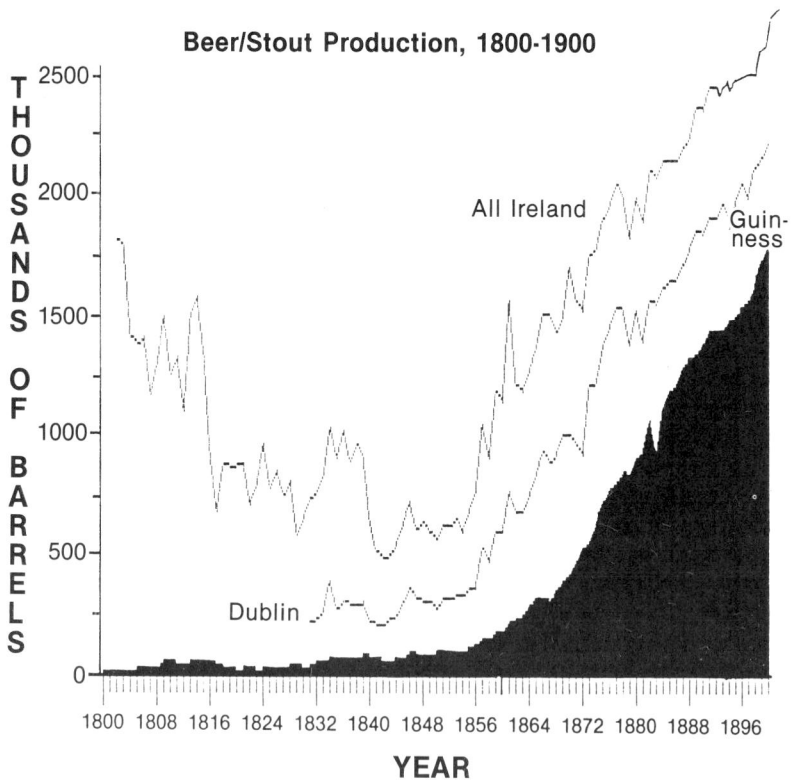

Source: BPP 1821 (147) XX 129; BPP 1823 (316), (571), XVI, 547, 549; BPP 1831-32 (223) XXIV 27 and annually to BPP 1901 (111) LXIX 191.

The success of the Harland and Wolfe shipyard, like the industrial growth of Belfast as a whole, rested on a far firmer foundation than the racist one suggested by Black: '[The reason] Ulster had so much industrial growth when the rest of Ireland had so little ... it seems to me that in most instances personal initiatives overcame the comparative lack of natural advantage.'[59] Ulster industrialization rested solidly on, and grew out of, the privileged garrison status of the Protestants of Ulster.

The British, Protestant settler farmers of Ulster, being part of the garrison ascendancy class, were of necessity armed. The relationship between these armed, Protestant settler farmers and the proprietors of the land that they farmed was very different from the relationship between the disarmed Catholic Irish peasants and the Anglo-Irish proprietors of the land that the Catholics farmed. The relationship in the first case was enshrined in the 'Ulster Custom', a body of practices that, as in England, implicitly recognized certain prescriptive rights of tenants in the land they farmed. These included security of tenure, subject to the payment of rents that were required to be 'fair'; and compensation on the termination of the tenancy for improvements effected. The relationship in the second case was reflected in a system under which the Catholic Irish tenants had no such right to the land farmed; had possession only subject to the payment of rack-rents that were extracted by middlemen; and received no compensation for improvements effected.[60]

A perfectly freely working land market that was uninhibited by any rights of Catholic Irish tenants made it possible, under appropriate price conditions, for young capital-less people to acquire land and to make, in the course of George III's reign, the cottier-coolies the largest social class in Ireland. The capital-less young could not acquire land so readily in Ulster, where Protestant tenants were under less pressure to maximize incomes by subletting land and where, if sub-tenants got possession of land, they could not be so readily evicted as in the rest of Ireland, where the Ulster Custom did not apply. Ulster during the reign of George III did not experience, therefore, the emergence to dominance of the coolie class that occurred especially in Leinster and east Munster. The Irish census returns of 1821, 1831 and 1841 provide abundant evidence of the different rates of growth of the proletariat in different parts of Ireland at the time. In Ulster the traditional Central Western European, capital-dominant structure of production was preserved. Because young people could not, under the Ulster Custom, get access to land, they were forced to remain dependent on their parents, who thus had exclusive tenancy of the land, the capital to finance its operation and the cheap family labour to operate it.[61]

The rise in European incomes after the Black Death created a demand for cloth and brought the English woollen industry into prominence, with all that that subsequently entailed (Chaper 3). The increase in British incomes, caused by the industrial revolution, gave rise to a similar heightened demand for cloth in the eighteenth and nineteenth centuries. The coolie-dominated agriculture of southern Ireland could not meet that demand: the capital-dominated agriculture of Ulster could. Potatoes, planted in March, can be marketed in the form of a fat pig by the following March. Flax sown at the same time cannot be marketed as yarn until the following September-twelve-months; at the earliest. Irrespective of the difference in returns, starving, rack-rented coolies had no option but to grow potatoes, which enabled them to meet their rental obligations at the earliest moment and so gave them a chance of renting another patch of land for another year. Neither could Leinster and Munster's more substantial farmers grow flax profitably. These, though they had the capital to grow grain crops and to stock land with cattle, did not have the high quality, low economic cost family labour that was needed to grow flax and process it into linen cloth. Their sons and daughters, on a freely working land market could and did rent a plot of land, grow potatoes, and thereby attain sufficient economic independence to become social units. In this way, outside Ulster, labour and capital became separated and gravitated into different production units or firms.

Ulster's farmers, protected by the Ulster Custom, had the capital and the cheap family labour to grow flax and to undertake the time-consuming (i.e. capital-consuming) work of processing it into linen cloth. Moreover, because of the spreading proletarianization of the rest of Ireland and the consequent difficulty there of processing yarn into cloth, the yarn produced in the 'flax counties' of the south was drawn to the north for processing. The south's decline thus furthered the growth of the linen industry in the north.[62]

The rest followed. An indigenous linen industry was solidly rooted in agronomic conditions of production; in institutional arrangements that recognized the prescriptive rights of armed, Protestant, garrison tenants in the land they worked, while denying similar rights to disarmed, garrisoned, Catholic tenants; and in the prevailing market conditions. It grew and adapted to changing circumstances. Part of that adaptation was the transition from cottage to factory production and the growth of Belfast. The factory production of linen cloth required different machines from those used in the British textile industry. It was necessary, in order to transform Ulster's cottage linen industry into a factory industry, to design and then to build machines suitable for processing flax into cloth. Hence the development of Belfast's engineering industry.

Abundant, deep-water dock space within rapidly growing Belfast, a labour force already accustomed to the discipline of factory production, and engineering skills acquired in the linen-machinery manufacturing industry; these were substantial attractions for the newly emerging industry of iron-shipbuilding. Traditional wooden-ship building yards, including Dublin's, could not easily adapt to the new technology. The old yards, in the old cities and towns, were hedged in by urban growth and, accustomed to building ships weighing at most hundreds of tons, they had neither the space nor the access to deep water necessary for handling ships ten or a hundred times larger, which the new age required. At least as serious as these problems was the fact that the old centres of the shipbuilding industry had become riddled with restrictive labour practices which had become embedded in the craft of building wooden ships. The new city of Belfast, uncluttered with the accretions either of urban sprawl or of craft regulation and tradition, offered both the space and the freedom to apply newly acquired local engineering skills to the highly innovative business of building iron ships in the nineteenth century.

Ireland's major industrial weakness of an inadequate domestic demand hardly affected shipbuilding. Relative to the volume of business transacted, little personal contact was required between vendor and buyer. The goods, which incorporated a tremendous amount of local value added to the crude, imported raw materials, could be sailed, under their own steam, to wherever the buyer wished to take delivery.

Belfast had a further major and unique attraction. This was the close identity of interests between the Protestant owners/managers and the Protestant craftsmen in the shipyards. Nineteenth century iron shipbuilding was, above all, an innovative industry. Innovation and flexibility were of the essence. Even in new, non-traditional British yards, these qualities were constrained by the basic class conflict between owners/managers and workers. Any such conflict that may have existed in Harland and Wolfe's Belfast yard was utterly overshadowed by the common interests of a Protestant settler garrison minority in the face of the implacable hostility of the garrisoned Catholic masses of Ireland. Disunity, or weakness of Protestant resolve, threatened to drown all — Protestant owners, managers and craftsmen alike — in the morass of poverty, social disintegration and famine that had engulfed Catholic Ireland. Fear of the Catholic enemy outside the shipyard, who had fallen upon the Protestant minority at every opportunity — in 1641, 1688 and again in 1798 — was a tremendously unifying factor that facilitated flexibility and adaptation in an industry where, and at a time when, these qualities were particularly important. A similar identity of interests and absence of class conflict was to be observed throughout the capitalist colonies among expatriate Europeans (including Catholic Irish) in the face of the overwhelming mass of hostile black or brown indigenes of Latin America, the Caribbean, Africa and Asia.

Flexibility and adaptiveness were the easier to achieve in as much as their cost fell mainly on the Catholic helots (as on the black or brown indigenes of the other capitalist colonies). When trade declined cyclically, or when innovation caused lay-offs, the marginalized Catholic workers could be fired, and the status and security of the established Protestant workers were preserved. Harland and Wolfe is a monument to

Protestant/Catholic antipathy in Ireland. That antipathy deepened as the value of Protestant privilege and the cost of Catholic disability grew in a Victorian Ireland that saw the Irish Catholic coolies wiped out. The depth of the aversion was the strength of Harland and Wolfe.

The Catholic Church was the fourth of the nineteenth century Irish successes which, by any standard, were remarkable; but which, in contrast to the decay of the society from which they sprang, were startlingly so. The success of the Church was remarkable in terms of the growth in the numbers of male and female clergy;[63] of the building of churches[64] and of schools and hospitals operated by Catholic clergy; and in terms of the world-wide spread of Irish missionaries and teachers. All of this occurred during the reign of Victoria, which also witnessed the destruction of Ireland's largest social class, the potato-growing coolies. It is possible to identify a number of factors which, while helping to account for the Church's remarkable growth, also throw light on the pathology of nineteenth century Irish society.

The most remarkable demographic characteristic of Irish society since the death of George III has been a very low marriage rate. Rather less than half those who were born in Ireland and who survived childhood acquired the basic socio-economic independence necessary for marriage (see below, Chapter 5). Never was sexual continence forced so rigorously on so large a proportion of any people. Celibacy is, for many, the greatest sacrifice required by the life of a Catholic cleric, male or female. But as celibacy was in any case unavoidable for very many Irish people, little additional sacrifice was involved in becoming a cleric. Only as marriage opportunities increased in Ireland in the 1960s and 1970s did becoming a Catholic cleric involve the sacrifice of celibacy, and since then the number of persons becoming clerics has dropped sharply.[65]

The Victorian reign marked the transformation of the market for Irish produce and thereby the destruction of the potato-based coolies and their replacement by the ascendant, cattle-grazing bourgeoisie. The rise of the Irish bourgeoisie meant also an upsurge of Irish nationalism (Appendix B); or an awareness of differences, particularly differences of economic interest, between the colonized and the colonizing. The unique, critical role of religion in Irish capitalist colonialism has already been noted. It was understandable, therefore, that as cattle prices rose fivefold relative to wheat and threefold relative to milk, and that as the coolies were destroyed and replaced by the bourgeois cattle-graziers, there should also have been a great upsurge of Irish nationalism and Catholicism.

The Irish bourgeoisie invested in cattle and sheep to secure their position in the harsh existing world; they invested in churches and convents to secure their position in the next. They favoured also Church-operated schools, where those of their children for whom there was no scope on the cattle-grazed land could get, at little cost, an education that would equip them better for a struggle for life that, in Ireland, was quite desperate.

Catholicism, for all its spirituality, supported and sustained property, particularly the property of its bourgeois members. It had contributed importantly to the growth of capitalism in Central Western Europe, in part by helping to enforce the celibacy that was necessary for capitalism's growth, and in part by preaching the divine origins of property and by imposing sanctions on those who infringed property rights (Appendix A). The restraint that the Catholic Church preached to the property-less had clear attractions for a bourgeois society struggling to curb the sexual license of the reign of George III, which had culminated in the Great Famine. The preaching of the Church was often a better bulwark to property than even the well organized Royal Irish Constabulary; at a time when the only defence the starving, potato-dependent coolies had against encroaching cattle was to hough or kill them. Moreover, Catholic teaching on property rights was sufficiently flexible and discerning to distinguish between Catholic and Protestant property. It allowed leading Church members to play a major role in the eventual confrontation between the Catholic owners of property in the form of livestock, and the predominantly Protestant owners of land, over the sharing of the agricultural product of Irish property.

Religion, finally, was one of a number of escapes or sources of solace from the grinding poverty and the unparalleled sexual deprivation that marked Irish society. Other escapes were alcoholism and lunacy, of which, together with celibacy and numbers of clerics, Ireland had the highest incidence in the world.[66] There was, of course, also emigration, which almost half the population chose.

It is, however, a misconception and a serious misrepresentation of the role of the Catholic Church to suggest that its pre-eminence was the cause of Irish socio-economic decline in the nineteenth century. Rather, the Church's role was like the success of the banks, of Guinness and of Harland and Wolfe; it was like the destruction of the coolies; it was like Irish socio-economic disintegration in the nineteenth century. These were all consequences of Ireland's capitalist colonization. It was the capitalist colonization of Ireland, uniquely among European countries, that gave to religion in Ireland the role that race played in the other capitalist colonies. That role was to distinguish easily the colonized from the colonizer, and of being a focus of anti-colonial sentiment (Appendix B). It was the capitalist colonial concept of land as a source of profit, combined with the fivefold rise of cattle prices relative to wheat prices that spelt the ruin of the Irish coolies; the rise of the Irish bourgeoisie; and of the Irish, bourgeois Catholic Church. It is interesting that, in the 1841 census, per 1,000 population, England had 1.29 and 'priest-ridden' Ireland had 0.88 clergy. But by 1901, per 1,000 population, England's 1.84 were dwarfed by Ireland's 4.33 clergy.[67]

The consequences (part 2). As colonial Spain decimated the agricultural population of Latin America, which constituted one of the great centres of pre-Colombian world population (Appendix B), so the profitable development of a livestock trade from Ireland to England required, as Petty perceived 300 years ago, Ireland's depopulation. But for 160 years, between the Restoration of Charles II and the death of George III of England, that livestock trade was incompatible with superior metropolitan interests. Landed profit was instead secured by an indirect, triangular trade in provisions produced by Irish coolie labour. A coolie class emerged and became the largest class in the land during the reign of George III. But when the market changed, the coolies and the production they supported ceased to be profitable. The socio-economic order established in colonial Ireland by metropolitan England obliterated the coolies. That occurred in the course of the reign of another English monarch: Queen Victoria. The class of self-employed persons, cultivating rented land with little more than a spade and a basket of seed potatoes, had virtually disappeared from Ireland by the end of the reign. Decline has persisted and now, in the Twenty-six counties, little more than one third as many people get a livelihood as in 1841, before the destruction of the coolies.

Ending colonialism. The ending of European colonialism is the eight and last of those threads that have been pursued here to help unravel as much of the great, tangled skein of a historic phase as is possible in this book, and as is necessary in order to give an adequate insight into a phenomenon that has shaped all modern life, but particularly the lives of the former capitalist colonies. The Irish experience, with some important exceptions that have been noted, fitted well enough into the overall pattern of capitalist colonialism that has been considered up to this. The Irish experience of decolonization also conformed to the world-wide pattern of the ending of European colonialism, which was everywhere achieved through the operation of three disparate sets of forces: a national elite pursuing its class interests; a sympathetic opposition in the metropolis; and the support of one or more metropolitan power (Appendix B).

Ireland's remarkable economic growth and relative domestic harmony in the eighteenth century inculcated in its Anglo-Irish, Protestant landed proprietors confidence in their ability to maintain, by their own efforts, their privileged position, and made them impatient of continued English tutelage and control. Grattan's Dublin parliament was representative of that class, which had been established and supported by metropolitan England, as the creoles of Latin America had been by Spain (Appendix B). Grattan's parliament, its members somewhat imbued with contemporary concepts of the rights of man — particularly the rights of property-owning man — and availing of England's preoccupation with the American War of Independence, sought and obtained 'the abolition of Poyning's Law in

1782, and the Renunciation Act of the following year. Every tie between Great Britain and Ireland was specifically removed, save that of a common sovereign'.[68]

The outbreak of the protracted French revolutionary and Napoleonic wars ten years later, in 1792, altered the position in regard to Irish decolonization in material ways. First, it radicalised the Irish independence movement, especially by challenging the Protestant ascendancy. Second, while it introduced the previously missing factor of foreign power support for colonial independence, the availability of that support from France awakened in England all the traditional fears about 'he who would England win, let him in Ireland first begin'. The third important effect of the wars with France was to unite English opinion against any concessions to Irish nationalism, as to all forms of liberalism in England itself.

The subsequent course of events in Ireland was dominated by the continued rapid growth, especially in east Munster and Leinster, of a Catholic coolie class that threatened to overwhelm every other interest.[69] The rise of this vast pauper class, combined with the progress of the revolution in France, weakened the confidence of the Protestant ascendancy, and of the considerable Catholic commercial class, in their ability to retain their privileges and their property in an independent Ireland. The move towards independence which they had initiated was, therefore, not pursued, although foreign support had become available. This was partly because the elite lost confidence in their ability to control an independent Ireland; and partly because of the absence of support for secession within a metropolitan Britain united in war against France. There was, on the contrary, general support among the Protestant landowners and among the Catholic commercial class — the classes which, 20 years earlier, had sought independence — for abandonment of the degree of autonomy that had been obtained in 1782, and for complete political and economic integration with Britain.[70] Ireland's landed and commercial classes in 1800 behaved like Belloc's little boy who 'clings to nurse for fear of worse'.

The obliteration of the coolies and their replacement by cattle and sheep in Victorian Ireland transformed the position of the Irish Catholic, farming, bourgeois class. That class's development had previously been cramped by pressure from the nether millstone of a burgeoning proletariat and the upper millstone of an Anglo-Irish ascendancy supported by metropolitan power. As already noted, Irish cattle exports, which had previously stagnated for 160 years, increased sixfold between 1821-25 and 1866-70; while sheep exports increased thirteenfold, from 50,000 to 681,000 annually over the same period. Livestock exports increased by a further 50% during the following decade.[71] Both processes — the destruction of the coolies and the growth of the livestock-grazing, farming bourgeoisie — as well as being opposite sides of the same coin of agricultural adjustment to changed market conditions in metropolitan Britain, reinforced one another in building up Irish bourgeois self-confidence. The owners of greatly enlarged, rapidly growing and profitable flocks and herds were of a very different calibre from the wretched coolies who had perished in millions from 1820 to 1850, with scarcely a murmur of protest.[72] The readiness of the bourgeoisie to challenge those who impeded their further progress was the greater because they had less to fear from the proletariat than any other bourgeoisie in the world. They had far less to fear than the landed Protestant and commercial Catholic classes of the 1790s who, with the example of the French Revolution very much in mind, opted for union with Britain rather than independence in an Ireland swarming with a seemingly ever-growing mass of potato-eating coolies.

The indigenous Irish middle-class farmers confronted metropolitan rule in the late 1870s. They made it clear through Parnell,[73] their spokesman in the Westminster parliament, that the price of Ireland's continued adherence to the Union of Great Britain and Ireland was the ending of the sharing of the large and growing profits from the livestock trade with the Anglo-Irish elites, who had titles to property in Irish land that were based on the increasingly anachronistic grounds of conquest, confiscation and royal munificence in an increasingly distant and irrelevant past.

Irish rebellion against the payment of rents to mainly Anglo-Irish landowners was facilitated and encouraged by the rise of the Liberal Party in England. The Liberals were the intellectual and political heirs to the Whigs, who, a century earlier, had encouraged the American rebels (Appendix B). The Anglo-Irish landed interest was a privileged interest, established and maintained in Ireland by metropolitan rule. Like all such privileged interests, it was incorrigibly reactionary; and in and outside the Westminster parliament, where its representatives sat, it supported the Conservative party. English Liberal fortunes were, as a result, advanced by the weakening of the Anglo-Irish landed interest and the support of the English Liberals was an important consideration in the success of Irish rebellion.

The third element in the movement towards independence, which was foreign power support for colonial rebellion against the metropolitan power, was supplied by the numerous Irish emigrants and their offspring in America, Australia and in Britain itself. These people, as evidenced by the very fact of their emigration, were perhaps the most hostile of the Irish to a colonial government that had made it impossible for them to secure a livelihood in their own country. The emigrants and their offspring in Britain gave important political support; and those in America and Australia gave financial support to Irish rebellion against the payment of rents to Anglo-Irish landowners.

The Irish middle-class farmers, together with their urban professional and commercial kin and class allies, quickly and easily won the concessions sought from an English government that was prepared to 'kill Home Rule with kindness'.[74] The 1881 Land Act established the principle of joint proprietorship in the land by the landlord and the farmer. That was followed by further legislation which, in the course of a few decades, effectively transferred the ownership of the land from some 10,000 Anglo-Irish landowners to Irish farmers, of whom some 20,000 graziers acquired about half of it. Property in Irish land, which had been confiscated by the Tudors from the clans and conferred on the ascendancy, garrison class, was, in this way, transferred to a larger, but still relatively small, farmer-grazier section of the Irish people.

The drift to independence. The steam having been let out of the independence movement by the 1881 and succeeding land acts, Irish nationalism, for some decades, followed a desultory course. That course was principally concerned with cultural matters, including drama, literature, and the revival of Gaelic games and Gaelic literature. The Anglo-Irish Protestants, stripped — by the land acts and by the sea-change of economic and political fortunes that underlay them — of their former economic, political and social dominance in Irish society, occupied a remarkably prominant role in this cultural revival. It was a role that probably assuaged their loss of power to the Catholic, Irish bourgeoisie.

The fiscal balance within the United Kingdom of Great Britain and Ireland had moved in favour of Ireland before the end of the nineteenth century, and was to continue to do so. Ireland, in 1901-2, contributed £9.8 millions, or 6.55% of total revenue to the UK exchequer. Non-military expenditure in Ireland in the same year was £7.2 millions, or 14.96% of total UK civilian expenditure that year. Ireland's contribution to Imperial Expenditure (i.e. the army and navy) was £2.6 millions, or 2.54% of the total. By 1913-4 these quantities had changed to an Irish revenue contribution of £11.1 millions, which was 5.71% of the total; non-military expenditure in Ireland was £12.4 millions, or 13.86% of the total, with Irish expenditure being subvented by a contribution of £1.3 millions from Imperial funds. Ireland had 12% and 10% of total UK population in 1901 and 1913 respectively.[75]

Notwithstanding the favourable shift in the fiscal balance, there was unease in Ireland about the course of the United Kingdom's public finances. Murray provides a partial explanation: 'A system of taxation which has been devised in the interests of a manufacturing country cannot be suited to the inhabitants of a poor agricultural country, where economic conditions and habits of living are in many ways so different'.[76] More fundamentally: the class structure of the Twenty-six Counties, where the proletariat had been virtually obliterated, was diverging increasingly from that of Britain, where the proletariat was in the ascendant. This divergence in class structure is shown in Table 4.2, which is based on the first censuses that provide the necessary information in both countries.

Table 4.2
Population by Social Class, Britain (1921) and Ireland (1926)

Occupation	England & Wales	Ireland
1. Farmers	250,024	268,930
2. Shopkeepers	470,842	29,106
3. Clergy and nuns	36,987	14,145
4. Other professional	387,274	21,896
5. Total of the above	1,145,127	334,077
6. Total occupied population	17,178,000	1,145,127
7. Total population	37,932,000	2,971,992
8. 5 as % of 6	6.7%	29.2%
9. 5 as % of 7	3.0%	11.2%

Source: Ireland: *Census of Population, 1926, Volume II, Occupations.*
England and Wales: *Census of England and Wales, 1921, Occupations.*

Understandably, given the broadening gap between the class structures of the Twenty-six Counties and Britain, southern Ireland was less than enthusiastic about the reform measures introduced by the Liberal government elected in 1906. These reforms, which were already in operation in a number of continental countries, included meagre old age pensions and unemployment insurance. Their financing necessitated the 'People's Budget' of 1909, which proposed higher liquor taxes and a land tax, and was 'intensely unpopular in Ireland'.[77] Anticipating somewhat the cutting by the Cosgrave government in 1924 of Irish old age pensions from 10 shillings to 9 shillings per week, and the more recent trenchent opposition to the introduction of a land tax in Ireland, the Irish Nationalist party at Westminster opposed Lloyd George's reforming 'People's Budget'.[78]

Table 4.3
Catholic Males as a Proportion of All Males and as a Proportion of Certain Occupations, Ireland, 1911

	Per cent
All males	74
Civil servants	59
Local and county government officials	52
Army officers	14
Barristers	44
Physicians, surgeons	49
Civil engineers	36
Veterinary surgeons	49

Source: BPP. 1912-13 CXVII (Cd. 6663).

The reservation of an unduly high proportion of administrative and judicial positions for Protestants was a further irritant to the Catholic bourgeoisie (see Table 4.3). Though of a second order of importance to the land and rent issue, it did tend to grow over time. A high proportion of Ireland's predominantly middle-class children received secondary education; and of those who did, a good proportion proceeded to take a university education at the Queen's Colleges in Cork and Galway, which were founded in 1845; or at the Catholic University in Dublin, founded in 1882. Catholic students previously had not generally attended the Protestant University of Dublin. All three colleges in Cork, Galway and Dublin, were consolidated into the National University of Ireland (NUI) in 1908.[79] The proteges of the Catholic secondary schools and of the NUI, who were emerging from the turn of the century onwards in increasing numbers, found their career prospects in Ireland impeded by the pre-emption of a high proportion of the senior positions by the Anglo-Irish Protestant elite (Table 4.3). The situation was not unlike that in colonial Africa some decades later, only there discrimination was based on race rather than religion (Appendix B).

Discontent with British 'welfare statism', which threatened Irish property with the ogre of socialism, or the difficulty the brightest and best educated Catholic youth had in securing high office in Ireland were not of themselves adequate grounds for secession. They were irritants that kept alive a drift towards secession which, once the key issue of property in land had been settled in favour of the Irish Catholic bourgeoisie, was otherwise of a desultory character. Irish nationalism during these decades was mainly concerned with cultural matters; matters that were the preserve of poets, dramatists and visionaries and that did not impinge on crucial bourgeois interests.

The Irish Conscription Act of 1917 did, however, present adequate grounds for secession. Large numbers of the remnants of the Irish proletariat had been swept into the British army at the outbreak of the Great War in 1914 and during successive recruiting drives. A soldier's pay and maintenance, with allowance for wife and children, was, for many of Ireland's residual proletariat, more attractive than the conditions that they could secure at home. The Anglo-Irish ascendancy, their economic, social and political position made as obsolete in Ireland by the land acts as cavalry had been made by the machine gun and barbed wire on the Western Front, also flocked to the colours in a final gesture of *noblesse oblige*.

The Great War brought unprecedented prosperity to the Irish bourgeoisie. The value of everything farmers sold, particularly cattle, rose rapidly and continuously. There was an unbroken rise in cattle prices from 1913 to 1920, the longest such rise that has ever been recorded.[80] Perhaps the best barometer of the self-confidence engendered by the continuously rising prices was the manifold increase in land values that occurred during these years. Farmers, many of whom themselves, and all of whose parents, had been rack-rented tenants before the passing of the land acts, found themselves, in the course of a few war years, proprietors of landed properties of very considerable value. The associated commercial and professional classes shared in the prosperity and self-confidence of the farmers.

The sons of Ireland's prospering bourgeoisie, in 1917, were the last surviving pool of well nourished, healthy manhood in the United Kingdom. They had not been caught up by the 1915 conscription legislation, which had only applied to Britain. They had not been driven by poverty, nor drawn by *noblesse oblige,* to the mud and and massacre of Flanders. As a police report of the time noted: 'Young farmers, shop assistants, clerks, school teachers and others of that class...in this country rarely if ever join the army'.[81] The imminent threat to the sons of the Irish bourgeoisie, posed by the Irish Conscription Act, mobilized the economically and politically dominant forces of the Irish bourgeoisie against English rule in Ireland. Overnight, those whose main concerns had been the maintenance of the established system of law and order, the value of property, and the generation of profits, were converted into rebels against those laws and that order which now sought to dragoon their sons to fight in a bloody war that, however profitable it had been, impinged on no vital Irish bourgeois interest. Farm, shop, office and pulpit resisted conscription with all the force and determination that a century of rapid bourgeois development made possible.[82]

The threat of conscription and the resistance it generated burnt bourgeois boats and threw the overwhelmingly dominant class in the land, which for half a century had toyed desultorily with independence, irrevocably on the side of secession from the United Kingdom of Great Britain and Ireland. Once the powerful bourgeoisie were committed to independence, independence could not for long be witheld. It was quickly conceded by post-war Britain, despite reservations that were held about the possible effects of Irish secession on India and other restive parts of the empire. Independence was conceded to the pastoral, Catholic southern Twenty-six Counties, in spite of the unwillingness of the Protestant, mainly industrial, settler majority of the six northern counties to throw in their lot with the seceding southern state.

Europe's Only Capitalist Colony

Ireland, with the important exceptions that have been mentioned, fitted well enough into the world-wide pattern of European colonialism. More specifically, it fitted into the pattern of capitalist colonialism which, as distinct from settler colonialism, was the colonization of non-individualistic, non-capitalist agricultural societies for the continuing benefit of metropolitan capitalist interests (Appendix B). Both the desire for land and the strategic defence considerations that motivated Ireland's colonization were common in the history of European colonialism; but the combination of both these motives was unique to Ireland. That unique combination arose from Ireland's proximity to England, which was the only country in the world 500 years ago where there was property in land, which yielded an income to those who had been able to establish title to it; and which, largely because of that fact, was a leading colonizing power. The unique combination of motives for the capitalist colonization of Ireland accounted for the general appropriation of land from agricultural indigenes, which was unique in the Old World and, apart from Ireland, only occurred in the New World of Latin America, where the agricultural indigenes lacked domesticated flocks and herds and were extraordinarily docile. The unique combination of land hunger and strategic defence considerations that motivated the capitalist colonization of Ireland and the unusual appropriation of land from indigenous agriculturists, also caused the Plantation of Ulster; a much rarer phenomenon. That seventeenth century replacement of indigenous farmers by settler farmers was one of five similar cases in the 500 year old, world-wide history of capitalist colonialism. The four other cases all occurred in Africa and none occurred until the nineteenth century, or 200 years after the Plantation of Ulster.

Finally, Ireland diverged importantly and uniquely from the general pattern of race distinguishing the colonists from the colonized. In Ireland, where both classes were Caucasian, religion distinguished the colonizers and their indigenous fellow-travellers from the colonized. Like caste, religion in Ireland has proved to be a much more durable barrier than race between colonizers and colonized.

The distinctive aspects of Irish capitalist colonialism derived from local circumstances; from Ireland's proximity, and strategic importance to, land-hungry, powerful, colonizing England. Similar local circumstances gave rise to distinctive aspects of capitalist colonialism in other regions, including the Caribbean, Latin America, Africa, South Asia and Southeast Asia (Appendix B). These local or regional distinctions enrich, but do not weaken, the generalization that all of these territories, which between them contain almost half the world's population, shared the experience of capitalist colonialism, which was also peculiar to them. The essence of that common experience was the superimposition by European colonists of European individualistic capitalism on non-individualistic, non-capitalist agricultural societies (Appendix B). That superimposition of cultures was marked in every case by the establishment by the colonial power of the essentially European institution of property. But that property, which in Europe (apart from England) and in the settler colonies was overwhelmingly in capital, took the form in the capitalist colonies of land; though, exceptionally, it took the form also of property in people (slaves or peons) in the Caribbean and Latin America.

Capitalist colonialism, which was common and unique to Ireland and the countries of the Third World, was a very different phenomenon from the hegemony that rulers of some European territories exercised over other European territories. Austrian emperors ruled Hungary and Belgium. Together with Russian and Prussian kings, they also ruled Poland; and together with the Spanish kings, they also ruled Italy. Sweden ruled Norway. And so forth. But all this was part of the millenia-old process by which individualistic capitalism emerged from the forest of Central Western Europe (Appendix A). As part of that process, politically distinct units emerged and coalesced. As recently as 800 years ago there were over a thousand of these distinct political units, which have since been reduced to around 25.[83] The general coalescence and occasional fragmentation of these units did not, however, imply change in the social order. Usually the only change was in the kings and so in the dynastic coffers into which the same taxes were paid. Peasants continued to be dragooned into armies, though under different banners; and if the princes happened to be of a different religion, according to the principle of *cuius regio eius religio,* they fought now for the Protestant and then for the Catholic interest.

The same organic, capital-based feudal order evolved throughout Central Western Europe. That feudal order first evolved in England to the stage where, in the seventeenth century, the owners of the property which was at all times the basis of Europe's economy (Appendix A), seized political and military power from the increasingly anachronistic feudal dynasties, and added it to the economic power which they already possessed. The owners of property rose to political dominance in Central Western Europe some 200 years later, with the French Revolution. With the general emergence thereafter of the property owners' state, the old hegemonic assertions of Europe's anachronistic feudal order quickly lapsed, especially in the more advanced west. Austria and Spain's hegemony over Italy, Spain's over Belgium, and Sweden's over Norway all ended; and they ended without the least socio-economic tremor. It was only then, indeed, with the property owners finally in control in many European countries, as they had been in England from the seventeenth century, that these countries too became engaged in capitalist colonialism. The bourgeoisie of Germany, Belgium and Italy were all concerned to grab capitalist colonies in Africa as vents for their surplus capital, labour and manufactured products.

Only in the marchlands of eastern Europe, which evolved very differently from the Central Western European heartland (Chapter 2), did hegemonic rule long survive the changes heralded by the French revolution. There, during Europe's post-revolutionary, industrializing era, developments occurred that contrasted remarkably with those in contemporary, capitalist-colonized Ireland. The contrast helps to elucidate the fundamental difference between the anachronistic, hegemonic rule of one territory by the king of another within the same social order, and the capitalist colonizing of a non-capitalist, non-individualistic territory by the property-owning colonizers of another territory and of another social order. In eastern Europe, as the demand for food in England increased, the nobles, who were the creatures and agents of the autocratic tsar, attempted to tie their serfs more firmly to the open plains and to squeeze from them more grain, for which there was now an expanding market in western Europe.[84] Their success contributed to holding down the price of wheat in England, so raising real incomes there. As a result demand shifted to meat as a higher quality food, which raised the price of cattle and sheep relative to the price of wheat in Ireland. The Irish landowner — who was a very different animal from the eastern European serfowner, whom the autocratic tsar could make or break at will — could thus declare at this very moment: 'the landlords of Ireland are at length deeply convinced that, though a stock of cattle or sheep will afford profit, a stock of mere human creatures, unemployed, will afford none.'

Ireland was an offshore island of an offshore island of Europe. The critical significance of England's insularity has been emphasized (Chapter 3). Ireland's location has made it different in fundamental ways from continental Europe. It was populated much later: not until some eight or ten thousand years ago, which was long after people had hunted and gathered throughout a continental Europe that included Britain, which, before the melting of the last Ice Age, was part of the European land mass. Its maritime climate prevented the evolution of an indigenous capitalism in Ireland, unlike neighbouring England and Central Western Europe (Chapter 2). The Tudor conquest of Ireland, therefore, implied a fundamental change in the social order; above all, it implied that land, which had been available for the support, however inadequately or ineffectively, of its occupants, was thereafter to be used for the profit of its proprietors. Nothing comparable ever occurred in continental Europe. People were never there cleared from land to make way for profitable cattle and sheep, as happened in early Stuart Ireland, as was proposed formally by William Petty in 1687 and again by the Irish government's national planners in 1962; and as actually happened in the nineteenth century, when the largest social class was obliterated to make way for cattle and sheep. The key differences, scarcely perceptible to those who have not attempted the impossible gamble of extensive crop-growing in Ireland, were a few more inches of rainfall and a few degrees less mean summer temperatures. So important were these difference that though the potato, imported from South America, was integrated also into continental Europe's agriculture, it never became there, as it did in Ireland, the rickety base on which an Irish coolie class developed.

If doubt remains that England's occupation of Ireland was not fundamentally different from, say, Austria's occupation of Lombardy, then the question must be raised as to why, alone in western Europe, the principle *cuius regio, eius religio* did not obtain in Ireland. The reason that the government and the property owners of Ireland were Protestant and the people of Ireland were Catholic was that Protestant property owners were the agents and beneficiaries of a new, individualistic, capitalist social order; while the Catholic people were the victims to be 'squeezed', who belonged to an older, tribal, pastoral society upon which the new order had been forcefully superimposed and from which the new order expected to profit. Nothing like that occurred elsewhere in Europe. But something very similar occurred in all the capitalist colonies of the Third World. Only, in the other capitalist colonies the differences and the clash between the new and the old orders were marked by race, while in Ireland these were marked by religion.

Ireland therefore is unique among European countries in having been a capitalist colony. Likewise it is unique among former capitalist colonies in being a European country. Ireland is linked geographically to Europe, which was the heartland of individualism and capitalism (Appendix A), and cannot help but share in that European heritage. But Ireland is linked too by every aspect of its history for the past 500 years to the other former capitalist colonies of the Third World. As Arnold Toynbee observed of Russia which, like Ireland, lies beyond the other, eastern, margin of European individualistic capitalism: 'To live between two worlds, which is an intelligentsia's function, is a spiritual ordeal...and in Russia in the nineteenth century this ordeal evoked a literature that was not surpassed anywhere in the world in that age.'[85] Something of the same 'spiritual ordeal' of living between two worlds may have accounted for Ireland's not insignificant achievements in creative literature.

V

Ireland: A Case of Capitalist Colonial Undevelopment (Part 1)

Introduction

The starting point of this book's inquiry was the coterminousness of undevelopment with capitalist colonialism: countries that have been capitalist colonized, undevelop; countries that have not been capitalist colonized, develop. The inquiry, to here, has been concerned with the nature of capitalism. It has considered the unique combination of ecological, technological and historical conditions that first gave rise to capitalist production in Central Western Europe several millenia ago (Appendix A). The inquiry has also looked at why, when, where and how Central Western Europe's individualistic capitalist culture interacted with other, non-individualistic, non-capitalist cultures, through the process of capitalist colonialism (Appendix B). How and why that cultural contact has left an enduring legacy of undevelopment in all of the 137 other former colonies which, conveniently referred to as the 'Third World', contain between them almost half the world's population, is considered in Appendix C. This and the following chapter are concerned with the manner in which the continuing undevelopment of Ireland has been the enduring, pathological consequence of British capitalist colonialism.

No two countries' colonial experience has been identical. Ireland's, while falling within the broad pattern of capitalist colonialism, has diverged in important respects from that pattern; and it continues to do so. It was, as noted in Chapter 4, the only European country that was colonized. It was, as noted, the only colony in which all, or most of the land was appropriated from cattle-keeping indigenes. And it was one of the rare cases where, on part of the land — Ulster — the indigenous farmers were replaced by settler, metropolitan farmers. It was, finally, the only capitalist colony where the colonizers were distinguished from the colonized by religion rather than race. The explanation for these important divergences is that Ireland was climatically too far from continental Europe to have permitted an indigenous growth of individualistic capitalism; but was strategically too close to Europe to have been ignored in the world-wide spread of capitalism in a maritime age. Ireland's proximity to Europe and especially to England, was the source of further peculiarities in Ireland's capitalist colonial experience. The closeness of the two countries offered the prospect of profit from land, centuries before land became generally profitable. Proximity to England caused Ireland to be caught up closely in England's industrial revolution from the start: England became a net grain importer from 1760 onwards, as the industrial revolution proceeded, and for 60 years neighbouring Ireland was the principal source of those imports.[1] That early metropolitan market for temperate zone food products triggered in Ireland, around 1760, the population explosion that occurred generally in the Third World a century or so later.

Ireland's proximity to Britain made it peculiarly vulnerable to the change in food demand that occurred in the metropolitan country as the era of factory capitalism progressed, from 1820 onwards. The change in demand, which in Ireland between 1820 and 1970 caused the price of beef to rise fivefold relative to the price of wheat and threefold relative to the price of butter, destroyed the precarious economic base on which an Irish coolie class had been created.

The extreme vulnerability of coolie agriculture 55 degrees of latitude from the equator, England's growing demand in the age of factory capitalism for fresh meat, and the capitalist colonial perception of land as a source of profit together gave rise to an implosion in the population of Irish primary producers. That was coincidental with the beginning of the rapid growth of the primary producing populations of the more distant capitalist colonies, which were located at lower latitudes, as these more distant colonies were increasingly drawn into the world-wide capitalist system. The relative decline in secondary and tertiary activity that occurred in the more distant colonies as the factories of the metropolises ousted indigenous craft products[2] was translated, in Ireland's exceptional case of a declining agricultural population, into a reduction also in the non-agricultural, urban population. A stagnating or declining agriculture precluded non-agricultural development. Irish industry, lacking an expanding supply of raw materials and an expanding home market, was easily wiped out by metropolitan England's growing factory industry. So far from industrial expansion being a substitute for a declining agriculture, industrial contraction was an inevitable consequence of a declining agriculture.

These objective economic conditions determined, within narrow limits, the course of the socio-economic and political histories of Ireland and of the other colonies of factory capitalism. It is remarkable that this should not have been perceived by — among very many other, less clear-thinking observers — a foremost exponent of historical materialism, Frederick Engels. He preferred a very different explanation: 'The sensuous and excitable nature of the Irish prevents them from undertaking tasks which require sober judgment and tenacity of purpose.'[3]

A European location, which in the age of factory capitalism underlay the collapse in the demand for labour in colonial Ireland, facilitated the social and economic integration of the surplus Irish into the accelerating, world-wide spread of capitalism under English leadership. Again quoting Engels, the Irish fulfilled 'the notorious function of supplying England, America, Australia, etc. with prostitutes, casual labourers, pimps, thieves, beggars and other rabble.'[4]

Population Implosion

The reduced demand for labour in Ireland coincided with the application there of those metropolitan-originating influences that world-wide have drastically reduced death rates. These influences include particularly the imposition of capitalist law and order and the application of elementary principles of public hygiene and disease control. The reduced demand for coolie labour in Ireland under these circumstances gave rise initially to two decades of chronic famine and then to the Great Famine of 1845-48, which was similar in character to the famines that have afflicted also the coolie population of India so frequently in the age of capitalist colonialism (Appendix B). Sufficient demographic adjustment, including particularly the broadening and deepening of the channels of emigration, occurred then to avoid further famine in Ireland. The resulting protracted decline in population has created in Ireland circumstances that prove most rules pertaining to economic development, in the sense of testing the limits of the validity of generalizations on the subject.

Part of the demographic adjustment that occurred has been the restriction, since around 1820, of reproduction in Ireland to about 40% of the females born there. Marriages in most societies are about 45% of births.[5] Not all marriages are first marriages; but neither are all cohabitations formalized by marriage. It is broadly true, therefore, that in most societies almost all the people mate. Bearing in mind the very low incidence of illigitimacy and the virtual absence of artificial birth control in Ireland until recent years,[6] it is clear that the very low level of marriages relative to births in Ireland — some 20% compared to a normal 45% — implies a remarkable degree of sexual continence.

69

Under the very different market conditions that obtained from 1820 onwards, the established social order imposed in Ireland those restraints on reproduction that had been a distinctive characteristic of society in Central Western Europe: people could not get married until and unless they commanded capital to operate land effectively (Appendix A). That capital in Ireland was livestock, or the money to buy them, as agriculture shifted from the production of grain and milk towards cattle and sheep production.

Opportunities to marry in Ireland, in the age of English factory capitalism, became much more restricted than they had ever been in continental Europe.[7] That was partly because of the labour-replacing nature of capital in Ireland's pastoral agriculture: between 1841 and 1981, the population of Ireland (Republic) declined from 6.5 million to 3.4 million, as the number of cattle increased from 1.8 million to 6.9 million.[8]

But opportunities to marry in Ireland were also greatly reduced by comparison with pre-industrial Central Western Europe as a result of influences deriving from Europe's industrialization. Chief of these was the reduction of death rates in Ireland, as in all other capitalist colonies of the time. But though death rates and opportunities to marry were both reduced, when people in Ireland did marry they proceeded, as in other capitalist colonies, to have biologically determined families. Thus birth rates in Ireland, at all times since the beginning of the nineteenth century, apart from the years of the Great Famine, have been substantially higher than death rates. Ever fewer members of this naturally increasing population could secure, in nineteenth century Ireland, the basic socio-economic independence necessary for marriage. Finally, as death rates declined, the possessors of capital lived longer than in pre-industrial Europe and delayed the intergenerational transfer of capital, without which marriage in Ireland was increasingly difficult. As people lived longer in Ireland ever fewer of those born there were able to marry there; and those who did married at an ever later age. Never was sexual continence enforced on so high a proportion of any population as on Ireland's population for 140 years after the death of George III in 1820.[9]

Systematic selection has occurred over some six generations of Irish people. 40% or less of those born there have married and reproduced in Ireland during those six generations. That was the 40% who opted not to emigrate, although remaining in Ireland implied a poorer prospect of attaining that degree of socio-economic independence which, among other things, makes marriage possible. It is at least conceivable that this rigorous, systematic selection has altered the genetic character of the resulting population. It is conceivable that the Irish population now is genetically more cautious, less disposed to change, than the population of 1820. Neither can it be discounted that, six generations on, Ireland now has a 'fat cat' population, with a genetically induced propensity for conservative caution.

Those metropolitan-originating influences had the effect in Ireland, where cattle and sheep were replacing people, of increasing the rate of emigration needed to achieve the economically dictated population decline. The large shortfall of death rates below biologically determined birth rates, coupled with the replacement of labour by grazier capital and the incorporation, through emigration, of the Caucasian Irish labour into the workforce of metropolitan capitalism resulted, in the long run, in almost half of those born in Ireland and surviving childhood, emigrating permanently from the country. Along with that half of the population there left also the political, economic, social and intellectual pressures that operate in, and are a fundamental part of, normal societies. The demographic pressures that are a key element in all the other former capitalist colonies have been inverted in Ireland. Reduction in death rates, which heightened social pressures in normal societies, caused their relaxation in Ireland, where reduced death rates simply led to higher emigration and the more thorough extrusion of the less contented.

The demographic change that gives rise in other former colonies to intense political, economic and social pressures that exacerbate undevelopment (Appendix C) has been inverted in Ireland to create, through the emigration of almost half the population flow, a social, political and intellectual vacuum. *'Solitudinem faceunt et pacem appellant.'* Ireland's 'peace' has been equally, though differently, inimical to development as have been the strife and pressures caused in other former colonies by population explosion. The inversion, through emigration, of the usual demographic pressures has permitted the exceptional enhancement of those socially detrimental interests which were established in Ireland, as in all capitalist colonies, by metropolitan rulers (Appendix C).

The responsiveness of the newly independent Irish state to the interests established by capitalist colonial rule and its anxiety to preserve and enhance those interests were manifested from the beginning. A major concern of the newly independent state was to stress that though the flag and the anthem had changed, though the language used on some official occasions had become Gaelic, and though the seat of legislation had moved from London to Dublin; despite these changes, the content of the legislation was substantially the same. It was very much 'business as usual' in independent Ireland. It was 'freedom from' rather than 'freedom for'. This was stressed,for example, by the Report of the 1925 Banking Commission.[10]

The new polity was peculiarly uninhibited and unrestrained by consideration of general social interests. The inversion through emigration of any pressure to the contrary is manifested, in the first instance, by an intellectual void that precludes radical thought and serious questioning of the *status quo*. The preservation and enhancement of individual interests inimical to social well-being has been facilitated, in the second instance, by the removal through emigration of the victims of that *status quo*. Those whose interests have been secured remained in Ireland and exercised political power; the half of the population whose interests suffered, emigrated. Important cases of the uninhibited pursuit of those individual interests are considered in the remainder of this chapter and in the following chapter.

Land Values

Irish land values have risen in response to the increasing demand from nearby, capital-rich Europe for Ireland's land-intensive products, especially cattle and sheep. Ireland's land values rose from around £10 per acre at the establishment of the state in 1922 to a peak of around £4,000 per acre in 1979.[11] Irish GNP at current prices increased much more slowly over the same period, from around £154 million in 1926 to £7,300 million in 1979.[12] Land prices fell after 1979 as the euphoria of entry to the EEC abated; but they have more recently (1985) recovered. Conacre, or competitive, rents for that 10% of Irish farmland that is rented have remained at around £100 an acre. That remarkable, eightfold enhancement of the value of land relative to GNP, in the 60 years of the Irish state's existence, reflects two disparate trends, which have been closely connected by the common nexus of emigration.

First, there has been an extraordinary political concern to protect and to increase land values. This has been done primarily by maximizing agricultural prices. With the possible exception of the early 1930s, state policy has been concerned to secure for Irish agricultural produce the freest access to the traditional British market, which was for long the most buoyant in the world; and more recently, to the EEC's even higher-priced market. There has never been in Ireland any of that concern, common in other former capitalist colonies, to hold prices low for local consumers.[13] Irish consumers who objected to high food prices voted with their feet against them, by emigrating. Nor did Irish governments, as governments in other former capitalist colonies do, attempt to secure revenue by taxing agricultural exports.[14] Instead, they have provided central exchequer grants in relief of land taxes.[15] More recently, these local government land taxes, or rates, have been abolished. Irish farmers, as well as paying no land or property taxes, pay very little tax on their monetary incomes; and, of course, no tax at all on that much larger income that they derive from the secure possession of an appreciating asset. Of total taxes on income collected in 1983, which was £1,661 million, farmers, who had 10% of national income, paid £32 million.[16]

Coincidental with these efforts of government to maximize prices and to minimize taxes for Irish farmers, the provision of public services free for all farmers has at all times been a major concern of Irish governments.

Though most of the cost of these services are now borne by the EEC under its Common Agricultural Policy, their residual cost to Irish taxpayers in 1983 was £227 million, or 4.5% of total government current expenditure.[17]

The second and related trend contributing to the relative increase in land values has been the slow, long run growth of GNP since the state's foundation. That, in real terms, has been around 2% annually, compared to 3.5% in neighbouring Britain, where growth has been slow by world standards.[18] Slow economic growth has been due, in large measure, to the emigration of some 1,125,000 persons between 1922 and 1971; or the equivalent of some 40% of all persons born in Ireland during that period.[19] Emigration on this scale has been a major economic drain. Persons aged 19 years (which is around the median age of Irish emigrants) or younger, account for 40% of Ireland's population and some 30% of total consumption.[20] Consumption accounts for 85 per cent and upwards of Irish GNP;[21] or some 25.5% of GNP has been used for rearing young people up to the age of 19 years. As, over the long run, 40% or more of these young people have emigrated, approximately 10% of GNP has annually been used 'to produce emigrants', who are a form of virtually 'unrequited exports'.[22] These, like Irish capital exports (Chapter 4), enhanced production in recipient and competing countries, and 'cost to produce' the equivalent of about two-thirds of Irish physical capital formation. This drain of human capital was a major direct loss to the economy. It also impeded economic development by reducing the available labour supply and by reducing those important economies associated with scale.

The enhancement of land values relative to GNP, which has been taken further in Ireland than in any other country, has operated more effectively here than elsewhere to select out the least competent to operate land.[23] That fact, which is the paradox of property (Appendix C), combined with the market/institutional orientation of land use towards extensive, dry cattle and sheep farming, has resulted in the volume of Irish agricultural production remaining virtually unchanged over a period of 140 years, during which time world agricultural production has increased perhaps sixfold.[24]

Protection

Ireland has indulged in more comprehensive and intensive industrial protection than perhaps any other country[25]. This, like the emphasis on enhancing land values, was attributable mainly to emigration, though of course other factors also operated. Those in Ireland who were not among the favoured ones who were employed in the protected industries could, like those who objected to high food prices, emigrate as an alternative to paying high prices for the shoddy products of the highly protected industries. Their emigration weakened any political curbs on the vested interests that pressed for ever wider and more intensive protection.

Linked to emigration as a factor that facilitated protection was the fact that Ireland's principal exports were live cattle and sheep. These require very few inputs other than land so their costs were minimally affected by industrial protection. Thus no major producer group's interests were seriously affected by industrial protection. Matters would have been otherwise had not the island been partitioned at the time of independence in 1922 and had the northern counties been included with the Republic. (Indeed, fear of the effects of protection on northern export industries was a major consideration in influencing Northern Ireland to remain within the United Kingdom when the rest of Ireland seceded in 1922). As matters were, those non-agricultural Irish industries that exported either relocated in Britain (Guinness's stout, Jacob's biscuits); or their exports declined, as in the case of Irish distillers.

Ireland produced an annual average of 12.3 million proof gallons of whiskey in 1917-21, compared to Scotland's 21.6 million proof gallons.[26] Ten of Ireland's 23 distillers at the time were located in Northern Ireland, though by 1925 six of these had ceased to operate. Assuming that whiskey production within Ireland was *pro rata* to the number of distillers, southern Irish production at the time would have averaged just seven million proof gallons annually, or one-third of Scotland's. Scotland, in 1950, produced 38.1 38.1 million proof gallons, but production in the Republic was only 1.2 million proof gallons.[27] Therefore, in a period of 30 years the Republic's whiskey production had dropped from a third to a thirtieth of Scotland's. Cattle and sheep production, on the other hand, having few inputs other than land, were largely unaffected by industrial protection. As a result, they accounted for a much higher proportion of Irish exports in the 1950s than they did in the early 1930s, when industrial protection was introduced.[28]

The severe world economic recession of the early 1930s ended Irish emigration for a few years and caused a reversal of the established pattern of population decline.[29] Intensive industrial protection was one response to the unaccustomed pressures that arose for the creation of new jobs. But once protectionist interest were brought into existence they acquired their own momentum. That momentum was facilitated initially by emigration. But emigration on the Irish scale in time accentuated the limitations of industrial protection; the rapid disappearance of large sections of the market through massive emigration, especially in the 1950s, helped to make that protection impracticable.

However, the loss of customers through emigration was only one of the difficulties that undermined Irish industrial protection in the 1950s. The countries of Latin America, which in the 1930s were the only other independent former capitalist colonies, also adopted intensive industrial protection at that time. For them too the possibilities of the policy appear to have been exhausted by the 1950s, although their populations, unlike Ireland's, were increasing rapidly.[30] More recently, most of the African and Asian colonies, which became independent after the Second World War, also adopted 'import substituting' protectionism. But for them too, some 20 years after its initiation, as in the cases of Ireland and Latin America 30 years earlier, the policy has lost most of its attractions. 'After a short initial phase of rapid expansion, the industrial sector (in many former capitalist colonies) came up against the limits of the home market and went into a severe recession in many countries.'[31]

Protection is normally accorded initially to industries producing unsophisticated consumer goods, like footwear and textiles. The possibilities for industrialization of this nature are limited, especially by the size of the market and by the need to import raw materials and equipment. Further industrialization requires either the production of more sophisticated consumer goods, the machines that produce consumer goods, or of exports to pay for imported raw materials and equipment. The absence of economies of scale in the protected home markets of the former capitalist colonies makes protection at this later stage, reached by Ireland and Latin America by the 1950s and by the former colonies of Africa and Asia by the 1970s, prohibitively expensive. Only India, with its numerically vast domestic market, appears to have progressed much in 'producing machines to produce machines'.[32] Meanwhile, the creation of a structure of innefficient, protected manufacturing industry constitutes an additional handicap on the economic development of the former capitalist colonies.

The general difficulty experienced by all former capitalist colonies of pursuing protection beyond the initial stage of protecting unsophisticated consumer goods' industries was probably the main factor that made protection impracticable in Ireland in the 1950s. But the rapid escape of the captive home market exacerbated the situation and hastened the shift to free trade.

Deficit Financing

Europe's Renaissance rulers were forced by new technology and new economic relationships into increasing dependence on the market. But, deterred by the formidable opposition of property owners to taxation, they resorted to alternative fund-raising expedients as much as possible (Appendix A; Appendix B). Borrowing was the expedient most commonly resorted to by rulers and would-be rulers during the centuries when kings could no longer 'live off their own', though the property owners' state had not yet emerged (Chapter 3). Borrowing allowed rulers to incur expenditure now and to pay for it later by repayment of the debt, or by payment of interest on it, or — most commonly — by repudiating the debt.[33]

The original version of the property owners' state was the *polis* or *civis* of the Ancient Mediterranean. The reappearance of that political form in Central Western Europe reconciled the conflict inherent in government being required to protect property, as the basis of economic activity, yet being forced to prey on that property to secure the resources with which alone the state could discharge its functions (see Appendix A).

The firm establishment in England, following the 'Glorious Revolution' of 1688, of the first property owners' state of modern times was signalled by the initiation of a national debt. The national debt and the Bank of England were founded simultaneously in 1694. Britain, the USA and other metropolitan, capitalist, property owners' states, since then, have resorted occasionally to national debt expansion. They have done so especially in wartime, when this expansion has been a politically expedient way of incurring exceptional public expenditure in times of crisis. It has permitted necessarily increased expenditure without aggravating a crisis situation, which increasing taxes would do. Lenders transfer the needed resources willingly to government against claims for future interest payments. The future taxpayers, whom government thus commits to make the payments, have not been born; or they are unaware of the commitment made on their behalf; or they are indifferent to it. It is an expedient that works so long as the weight of debt does not become excessive relative to the GNP — from which the rentier holders of debt receive their interest payments — as that weight did become with the Bourbons in France in 1789.[34] In the cases of the United Kingdom and the United States, interest payments on the national debts, which were incurred principally to finance the two World Wars, were 4.06% and 1.97% of their respective GNPs in 1950. These proportions had changed to 2.58% and 2.85% respectively by 1980.[35]

National debt expansion has been resorted to by the governments of former capitalist colonies since the first of these, in Latin America, became independent in the 1820s. Domestic borrowing by these governments was limited, partly by the inadequacy of domestic savings and partly by the reluctance of citizens to lend to their governments. Reliance was placed instead mainly on foreign borrowing. The servicing of these foreign debts was not infrequently enforced by 'gunboat diplomacy', as when, 'in 1902, the British government joined with the German and Italian governments in blockading the ports of Venezuela in an effort to force the Venezuelan dictator, Cipriano Castro, to honour obligations to British, German and Italian nationals.'[36] An example of the many United States military interventions in Latin America was when 'in 1913 US marines entered Nicaragua, ostensibly to protect the lives and property of American citizens endangered by a bitterly fought revolution. Again an American receivership of the customs was established, and a British loan was refunded through New York bankers, while new loans were extended for various Nicaraguan government purposes'.[37] The 'Suez incident', in 1957, when Britain and France attempted to re-establish title to the profits from the Suez canal, marked what appears to be the end of the era in which foreign creditors enforced repayment of debts by the use of military force against sovereign governments.

Circumstances that are again closely associated with emigration have, in Ireland, relaxed the constraints on public debt expansion that have operated in other former capitalist colonies. First, because of the relatively high incomes since the mid-nineteenth century of the residual Irish population, savings have been correspondingly higher in Ireland than in the other former colonies. Elsewhere savers have been a relatively small minority of rapidly expanding proletarian populations; in Ireland, the increasingly dominant bourgeoisie comprised a much larger proportion of the population than elsewhere (Table 4.2).

Opportunities for investment in Ireland were poor for those reasons considered above (Chapter 4). They deteriorated over time, especially when cattle numbers became stabilized around the end of the nineteenth century.[38] Bank deposits were the only outlet for most savings, and the acceptance of these deposits and their transfer to the London money market laid the foundations for the grotesque prosperity of the Irish banking system (Chapter 4). The paucity of alternative outlets for savings increased Irish savers' willingness to lend to government.

A record of political stability and public financial rectitude enhanced the attractiveness of lending to Irish governments. The change in Ireland, between 1820 and 1850, from a situation of expanding to one of contracting population occurred in a cauldron of social pressures that were contained by the rigorous, efficient application of force by the metropolitan power. Thereafter, social pressures have been dissipated by the emigration from Ireland of those who objected most to social conditions. The extermination of the proletariat, the emergence to dominance of the bourgeoisie and political independence were all facets of an Irish historical process that resulted in the removal simultaneously of both social pressures and the metropolitan-controlled forces that had been needed to contain those pressures when they existed. The result in Ireland has been an extraordinarily protracted record of political stability. Associated with this, Ireland's financial affairs, until recent decades, were conducted with extreme conservatism. This was done, first, by the metropolitan authorities and subsequently by native governments, which latter were not exposed to the political pressures that existed in other former capitalist colonies.

The relatively high incomes and savings of an exceptionally bourgeois society, the lack of local investment opportunities, and the long record of political stability and financial rectitude made it possible for Irish governments to borrow exceptionally large amounts domestically. The exceptional domestic borrowing capacity, when used in the post-Second World War years to finance expenditure on housing, schools and hospitals, quickly led to balance of payments difficulties in the mid-1950s. That crisis caused a shift in deficit-financed government expenditure towards encouraging exports in various ways, particularly through Industrial Development Authority (IDA) grants and through tax holidays for exporters (see Chapter 6). That use of government credit relaxed the foreign exchange constraint that precipitated the crisis of the 1950s, and it allowed the economy to grow through the 1960s. But as the cost of servicing the public debt has grown, the economy has become increasingly less competitive and balance of payments deficits have become absolutely and relatively larger than in the 1950s (Table 1.2).

T.K. Whitaker, sometime Secretary of the Department of Finance and sometime Governor of the Irish Central Bank, has written feelingly of Ireland's difficulty, shared by other potential borrowers, of borrowing abroad in the 1950s. 'I have unpleasant recollections of the difficulty of raising even a few million pounds on a short term basis in London in 1956.'[39] The availability of 'Eurodollars' in the 1960's and of 'petrodollars' in the 1970's removed the constraints on foreign borrowing experienced by Whitaker. Borrowing by former capitalist colonies expanded over fourfold in the 1970s. 'This rapid increase in lending to [former capitalist colonies] was a result of changed conditions in the Euro-currency markets. The credit demands of traditional clients slowed down as a result of the recession at the same time that deposits from oil-exporters were growing fast. This prompted the banks to lend to borrowers previously regarded as marginal.'[40] The availability of foreign exchange to 'borrowers previously regarded as marginal' has made it possible for Irish governments to persist in deficit financing over a protracted period and on a scale that is without precedent (Chapter 1).

The particular facility with which Irish governments have been able to borrow abroad is due precisely to those circumstances that have enabled them to borrow domestically, namely, relatively high incomes, which the other major international debtors, Mexico, Argentina, Brazil and Poland have;[41] coupled with a long record of political stability and public financial rectitude.

Credit-worthy persons and institutions must be willing, as well as able, to borrow. It has been the hallmark of developing countries (i.e. those of metropolitan Europe, the settler colonies of North America, South Africa and Oceania, Russia, the uncolonized countries of East Asia, and the city states of Hong Kong and Singapore), that their governmments have resorted to deficit financing only in exceptional circumstances, such as war-financing or as an economic stimulus in cyclical recessions. On the other hand, it has been the hallmark of those western countries, before the establishment there of property owners' states (Appendix B), as well as being now the hallmark of the undeveloping former capitalist colonies, that their governments have borrowed as much as possible. That borrowing has usually been to serve the personal interests of rulers: for dynastic glorification, as in the case of France's 'Sun King', Louis XIV; or for the retention of office by the politicians of former capitalist colonies. Emigration, as well as creating an unprecedented government borrowing capacity, has created in Ireland too the political and intellectual void within which Irish politicians have been able to borrow, without hindrance, to the limits of that capacity.

Apart from the occasional warning in the Irish Dail, or parliament, about the unPickwickian spending of £1 and sixpence from a revenue of £1 — references invariably prefaced by a ritualistic assertion of 'the fundamental soundness' of the country's public finances — there has been neither intellectual nor political opposition to the creation, during the last forty peacetime years, of a public debt that, relative to population or GNP, is the largest in the world. Irish social scientists have chosen not to recognize the fundamental difference between the Irish situation and that in those countries where Keynesian 'demand management' has had some, though increasingly questioned, relevance.[42] Irish social scientists have chosen not to question the appropriateness, or the long term consequences, of governments adding to demand in the short term as the principal means of rectifying those profound structural defects that are the essence of undevelopment, that prevent all former capitalist colonies from providing a livelihood for their people, and that in Ireland's case have forced half the population to emigrate or starve. The Irish political establishment, well accustomed to pursuing policies that ignored the interests of the emigrant half of the population who, by ceasing to vote, became politically impotent, for its part has had no qualms about ignoring the interests of the future taxpayers who will be required to service, but have not been present to vote against the debts created by the current establishment.

Emigration gave Ireland higher living standards than any other former capitalist colony. It gave it an unparalleled record of political stability and public finance rectitude. It created an intellectual and political void wherein policies are cursorily or superficially examined; and wherein governments, accustomed to act regardless of the interests of the emigrant half of the population, have had no difficulty in neglecting the consequences of their actions for future generations, who are as powerless as the emigrants to effect the present course of Irish politics. All these factors, combined with the accidental circumstance of the creation of the 'Eurodollar' market in the 1960s and the 'petrodollar' market in the 1970s, gave to Irish governments both an unparalleled ability and an unparalleled willingness to borrow domestically and externally. This borrowing has made possible the sustained economic expansion of the past 40 years or so. It has enabled

Irish living standards to rise in line with those in Britain and elsewhere in the West, without a serious decline for almost 30 years in the number getting a livelihood in Ireland. Borrowing has papered over the fundamental flaws in the economy of an undeveloping former capitalist colony: the flaws that in the past caused half the population to starve or emigrate; and the flaws that, during the past 30 years, have caused the immizeration of billions of people in the Third World. As in the case of the expedient of industrial protection practiced in the 1930s, the expedient of sustained, massive government deficit-financing, which has wasted domestic savings and has exhausted foreign credit, leaves the economy structurally weaker now, with 'the government's capacity to borrow abroad virtually exhausted.'[43]

A peculiar combination of production, market demand and institutional conditions brought about a remarkable growth in the eighteenth century Irish economy (Chapter 4). That growth, under colonial rule, created Georgian Dublin, most of urban Ireland and the multitude of elegant Georgian residences in the countryside. It was based entirely on the potato, a plant from the Andean highlands of South America that had hardly been known in Ireland 100 years earlier but by the nineteenth century had become the exclusive diet of half the people and the principal diet of virtually all the rest. Inevitably the exotic potato failed and its failure hurled the society that had been forced into dependence on it into chaos. Another peculiar combination of circumstances has enabled Irish governments to borrow during the past forty years far more relative to population and national wealth than the government of any other country. With these borrowings they have been able to draw on foreign resources to finance, after a century-and-a-half of economic stagnation, a latter day 'economic miracle' comparable only to Georgian Ireland. But now too Irish society has been forced into a dependence on foreign resources as complete as that on the exotic potato 140 years ago. As the failure of the potato was inevitable then, so is the eventual witholding of the foreign credit which now alone sustains the economy. Then mass famine ensued; now utter economic, political and social collapse will be the consequence.

Trade Unions

Labour and capital in the age of factory capitalism operate in the metropolises in an economic milieu where land remains effectively non-limiting (Appendix A). Two factors have had particular influence. The first has been the stabilization of population and of the labour supply following the rapid increase in incomes associated with the industrial revolution in the metropolises (Appendix B). The second has been the ability of the industrialized metropolises to exchange their factory-made products for the food and raw materials of the capitalist colonies. Unlike the situation

in the former capitalist colonies, human endeavour, either in the form of
more-or-less skilled labour or in the form of saving for capital formation,
rather than land resources, has continued to determine the level of output
in the West. That continued pre-eminence of human endeavour has served
to maintain traditional individualistic values in the West (Appendix A).

Factory capitalism in the metropolises caused a break in the earlier
identity between the owners and the operators of 'penny capitals'. It gave
rise to a distinctive new class, a proletariat which lived by operating capital
that others owned.[44] It did so in a milieu where, as noted and for the
reasons given elsewhere (Appendix B), land continued to be non-limiting
and where the proletarian labour of the metropolises could normally earn
enough not merely for its maintenance and reproduction, but to maintain
these at rising levels of consumption. Despite the divorce of capital from
labour under factory capitalism, the traditional significance of the individual
in the West has been maintained. Trade unions, by strengthening labour's
bargaining power, may have contributed to maintaining returns to capital-
less labour. The point, however, is debatable.[45]

The ability of labour to secure, by its own efforts, sufficient for its
maintenance and reproduction at acceptable living standards has come under
serious strain in recent years. This has been so notwithstanding a declining
labour supply as birth rates in the West have dipped below death rates that,
having already been greatly reduced, cannot easily be reduced further. The
ending of capitalist colonialism has contributed to the growing structural
inability of labour in the metropolises to secure a livelihood. This has been
because the former colonies now have more control over their foreign trade
and, to some extent at least, have prevented the metropolises from
'exporting their unemployment' in the form of manufactured goods that
compete with colonial products.

Not only can the metropolitan countries no longer so easily export their
unemployment; the newly developed, non-western, non-colonial countries
— Japan, Korea and Taiwan — and, in the same category Hong Kong and
Singapore (Chapter 1) have become major exporters of sophisticated
manufactured goods to Central Western Europe and to its New World
settlements. Central Western Europe and North America, no longer able
to 'export their unemployment', have also become 'importers' of the
unemployment of other countries.

Finally, the character as well as the volume of capital formation in the
metropolises have changed. Following a trend that has existed from the
beginning of capitalism, as incomes rise, savings and capital formation
become easier (Appendix A). The greatly accelerated increase in
metropolitan incomes since the Second World War has led to corresponding
acceleration in the rate of capital formation. Increasingly, through
automation, that capital has been labour-replacing rather than labour
complementing.[46]

The post-colonial, automated, metropolitan West, despite a decrease in the labour supply, is paradoxically moving for the first time towards a condition of chronic labour surplus. It is moving towards the situation that has always obtained outside the individualistic, western world. The western world, the distinctive characteristic of which has been the capacity of individuals, by their own efforts, to secure a livelihood, is moving into a situation of massive, chronic, structural unemployment, where the individual's efforts no longer contributes to output. The West is moving towards a situation that is similar to that of Pharaonic Egypt, of other riverine societies, or of the Russian steppes, where the efforts of the individual no longer count (Appendix A). Typically in the western, British case, the disappearance of one or two million unemployed persons would leave GNP unaffected, but would raise the shares available to those remaining. The West, under these radically changed circumstances, is slowly adjusting the manner of distributing wealth. It is relying less and less on the market to determine the share, large or small, going to individuals. Instead, it is adopting the fundamentally non-western approach of recognizing people's claims to a share in the total product, simply because of their membership of the society where the product occurs.[47] The increasingly distributive role of the modern state is acquiring, in modern democratic form, the guise of the Pharaonic Egyptian state, which distributed the surplus produce of the Nile valley to those people not required for its production, by using the supernumerary population for pyramid building. The modern distributive state of the West is adopting implicitly the values of tribal society, in Ireland and elsewhere: that members of the tribe, *ipso facto*, share the tribe's resources.

However efficacious trade unions may be in securing a larger share of the product for labour under factory capitalism in the metropolitan West, the power of trade unions in the former capitalist colonies has been much more circumscribed. The power of western-originating unions has been circumscribed by the chronic surplus of labour in these economies where land has always been the most limiting factor; and where wealth has traditionally been distributed according to status in society rather than the recipient's contribution to wealth production (Appendix A). Union power has become increasingly restricted by the population explosion that exacerbates the labour surplus in the former capitalist colonies. Trade unions are limited to securing better conditions for small elite groups in key positions. They are powerless to improve living conditions for the masses, who have tenure neither of land nor jobs and whose conditions deteriorate as those of elite trade unionists improve (Chapter 1).

Trade unions have been extraordinarily active and effective in Ireland, even by western standards. Of nine countries for which appropriate data are available, Ireland has the highest but one number of days lost through industrial disputes per 1,000 workers. Only in Italy are more days lost per

Table 5.1
Workforce, Working Days Lost and Trade Union Membership

Country	Wage-earners (000s)	Working days lost	Trade union membership (000s)	Days lost per wage-earner	Proportion of wage-earners in trade unions %
United States	89,596	33,761,800	22,463	376.82	25.1
Belgium	2,999	645,579	2,641	215.26	88.1
Denmark	2,023	578,740	1,588	286.08	78.5
France	17,469	3,262,230	5,550	186.74	31.8
Germany	21,855	725,559	9,400	33.20	43.0
Ireland	849	541,564	671	637.88	79.0
Italy	14,664	17,168,100	7,148	1170.77	48.7
Netherlands	4,333	136,450	1,459	31.49	33.7
United Kingdom	21,244	12,040,300	12,250	566.76	57.7

Source: OECD, *Labour Force Statistics 1962-1982*; K. Walsh *Strikes in Europe and the United States* pp. 156, 196.

1,000 workers; and there many of the days lost are due to strikes of a political rather than industrial nature.[48] Only in Belgium is a higher proportion of the workforce in trade unions; but there 'the unions also count among their members military personnel, the unemployed and certain people over retirement age.'[49] Ireland lost on average between 1972 and 1981, 638 workdays annually, compared to 392 workdays lost per 1,000 workers in the other eight countries. Ireland has 79% of its workforce in trade unions compared to 36% in the other eight.

The aggressiveness of the Irish trade unions is reflected in the relatively high level of Irish wages. In the three years 1980-82, which are typical of the long term trend, UK wage rates, adjusted for differences in the UK and Irish currencies, were, on average, slightly less than 10% higher than Irish wage rates (Table 5.2). Output per person, or gross national product at factor cost per head of population was, by contrast, 76% higher in the United Kingdom in those years.[50] The difference between the excess of output per person in the UK and Ireland and the excess of wage rates per man is a measure of Irish trade unions' effectiveness in forcing up wage rates for their members in a relatively poor country. They have, according to the above criteria, been phenomenally successful. They have been more successful than their counterparts in other former capitalist colonies, where trade unions serve small, elite groups. Ireland's population implosion is the key to the success of the trade unions, as it is the key to many other Irish phenomena.

Table 5.2
**Hourly Wage Rates in Manufacturing Industry, Ireland & UK
1980-1982 (IR£)**

	Ireland	United Kingdom	UK as a % of Irish Rate
1980	2.620	2.743	1.05
1981	3.120	3.515	1.13
1982	3.560	3.942	1.11

Source: ILO *Bulletin of Labour Statistics,* 1984, Vol 2, pp.93-5; Central Bank *Report 1984,* appendix p.24.

The emigration of up to half the oncoming population stream has removed from Ireland the overhang of labour that exists in all other former capitalist colonies. People made unemployed, by trade unions forcing wage rates above the level at which people would have been willing to work rather than be unemployed, have not remained in Ireland. Neither have those made unemployed by the substitution of livestock for people. Emigration has given to Ireland, for over a century, conditions approximating to 'full employment', with no large pool of unemployed labour to form a source of competing non-unionized labour, working either as self-employed persons or for non-union firms. These virtually 'full employment' conditions, brought about by mass emigration, have been fundamentally different from the normal conditions of massive, growing labour surpluses in the former capitalist colonies.

The position of the Irish trade unions has been secured by the poor quality as well as the small size of the 'reserve army' of unemployed. Apart from those made temporarily unemployed by seasonal, technical or trade factors, Irish hard core unemployment has traditionally comprised those who have been unwilling to emigrate to England or to the settler colonies where, in the past, employment has been available for Ireland's surplus labour. The double selection, of people unable to get work in Ireland and unwilling to look for work abroad, implied that the hard core of long term Irish unemployed was of exceptionally poor quality and offered little if any threat to the privileged position of employed trade unionists.

Additionally, Irish governments' uninhibited borrowing has greatly contributed to trade union status. It has done so in four principal ways. First, it has allowed the provision of a given level of public services at lower levels of taxation and hence at higher levels of real wages for a larger work force than would otherwise have been the case. It has, in particular, allowed governments, while taxing incomes and expenditure heavily, to avoid taxing the profits of manufacturing industry. This has been a major incentive for foreign firms to locate in Ireland where they account for 40% of the total employment in manufacturing (Chapter 6). Without massive, sustained government deficit financing, trade union pressure to raise wages would either have been less successful or would have resulted in fewer persons being employed and more having to emigrate. Either outcome would have been detrimental to the trade unions.

The second way in which government deficit financing has contributed to trade union strength is the expansion in the public sector which it has made possible. Public sector expenditure accounted for 69% of total national expenditure in Ireland in 1981.[51] Public sector expenditure, of course, is linked to public sector employment. There are in public employment some 325,000 persons, or 38% of the total number of employees.[52] An exceptionally high proportion of public sector employees, being free from the discipline of market forces, are in trade unions.

The third important way in which government deficit financing has helped to strengthen Irish trade unions has been through the relaxation that it has permitted in balance of foreign payments constraints. Without large government borrowing to finance the external payments deficits, either economic activity would have had to be at a much lower level, employing many fewer people; or domestic costs would have had to be reduced, mainly through lower wages. Either way, trade unionists would have been worse off.

Finally, deficit financing has made it possible for the Irish state, alone of all the states of the 138 former capitalist colonies, to pay unemployment benefit or assistance. These state payments to the unemployed dampen the pressures from the unemployed that exist elsewhere in the Third World to force down wages.

That the strength and success of Irish trade unions reflects the licence accorded to them by population implosion rather than the radicalism of the Irish workforce is evident from the voting patterns of trade unionists in parliamentary elections. The two main right-of-centre parties, Fianna Fail and Fine Gael, have together on average won 80%, and have never won less than 59% of the seats in the 23 general elections since the state's foundation. The Labour Party, on the other hand, though supported officially by the trade unions, won on average only 10% of Dail, or parliamentary, seats in the general elections and have never won more than 15% of them. In the most recent, 1982, general elections, the two right-of-centre parties won 78% of the seats and the Labour Party secured rather less than 10%.[53] Irish workers join trade unions to get better paid, more secure jobs. They vote for right-of-centre political parties in order to perpetuate a socio-economic order that enhances the value of tenure in land and tenure in jobs and that, since the state's foundation, has denied a livelihood to half the people.

VI

Ireland: A Case of Capitalist Colonial Undevelopment (Part 2)

Whitakerism, the IDA and 'Economic Take-Off'

The coalition government that came into office in Ireland in 1948 were among others who argued that, if it was economically correct for the Allied powers to borrow to finance the Second World War, it was in order too for an Irish government to borrow for 'nation building'.[1] But deficit financed public expenditure on houses, hospitals and schools brought about a major balance of payments crisis in the mid 1950s. It was symptomatic of the intellectual and political vacuum within which Ireland existed[2] that the initiative for dealing with the crisis did not come from politicians, which would have been normal in western states; nor from the military, which would have been normal in other former capitalist colonies. The initiative instead came from T.K. Whitaker, who had joined the Irish civil service as a youth of eighteen, spent all his working life there, and by the time of the crisis had duly reached the apex of the service as Secretary of the Department of Finance.[3] Among the most vigorous supporters and popularisers of Whitaker's initiative was the present (1986) taoiseach (prime minister), Dr Garret Fitzgerald. Fitzgerald was at the time an economic journalist and subsequently drew on his involvement in supporting the Whitaker initiative for his Ph.D. thesis, 'Planning in Ireland'.[4]

The essence of the Whitaker initiative was the scrapping of protection and the closer integration of Ireland, through expanded foreign trade, into the world economy. Agricultural exports were to be increased, in part by the intensification of existing methods, particularly agricultural extension; and in part by securing better foreign markets, mainly as the *quid pro quo* for dismantling Irish industrial protection. Immediately, the aim was to secure access on more favourable terms for Irish agricultural exports to the traditional British market; the longer term aim was membership of the EEC, with its very high, administered agricultural prices.

Simultaneously, established manufacturing industry was to be encouraged to shift away from production for the home market, protection on which was to be dismantled over a period, and into production for export. New, export oriented industries were to be established in Ireland. Many of these would, in the first instance, be from countries seeking to get better access to the United Kingdom market under the Anglo-Irish free trade agreement of 1965. Subsequent to Ireland's joining the EEC, Japanese, US and other industry was to be attracted to Ireland as a base within the EEC from which to supply that major market.

A package of grants, subsidies and tax holidays was offered to industries producing for export, whether these were old Irish industries switching from the domestic to foreign markets, or newly established export industries. The latter were mainly subsidiaries of foreign-owned, multinational corporations. The tax holidays were subsequently extended, which 'effectively means a negligible tax for manufacturing projects in Ireland'.[5] The Industrial Development Authority (IDA) was the principal state agency through which inducements to industry were offered. The state-owned Industrial Credit Corporation provided capital. The commercial banks and the ICC were exempt from taxes on that part of their profits which was attributable to interest on loans to exporters. Because of this, the ICC and the commercial banks were able to make loans to exporters at low interest rates, which were normally well below the current rate of Irish inflation.[6]

The Whitakerian-Geraldine policy of fostering exports, towards which the country gravitated from the late 1950s onwards, had an intellectual basis in an amalgam of the Keynesian deficit financed 'demand management' economics that had precipitated the acute balance of payments crisis of the the mid-1950s; and of the currently popular teaching by Rostow on 'economic take-off'.[7] Keynes had made deficit financing intellectually respectable. Rostow purported to show that economies, having been assisted by the state through various preliminary 'stages of growth', reached a point of 'take-off' when they could generate 'self-sustained growth' and further public assistance would become unnecessary.

The argument for public assistance to export industries was subsequently fleshed out in a cost-benefit analysis of the IDA's operations by J. McKeon, an IDA economist.[8] This showed that the public benefit from the policy, which included the unemployment benefits that persons employed in exporting industries would otherwise have had to receive and the income taxes that they paid when they were employed, exceeded the public cost of the policy.

Typically, there was little debate on the new departure which easily gained virtually universal acceptance. It was the more acceptable in that no immediate costs were involved. The various grants and tax concessions to exporters were financed by borrowing, which meant higher interest rates for savers. Provided that borrowing stimulated exports and attracted capital inflows and so relaxed the balance of payments constraint, there was no perceptible limit on Irish governments' capacity to borrow. True, the policy posed a threat to protected industry; but that threat was in the future when tariffs would be removed, while the benefits of the new departure were palpable and immediate. Meanwhile, the people and plant engaged in protected industry, aided by liberal public subsidies, could 'recoup lost domestic sales by increased exports'.[9]

The public commitment to encouraging exports had very substantial attractions for Irish landowners, over one third of whose produce was exported and whose incomes were in large measure determined by the prices realized for those exports. The prospect particularly of membership of the EEC and the very high prices that that held ensured the enthusiastic support of the Irish farming interest for the Whitakerian-Geraldine policy of export promotion.

Irish people, unlike the people of the other former capitalist colonies, had never been concerned about higher food prices caused by agricultural exports to the metropolises (Chapter 5). Those who might have objected, emigrated. Even the prospect of the very high food prices that would result from Irish membership of the EEC did not trouble a people who had become accustomed to trade unions ensuring that wages and salaries rose more rapidly than prices (Chapter 5).

A European location made Whitakerism, the IDA and the pursuit of Rostovian 'economic take-off' uniquely attractive, feasible and durable in this former capitalist colony. First, the policy depended absolutely on the state's ability to borrow, which permitted the benefits of the policy to be enjoyed immediately, while its costs could be deferred to a future when, in the Keynesian aphorism, 'we are all dead'. Ireland's European location, in the manner discussed above (Chapter 5), principally accounted for the state's remarkable credit. Second, a European location made EEC membership possible. That, as noted, had enormous attractions for Irish landowners while Ireland, as a member of the EEC, also had an attraction, which was unique among former capitalist colonies, for non-European manufacturers wishing to secure a footing within the large EEC market. Third, Ireland's shedding of the less contented half of its population flow, which also arose from its European location (Chapter 5), conferred a political stability that was unique in its way and that, as well as facilitating state borrowing, further enhanced the country's attraction for foreign manufacturers.

The Whitakerian-Geraldine policy of promoting exports and integrating the Irish economy more closely into the European and world economies has had successes. Those successes prompted Dr Fitzgerald in the 1960s and early 1970s to refer frequently to the country's economic growth, which was as remarkable in its way as the economic performance of Germany, as 'Ireland's economic miracle'. The successes of Whitakerism prompted Mr Haughey, the leader of the Fianna Fail opposition party, to declare on television in 1969, when he was Minister for Finance, that Ireland had solved its economic problems and had now only to deal with the social problems of distributing its wealth.

The flaws. There were however major flaws in Whitakerism, which are more obvious now than they were 20 years ago.[10] To begin with, whatever the case for Keynesian deficit financed 'demand management' as a means of countering short run cyclical fluctuations in metropolitan economies (and that case is being increasingly questioned not merely by Friedmanite monetarists but by a widening body of neo-Keynesians[11]) no one has seriously sought to justify public sector deficit financing sustained, without a break, for 40 years. Following on that, the defects of the Irish economy, as of the economies of all the undeveloping former capitalist colonies, are deep-seated and structural, unlike the cyclical problems that affect wealthy metropolitan developing countries that Keynes was concerned to rectify. Faults similar to those in the Irish economy have precluded, in every former capitalist colony, the 'economic take-off' about which Rostow facilly wrote, but which occurred virtually spontaneously in countries that were not capitalist colonies (Chapter 1; Appendix C).

The character of the industries attracted to Ireland presented another fundamental problem. The industries attracted are (1) dirty; (2) subsidiaries of multinational companies practicing transfer pricing; and (3) capital intensive and labour extensive.

Pressure to create jobs causes Ireland to accept exporting industries that, in one way or another, are 'dirty', and thus less acceptable to more discriminating metropolitan host countries. The Merck, Sharpe and Dohme chemical complex near Clonmel, Co. Tipperary, is an example of a physically polluting industry that would have been less welcome in other EEC countries, where the pressure to create jobs is less and concern for the environment is greater.[12]

The Aughinish Alumina Company (AAC) is an example of an enterprise that is 'dirty' in the sense of having an undesirable political/ethical status, which would be less welcome in other EEC countries where public concern for equity to poor Third World countries is greater than in Ireland. With access to the EEC market assured by Irish membership, the AAC, of which 65% is owned by Alcan and the balance by Billicon (a subsidiary of the Shell Oil Company), is strategically located on the Shannon estuary to draw bauxite from either the West Indies or West Africa. It is thus ideally placed to play off against each other the impoverished bauxite producers on both sides of the Atlantic, thus enabling it to continue to pay less than 2% of the value of forged aluminium for the bauxite raw material.[13] The policy of minimizing payments to bauxite producers in the former capitalist colonies has enabled Alcan, the major partner in the AAC, to become the 77th largest company in the world.[14] Established in the 1920s, Alcan drew all of its bauxite from Guyana until recently. Guyana, meanwhile, is one of the poorest countries in the world, with incomes, on average, one-sixth those of Ireland.[15] Irish government practice in this regard departs greatly from Irish government preaching. Dr Fitzgerald drew warm applause when, addressing the General Assembly of the United Nations in New York, he declared that as a first condition for equity between the nations 'there must be an assurance of a continued, long-term improvement in the relative prices for (undeveloping) countries viz-a-viz the prices of industrial manufactures.'[16]

The AAC, which is typical of the enclave industries industries attracted to Ireland by the IDA, is a subsidiary of multinational companies that practice transfer pricing. It charges into the Aughinish plant the 1.6 million tons of bauxite it uses annually at a price so low that the parent company's bauxite mining operations cannot show a profit and as a result minimizes their obligations in respect of taxes and royalties payable in Guinea, which is now the principal source of bauxite for Aughinish and where per caput incomes, at one-thirteenth those of Ireland, are among the lowest in the world. The alumina from Aughinish is charged out to the downstream aluminium smelting and fabricating operations of Alcan and Billicon at a sufficiently high cost to show these operations to be marginal, thereby minimizing tax liabilities and maximizing concessions from governments in the metropolitan EEC countries where the downstream operations are located.[17] Most of the profits from the combined operation — of mining bauxite to fabricating the resulting aluminium — are, therefore, shown as accruing to the Aughinish alumina producing plant where the profits carry no tax.

Because the enclave industries brought in by the Whitakerian-Geraldine strategy have been branches of multinational companies practicing transfer pricing, upstream and downstream integration with Irish industry has been minimal. 'Little spinoff has occurred from multinationals in Ireland...Irish companies are not successfully supplying sub-supplies to foreign owned industries.'[18] That is understandable. The controlling company charges in the enclave inputs at low prices against which Irish producers cannot compete; and it charges out the product at high prices, which Irish processors cannot afford to pay.

The AAC illustrates the characteristics of such industries. It imports annually 1.6 million tons of bauxite and 200,000 tons of crude oil, both supplied by upstream subsidiaries of the parent Alcan and Shell companies.

It exports 800,000 tons of alumina to smelters and fabricators owned or controlled by the parent companies. Its only local acquisitions are 1,000 tons of flour and 11,000 tons of limestone annually, as well as electricity which it buys at a small fraction of the cost Irish consumers pay.[19]

The industries brought to Ireland by the IDA are also capital-intensive and labour-extensive. Most of their costs, therefore, represent returns to capital, which is given as a grant by the IDA, or supplied either by Irish banks at negative real interest rates or by the companies themselves. No tax is paid on these returns, which are repatriated. Again the AAC illustrates the point. The cost of the project was £650 million. The IDA gave at least £16.8 million of this as a grant. More of the capital was supplied by Irish banks at negative real interest rates. The AAC employs some 700 persons, or around one person per £1 million invested. Only 33 persons are needed to operate the plant through a shift.[20] The enclave operations absorb large quantities of capital, which Ireland does not have and is therefore forced to borrow; while they employ relatively little labour, of which Ireland has a chronic surplus.

The Whitakerian-Geraldine initiatives of the 1950s and 1960s were also seriously flawed by their assumption that higher agricultural export prices would result in a large increase in the volume of agricultural output. That anticipation ran counter to Irish experience throughout the nineteenth century, when its agriculture had completely free access to Britain, which was then the largest, most rapidly growing market for food in the world: and when Irish agriculture stagnated (Chapter 4). The expectation of increased production was unwarranted because of those deep-seated structural and institutional defects which in all former capitalist colonies preclude the efficient use of agricultural resources (Appendix C). The volume of net agricultural output was in fact lower in 1984 than in 1973, when Ireland joined the EEC.[21]

The cost. The Whitakerian-Geraldine strategy, while wildly overestimating the benefits also gravely underestimated the costs to the undeveloping Irish economy of those initiatives. Integration of Ireland's economy, first with the British, then with the EEC's and later with the world's, which was the linchpin of the strategy, is a two-directional process. Access to EEC markets, for Irish agricultural produce and for the manufactured products of foreign-owned enclave industries, is conditional on the Irish market being open to imports from the EEC and from countries with which the EEC has trade agreements. Irish manufacturing industry was obliterated in the nineteenth century, when it first experienced free trade under factory capitalism (Chapter 4). The fundamental structural and institutional flaws at the root of that persist; the economy continues to be small and isolated with a stagnant agriculture. The competitiveness of Irish industry and its ability to withstand foreign competition has meanwhile, in material ways, been lessened.

Much of Irish industry developed on the basis of the intensive protection that was practiced in the pre-Whitaker decades. These twentieth century, protected industries were even less competitive than the cottage and craft industries of the nineteenth century which had emerged without the benefit of protection but were, nevertheless, destroyed by free trade in the age of factory capitalism.

The EEC's Common Agricultural Policy (CAP), under which farmers receive artificially high prices for their produce and consumers pay artificially high prices for food, benefits Irish farmers but is particularly harmful to Irish industry. This arises from the fact that incomes are lower in Ireland than in the rest of the EEC (apart from Greece). It follows that for a given value of output, more labour is employed in Ireland than elsewhere in the EEC, again apart from Greece. People with low incomes of necessity pay a higher proportion of their incomes on food; the Irish on average spend 28% while the poorer classes of the Irish spend 40%.[22] Because, for a given value of output more labour is used in Ireland, and because Ireland's relatively low paid workers spend more of their earnings on food: the CAP's high food prices are more harmful to industry in Ireland than in the other EEC countries.

Ireland's relatively labour-intensive, indigenous industries, like textiles and footwear, suffer from the obligation to accept the imports of Third World countries with which the EEC has trade agreements. These trade agreements secure better access to Third World markets for the capital-intensive, technologically advanced industries of the metropolitan EEC. The resulting imports of less advanced, more labour-intensive, manufactured products from the Third World are of little consequence to the metropolitan EEC, where the industries producing these goods are all but obsolete. Industries of this sort, however, continue to account for the bulk of Irish indigenous manufacturing, which in addition has very few technologically advanced products of its own to market in the Third World.

One aspect of the EEC arrangements is particularly unfavourable to native Irish industry. High EEC food prices result in surplus 'mountains' of butter, skim-milk powder and beef. These surpluses are exported to the Third World, either at heavily subsidized prices or free as 'food aid'. These dumped 'food aid' surpluses, apart from the problems that they create in the recipient countries (Appendix C), cause special difficulties for Ireland. The Third World countries are enabled to produce manufactured exports cheaper, partly because their costs are reduced by getting beef at half the EEC price and dairy produce free as 'food aid'.[23] Thus, for example, workers in the Irish textile industry have to compete with an Indian textile industry, the workers in which receive free from Ireland milk products for which the Irish are charged so much that they can only consume a small part of total production.

Part of the Whitakerian-Geraldine and McKeon thesis was that the jobs created in IDA-attracted enclave industries reduced the state's obligations to pay unemployment benefits or assistance, and the taxes paid in wages and salaries in those industries was an additional source of revenue. In turn, these savings and new tax revenue would constitute an adequate return on the outlay by the IDA in bringing the industries to Ireland. This argument, which was most clearly enunciated by McKeon,[24] overlooked the fact that the state's obligations did not end when factories were built and people got jobs. The factory's operations were dependent on the availability of the whole range of public services, from basic policing to advanced communications. The factory workers expected and received for their taxes the range of consumer public services, including policing, health, housing and education. If the factories themselves paid no taxes and if the factory workers' taxes were pre-empted to offset the cost of establishing the factories, the increase in government's current costs arising from their establishment had to be financed otherwise. That, in the final analysis, meant the remainder of the economy which did not receive subsidies, grants or tax holidays.

A militant trade union movement (Chapter 5) ensured that wages rose at least as rapidly as prices whether prices rose as a result of higher EEC agricultural prices or because of higher taxes. The unions also ensured that wages rose sufficiently to compensate for rising PAYE taxes on salaries and wages, which are pre-empted to service a rapidly expanding national debt. This transfer of the cost of fostering exports into higher wages, through higher agricultural prices and borrowing to finance the IDA's grants and tax holidays, bore on industries that did not export and that, as part of the Whitakerian-Geraldine policy, were deprived of protection from competing imports. Most of that part of Ireland's indigenous manufacturing industry, competing with imports under these conditions, was wiped out. The process of destruction is illustrated below by reference to the case of the Aughinish Alumina Company.

The AAC case. IDA grants and tax exemptions to projects like the AAC have been financed in the past by government borrowing. The cost of servicing the resultant debt was £1,710 millions in 1984, which was almost identical with the expected revenue from the PAYE tax system. Because of its commitment not to tax the profits of the AAC and of other manufacturers, government is forced to finance welfare payments by PRSI levies on workers and employers. PAYE and PRSI contributions together in 1984 yielded some £2,500 millions, or the equivalent of 30% of total wages and salaries. Labour costs are raised further by VAT on the goods and services that workers buy, upon which tax, in the absence of land or profit taxes, government is forced to rely for a quarter of its tax revenue. Labour costs are also raised by the high food prices that have resulted from Irish membership of the EEC; a membership that ensures duty and quota

The Aughinish Alumina Co. Case

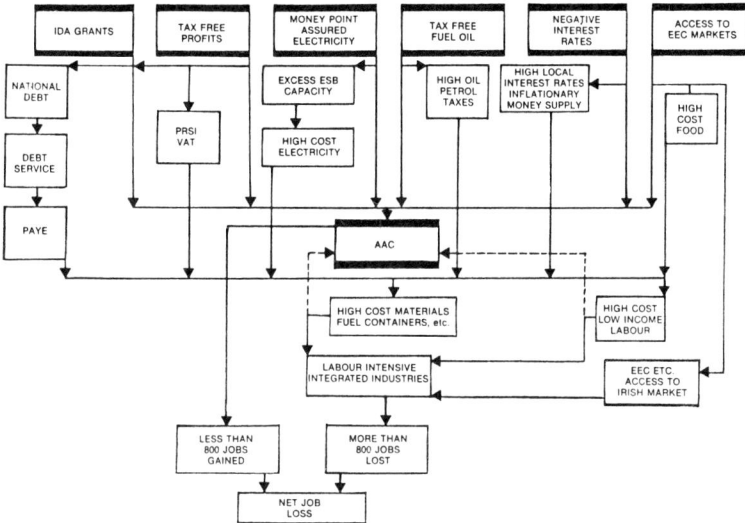

IDA GRANTS | TAX FREE PROFITS | MONEY POINT ASSURED ELECTRICITY | TAX FREE FUEL OIL | NEGATIVE INTEREST RATES | ACCESS TO EEC MARKETS

NATIONAL DEBT | EXCESS ESB CAPACITY | HIGH OIL PETROL TAXES | HIGH LOCAL INTEREST RATES INFLATIONARY MONEY SUPPLY

PRSI VAT | HIGH COST ELECTRICITY | HIGH COST FOOD

DEBT SERVICE

PAYE

AAC

HIGH COST MATERIALS FUEL CONTAINERS, etc. | HIGH COST LOW INCOME LABOUR

LABOUR INTENSIVE INTEGRATED INDUSTRIES | EEC ETC. ACCESS TO IRISH MARKET

LESS THAN 800 JOBS GAINED | MORE THAN 800 JOBS LOST

NET JOB LOSS

free access for the AAC's alumina to the EEC's market. Costs are raised also by the banks' expansion of the money supply which, by inflation, forces the public to save to provide the funds to loan to the AAC at interest rates below the rate of inflation.

The banks are secured against default of the Irish currency loan to the AAC by the collateral of the AAC's parent companies. They are secured against currency exchange loss by the Irish government's currency restrictions and its borrowing to finance the balance of payments gap generated by the banks' inflationary increase in the money supply.

Living and labour costs are increased by electricity costs to domestic consumers that are the highest in western Europe, to a considerable extent because of the high capital cost of the Moneypoint station, which was built largely to ensure abundant electricity for the AAC but which is surplus to the nation's needs.[25] Costs are finally raised by the exemption from excise duty of the 200,000 tons of fuel oil used by the AAC and the correspondingly higher rates of duty that must be charged to other users to secure a given revenue from this source. These taxes result in Irish fuel oil and petrol prices also being the highest in western Europe.[26] PAYE, PRSI, VAT, high electricity, petrol, fuel oil and food costs, and inflation: all raise the cost of labour and/or reduce real wages. High electricity, petrol and fuel oil costs and inflation also raise the cost of materials, fuel, containers, etc. which account for 64% of the gross output of manufacturing

95

industry.[27] Costs of these inputs to manufacturing industry are also raised by high labour costs.

Materials, fuel, containers, etc., as noted, represent 64% of the value of Irish manufacturing output. Labour costs account for another 15% of gross output. In alumina production at Aughinish, where almost £1 million of capital is employed per worker, labour accounts for no more than 5% of gross output.[28] However, labour accounts for over 40% of the value added by Irish manufacturing industry as a whole, and over 80% of the value added by service industries.[29] The various measures taken to attract the AAC to Ireland, while seriously increasing the cost of labour, materials, fuel, containers, etc., which together account for almost 80% of Irish industrial output and for an even higher proportion of the costs of the service industries, hardly affect the AAC's production costs at all.

Part of the price of securing tariff and quota free access to the EEC's market for the AAC's alumina is the similar access to Irish markets for the products of other EEC countries and of countries, including some in the Third World, with which the EEC has trade agreements. Most of these countries have much larger local markets, which allow them to to achieve greater economies of scale than are available to most Irish manufacturers. None of them has a structure of policies that raise factor costs as much as Irish policies do. Moreover, producers in the non-EEC countries that have access to Irish markets can buy food well below EEC prices; and in some cases, as for example Indian textile workers, they can get free as 'food aid' from the EEC, dairy produce that has been priced too high for Irish workers to be able to buy.[30]

The policies that have been described withdraw resources, through higher prices, from industries that use much labour; and they give these resources to industries like the AAC, which have minimal inputs of Irish labour, materials, fuel, containers, etc. The policies, in effect, discourage the employment of labour, much of which is unemployed, and they encourage the employment of capital, much of which is borrowed abroad. While attracting some of the latter, capital-intensive and labour-extensive industries, the policies force out of business the former type of industry, which is labour-intensive and capital-extensive. The operation of these policies in the case of the AAC is illustrated in Figure 6.1.

Industrial concentration. The Whitakerian-Geraldine policies have been a charter for the 'take-over' merchant who, borrowing at negative real interest rates, acquires competing firms; 'rationalizes' them (i.e. adds their labour to the half of the nation's workforce that has never been employed in Ireland) with capital that has been borrowed abroad by government and, by alchemy, makes a profit.

But the possibilities for take-over merchants in non-trading industries are quickly exhausted in a small economy where conditions for takeovers have been made so extremely attractive. Understandably, therefore, firms like Allied Irish Banks, Cement Roadstone, the Insurance Corporation of Ireland and the Jefferson Smurfit Group which, through takeovers, have become dominant in Ireland's non-trading industries, have spread their activities abroad in a spate of foreign investment that is altogether out of character for a country as small and poor as Ireland. The dominant non-trading Irish firms, with foreign exchange acquired in the first instance by Irish governments borrowing in the name of, and to the account of, the plain people of Ireland, pursue the takeover game on a broader, grander, international scale. As the Telesis report puts it: 'Most of the largest and strongest companies are investing abroad in businesses only minimally related to Irish employment and exports....From the national point of view, this cannot be the best use of the managerial, financial and organizational capabilities of these companies.'[31]

The case of the Aughinish Alumina Company illustrates how Irish economic policies cause the destruction of indigenous trading industry. The Jefferson Smurfit Group, now by far Ireland's largest firm, illustrates how these policies also destroy jobs in Ireland's indigenous, non-trading, manufacturing industry. Young Jefferson Smurfit, from Sunderland in England, acquired a small box-making firm in Dublin in 1934. The firm's progress over the following 30 years was unexceptional. Matters changed in 1964, when Whitakerian-Geraldine policies had already begun to swing the balance in favour of capital and against labour; and when Jefferson Smurfit got a stock exchange quotation that gave him access to Ireland's now virtually free capital. Thereafter the company's progress, by taking over other companies, was meteoric, especially when, in 1972, it commenced to cast its acquisitive net overseas. The company's progress during the most recent seven years for which data are available is charted in Table 6.1. The Irish share of the Group's operations, as measured by sales, declined over the period from 28% to 13%. Allowing for the 68% increase in Irish wholesale prices for the paper and paper products that Jefferson Smurfit produces, the volume of the Group's production in Ireland remained virtually unchanged.

Separate particulars are unavailable for the shares of the Group's total assets that are employed in Ireland. Assuming that these are *pro rata* to sales, the estimated quantities are:

	1978	1984
Assets employed in Ireland (£000s)	18,981	54,927
Persons employed in Ireland	2,458	1,552

These figures indicate that the Jefferson Smurfit Group increased its net investment in Ireland by some £36 millions over the period and, by so doing,

Table 6.1
Jefferson Smurfit Group, 1978-1984
(Values in IR£000s)

Year	Total Assets	Of which, loans, creditors & provisions	Sales Total	Sales Ireland	Profit after tax	Employees
1978	68,030	13,128	175,686	49,019	11,139	8,810
1979	77,999	17,541	190,989	56,153	12,747	9,179
1980	164,027	46,759	279,797	64,406	14,079	12,711
1981	180,630	52,051	401,429	67,269	14,779	11,722
1982	212,449	60,151	491,651	84,716	17,532	11,207
1983	270,243	93,768	501,006	86,446	15,714	10,046
1984	428,796	184,196	685,985	87,872	20,939	12,119

Source: Jefferson Smurfit Group, *Annual Reports.*

was able to secure the same volume of output with about 900 fewer people. That is to say, the Group was able to wipe out, on average, one job for every £40,000 of investment. The IDA, by contrast and over the same period, was spending around £29,000 for every new job it managed to create![32]

The situation has been analogous to that of nineteenth century Ireland. Then a stagnating agriculture provided livelihoods for a declining number of people. The number of people who, at any time, in any situation, could get a livelihood depended on the number and price of cattle and on the success of the 'land grabbers' in acquiring land on which to replace people with capital in the form of more profitable cattle (Chapter 4). Because the output of Ireland's non-trading industries is determined by the size of the economy (which in turn in Ireland is determined almost entirely by foreign trade) the number getting a livelihood in these non-trading industries in recent years has been determined by the extent to which capital, in the form of plant, has replaced people. As in the nineteenth century the number of livelihoods depended on the success of the 'land grabbers' in replacing people with cattle, so in recent decades, the number of livelihoods in the non-trading industries has depended on the success of the 'job grabbers' in replacing people with plant. As the form of tenure and prices in the British market made it profitable for the nineteenth century land grabbers to replace people with cattle, the Whitakerian-Geraldine policies make it profitable to replace people with capital in Ireland's non-trading industries in the twentieth century.

Then as now there was no outlet for investment in Ireland for the profits made by replacing people with capital and, as a result, these were transferred abroad. This was done in the nineteenth century through the new system of branch banking that emerged and that profited hugely from transferring Irish savings to London, where they helped to finance English factory capitalism which was destroying Irish cottage industry (Chapter 4). Now, as then, the Irish banking system is profitably engaged in destroying livelihoods in Ireland. It does so now by inflationary credit expansion, which forces people to save and passes these forced savings, at negative real interest rate, to the job-grabbers. Now the profits made by replacing people by capital are no longer lodged with the London money market. They are now spent abroad in acquiring foreign businesses that are 'minimally related to Irish employment and exports'.

Phenomenal successes, in the nineteenth century as now, emerged from, were the product of, and contributed to, socio-economic dissolution. The successes of the nineteenth century were Guinness, the banks and Harland and Wolfe (Chapter 4). The latter day successes are the Irish firms producing non-traded goods and services that have 'gone international' by buying foreign assets with foreign currency borrowed, in the first instance, by Irish governments on behalf, and to the account, of the Irish people.

There are contrasts too between the capitalist colonial and the post-capitalist colonial eras in the circumstances under which the profits made by replacing people with capital are being transferred abroad. Thanks to massive foreign borrowing by the governments of the Republic, the foreign investment has not now to be financed, as it was in the nineteenth century, by low domestic consumption. In the same way, the job losses are now, in a measure, compensated for by unemployment benefits and assistance which, alone of all the former capitalist colonies, the Irish state pays. The apparently limitless willingness and ability of the governments of an independent Ireland to pawn that independence against foreign credits has, for the moment, taken the sharp edge off want and has altered attitudes. The 'land grabbing' destroyers of peoples' livelihoods in the nineteenth century were, if fortunate, merely boycotted. But in a more affluent Ireland, a less jaundiced view is taken of Ireland's own princes of commerce and captains of industry who profit now by grabbing the jobs, if no longer the land, of the Irish people.

The impact of Whitakerian-Geraldine policies on Ireland's indigenous industry, both trading and non-trading, has been devastating. The total number engaged in manufacturing industry in Ireland in 1951, five years before Whitaker became Secretary of the Department of Finance, was 212,000.[33] That total had declined to 197,000 by September 1984 and was then still declining.[34] The number engaged in the IDA's enclave industries in 1984 was 80,000.[35] The number continuing to work in Ireland's indigenous manufacturing industry was, therefore, some 117,000, or only about 55% of the pre-Whitaker level. That 45% fall in employment in indigenous Irish manufacturing industry over a 33-year period was paralleled only by the collapse in industry during the last decades of British rule in Ireland.[36]

The total number at work in Ireland declined from 1,217,000 in 1951 to 1,112,000 in 1984, or by 9%.[37] The total loss of livelihoods would have been greater but for the expansion of public service employment, which was made possible by the country's large and sustained borrowing. Public sector employment increased by 87,000 between 1970 and 1984, having previously grown by an estimated 16,000 between 1951 and 1970.[38] The loss of livelihoods, which was contained during the first 30 or so years of the state's existence, has recommenced during the past 30 years when the number at work declined by 105,000 or, as noted, 9%. This is approximately the number of jobs lost in indigenous manufacturing industry.

The ultimate consequence of the Whitakerian-Geraldine policy of reintegrating Ireland's former capitalist colonial economy with the economies of the metropolitan capitalist countries has been to intensify Irish economic dependence. It has given rise to a high cost agriculture that produces with little reference to consumers' needs. A major element of

Irish agriculture's additional cost is the increase of bank and Agricultural Credit Corporation indebtedness, from £87 millions in 1970 to £1,081 millions in 1984.[39] Interest alone on that debt in 1984 was £221 millions.[40] This increase in farmer indebtedness was, in many if not most cases, caused by 'the desire of commercial banks to increase advances and thereby their profits, and of the ACC to increase its advances and thereby its corporate status and the status and salaries of its executives.'[41] These advances, which were made without regard to their impact on agricultural output, the volume of which declined over the period,[42] were highly inflationary. Because of the inflationary character of the advances, even farmers who did not wish to invest, but who had not savings to cushion them against rising production costs (especially for replacement livestock) and against rising living costs, were forced to borrow and became entrapped in the morass of agricultural debt created by the banks and the Agricultural Credit Corporation. Largely as a result of the higher debt charges, farmers' real incomes hardly increased during these years, although Irish agricultural prices rose in nominal terms almost fourfold and in relation to the consumers' price index by nearly 50%. Meanwhile the value of manufacturing milk production has increased from 21% to 33% of total agricultural output at a time when the consumption of milk and milk products in metropolitan countries has been declining and when Irish milk products can be disposed of only by the EEC adding them to its 'mountains' of skim milk powder and butter, or by selling them to Russia at less than half their cost, or by giving them away free as 'food aid'. Irish cattle and beef exports, which in the past have been exported so profitably as to give rise to major social and macro-economic problems (Chapter 4), now require an EEC export subsidy equivalent to about half of the price paid to producers.[43]

Indigenous Irish manufacturing industry has been eclipsed in the manner indicated and its decline continues. New manufacturing jobs now come almost exclusively from foreign firms. Irish dependence on the metropolitan capitalist economy is clinched by its large and rapidly expanding national debt, which is the inescapable consequence of fostering exports through government deficit financing, which has been the nub of Whitakerian-Geraldine policy. Ireland is now so dependent on foreign borrowing that the entire economy would collapse overnight and the polity would disintegrate if foreign credits ceased to be available.

Ireland's metropolitan dependence, with respect to agricultural prices, jobs and credit is now far more complete than that of any other former capitalist colony. This extreme dependence arises from, and is the corollary of, Ireland's uniqueness among former capitalist colonies in being located in Europe. That European location, while not sparing Ireland the experience of capitalist colonialism, has made it possible for Irish governments to borrow relatively far more than the government of any other former capitalist colony; and for Ireland to join the EEC. It is the realization of both these possibilities, which was the essence of Whitakerian-Geraldine policy, that has locked Ireland into a condition of more complete metropolitan dependence than any other former capitalist colony.

Patrons and Clients

Institutions and technology that ensure inefficient land use, and birth rates well in excess of death rates and therefore rapidly expanding populations: these are the key elements of the capitalist colonial heritage. That heritage, throughout Latin America and the Caribbean, Africa, South and Southeast Asia, is the source of chronic political instability and deteriorating living standards for the burgeoning landless and jobless masses (Appendix C). The same heritage results in Ireland in even more inefficient land use, insofar as Ireland is the only part of the world where agricultural output is not substantially greater now than it was 140 years ago.[44] But Ireland's capitalist colonial heritage has included the removal through emigration of virtually every element of discontent in Irish society. This has made it possible for Ireland's declining population to achieve living standards approaching those of the metropolises. Partly because of improving living standards and partly because of the removal of discontent through emigration, a 'fat cat' Irish society has experienced more political stability than other former capitalist colonies and even most metropolises.

The non-radical character of pre-independent Ireland's politics was reflected in the dominance in the political scene, from the death of Daniel O'Connell in the 1840s to the emergence of W.T. Cosgrave as head of government in the Irish Free State in 1922, of a heterogenous succession of individuals with tenuous Irish connections (Chapter 4). The conservatism of post-independence Irish politics is best reflected in the continuity of the parties and persons involved. The major parties, Fianna Fail and Fine Gael, have dominated politics since the state's foundation. They are ideologically indistinguishable — a case of 'tweedledum and tweedledummer' — and they jockey for power in the centre of a road from which almost all elements of right and left wing extremism, as well as all shades of radicalism, have been removed by emigration. The claims of the parties to office, in the absence of ideological or policy differences, are based on their records as patrons in serving the interests of their client constituents.

The political groupings that offer to serve their supporters' interests, through their control of the public purse when in office, have much of the character of the Guelph and Ghibelline factions that dominated Renaissance Italian politics; or the factions that now play so large a part in Indian and African politics.[45] They have nothing in common with Edmund Burke's concept of a political party as 'a body of men united, for promoting by their joint endeavours the national interest, upon some principle in which they are all agreed.'

The factions serve their clients' interests through their control, when in office, of a public expenditure equivalent to over two-thirds of GNP; one third of which expenditure is financed by borrowing and, therefore at the cost of future taxpayers and not at the cost of their present clients. The remarkable extent to which governments have been able and willing to finance their expenditure by 'painless' borrowing, in much the same way as the absolute monarchs of Renaissance Europe (Chapter 5), has conferred on Irish governments a fairy-godmother character. Sustained, large scale borrowing has made government in Ireland a cornucopia of public and private benefits. Access to the fount of plenty is not automatic. It is reached through the mediation of politician patrons who, of necessity, devote a major part of their time and resources to constituency 'clinics' where they serve their clients' interests by negotiating them through the webs of bureaucratic inertia and of competing interests, and at the expense of those who omit to secure patronal services.

As the emigration of Irish radicalism left the field clear for the remarkable dominance of Irish politics, from O'Connell to Cosgrave, by a polyglot collection of non-Irish persons, so the continued removal by emigration of normal political disciplines facilitated the subsequent dominance of Irish politics by persons with a less than usual regard for the public good. The 166 members of parliament, or Dail deputies, collectively have the power to allocate the £2.6 billions that the political establishment annually raises by the painless expedient of expanding national debt. Each deputy/patron has, on average, the power to dispense among his clients £16 millions annually of public funds, secured free from the odium of taxation. The personal nature of patron/client relationships, which are the essence of politics in the Irish Republic, is reflected in the exceptionally dynastic character of those politics. A remarkably high proportion of sitting members of the Dail are the widows, children, grandchildren, nephews, nieces, sons and daughters-in-law of former members. The Dail in 1986, out of a total membership of 166, has 22 sons, four daughters, five nephews, one brother and one son-in-law of former members. Three members are sons of former senators, or members of the upper house. There are four pairs of siblings. The leader of the largest party, Fianna Fail, is the son-in-law of a former taoiseach. The leader of the second largest party, Fine Gael, and present taoiseach, is the son of a former minister of government. The leader of the third largest party, Labour, is the son of a former member of the Dail.[46] The sons of the country's two first prime ministers, William Cosgrave and Edward de Valera, have duly passed on the Dail seats that they inherited to their children, who are now the third generation of two opposing political dynasties.

Control of the expenditure of public funds equivalent to over two-thirds of GNP in an Ireland where, for generations, only half the oncoming population have been able to get a livelihood, creates an extreme dependence on the part of the public on the politicians. Or as Thomas Paine would have put it: the governors are furnished with the means of corruption and the governed are put in the condition of being corrupted. Perhaps the closest parallel in history to the dependence of the Irish public on their politicians is that of the plebeian clients on their patrician patrons in the final decades of the Roman Republic.[47]

Just as the patron-client relationships of the later Roman Republic gave rise to unbearable tensions as parties contended for the power that had become concentrated into the hands of a few leading citizens, Irish politics are increasingly and inescapably conducted with a view to securing office and thereby control of the public purse. Control of an exchequer bloated by borrowing enables patrons to reward clients who, in a fatally flawed economy, are utterly dependent on these rewards. The actual or prospective reward of clients, on the other hand, is the condition of the clients' support for factional politician patrons, who would be nothing without that support. The struggle by politician patrons to secure from the public purse largesse for their clients, like the disastrous civil wars of the final years of the Roman Republic, adds another dimension of inefficiency, iniquity and corruption to the former capitalist colonial Irish scene.

The Spectre of Northern Ireland

Half the world's population are the descendants of agricultural people who, in 138 or more countries during the past 500 years, were colonized by individualistic, capitalist European countries. Commencing in Latin America 160 years ago, the peoples of these former colonies have almost all recovered the sovereignty and the land that were taken from their agricultural forebears (Appendix B). Only in Northern Ireland and South Africa has this not happened.

These are the two surviving cases not only of capitalist colonialism, which applied to half the world's population, but of five cases in all where the land of the indigenes was not merely appropriated but was operated by settler farmers from the metropolises. The other cases were Algeria, the white highlands of Kenya and Rhodesia/Zimbabwe (Appendix B). Capitalist colonialism ended in these three colonies only after fierce, protracted, rearguard struggles by the metropolitan settlers to retain the capitalist colonial *status quo* had been overcome.

Clearly the situation in both Northern Ireland and South Africa are transient and unstable. The rising incomes of the dispossessed stimulates resistance to the settler regimes. The black townships, like Sharpville and Soweto, where incomes, literacy and levels of political consciousness are far higher than anywhere else in black Africa, are the chief centres of opposition to white South African supremacy. As incomes, literacy and political consciousness rise further in the townships, the effect is to sharpen consciousness of deprivation and to heighten the struggle against remaining white privileges. Similarly, in Northern Ireland, as incomes and standards of education of the Catholics approach those of the Protestant settlers, impatience with the surviving Protestant privileges and with the surviving Catholic disabilities intensifies.

Undevelopment of the former capitalist colonies of Africa and Southern Ireland stimulates both opposition to, and support for, the maintenance of settler privilege in South Africa and in Northern Ireland. Using the standard ploy of diverting public discontent from domestic failure by foreign adventurism, political leaders in black Africa and in the Irish Republic seek to distract attention from domestic affairs by stimulating discontent among their racial followers in the settler colonies; and by attacking the defenders of white and Protestant privileges, the one located in Pretoria and the other in London. The animosity and indignation of their own peoples are diverted from domestic failure and against the disabilities suffered by their fellow blacks in South Africa or their fellow Catholics in Northern Ireland. The inferiority of employment opportunities, of wages, of social services and of political status vis-a-vis those of the ascendancy whites of South Africa or of the Protestants of Northern Ireland is emphasized. The much wider disparities between the blacks of South Africa and those of the rest of Africa, and between the Catholics of Northern Ireland and those of Southern Ireland are ignored. The political leaders find excuses for domestic failure in the insecurity and economic dislocation caused in their territories by the struggles of the indigenes against white supremacy in South Africa and against Protestant ascendancy in Northern Ireland.

The socio-economic failure of the former capitalist colonies, on the other hand, strengthens the resolve of the metropolitan settlers to cling to their positions. As mega-famine threatens or envelops black Africa, the white settlers are made more determined to cling to the superior life that they have secured for themselves on the lands that they appropriated, mainly from the Khoikhoi hunter-gatherers, but also from the Bantu agriculturists. The transformation of Rhodesia/Zimbabwe, within a decade of independence, from a food surplus to a food deficit country is an immediate example on South Africa's border of the consequences for white settlers of black rule. The Zimbabwe case confirms the earlier experience of the white settlers of Kenya and Algeria.

The loss of livelihoods in the Republic confirms Northern Protestants of the correctness of their choice in maintaining the Union with Britain in 1922. The fact that this was particularly severe among non-Catholics, who declined from 10.4% of the Twenty-six Counties' population in the last pre-independence census of 1911, to 4.6% of the total in 1971,[48] reinforces Northern Protestant conviction of the need to avoid absorption by the Catholic majority. The prognoses for black Africa and for the Irish Republic strengthen resolve in both territories. Black Africa is patently sinking into chaos. The Irish Republic is sinking under an impossible burden of public debt at a time when its surplus population can no longer emigrate. These prospects leave little option for the settlers but to cling to their privileges and to try to contain the violence.

Ireland then, as well as being the first of the capitalist colonies, is also fated to be one of the last two arenas for the struggle against capitalist colonialism. That struggle has already recovered sovereignty and land for half the world's population under similar circumstances. It can hardly fail to do so for the half million Catholics of Northern Ireland. But resistance by the Protestant settlers to that struggle is likely to be as bloody and protracted as that now being offered, under similar circumstances, by the whites of South Africa, and as was offered by the metropolitan settlers in Kenya, Algeria and Rhodesia. That is the spectre of Northern Ireland.

End of an Era

Ireland, more than 60 years after independence, remains 'the old sow that eats its farrow' and from which escape lay in 'silence, exile and cunning'.[49] Only exile is no longer an available option. Now too the excluded half of the Irish are not as they were in the past, malnourished, potato-fed, illiterate coolies. Nor is there a highly efficient, paramilitary Royal Irish Constabulary, supported if necessary, as de Beaumont observed, by English artillery, to ensure that the coolies perished quietly but paid their rents to the last, as Daniel O'Connell, their leader and himself a landlord of substance, proudly acknowledged. And because exile is no longer possible for the excluded half, unemployment has increased fivefold in little more than a decade. It will multiply overnight when the foreign credits, on which Ireland is now as dependent as it was on the exotic potato in the 1840s, are withdrawn. At or before that stage, the number of the unemployed will no longer be counted and they will cease to be paid dole, unemployment benefit or assistance, as is now the case in every one of the other 137 former capitalist colonies.

The excluded half of the Irish, better fed and read than their predecessors of the early nineteenth century, no longer overawed by a metropolitan controlled army of operation, nor able to emigrate, nor placated by doles from a bankrupt state, will be an explosive force. Sooner or later, unless integrated into a reformed social order, it will explode and destroy the interest groups that deny it a living. That explosion is the more certain and the more imminent in that, unlike the nineteenth century situation, a torch of rebellion already burns within Ireland.

As the capitalist colonial influences that have shaped society in Southern Ireland change profoundly and dramatically, and in so doing force change on an exceptionally unresponsive society, the situation in Northern Ireland proceeds to a denouement that has already taken place in the other capitalist colonies. The recovery by the Catholic Irish of the sovereignty and lands that were taken from their agricultural forebears is resisted in Northern Ireland by the descendants of the metropolitan settlers, just as it was in Algeria, Kenya and Rhodesia/Zimbabwe, and as it continues to be in South Africa (Appendix B). The intensification of the struggle of the Catholics of Northern Ireland has already brought about the dissociation of the Catholic third of the population from the Protestant government of Northern Ireland. That dissociation of the Catholics is the base for the politico-military Sinn Fein/IRA movement. This movement plays in Northern Ireland a role similar to that of the FLNA in Algeria, of the Mau Mau in Kenya, of ZAPO and ZANU in Rhodesia during the wars of decolonization in those countries; and of the African National Congress in South Africa now.

The politico-military Sinn Fein/IRA movement already has widespread, if numerically limited, support in the Republic, where, for the most part, the various established interests wish it would go away and cease to threaten those interests. As economic conditions deteriorate and dissillusion heightens with the political establishment, support will grow for a Sinn Fein/IRA movement that carries the lighted torch of nationalist rebellion against an intolerable, metropolitan-imposed, social order within part of the island. Moreover, it has no responsibility for the economic debacle that discredits the Republic's other political organizations. The growing strength of the Sinn Fein/IRA movement heightens instability and increases the probability of catastrophic collapse as the crisis deepens.

VII

A Radical Alternative

Introduction

This work has had two principal concerns. The first has been to place Ireland's record of undevelopment in the context of Third World undevelopment. The second has been to analyse the nature of that undevelopment, showing how and why none of the 138 or so former colonies has developed, although some have been independent for 160 years. The enduring heritage of capitalist colonialism has everywhere been an impenetrable barrier to development; an impossible handicap that drags societies down into the trough of undevelopment. It would not be unreasonable to conclude in light of the record of these 138 countries, including so many people and extending over so long a period and over such varied conditions, that the heritage of capitalist colonialism is irreversible undevelopment. The concomitant of contact between western, individualistic capitalism and non-western, non-individualistic, non-capitalist cultures, through the experience of capitalist colonialism, has universally been the persistent undevelopment of the colonies.

A chief purpose of scientific study is, through knowledge and understanding of the phenomena studied, to change them. A chief purpose of studying and seeking to understand the laws of the undevelopment of former capitalist colonies is to discover ways of influencing the manner in which they are undeveloped The better, more clearly, these laws are understood, the better is the prospect of influencing their operation. Recognizing that no former capitalist colony has developed makes clear the intractible character of undevelopment and the futility of existing approaches to development. These approaches are invariably based on false paradigms with developing western countries that are not former capitalist colonies; and made, as they are, by 'experts' from those countries. The Telesis report, *A Review of Industrial Policy,*[1] is typical of such approaches. They are made in every former capitalist colony by innumerable 'experts' from rich countries who have no intuitive conception of the problem of transforming undevelopment into development. The Telesis report traces the various stages through which developing countries develop, quoting in particular a model of such progress that has been used by the Japanes Economic Planning Agency. The report typically fails to recognize that none of the countries it quotes to illustrate the process of economic development is a former capitalist colony. Nor does it recognize the basic development/undevelopment issue: countries that have not been capitalist colonized, develop; countries that have been capitalist colonized, undevelop. The half of the world that has not been capitalist colonized develops, under enormously diverse regimes. These regimes range, in the matter of government intervention alone, from the *laissez faire* of Hong Kong to the centralized planning of Russia.

The half of the world that has been capitalist colonized, undevelops. It has done so at all times since it was colonized; and it does so notwithstanding the application (nowhere more so than in Ireland) of all the measures that all the experts have ever perceived as being associated with the development of non-capitalist-colonized developing countries. If a country has not been capitalist colonized, it develops in spite of government and experts; if it has been capitalist colonized, it undevelops in spite of (or because of) government and experts. Recognition of this fact is an essential step towards the achievement of that degree of understanding of the laws of undevelopment which offers a prospect of effective, purposeful intervention.

This work, in the body of the text and in the appendices, has sought to identify and to explain the origins and the persistence of grievous defects in the social order of the undeveloping, former capitalist colonies. It has been argued that those fundamental defects stem in all cases from the imposition of western, individualistic capitalism on non-western, non-individualistic, non-capitalist societies. Very peculiar ecological and historical conditions permitted the spontaneous growth of individualistic capitalism when and where it did (Appendix A). Those conditions made it possible for myriads of individuals to seek to better themselves and to do so, not necessarily at the expense, but to the benefit of society (Appendix A).

That force of individualism, or the striving of individuals to better themselves while simultaneously and incidentally benefiting society, has been the most potent social force in human experience. It made possible the transformation of the dark, cold forests of Central Western Europe into the modern world of science and affluence. But it has, in doing so, superimposed, through the process of capitalist colonialism, the culture of individualistic capitalism on societies that existed in non-individualistic and non-capitalist ecological and historical environments (Appendix B). Out of context, that superimposed capitalism, has everywhere been inverted and, throughout the Third World, is proving as socially destructive as it has been constructive in the West.

Two key aspects of western culture have been particularly ruinous in the Third World. One of these is the institution of property, without which Central Western Europe could not have developed as it did. The other is the extension of life expectancy by strong western-type states and by hygiene and medical science, which are a major component of the corpus of scientific knowledge and method, without which western life would be inconceivable (Appendix C). Property in a non-western context invariably attaches to land and results in inefficient land use. Superimposed metropolitan capitalist institutions and the western technology of death prevention, in non-western contexts, normally cause population explosions. The result in Ireland's exceptional case, has been to intensify emigration and the profound problems associated with it (Chapter 5).

Individuals benefit from the retention of the heritage of capitalist colonialism while society loses, in Ireland's case as in that of every former capitalist colony. The palpable inefficiency and iniquity of the social order are maintained by powerful, western-type states everywhere in the Third World; and no less so in Ireland.

To repeat a point made at the outset of this chapter: a main purpose of scientific study is to increase control of the phenomenon studied, with a view to altering it in desirable ways. The cause of Third World undevelopment is here perceived to be the enduring consequence of the impact of western capitalist culture on non-capitalist, local cultures. It follows that reducing or reversing undevelopment requires countering the effects of western culture on non-western societies. Here it is emphasized that there can be no question of an atavistic return to a lost, pre-colonial innocence. Even if it were possible to recapture a lost innocence, few people would wish to return to an age that was also one where 'life was short, nasty and brutish'. Pre-capitalist societies were homeostatic, but at a low level of attainment. Reducing the scale of world poverty by making lives that are already 'nasty and brutish' shorter is neither an acceptable nor a feasible solution. Reversion to a pre-capitalist-colonial status which was also far from ideal, is clearly ruled out.

There is no precedent for halting and reversing the undevelopment that is characteristic of, and peculiar to, former capitalist colonies. The only grounds, therefore, for believing that the undevelopment of these colonies is not irreversible is faith in man's limitless capacity to transform his environment. That capacity for constructive change depends absolutely on studying, knowing, understanding, empathizing and reasoning about the transformation problem.

An encouraging aspect of the problem of changing undevelopment into development is the recognition that all categories of countries, except former capitalist colonies, have succeeded in developing (Chapter 1). The noncolonized, East Asian countries, Japan, Korea and Taiwan, are now developing much more rapidly than metropolitan capitalist and settler colonies (Appendix C). Their experience is clearly relevant. However, their success in eclectically borrowing from the West emphasizes the need for former capitalist colonies, likewise, to borrow with great discrimination from the experience of Japan and of other non-western developing countries. An indiscriminate emulation of the Japanese (or Chinese, or Russian) path to development would almost certainly ensure an equal or even greater degree of undevelopment to that which has resulted from failing to adapt superimposed western institutions and technology in the post colonial era.

Trust in man's ability to transform the environment ought not to obscure the enormous momentum of Third World undevelopment. Nearly 2,000 million people live in former capitalist colonies, all of which are undeveloping and some of which have done so for over 160 years. Escaping from the mould presents a formidable challenge to man's abilities. Yet there are aspects of the Irish situation now which suggest that it offers the best available prospect for creating the precedent of transforming former capitalist colonial undevelopment into development.

Ireland, as emphasized in the two preceding chapters, while conforming to the general pattern of undevelopment, also has features that make it *sui generis* among former capitalist colonies. These distinctive features have led Ireland to a turning point where presently it must either change direction or collapse into revolutionary chaos. That revolutionary chaos is unlikely to be contained in Ireland, as it has been in illiterate, impoverished Latin America, Africa and Asia, by military regimes; or indeed as it was in Ireland by 'firm' paramilitary government during the quarter century of chronic famine that culminated in the Great Famine. The cost in terms of lives and money of containing the mildly disaffected Northern Ireland Catholics is an augury of the force that would be needed to contain, within a social order that has been inherited from capitalist colonialism, that half of the Irish population stream which, since the early nineteenth century, has failed to get a livelihood in Ireland, which can no longer emigrate, which now has living standards that are among the highest third in the world and which, once the country's credit is exhausted, will no longer be placated by government doles.

It is timely, under these circumstances, to show that there is a feasible alternative to the inefficient and inequitable social order that has degraded Irish society for the five centuries during which it has existed and that has finally taken that society to the brink of chaos. That alternative need not be a pathetic attempt to apply, in a former capitalist colony in the 1980s, the insights that Karl Marx acquired into the nature of metropolitan English society in the 1850s. Nor need it be rule by a jumped-up barbarian: an Amin in Africa, a Pinochet in Latin America, or a Zia in Asia, equipped with advanced western methods of repression (Chapter 2).

Measures that seek to reverse capitalist colonial undevelopment, to have any prospect of success, must *a priori* have certain characteristics. They must, first, be concerned with efficiency, or securing a better relationship between needs and the means of satisfying those needs. In Ireland's case, that means securing the livelihoods that the existing social order destroys; and in the case of the other former capitalist colonies, reducing the scale and intensity of poverty. Second, the measures must be equitable, inasmuch as in the post colonial era, in a world of increasing literacy, with metropolitan armies withdrawn, the choice is between equity, on the one hand, and the inefficiencies and the brutalities of the party commissars, the Amins, the Pinochets, or the Zias on the other hand. Or, in Ireland's case hitherto, between equity, on the one hand, and massive emigration and massive state borrowing on the other. Finally, it is clear that these measures must be radical. They must be radical in the sense of aiming at the root causes of the widespread and persistent undevelopment which they seek to transform. If any of these characteristics is missing, the others are unlikely to be effective. A transformation will not be effected.

Incorrect Factor Pricing

Undevelopment, it has been suggested above (Chapter 1), is a failure of production relative to needs, so that more are worse off and/or fewer are as well off as formerly. It has also been suggested that capitalist colonialism, in all cases, has been the ultimate cause of undevelopment. Its operation has resulted in inefficient production and in generating needs that expand more rapidly than the capacity to meet them (Appendix C). Ending this imposed undevelopment requires both an increase in output and a curb on needs relative to the means of meeting them.

The causes of low output in the former capitalist colonial Third World in general, and in Ireland in particular, have been seen to be the inefficient use of resources (Appendix C; Chapters 4,5,6). Irish land now produces little more than it did 140 years ago. Irish capital has been prodigiously wasted. Half of Ireland's labour has never been employed in Ireland. The ultimate cause of this inefficient resource use is a social order, which retains, out of its original context, critical elements of the West's individualistic capitalism. The proximate cause of inefficient resource use has been incorrect factor pricing. The cost to landowners of holding land has been minimized by first freezing and later abolishing land taxes or rates. Simultaneously, the attraction of holding land has been enhanced as a result of the accumulation of population and capital in neighbouring continental

Europe, to the markets of which Ireland has gained preferential access by joining the EEC. In addition to the elimination of land taxes and the increased effective demand for its products, land's attractiveness as an asset to hold has been enhanced by the inflationary increase in the money supply. The more people discount future inflation, the more land prices rise relative to land's net current income. So Irish land prices have been rising much more rapidly than GNP (Chapter 5).

Capital has been virtually free to the politicians, who borrowed domestically and abroad and who have been able to service older borrowings by rolling these over into new debt. They have got money other than by unpopular taxation. The cost of the savings imposed by the banks on the public, through their inflationary increase in the money supply, has also been low, and in some cases negative, for those with property and therefore able to borrow from the banks (Chapter 6).

The corollary of low cost land and capital has been high cost labour. All of the revenue raised by PAYE is pre-empted to service the public debt. Because government taxes neither land nor capital, it must impose PRSI contributions on workers in order to finance welfare payments. These, combined with PAYE, amount to the equivalent of 30% of all wages and salaries. The need for revenue, while simultaneously avoiding taxing land or capital, causes government to enforce rapidly escalating PAYE and PRSI charges so that, at the relatively modest salary of £12,750, it costs an employer £4.08 to place an additional £1, net of deductions, in an employee's pocket.[2] Again because government does not tax wealth, it must take through VAT on average 15 pence out of every residual £1 the worker gets and spends on goods and services. These cost-increasing taxes on labour are reinforced by trade union action that is particularly effective in Ireland and that further forces up labour costs (Chapter 5). Labour costs are also enhanced by unemployment benefits and assistance, which are paid conditionally on the recipients not working (Chapter 5). Labour costs that are forced up by taxes on labour and on things that workers buy, by trade union activity, and by subsidies on unemployment, result in only half those who wish to work getting employment in Ireland. The other half emigrated in the past. The replacement of dear labour by cheap capital found its ultimate expression in the Whitakerian-Geraldine strategy initiated in the 1950s and epitomized by such cases as the Aughinish Alumina Company and the Jefferson Smurfit Group (Chapter 6).

The heritage of capitalist colonialism, like infection with an incurable disease, persists in all of the 138 or so former capitalist colonies. The remarkable durability of this heritage is everywhere attributable to its profitability for powerful, entrenched interests that are part of it. Irish landowners profit from the capitalist colonial institution of property in land, the value of which has increased a million times since Cromwell financed the reconquest of Ireland by selling Irish land in London at one old penny an acre.³ The value of land now in Ireland appears to be greater, in relation to GNP, than in any other country.

The Irish banks have profited enormously, first by transferring Irish savings to England. More recently they have made much greater profits by appropriating to themselves 'the things that are Caesar's' and using their misappropriated sovereign power to inflate the money supply. The resulting balance of payments deficits understandably have had to be financed by Caesar, in the form of foreign borrowing charged to the sovereign Irish people. Irish banks, relative to Irish GNP, are the most profitable in the world, as well as being among the most long lasting: an obscene contrast to the condition of Irish society. Specially favoured firms, like the Aughinish Alumina Company, have profited from concessions made at public expense. Others, like the Jefferson Smurfit Group, have profited by replacing heavily taxed and otherwise encumbered labour with cheaply available capital and by investing the resulting profits abroad (Chapter 6).

Irish politicians have profited from the great enhancement of their patronal powers through the disposal of borrowed funds. Trade unionists have been able to secure privileged positions in the scramble for livelihoods in a country where there have been livelihoods for only half those who sought them. Innumerable bureaucrats and functionaries profit from a capitalist colonial heritage that has secured for them permanent and pensionable employment in a world of uncertainty. The majority who lose by the preservation of the heritage of capitalist colonialism, are coerced, in almost all cases except Ireland, by power-based, extremist right or left wing governments. In Ireland those who lost emigrated.

The low cost of holding land, the low cost of borrowing capital, and the high cost of employing labour in all the former capitalist colonies are major elements of the capitalist colonial heritage. Everywhere this heritage results in inefficient land use, the waste of capital and the unemployment of labour. Production in all the former colonies is depressed by this incorrect pricing of the factors of production (Appendix C).

The second of these major components of the capitalist heritage are those colonial-induced influences which cause a drastic reduction in death rates, viz. the power of centralizing, western-type states and the application of the principles of hygiene and medical science (Appendix C). Reduced death rates, outside the very peculiar, western context, generally cause an explosion in population and in the need for the products which their economies, crippled by incorrect factor pricing, cannot supply. Those death rate reducing factors, which are also a major element of Ireland's colonial heritage, have, in this exceptional case, determined the level of emigration. This emigration has been the safety valve of Irish society which has permitted, to an extraordinary degree, the perpetuation and flourishing of the heritage of capitalist colonialism in the post-colonial era.

The retention of an inappropriate system of factor pricing in Ireland as

115

in all former capitalist colonies, as well as serving the powerful entrenched interests bequeathed from the capitalist colonial era, also owes much to persistent intellectual imperialism. This is especially dominant in the intellectual void caused by massive, sustained emigration from Ireland. Inappropriate factor pricing survives, in part at least, because of the failure in the former capitalist colony to recognize how fundamentally different economic circumstances are in Ireland from those of the metropolises and of the the former settler colonies; and therefore how misleading and irrelevant are paradigms drawn from the latter countries when applied to the former. It is a system of factor pricing that makes the criterion of efficiency the level of output per unit of labour, although half the supply of Irish labour has been unused for generations; that ignores output per unit of land, though land values are higher in Ireland, relative to GNP, than anywhere else; and that ignores output per unit of capital, although the country now absolutely depends on borrowing abroad £4 million every day.

Land has never been limiting in the metropolitan capitalist and settler capitalist countries (Appendices A; B). It has, therefore, in accordance with the paradox of property, been used efficiently there. This is in contrast to the situation in all the former capitalist colonies, where land has always been limiting and where, also in accordance with the paradox of property, it is used inefficiently once it becomes private property (Appendix C).

Capital has always limited production in the metropolises and in the settler capitalist colonies. Capital formation there has been the condition of expanded output. The role of capital in the former capitalist colonies has been much more ambiguous. Capital formation in tribal, pastoral Ireland was in the form of more livestock, probably leading to overstocking and to reduced output from the communally grazed pastures (Appendix A). Capital formation in the nineteenth century was again in cattle and sheep, which replaced people and crops and reduced total output (Chapter 4). Capital formation by the Jefferson Smurfit Group made it possible to maintain the same output while destroying the livelihoods of 40% of the producers (Chapter 6).

'Thou shalt earn thine bread by the sweat of thine brow' was part of the western, individualistic, capitalist ethic long before John Calvin and the Puritans appeared on the scene. It was a close enough reflection of reality in Central Western Europe where, until the eighteenth century, population was constrained by the dowry system, by the low marriage rate and by high mortality rates (Appendix A). The value judgment that people's consumption should be related to the productivity of their labour bears little if any relationship to the pre-colonial circumstances of Ireland and of the other capitalist colonies. Custom and status, not marginal labour product (which in any case was virtually zero) determined the individual's share of the total product, both in riverine, crop-growing societies and in tribal pastoral ones like Ireland (Appendix A; Chapter 2). The continuing inappropriateness and irrelevance to the Irish scene of the metropolitan capitalist stricture about bread and sweat is manifested by the failure of half of six generations of Irish people to get any bread according to that rubric.

Getting Factor Prices Right

The argument of this book so far shows, it is suggested, that it is essential to counteract, directly and purposefully, the malign influences of the capitalist colonial heritage if the undevelopment of the Third World is to be transformed into development. That is no less necessary in Ireland. Doing so involves, principally, rectifying the inefficiency and concomitant iniquity that are a major part of that heritage. This involves above all rectifying the system of factor prices so that the prices of factors of production are made to reflect the economic realities of the former capitalist colonies rather than the privileges created there by capitalist colonialism; and then securing the benefits of this correction equally for all members of society in the manner that, by and large, all the peoples of the non-individualistic, non-capitalist societies did prior to capitalist colonialism. The application of these principles implies in the Irish case the specific measures outlined below.

New and higher taxes. 1. Taxing land, urban and rural, up to the point where property in land, created by capitalist colonialism (Appendix B), ceases to have value. Land will then be freely available against the payment of taxes. Irish land would become free, as it was before the Cromwellian conquest of the 1650s. A land tax of the order proposed would undo the conquest in the very profound and explicit sense of recovering for all the people of Ireland the wealth that, since the conquest, has been appropriated by the few upon whom the conquest conferred the proprietorship of the country's land and whose heirs and assignees have persistently and inevitably used that proprietorship in ways that have been highly inimical to the social well-being.

Only those who use land efficiently will be able to pay the tax on it; and only they will wish, or be able, to retain land. The taxes would reflect the current, market-determined value of land, varying from field to field, from street to street, and from year to year. The taxes would be adjusted periodically to reflect changes in current market values, just as conacre rents for farmland now vary from year to year and as rents of flats and apartments vary over time.

Overtaxed land would be abandoned and its abandonment would indicate an over-correction of the present situation, where users pay too little for land. Overtaxed, abandoned land would involve an even greater waste than undertaxed, neglected land. There is an extensive literature and a large corpus of experience of modern land valuation from which it is clear that both over and under taxing land can be easily avoided.[4]

2. Taxing bank deposits at a rate approximately equal to the difference between the rate paid by the banks on deposits and the rate charged by the banks on overdrafts and loans.[5] That level of taxation would remove the banks' incentive to create inflationary additional money, which compels people to save by reducing their consumption; and which enables the banks to supply capital to privileged borrowers at negative real interest rates in order to substitute that capital for labour. The proposed tax would force the banks to direct their funds to those able to make the best use of them, rather than as now, to give them to those who, like the Jefferson Smurfit Group, with inflation-induced, appreciating assets, give the banks the most attractive combination of profit and security; or to those who, like the Aughinish Alumina Company have been chosen for favoured treatment by office-seeking politicians. The proposed bank tax would destroy the capitalist colonial created malign bank interest, just as the proposed land tax would destroy the malign landed interest.

Taxation will be excessive when the banks, which have profited inordinately from, and have contributed importantly to, the undevelopment of Ireland (Chapter 4; Chapter 6), are forced into liquidation. The need to maintain a banking, or post office giro system, that is adequate to effect commercial transfers and to mobilize and direct voluntary savings into the market-determined most productive use, limits the potential revenue from taxing banks.

3. Government creates many quasi-monopolies. These reduce to users the current cost of the assets involved, which tends to their being inefficiently used. Further, by impeding the inflow of labour to the occupations affected, they reduce the demand for, and the return to, labour. It is proposed to maximize revenues from taxes on these government-created quasi-monopolies.

Taxing government-created monopolies, apart from property in land and banking, so as to maximize the revenue from these taxes will result in all citizens having equal access to the trade or profession concerned, subject to payment of the tax, to being of good standing in law and being adequately qualified. Maximizing revenue from these sources would normally involve raising existing taxes. Included would be taxes on public houses, adjusted to local demand for public house services; taxes on licenses to transport people or goods for hire, which would be expected to result in taxis, or 'jitneys', plying for hire as buses do now, within and between cities;[6] taxes on radio and television broadcasting.

There is a good case for taxing advertising of a persuasive rather than an informative character.[7] The objections to taxing advertising would have less force if the tax on advertising were, as proposed, part of a radical restructuring of the social order.[8] They would have less force also given the proposed use of the tax revenue.

The envisaged maximum revenue from these taxes is:

	£ millions per annum
Rural land	1000[a]
Urban land	1000[b]
Banks	500[c]
Other monopoly taxes	500[d]
Total	3000[e]

NOTES

a) This is based on current conacre, or competitive rents of around £80 per acre per annum, for 12 million acres of farmland, plus some five million acres of rough grazing and mountain land. Further changes suggested below would raise demand for rural land and so would raise further the potential tax revenue from it.

b) Total urban land values are twice as great as total rural land values in Denmark, a country where the proportion of GNP deriving from agriculture is not unlike that in Ireland; and where there is a long tradition and considerable experience of efficient land value taxation.[9]

Reports of sales of urban land in Ireland, particularly in Dublin (e.g. £4.4 million for six acres at Cornelscourt, Co. Dublin[10]) indicate the high value of urban land for residential, commercial and amenity purposes. The total value of urban land is here taken to be the same as the total value of rural land, or half the proportionate value of urban to rural land values that obtain in Denmark.

c) The total Irish money supply in December, 1983 was £11,035 millions. Of that, £6,600 millions was in the form of non-government bank deposits.[11] The suggested tax revenue would represent rather less than 7% annually on those deposits. The banks charged 17.75% interest on loans and paid 7% interest on deposit accounts (though nothing on current accounts).[12]

A tax of £500 millions would absorb much of the margin between the interest paid to depositors and that charged to borrowers. The banks, in order to pay the taxes, would need (1) to reduce their operating costs; (2) lend to people who can pay the most for scarce savings, who are most likely to be young, landless, capital-less and jobless people; and (3) to draw on their reserves. These reserves are the accumulated profits from transferring

119

savings out of the economy between 1820 and 1950; and from the appropriation, since around 1950, of the sovereign right of the state to create money.

d) This is a crude 'guesstimate' based on such indicators as Dublin public houses being sold for over half a million pounds, staff at the Carriage Office fraudulently issuing taxi licenses for £6,500, and the published profits of the advertising industry.[13]

e) It is possible that, even following the other changes suggested below, the revenue realized from some or all of the taxes may be less than the indicated amounts. That is of a lower order of importance than the fact that a very large revenue can be raised from each of these taxes; and that raising that revenue will contribute powerfully in every case towards raising economic efficiency. Moreover, any shortfall in the actual as compared to the indicated revenue from the suggested taxes can be made good by retrospective taxes on the users of, and beneficiaries from, these national resources.

Reducing expenditure. National debt creation, as well as making possible a vast, protracted misuse of savings by buropoliticians and their clients, is also an expedient that is now nearly exhausted, as more and more of the borrowing must be from abroad, where lenders are free to refuse credit. It is also an expedient that has now become enormously expensive, in as much as debt servicing costs absorb resources that are equivalent to over 10% of GNP. Repudiating the national debt, which already is on a scale that makes repudiation unavoidable in one way or another, will preclude further debt expansion and the irresponsible government that is the concomitant of public debt expansion. It will reduce public expenditure by one fifth.

Scrapping public sector capital formation. The Irish state, since the Second World War, has undertaken capital formation on its own, through various state corporations and bodies, and by grants to private enterprises. Borrowing to finance public sector capital formation has been on a greater scale than in virtually any other country outside the Communist bloc (see Table 1.3). The purported purpose was the development of the economy and especially the creation of jobs. The reality has been a very poor relationship between capital formation in Ireland, of which an exceptionally large proportion has been attributable to the public sector, and economic growth. Every £1 growth of Irish GNP has been accompanied by £14 capital formation, whereas a more normal proportion is £1 growth of GNP and £3 — £4 of capital formation. The unproductiveness of Irish public sector capital formation is reflected in the lag between the rate of growth of GNP and the rate of growth of government indebtedness. The result has been that the cost of servicing public debt, which was virtually zero 40 years ago, has now grown to over 10% of GNP.

Yet no additional jobs have been created. Ireland, where public sector capital formation has been exceptionally large, has the unique distinction of having substantially fewer people at work now than when public capital formation, financed by national debt expansion, commenced in 1948.

The ineffectiveness of public sector capital formation is understandable, if not inevitable. It has been financed by national debt expansion, which implies a virtually zero cost of savings to the buropoliticians who undertake their expenditure (Chapter 5; Chapter 6). This is a prescription for irresponsible government, now as it has been in the past (Appendix B). It is therefore proposed to terminate public sector capital formation financed by national debt expansion.

Scrapping existing taxes. Taxing land will raise the cost of land to its users. Taxing the banks and repudiating the public debt will raise the cost of capital to buropoliticians and to private sector borrowers who are favoured by the banks or are the clients of buropoliticians. The corollary of these measures to raise the cost of land and capital to their true economic level is to reduce the cost of labour, only half the available supply of which has ever been used in Ireland since the commencement of the era of factory capitalism in England.

The existing taxes on labour, PAYE and PRSI, absorb about 30% of the total value of wages and salaries. At quite moderate incomes, these taxes absorb 75% of marginal wages and salaries. Scrapping these taxes would allow the money cost of labour to fall by 30% without affecting the net-of-tax return to labour.

VAT absorbs around 15% of total consumer expenditure. Scrapping it would allow prices to drop on average by 15%. This would make possible a further decline in money wages and salaries without reducing the net-of-tax return to labour.

The combined effect on the money cost of labour of scrapping PAYE, PRSI and VAT may be illustrated by the example of an individual with a representative gross wage of £150 per week, none of which is saved. The individual now has a wage net of PAYE and PRSI of £105. Given that all is spent on goods and services, the amount paid in VAT, at an average of 15%, is £15.8 per week. The VAT free cost of the goods and services would be £89.2. Scrapping PAYE, PRSI and VAT would, therefore, allow the representative wage/salary earner to accept a 40.5% lower cash return for his/her labour and still be no worse off than now.

Wages and salaries account for about 77% of net domestic product at factor cost.[14] Therefore, if wages and salaries were reduced in nominal terms by 40%, while leaving them unchanged in real terms as a result of abolishing PAYE, PRSI and VAT, the effect would be to make possible a further 77% x 0.40 = 30.8% reduction in prices. The final effect on prices, therefore, of scrapping PAYE, PRSI and VAT would be to allow these to fall by at least 45% below their 1984 level.

Financial Implications

Factor prices now in Ireland, as in all former capitalist colonies, reflect the perpetuation of interests that were originally established under capitalist colonialism for the purpose of advancing metropolitan interests. The perpetuation of those interests, as reflected especially in established factor prices, has precluded development and has caused undevelopment in Ireland as in every one of the 137 or so other former capitalist colonies. The proposed changes in the public finances, which involves some new or higher taxes, some reductions in public expenditure, and the scrapping of other taxes, are designed to change factor prices with a view to causing them to reflect the economic realities and needs of Irish society, instead of perpetuating interests that have been, and are, incompatible with the well-being of that society. The financial implications of the proposals are set out in the following tables, which are based on the *1984 Budget*.

The proposals involve credits and debits to the exchequer on an annual basis as shown in Table 7.1.

Table 7.1
Exchequer: Credit/Debit Implications of Proposals

Credit	£m.	Debit	£m.
New or higher taxes	3,000	Ending PAYE and VAT	3,079
Reduced expenditures: cancelling public debt servicing	1,710	Ending public borrowing	2,142
Ending public capital expenditure	1,022	Balance	511
Total	5,732	Total	5,732

Source: Budget, 1984.

The net effect of the proposed changes would be an exchequer surplus of £511 millions.

The *1984 Budget* proposed revenues and expenditures as in Table 7.2. The proposals that have been advanced above, if implemented, would change government revenues and expenditures as in Table 7.3.

Further Expenditure Reductions

An unprecedented and unparalleled use of borrowed funds has permitted the state, while helping to shore-up in the short term an inherently

Table 7.2
Budget Revenues and Expenditures, 1984

Revenues	£m.	Expenditures	£m.
Tax and miscellaneous		Debt service	1,710
revenues	5,881	Public capital	
Borrowing	2,142	expenditure	1,022
		Other recurring	
		expenditure	5,291
Total	8,023	Total	8,023

Source: Budget, 1984.

Table 7.3
State Revenues and Expenditures, with Proposals Incorporated

Revenues	£m.	Expenditures	£m.
Tax and miscellaneous		Other recurring	5,291
revenues	5,802[a]	Surplus	511
Borrowing	—		
Total	5,802	Total	5,802

(a) A net reduction of £79m. on the *1984 Budget,* resulting from increased taxes (£3,000m.) and abolishing PAYE and VAT (£3,079m.)
Source: See text.

unsustainable social order, meanwhile to exacerbate the associated inefficiencies, iniquities and corruption. The measures already proposed are designed to make the Irish social order efficient and equitable. It is germane in that context to consider the diminution of the Irish state and the further enhancement of efficiency, equity and integrity by an appropriate use of the resources saved by that diminution. These qualities can all be maximized by distributing the resources saved in the form of an equal national dividend paid to all resident citizens on the voters' register.[15] Examination of the recurring expenditures proposed in the *Budget 1984* indicates how the state can be diminished and also the amount of resources that could be freed for distribution as a national dividend.

The principal heads of recurrent state expenditure, other than service of the public debt, as given in *Budget 1984,* are summarized in Table 7.4, together with the reference numbers of the parliamentary votes under which the expenditures were approved. These heads of expenditure are considered below seriatim to identify the extent to which they could be reduced, the saving effected being distributed as a national dividend.

Ireland in Crisis

Table 7.4
Budgeted State Expenditure, 1984

Item	Cost (£m.)	Votes
1. Regulatory functions	558	22, 23, 24, 25, 43, 44
2. Economic services	630	35, 36, 38, 39, 40, 41, 49
3. Environment	533	28
4. Social welfare	1,185	47
5. Health	964	48
6. Education	776	30, 31, 32, 33
7. Government overheads	669	
Total	5,315	

Source: 1984 Estimates for Public Services.

Regulatory functions. A large, metropolitan-controlled army of occupation and subsequently the very efficient paramilitary Royal Irish Constabulary imposed capitalist colonial institutions and technology on Irish society and forced that society, within a capitalist colonial institutional framework, to adapt to changing external market conditions (Chapter 4). Subsequently the emigration of the less contented half of the Irish, coupled with large, sustained government deficit financing, has made it easier to maintain an alien, imposed social order. Nevertheless the Irish state is spending an increasing proportion of GNP on repressive functions. That proportion was 2.5% in 1974; it increased to 4.1% in 1984. These repressive forces would be largely unneeded under a reformed social order. A small, possibly mainly volunteer police force would probably be adequate and would be unlikely to cost more than a tenth of the present cost of police and prisons. The army would be disbanded. This reduction of the repressive forces of an inefficient, inequitable and corrupt state would release over £500 millions annually.

Economic services. The proposals made above would establish economically accurate factor prices, which would make the economy efficient. Those departments of state that now are supposed to raise output, but by their presence and cost add to the output-depressing forces they purportedly seek to counter, would be clearly superfluous. The departments concerned are: Fisheries, Forestry, Agriculture, Labour, Trade, Commerce and Tourism, Transport, and Industry and Energy. Closing these departments would save £630 millions annually.

124

Environment. A major component of this expenditure is in respect of grants to local authorities for housing subsidies (£193 millions). Terminating these subsidies would make it possible to increase the national dividend by just £90 per person, while simultaneously contributing to a more efficient use of the stock of houses.

Subsidies to local authorities in respect of relief of local government rates (property taxes) comprise another major outlay under this heading. These subsidies, if abolished, would cause an equivalent reduction in revenue from the proposed land tax. While it would obviously be senseless to continue to pay grants in relief of land taxes, so as to maximize in a circular manner the revenue from those land taxes, it is here assumed, in order to avoid both the complexity of reducing the assumed revenue from a land tax (£2,000 million annually) and double counting, that grants in relief of rates continue at £280 millions annually. Terminating other expenditure under this heading would release £253 millions annually.

Social welfare. It is proposed below to pay to every resident citizen a national dividend of some £80 per week in 1984 purchasing power. This will exceed the amounts now paid under every form of welfare payment and unemployment benefit.[16] It is proposed, therefore, to cease all welfare payments, apart temporarily for children's allowances. As the national dividend would be paid irrespective of income from other sources it would be neither a subsidy to unemployment nor a tax on employment, which unemployment benefit and asssistance now are. The replacement of unemployment benefit and assistance by a national dividend, as well as making recipients financially better off, would reduce the unattractiveness of work, which is now effectively taxed by the amount of unemployment benefit or assistance that is withdrawn when people work.

All but one class of recipient will get more from the proposed national dividend than they get from social assistance now. Persons in receipt of children's allowances, especially for large families, may not get as much in the national dividend as they now receive in children's allowances. It is proposed, therefore, to retain these allowances for the present, at a 40% lower rate to allow for the reduction in retail prices made possible by the removal of VAT, PAYE and PRSI, and by the payment of a national dividend. However, it is noted that the birth rate, at over 2% per annum, is about twice the death rate in Ireland. On the grounds that a stable, or only slightly increasing, population is preferable to the country's now quite rapidly growing one and that therefore a lower birth rate is desirable, it is proposed that children's allowances be withdrawn in respect of children born after a specified early future date.[17]

The economies attainable under this heading are £1,083 million annually.

Health. The cost of the Department of Health in 1984 was about one billion pounds; or some £9 per week per citizen on the voters' register and entitled to a national dividend. Better, cheaper health services would be got by greatly reducing the scale of publicly provided health services, which would make possible a larger national dividend while leaving it to the individual citizen to provide for his/her own health service by insurance, saving or otherwise. Public provision could still be made for the old and the chronically ill and for persons on low incomes; though that provision would make allowance for the fact that those supplying and those receiving the service would be in receipt of a national dividend; would be paying no VAT, PAYE or PRSI; and would be paying prices not much more than half their present level.

There might also be, in an efficient and equitable society, where producers paid the full cost — but no more — for factors of production and where citizens benefited equally from that through a national dividend, a case for relying much more on voluntary work to provide for exceptional cases of hardship. Individuals are likely to be more caring about others in an efficient, equitable and less corrupt society, where fewer people will require such care and where more will be in a position to render it.

Education. Budgeted current expenditure on education in 1984 was £776 millions. Of this, £692.7 millions was in respect of primary and secondary education and £33.3 millions was for higher education. Expenditure on primary and post-primary education is now equivalent to some £800 per person in the age groups from five to 17 years, of whom there are some 850,000. Allowing for the 45% price reduction made possible by scrapping PAYE,PRSI and VAT, the parents/guardians of these young people would have command over greater educational resources than now if paid a grant of £400 per young person annually. They could use these resources much more effectively than now, by getting the education for their children that they, and not the buropoliticians, deem best.

The state would cease to support higher education. Persons aged 18 years and over could use their national dividend and other resources, including earnings and borrowings, to pay for the higher education of their choice which, because of the other proposed reforms, would be available at around half the present cost. Again, because the recipients would be paying for the higher education of their choice and not one foisted on them, the quality of the education would be greatly improved.

The state's educational role would be reduced to ensuring that the right of the individual young person to adequate education, as well as to adequate nutrition, clothing and housing, was being met by parents or guardians. Allowing for this residual role of the state in education and after providing for the payment of an educational grant of £400 annually in respect of every person aged five to 17 years, the savings possible under this heading would be £430 millions.

Government overheads. The proposed economies in the executive departments of the state would involve a reduction in their expenditure from the 1984 level of £4,621 millions (Item 1 to 6, Table 7.4) to a little over £400 millions (which would include temporarily retained Children's Allowances of £102 millions, but would exclude the payment of £400 annually to parents/guardians in respect of every person aged five to 17 years). The outstanding item of public expenditure to be considered is item 7 in Table 7.4, which is here referred to as government overheads and which in 1984 amounted to £670 millions.

The concentration of power into the hands of Irish politicians necessitates a costly apparatus of state. This arises from the patron-client relationship between politicians and public. It takes such forms as the provision of cars, drivers and security guards for senior politicians, comparable to the original *fascisti* who, in the final years of the Roman Republic, beat off importuning clients when powerful patrons went abroad. Or it takes the form of a clamour to expand the resources available to Dail members to enable them to monitor better the state's burgeoning activities, which they have brought into existence.

The return of power to the people, which will accompany the national dividend, will strip power from the state and from the buropoliticians who operate the state. Even the most senior politicians, under these circumstances, will have no more power, authority or status than the mayor of a substantial town now has. A situation similar to that which obtained in England 60 years ago would be appropriate. Then prime minister Ramsey McDonald, who had no official transport, walked to the end of Downing Street to catch a bus or taxi to his destination.[18] Given the much reduced role of the state and of the buropoliticians who operate it, it would be feasible and desirable to reduce very much the cost of such items as the presidential establishment, the oireachtas (houses of parliament), the office of the taoiseach, and to reduce also the cost of the services provided for these institutions by the other arms of government.

It is proposed to reduce expenditure under this residual heading of government overheads from £670 millions to £50 millions annually, effecting a saving of £620 millions. It might well be deemed expedient, in this connection, to appraise critically the appropriateness of parliamentary-type government to former capitalist colonies. While that form of government, like the institution of property, has served well the interests of the metropolises and of the settler capitalist colonies (Appendix C) it has failed singularly in every one of the former capitalist colonies. However, the principal reform of government in Ireland that is proposed here is one of scale rather than format. The proposal is to reduce the annual level of expenditure by buropoliticians from the present (1984) £8,023 millions to some £500 millions annually.

Summary

The 1984 budget and the proposed expenditures of the Irish state are given in Table 7.5. The proposed saving on recurring state expenditure of £4,820 millions, together with the surplus of £511 which would exist without the proposed savings (Table 7.3) would make £5,331 millions available annually for distribution as a national dividend. Allowing for the 45% reduction in prices made possible by the elimination of PAYE, PRSI and VAT, that would allow a weekly national dividend payment of somewhat over £80 in 1984 purchasing power to every person on the voters' register and resident in Ireland.

Table 7.5
Budgeted and Proposed
Expenditures of the Irish State, 1984

Item	Budgeted Expenditure £m.	Proposed Expenditure £m.	Proposed Saving £m.
Regulatory	558	58	500
Economic	630	—	630
Environment	533	180	353
Social Welfare	1,185	102	1,083
Health	964	100	864
Education	776	346[a]	430
Government overheads	669	49	620
Total	5,315	835	4,820

Note: (a) Includes education grant of £400 per person aged 5-17 years.

The brief review in this chapter thus indicates that it is financially possible:

1. To abolish PAYE, PRSI and VAT.
2. To pay every person on the voters' register and resident in Ireland the equivalent of £80 weekly at 1984 prices.
3. To pay an education grant in respect of every person aged 5-17 years equivalent to £750 at 1984 prices.
4. To retain, at a reduced rate to allow for an anticipated reduced cost of living, children's allowances for the present child population, but not for children born subsequent to a future date to be announced.
5. To retain public health services for the old and the chronically ill.

VIII

Other Issues Briefly Considered

A profound crisis develops in Ireland. The elements of that crisis are a population that is growing more rapidly than anywhere else in the West and that has higher incomes than anywhere else among the former capitalist colonies; the unwillingness of foreign creditors indefinitely to lend to Irish governments the money on which the economy is now absolutely dependent — some £3 millions daily — but which must inevitably increase with the logic of compound interest and which can never be repaid; and the presence in Ireland of a substantial Catholic population who are already alienated from the state in Northern Ireland. Proposals have been made in the preceding chapter for changes in the Irish social order that are designed to transform Ireland from an undeveloping to a developing society. That transformation, if achieved, could save the country from the chaos that is characteristic of much of the Third World. The financial implications of the proposals have been examined and found feasible in the preceding chapter. The major political and economic implications of the proposals are now considered.

Political Implications

The changes proposed are, first, the establishment by appropriate fiscal means of factor prices that reflect economic realities and social priorities. Factor prices now preserve individualistic interests that are part of the capitalist colonial heritage and that are socially destructive. The establishment of economically correct factor prices will cause resources to be used efficiently. It is proposed to distribute the social surplus that will accrue from efficient resource use as a national dividend, paid equally to everyone on the voters' register and resident in Ireland. These measures would effectively undo the Conquest. They would replace an inefficient and iniquitable social order with an efficient and equitable one and they would secure a livelihood for all the people of Ireland in Ireland.

Repudiating commitments. The measures proposed involve a unique exercise of the sovereignty that is the concomitant of political independence, for the purpose of casting off the debilitating heritage of capitalist colonialism. The measures proposed are perceived to be the means by which a sovereign, independent people, responding to a unique challenge, can save itself from continuing, and now accelerating, undevelopment. An exercise of sovereignty of this nature cannot be bound by the past, any more than it can bind the future; except insofar as the present deems it expedient to accept past commitments and in so far as the future deems it expedient to accept present commitments. Sovereignty implies the rejection of what Thomas Paine called 'the vanity and presumption of governing beyond the grave [which] is the most ridiculous and insolent of tyrannies.'[1] The imperative need to escape from the present situation makes it expedient now to reject commitments made by those who in conducting the affairs of the Irish state have sought to broaden, deepen, enhance and preserve the colonial heritage.

The exercise of sovereignty now requires the rejection of the commitment by past sovereigns of the exclusive right of some individuals, their heirs and assignees to the use of Irish land (by which commitment most of the Irish are excluded from access to land); the commitment to others of the exclusive right to create and to allocate money; to others the exclusive right to sell intoxicating liquor, to provide transport for hire, etc.; to others the right to receive interest on, and the repayment of, money that was advanced to politicians who used it to buy office and left no assets to service the debt. The exercise of sovereignty requires the rejection of the commitment to others of the right of permanent and pensionable employment in the public service. The justification of this exercise of sovereignty — if such an act ever needs justification — is that the commitments mentioned have caused the undevelopment of Ireland, as similar commitments have caused the undevelopment of all the other former capitalist colonies (Appendix C). Only this exercise of sovereignty can ward off a crisis of unparalleled severity in the affairs of the Irish people; a crisis that threatens to hurl Ireland into a chaos comparable to any witnessed in the most disturbed and distressful parts of the Third World.

The repudiation of public debt, of tenure of public office and of state and quasi-state pensions is an exercise of sovereignty that perceives these commitments to be excessive, unreasonable, 'the most ridiculous and insolent of tyrannies', and a barrier to the efficient and equitable reorganization of the economy. The proposed reorganization should result in most of those who lose by the proposed repudiations — including non-government employees whose pension funds are invested in public debt — gaining more from their share in the social surplus, or the national dividend, and from the better demand for labour. Only those with exceptionally large claims on public funds will lose more from the repudiation of those claims than they can expect to get from the reorganization of the economy made possible by that repudiation. Exceptionally large claims on public funds imply exceptional responsibility for ensuring the conduct of public affairs in a responsible manner which provided reasonably for citizens' needs over a sustained period. The present debacle clearly indicates that Irish public affairs have not been so conducted; and, to that extent, those with the largest claims on public funds have most grievously failed in their responsibility. The scale of the individual's claim against an inefficient, iniquitable and corrupt state is also the scale of the individual's responsibility for the present condition of that state. That responsibility more than cancels any claim in equity for the loss of rentier incomes from public sources.

Repudiating public commitments, as well as removing the ability of politicians to borrow money and therefore to waste it, will also destroy the permanent and pensionable character of public employment, which is attractive for many. Against that, under the circumstances posited, there would be a very great diminution of the role of the state and a corresponding decrease in the need for public and semi-public employees. An adequate supply of persons of suitable calibre would almost certainly be forthcoming to discharge the duties of a greatly diminished state, notwithstanding the loss of the permanent and pensionable character of public and semi-public employment. Indeed, it might well be that persons of a superior quality would be attracted to the public service than are now attracted by its present character. A high preference for permanence and pensionability is not characteristic of the world's achievers.

An exercise of sovereignty that included the repudiation of debts incurred by non-mandated politicians and held overseas might generate a potentially damaging overseas reaction. The day passed, with the Suez incident in 1957, when metropolitan powers dispatched warships to enforce repayment of debts incurred by former colonies. (This was usually done by rolling over existing debts into bigger, new debts, at higher interest rates until, as in the 1930s, the whole shakey edifice collapsed). But since the flooding of metropolises with petrodollars in the 1970s and the vast expansion in lending to the governments of former capitalist colonies to which that has given rise (Chapter 5), there has been increasing nervousness about the global consequences of a general defaulting by debtor states in honouring these debts.[2] An explicit statement by Ireland of its intention not to service either internally or externally held public debt might provoke reaction of an exemplary nature, aimed at discouraging a general pursuit of the same course by other former capitalist colonies.

The principal and most likely retaliatory action would of course be the cutting off all future credits. Though the Irish economy is now absolutely dependent on these, to the extent of around £1,000 millions annually, or nearly 8% of GNP,[3] the restructuring of the socio-economic order that has been proposed would transform that dependence. The major part of current foreign borrowing is for funds to service existing foreign debt.[4] These funds will no longer be needed once the debt is repudiated, which will greatly reduce the balance of payments deficit.

All the balance of payments deficit is accounted for by capital inflows.[5] These capital inflows are encouraged by those policies which have already been considered and which reduce the cost of capital, as well as of land, to users. The changes suggested would cause the substitution of labour for capital and thereby, at a given level of GNP, would reduce the need for capital imports.

Raising the cost of land and capital, reducing the cost of labour, and transferring decisions on spending money from buropoliticians to citizens, as proposed, should greatly increase Irish economic efficiency. This would be manifested, among other ways, by the greater competitiveness of Irish goods and services on home and export markets. Exports would be increased and imports would be decreased for any level of total output. An increase of 10% in exports and a decrease of 10% in imports would, at the present level of GNP, bring foreign trade in goods and services into balance.

The cessation of service payments on foreign debt, the substitution of labour for capital in production, and the increased competitiveness of Irish goods and services should not merely wipe out Ireland's chronic external deficit, but should give rise to sustained balance of payments surpluses. These surpluses could be used, first, to augment the country's external reserves; and second, to finance an upward revaluation of the currency, so that the country would need to export fewer goods and services to acquire a given level of imports: or so that Mediterranean holidays would cost Irish citizens less!

A more efficient Irish economy that secured balance between present and future needs, and between imports and exports, at a far higher level of consumption than now, would be freed from the need to resort to the kind of exigencies that are now practiced by the IDA and that, as illustrated by the Aughinish Alumina Company case, are both disreputable and unprofitable for the nation (though of course profitable for the AAC and the IDA). There would be no scope in such an economy for 'job-grabbers' like the Jefferson Smurfit Group to syphon resources out of Ireland to buy foreign assets. Ending these abuses would also reduce the need for foreign currency.

The withdrawal of further foreign credit, which a repudiation of foreign debt would entail, should not be a problem in these circumstances. Punitive action against Irish exports by the foreign holders of Irish public debt would, however, remain a danger. Two lines of action are indicated to guard against it.

First, as a former capitalist colony, Ireland should identify closely with the other former capitalist colonies of the Third World. Correspondingly, it should distance itself politically, as far as it is feasible to do so, from its main European trading partners. With the inclusion of Spain and Portugal, the European Economic Community is a community of all the former capitalist colonial powers. Two members only of the EEC are not former capitalist colonial powers: Greece, and Europe's only former capitalist colony; Ireland.

Ireland should seek to demonstrate the irresponsible character of the lending by metropolitan banks to the governments of the former capitalist colonies. These funds have generally been used, as in the Irish case, by local politicians with a view to securing immediate political support, but with little if any regard to the generation of foreign exchange earnings to service the debts.[6] Metropolitan banks, to that extent and for the purpose of an immediate enhancement of profits, have been highly culpable in facilitating irresponsible, wasteful, iniquitable and corrupt government in many former capitalist colonies.

The great public concern that exists in the metropolitan countries about the undevelopment of the former colonies, including that aspect of undevelopment that is manifested by sectarian violence in Northern Ireland (see following section), should be alerted and informed of the role of metropolitan lending in perpetuating undevelopment. A metropolitan public, informed about the way their own banks, with a view to profit, lent money irresponsibly to Ireland and to other former capitalist colonies, without any competent appraisal of the purposes for which the money was to be used or the possibility of its being repaid,[7] would be unlikely to support politically action in metropolitan countries against imports from Ireland. That would be especially so if it were made clear that the repudiation of internally and externally held public debt was a key element in purposeful, socio-economic restructuring in order to undo the consequences of capitalist colonialism and to develop.

It should be emphasized, in relation to foreign held Irish public debt, that the creation of that debt has helped to perpetuate a socio-economic order in the Republic that has failed to provide a livelihood for half the area's population for generations and that results in less than half as many people having employment in Ireland now as formerly. It should be emphasized that under the socio-economic order that has been sustained by foreign borrowing, there is no prospect of terminating Irish partition and the murderous competition for livelihoods between Catholics and

Protestants that now occurs in Northern Ireland. The changes that can provide all the Irish with a livelihood in Ireland and that can therefore end partition and murderous sectarian competition for jobs require the repudiation of both internally and externally held public debt.

Arguments could be advanced in relation to foreign held Irish debt similar to those Keynes put to the victorious Allies with regard to German reparations after the Great War of 1914-18.[8] If the bankers are to receive interest and repayment of the funds that they lent irresponsibly to Irish politicians, who spent them without creating productive assets to service the debts, then Irish exports cannot be used to pay for current imports from trading partners. A choice is unavoidable between servicing the debts of profit-hungry, irresponsible, metropolitan bankers, or buying the goods and increasing the exports of metropolitan countries, and expanding employment in those countries.

Provided that a firm though placatory posture is adopted by the Irish authorities, foreign holders of Irish public debt and their governments are unlikely to be provoked into retaliatory action, which would be likely to be as damaging to them as to Ireland. Elements of the economy would, however, be vulnerable in the event of a general repudiation of the public debt. Foreign holders of that could secure easy redress against the assets of Irish nationals and of Irish firms held overseas. As already noted (Chapter 6), 'most of the largest and strongest [Irish] companies are investing abroad.' The foreign held assets of these firms, as well as those of individual Irish nationals, would be highly vulnerable and would almost certainly be sequestered as part compensation in the event of repudiation of the Irish public debt. The case for sequestration would be the stronger in that these overseas assets are owned by non-trading Irish firms, which did not themselves earn the foreign currency to buy these assets but bought them with foreign currency borrowed in the first instance by the Irish state.

To allay further any tendency on the part of foreign governments to take retaliatory action, the Irish authorities, in order to appear as conciliatory as possible, might let it be known that they would raise no legal or political objection to the confiscation of the foreign held assets of Irish firms and individuals. The losses, no doubt, would be severe for the individuals and firms involved; but they would not adversely affect the economy. As the Telesis report observed in relation to these foreign investments by Irish firms, they are in businesses that are 'only minimally related to Irish employment and exports'. In so far as the envisaged confiscations made explicit the real risks for Irish persons and firms of foreign investment, such investment would be discouraged in future, which would make available more Irish savings for internal investment.

Finally on this issue, it may be recalled that foreign held public debt comprises almost entirely entries in bank balance sheets. The primary concern of the banks is that the debts should retain, or appear to retain, the value of these entries; and that is a matter of the debts continuing to be serviced. Bank managers are usually no more heroic than others, including such others as Louis XV of France who, with the quip *'apres moi le deluge'*, deferred the inevitable. Rather than have items wiped off their balance sheets, banks are sometimes willing to finance the servicing of existing debt by an expansion of it. 'The banks have to keep on lending to the Mexicos and Polands. The alternative is to call in their loans, declare the borrowers bankrupt and swallow huge loan losses. Since more red ink is the last thing they want on their books, the banks keep lending while hoping that somehow things will get better.'[9] Conceivably, foreign bankers might take that view if government proposed to repudiate external debts, especially if they feared that Irish repudiation would trigger off general Third World defaulting. It would be churlish of any Irish government, under such circumstance, not to collaborate with foreign bankers in maintaining the fiction of an Irish public debt that would some day be repaid: as long as that collaboration only involved the further expansion of foreign debt and did not cost the Irish people anything.

The role of the state. There is a powerful bias in favour of extending state activity in all former colonies. The post-colonial state is everywhere looked to to protect the individual interests established by capitalist colonialism; which interests, in every case, have played the leading role in establishing the independent, post-colonial states (Appendix B). Others look to the post-colonial state as a potential source of individual benefit, if only to the extent of alleviating illness and so reducing death rates below approximately biological birth rates (Appendix C). Most post-colonial states sustain the socio-economic order inherited from capitalist colonialism by the use of military power, exercised by political regimes of the extreme right or left. In Ireland the state seeks to sustain the inherited socio-economic order by a frenetic expansion of economic activity.

Central to the state's extraordinary economic activity, on a scale equivalent to two-thirds of GNP, is the money borrowed by the state and other public agencies. That, in 1984, was some £2.8 billions, equivalent to 20% of GNP in that year. The possibility of receiving a portion of this largesse, distributed by the state at the cost of future taxpayers or unpaid creditors, creates in Ireland a powerful additional demand for state action. The great scale of state action in such matters as allocating savings for purposes that cause little if any growth in GNP, or in providing health, educational and transport services that buropoliticians rather than users think best, exacerbates the inefficiencies and iniquities that are the common heritage of capitalist colonialism. State action creates a need for more state action, but increasingly of a repressive character in the form of soldiers, police and prisons.[10]

The proposals made in the preceding chapter imply removing, or neutralising, the enduring consequences of capitalist colonialism. They imply offsetting by countervailing obligations those individual interests that were created by capitalist colonialism and everywhere outside a metropolitan context have caused undevelopment (Appendix C). To that extent, the proposals would rectify the bias that now exists in favour of extending state activity. They imply, not so much the 'withering away of the state', as the purposeful diminution of a state that is inefficient, iniquitable and corrupt; and that has been the means of perpetuating capitalist colonial undevelopment. The proposals imply the taking of power from the buropoliticians and the giving of money and power to the people.

The proposals, by reducing greatly the scope of state action, would substantially improve living conditions, especially for those who are now poorest. That improvement would be effected, not as an act of public munificence, but as explicit recognition of all citizens' right to an equal share, through the national dividend, in the social surplus. The indicated level of the national dividend would be higher than present old age pensions and unemployment benefits and would be paid as a right and not subject to a means test. People who are now unemployed would also benefit from the taxing of land and banks, which would channel land and savings towards those best able to use them; and these, for the most part, are the young, the landless, the capital-less and the jobless.

It is very conceivable that, notwithstanding these substantial improvements in equity — indeed, probably because of them — further amelioration of conditions for specific groups may seem desirable. A national dividend equivalent to £80 per week in 1984 prices remains short of affluence. The possibility of voluntary action to secure that amelioration should not be overlooked. Voluntary action to relieve the worst excesses of an inefficient, inequitable and corrupt regime, apart from indulging the donors in 'a cheap and selfish philantrophy',[11] merely seeks to perpetuate the malorder by concealing some of the more shocking and disagreeable symptoms. Voluntary action, in conjunction with good national dividends, probably can contribute usefully to alleviating residual problems. It is the more likely to be forthcoming and to be effective if people do not, as now, feel they are already being compelled, through PAYE, PRSI and VAT, to contribute excessively to the relief of less fortunate citizens. The same consideration should also make more readily available than now resources for the voluntary endowment of education, research and other activities of an essentially social character. That endowment should also be more effective in a restructured society.

If, having exhausted the possibilities of voluntary action, an extension of public sector activity beyond the role envisaged here seems desirable, then it would be clearly wrong to curtail that activity because of a doctrinaire concern to minimize public or state activity. Given the malign role of the state in all former capitalist colonies, it is true that 'the least government is the best government'. But government under a new socio-economic order would not be inherently malign. There would be no objection in principle, as there is now, to extending the role of the state. The combination of taxes, government services and national dividend proposed above is only one of a spectrum of such combinations that would be consistent with an efficient, equitable and incorrupt social order. It would be feasible to contract or to expand state expenditure below or above the £500 million level mentioned above. Every £220 millions increase or decrease in public expenditure would give rise to a corresponding £100 decrease or increase in the citizen's total annual national dividend. It would be for citizens to decide democratically what particular combination of public service and national dividend is preferred.

Once the capitalist colonial conquest has been undone the repressive role of the state, which is the enforcement in Ireland of the law and order imposed here by metropolitan England, will be obsolete. Once the principle of sovereignty is established, which is that today's sovereign people cannot be bound by the past and cannot, in turn, bind tomorrow's sovereign people, the cornucopia of government borrowing will be exhausted. A national dividend will provide an efficient and equitable way of distributing the social surplus. These are the considerations that point to the likelihood of a greatly reduced role for the state under the new order that would result from the implementation of the proposals made in the preceding chapter. There would appear to be no place in that new order for the corrupt, patron-client politics that govern Ireland now.

Politicians are now supported by clients, on whose behalf they incur public expenditure that is financed by borrowing or by taxation of uncertain incidence. The benefit to the clients is palpable; the cost to society and to individual members of society is indeterminate. The clients support the expenditure; society's members do not oppose it. The proposals made envisage public expenditure being financed from the social surplus, with increases or decreases in public expenditure resulting in corresponding decreases or increases in the individual citizen's national dividend. Aspiring politician-patrons would have to weigh the support to be gained from clients as a result of public expenditure incurred on their behalf against the opposition generated by the reduction in the national dividend caused by the expenditure. Political success would come to depend on offering the public the most acceptable combination of taxes, public expenditure and national dividend.

Regular opinion polls might be a feature of government to ascertain citizens' views on the balance between increasing or decreasing their share of the social surplus disbursed in cash, on the one hand; and of curtailing or expanding specific public expenditures on the other hand. Groups of citizens of a specified size — say 1,000 — might be empowered to petition for the inclusion of a specific item of expenditure in any such opinion poll.

Politicians could accept or reject the majority view as expressed by opinion polls. Citizens would in turn probably return to office, or reject, those politicians whom they thought would support the voters' preferred allocation of the social surplus between a national dividend and publicly provided goods and services.

The role of politicians, in these altered circumstances, would be much diminished. Politicians would cease to be the power brokers they now are. Diminishing the role and power of politicians would be the corollary of the enlargement of the individual citizen's control of, participation in, and benefit from, the conduct of public affairs. The patron-client relationship that now exists between politicians who expend the equivalent of over 60% of GNP annually and citizens whose share in that expenditure depends mainly on the whim of politicians, could not survive in a situation where public expenditure was financed from a social surplus that was explicitly recognized as the property equally of all citizens.

Deprived of the tremendous power that the political establishment commands under the present dispensation, where on average every Dail member can dispense nearly £20 millions annually from borrowed public funds, public office would become much less secure and valuable. The political dynasties would terminate (Chapter 6). The paradox of property would apply (Appendix C): only those most willing and able to reflect public opinion could, or would, secure or retain public office. The existing system selects out those who are least fit to hold public office, to invest the nation's savings and to operate its land. Under the proposed dispensation, the most competent would be selected to hold public office as well as to operate the nation's land and capital.

The choice would not always, or even in most cases, lie between public action at the national level and individual action; between state expenditure and cash distribution to the citizen. Joint action may be desirable at the regional, county, parish or community levels. The efficiency and the democratic control of local government could be greatly enhanced. Statutorily recognized local authorities could have the right to have allocated to them, as their sole source of revenue, various maximum proportions of the share of the social surplus accruing to citizens resident within their boundaries. The actual amounts so allocated and spent would be determined by elected local representatives. The citizen might then get periodic statements along the following lines:

Credit	Debit	
Citizen's share in the social surplus £...	Citizen's contributions to:	
	a) Central government	£...
	b) Regional government	£...
	c) County government	£...
	d) Parish government	£...

                                    e) Community government £...
                                    Total public expenditure   £...
                                    Balance, being national
                                            dividend   £...
Politics would become largely an argument as to whether social
expenditure should be increased or decreased under the above various
headings, with a corresponding decrease or increase in the national
dividend. That argument would, of course, extend to whether public
expenditure should be undertaken now, with a view to increasing the future
social surplus; or whether public expenditure should be curtailed now, at
the cost of reducing the future surplus. The reduction of the power and
patronage of politicians would ensure that these and similar arguments
would be resolved in ways that closely reflected citizens' wishes. The right
of individuals to attempt to influence what citizens wished need not be
diminished; but the financial resources and incentives to do so would be
very greatly reduced.

The Economic Implications

The economic affairs of Irish society as of society in all the former capitalist
colonies have been conducted in ways that serve the interests that were
established under colonialism (Appendix C). Those individualistic interests,
established for metropolitan benefit without reference to the well-being of
local society, are the principal part of the capitalist colonial heritage.
Catering for these interests has required, above all, an unceasing concern
for markets; or, in the Keynesian jargon, for 'demand management'. This
emphasis on markets for the products of the controlling interests has raised
the profits of land ownership, as is reflected in the eightfold increase in
the value of land relative to GNP since the state's foundation (Chapter 5).
It has enabled the banks to expand the money supply to the extent of making
the Irish banking system, relative to GNP, the most profitable in the world.
It has enabled those to whom the banks channelled the expanded money
supply, which reflected the nation's forced savings, to found political
dynasties, if they were politicians; or, if they were business people, to grow
into big commercial fish, too big for the small Irish pond. Finally, the
emphasis on securing markets has made it possible for the smallest
workforce that has existed in Ireland for 250 years to get incomes that,
on average, are among the third highest in the world.
    The assumption implicit in the conduct of affairs in this manner has been
that, even if Irish people did have to pay more for their meat and butter,
or for their shirts and shoes, the benefits accruing to the landowners,
bankers, business people and trade unionists would 'trickle down',
eventually to benefit all the people.

Part of the cost of the state's demand-oriented economic policies has been the continuous failure of Irish people to get a livelihood in Ireland. This was reflected, up to recent years, in the emigration of almost half those born in Ireland; and, more recently, in the rapid growth of unemployment. More of the cost of the state's economic policies has been wished on to future generations of taxpayers through a massive national debt. These costs of policy can no longer be met: emigration at a demographically significant scale is no longer possible; and, as Whitaker pointed out, 'the government's capacity to borrow abroad is almost exhausted'.[12] Radical change in economic policy or collapse is unavoidable.

The proposals in this book imply a rejection of the socio-economic order established in Ireland by the sixteenth century Tudor conquest and perpetuated by the Irish state since 1922. That order holds that the individual's income shall be determined by the marginal product of whatever resources are commanded by the individual regardless of the means by which they have been acquired or are used. The proposals imply the replacement of that order by one that holds that an individual's income shall be determined, in large part, by the size of the total social product and by the number of those who share that product; and in part only by the contribution the individual makes to the social product by work, saving or entrepreneurship. That socio-economic order would imply the reversion, in a fundamental sense, to the sort of society that existed in Ireland, as in other former capitalist colonies, before their colonization. It would, however, be a reversion that took account of the vast advances in technology and in human understanding that have been made during the past 500 years, to which advances the sufferings and degradations of the capitalist colonies contributed, in their way, as much as did the saving, investment, entrepreneurship, adaptiveness and thrust of the individualistic, capitalist societies contribute. Those advances make possible a manifold increase in the output of an Irish economy that is efficiently organized through correct factor pricing; and increasingly these advances will cause the size of the population of citizens over which the product is to be divided to be determined by rational, individual choice instead of by the interplay of blind biological and economic forces.

Rejection of the western, individualistic, capitalist concept of the individual's income being determined by the productivity of the resources commanded by the individual is essential for the economic development of former capitalist colonies. The application of that concept or principle in former capitalist colonies results in great waste of resources in these countries and in the impoverishment of the bulk of their populations, the marginal product of whose labour is close to zero. Even if the former capitalist colonies were able to produce at low cost with their low cost labour, because of inadequate domestic purchasing power most of what they produced would have to be exported to the metropolises. There alone the purchasing power is adequate, but there also mechanization and automation largely offset the low labour costs of the former capitalist colonies. Before these could compete successfully, labour costs would have to fall so low that workers would starve and society would disintegrate, as happened in Ireland in the 1840s (Chapter 4) and as is happening in countries like Bangladesh now. Determination of income largely by the size of the social product and the number of persons among whom it must be shared, on the other hand, makes it possible for the price of labour to fall towards its true, very low marginal value, while incomes would be determined by the equitable distribution of the large social surplus from an efficiently organized and operating economy. The individualistic, capitalist nexus between incomes and marginal product would be shattered and would be replaced by the determination of incomes in part by the social product and in part by individual effort.

High incomes would create a strong local demand, which has always been the basis for successful exporting. High incomes, within an equitable social order, would evoke skilled, reliable, responsible labour, which would nevertheless cost little. The structural reforms proposed would make possible highly paid, high quality, but low cost labour: the sort of labour, for example, that existed for millenia on the family farms of Central Western Europe and that transformed it into the modern world (Appendix A).

The combination of efficiently used land and capital with high-income, high-quality, low-cost labour would make possible a very great increase in output. Some of that increased output would reward any additional savings/investment, entrepreneurship and labour employed, while the balance would be available for increasing the national dividend. Some of the envisaged increase in output would probably come from agriculture where competent farmers, able to pay land taxes equivalent to competitive rent and in receipt of a national dividend, could easily double output. Some of the doubled agricultural output would be available for domestic consumption, which would increase as a result of higher domestic incomes; some of the additional agricultural output, produced at low cost, would replace food imports; and the balance of high quality products, produced at low cost by an efficient agriculture — such as free range eggs and chickens, disease-free breeding stock and immature cattle — would be available for export.

Indigenous Irish manufacturing industry, whether based on the processing of locally available primary products or based on supplying the home market, would expand, in part because of the larger quantity of better quality, low cost agricultural produce available for processing; and in part because of the expanded local demand from an efficiently and equitably organized economy. These industries would also expand because of the increase in the quality and reduction in the cost of labour, which they employ in relatively large amounts. These manufacturing industries, operating at low cost, with high quality labour and with a secure base of abundantly available local materials and/or a thriving domestic market, would be well positioned to replace much that is now imported and to expand exports.

A regime of high cost land and capital and of low-cost/high-quality labour would be most favourable for the expansion of service industries, which is the principal growth sector in all high-income, modern economies. Ireland's insular location and small size, which are a handicap in the production of goods, can be a boon in the production of services. There economies of scale are less important. Often, 'small is beautiful'; and being a step outside the hurly-burly and the violence of the mainstream can be advantageous.

The small size of the domestic market makes it difficult for Ireland to achieve economies of scale in manufacturing industry without relying heavily on exports. An insular location is a handicap to manufacturing Irish industry on two accounts. Firstly, it adds to the cost of raw materials, fuel, containers, etc, which account for over two-thirds of the gross value of manufacturing output and over half of which are imported in Ireland's case. An insular location penalizes manufacturing secondly when, as in Ireland's case, well over half the output must be exported. These handicaps do not apply to service industries because labour, which is locally available, accounts for almost all the inputs, and because most of the services are consumed within Ireland. An Ireland where, uniquely in the world, labour would have a high income and be of correspondingly high quality, yet cost little, would be extremely well placed to become a major producer of services.

Demand for Irish services would come, first, from domestic consumers, who would require more as their incomes increased. Given the changes proposed, Ireland would be exceptionally well placed to cater for a world-wide demand for services which is growing far more rapidly than the demand for manufactured or agricultural products. The services that Ireland could provide for non-nationals might include, for example,providing for retired persons. A small, insular, efficient, equitable society, where crime would be minimal and medical and personal services would be of high quality and inexpensive, would be highly attractive to retired Americans, British and continental European persons.

High domestic incomes and low labour costs should stimulate the Irish education industry. A thriving, efficient, low cost, Irish education system should be extremely attractive to a wide range of foreign students seeking education outside their own countries and especially an education in an English-speaking country. As the first former capitalist colony to escape the heritage of capitalist colonialism by transforming undevelopment into development, Ireland should also be especially attractive for people in all parts of the world who are interested in the problems of development and who have hitherto sought in vain for the means of changing undevelopment into development.

Effective demand for medical services should expand. A medical industry that satisfied that demand by being made much more responsive than now to market forces should be much more efficient and would cost much less than the present Irish medical service. The cost of medical services should also be greatly reduced by the fiscal changes suggested, including the elimination of PAYE, PRSI and VAT. The payment to people of a national dividend, which would allow them to buy the goods and services they wished to acquire rather than those that buropoliticians think they should have, combined with the elimination of PAYE, PRSI and VAT, would make Ireland a most attractive location for medical, nursing and recuperative services. The provision of medical and ancillary services would complement the country's other envisaged service roles, as a retirement sanctuary and as an educational centre.

An efficiently and equitably organized Ireland, where labour was of high quality, with high incomes, yet of low cost; where labour was not taxed; where medical and educational facilities were of high quality and low cost; an Ireland that was linked to the mainstream by good communications, yet insulated from the less congenial aspects of the mainstream by its offshore location: such an Ireland would be highly attractive for a number of other service industries, including especially research and development, computer software, offshore banking and tourism.

It is not a defect of the provision of services to non-nationals that it represents the ultimate realization of the mindless, autarkic cant about 'maximizing value added', which is only achieved when all agricultural and manufactured goods are sold retail on the domestic market. 'Maximizing value added' to agricultural and manufactured goods in a small economy is possible only when the goods are consumed by persons providing or using services, with a high proportion of those services being sold to non-nationals.

The increase in national output foreseen would result from an organically more efficient use of the country's land, capital and labour, secured through fiscal measures that caused users to pay the economic price, no more and no less, for those resources. An organically more efficient use of resources would require neither protection against imports nor subsidies to exports financed by public debt expansion. The efficient economy of a small island would inevitably continue to be closely integrated into the world economy, but less so than now and far more so on its own terms. Instead of an inefficient, unproductive agriculture, producing food at high cost to be added to EEC surplus stocks while an increasing proportion of the country's food is imported, an efficient, low cost agriculture would make unnecessary virtually all temperate zone food imports. Labour intensive indigenous industries would produce most of the manufactured products now imported, while also contributing to exports. Most foreign earnings would come from service industries, using Irish resources almost exclusively, and operating and controlled almost entirely within the country. That situation would contrast sharply with the present one. Now, conglomerates in Irish non-trading industries, with profits syphoned from their Irish activities, 'are investing abroad in businesses only minimally related to Irish employment and exports';[13] while most Irish manufactured exports are the products of fly-by-night, foreign-owned, enclave industries that import almost all of their inputs, export almost all of their outputs, repatriate all their profits, and move their operations into and out of Ireland according to international circumstances which Ireland is powerless to influence. Finally, an organically efficient Irish economy would not depend on foreign borrowing.

An organically efficient Irish economy will depend far less on buropoliticians for decisions as to what and how to produce. The envisaged drastic reduction in the state's budget will be the corollary of the transfer of purchasing power (and political power) to the people via a national dividend. This will shift demand, from the goods and services that buropoliticians think people should have, to the goods and services that people themselves think they should have. That alone will enormously enhance the value to people of what is produced.

Unemployment and Jobs

The individualistic, capitalist West is preoccupied with the problem of growing, structural unemployment. The widespread failure of large numbers of people in the West to secure remunerative employment is, as explained above, a new phenomenon (Chapter 6). Ireland is no less concerned about its exploding numbers of unemployed. Its growth is also a new phenomenon and related to the broader, western phenomenon of chronic structural unemployment. This is because chronic unemployment in the West now prevents the emigration of that half of the population which, since the beginning of English factory capitalism, has failed to get a livelihood in Ireland. But the Irish case, despite its connection with metropolitan unemployment, is a fundamentally different phenomenon. The difference stems from the difference between the character of metropolitan, capitalist society and the character of former capitalist colonies.

An era now appears to be ending in the metropolitan West. The capital-less, proletariat class, which has been the product of factory capitalism, can no longer earn a living by their labour. This appears to be due to the combination of (1) the ending of capitalist colonialism and of the export of metropolitan unemployment to the colonies; (2) an increasing inflow of products from non-western, non-colonized Japan, Korea, Taiwan, and also from Hong Kong and Singapore; and (3) labour-substituting automation. Western countries, where incomes are high and populations are stable or declining, have begun to adjust to this new situation, principally by income transfers from the holders of property and jobs to the propertyless and jobless. This involves a major extension of state welfare services. It is an adjustment that recognizes implicitly the impossibility, in the post-colonial era, even under conditions of a static or declining labour supply, of large sections of population securing a livelihood by their individual effort. It appears to be an adjustment by the developed, individualistic West towards a social order that accords to members of society a livelihood on grounds other than their contribution to GNP. It marks a repeal of the key, individualistic, millenia-old ordinance, 'thou shalt earn thine bread by the sweat of thine brow'.

It is futile to imagine that Ireland, which has failed to provide a livelihood for half its population throughout the era of factory capitalism — when the world's workforce increased fourfold and Ireland's declined by two-thirds — can now, when metropolitan employment is declining, provide employment for all its people. The limitations on preserving jobs in Ireland by curbing wages — 'incomes policy' — were brutally demonstrated in the 1840s when wages dropped below the subsistence level, workers starved, and the number at work collapsed (Chapter 4). The limitations on creating jobs in Ireland by public debt expansion have been reached after nearly 40 years of public borrowing. Other strategems, such as 'job-sharing' or the IDA's inducing foreign firms to locate enclave industries here at great cost to indigenous, integrated industries, are more likely to cause accelerated job decline than to provide new jobs (Chapter 6). One of the results of the job-creating efforts of the Whitakerian-Geraldine era is a system of taxation that raises the cost of labour to its users to over four times what the supplier receives (Chapter 7).

Not only is it futile for Ireland to attempt to create jobs for all its people; it is incongruous that it should contemplate doing so, especially now when the western world is adjusting to the need to distribute wealth on different principles. Ireland's preoccupation with job creation is indicative of an utter failure to grasp the nature of the social, economic and political problems confronting the country.[14] Under the socio-economic order that exists in all former capitalist colonies, there is no possibility of achieving anything like full employment. There is, under *that* socio-economic order, no possibility of providing a livelihood for all the people in Ireland, any more than in the other former capitalist colonies.

Under a different socio-economic order, where development had replaced undevelopment, employment creation would cease to be a policy objective. The over-reaching policy objective of the socio-economic order proposed would be the efficient use of land, capital and labour in order to secure the largest possible output of goods and services; and the distribution of that output in the most equitable manner possible. That would of necessity involve the reintegration into society of the landless, jobless masses that everywhere in the Third World are the enduring consequence of capitalist colonialism. That policy objective, which implies the ending of unemployment, is very different from creating jobs. Creating jobs is a policy that appeals to the idle rich, who believe the devil finds work for the idle hands of the poor; and to the incorrigibly unimaginative who can perceive no greater attainment in life than their own success in securing permanent, pensionable and usually utterly unproductive employment.

GNP, under the proposed changes, would be maximized by charging users the full economic cost, but no more than that, for land, capital and labour. The difference between the amount produced and the amount needed to secure the required supply of factors of production — which is the social surplus — would be distributed equally by means of a national dividend to all resident citizens. That arrangement would, in Ireland's case, effectively reintegrate into society the landless, jobless masses, who formerly emigrated and who now comprise the country's burgeoning unemployed.[15] That arrangement would end unemployment and would make emigration unnecessary.

The proposals that have been made here, which are specifically designed to end undevelopment and concurrent unemployment, would also cause an increase in employment. However, that would be quite incidental to, and would in no sense be an objective of, the measures proposed. More work, like more savings or higher prices (and their corollaries, less leisure and lower consumption) can be warranted only in so far as they make possible higher consumption now, or less work and/or higher future consumption. The measures proposed would, however, reduce greatly the supply price of labour, which is now in surplus.

Demand for labour would be increased at the same time as its supply price would be reduced. The various fiscal and redistributive measures proposed, by increasing the demand for goods and especially for services, would increase the demand also for labour. Taxing land and other government-created monopolies would force into retirement or semi-retirement many who are now unable to operate efficiently the land and capital they control, which would make these resources available for operation by more competent and, generally, younger people. Both bank and land taxes would have the effect of redistributing bank credit. Banks now optimize by lending to owners of property, the value of which is increasing because of the banks' inflationary increase in the money supply. Bank taxes would remove the banks' existing incentive to expand inflationarily the money supply, which now increases property values. Land taxes would simultaneously appropriate for society the value of landed property. Just as a land tax forces landholders either to use it effectively or to surrender it to those who can do so, a bank tax would force banks either into liquidation or to lend money to those able to pay the highest interest on it and therefore able to make the best use of it. These people would, again, for the most part be young, virile, able persons, possessing little or no capital or land and therefore best able to use both capital and land productively. This redistribution of the nation's savings would add very much to the demand for labour.

The simultaneous reduction in the cost of, and increase in demand for, labour will transform the status of the individual supplier of labour from that which has obtained in Ireland since the sixteenth century Tudor conquest. The individual, by the fact of being a member of society, will share in the substantial portion of the total product of that society that properly accrues to society: the social surplus. Thereafter he will be free to contribute to the total product, by 'deferred gratification' or working, increasing by individual effort both the portion of the product that properly accrues to him as a return for his labour and savings; and the portion that properly accrues, though increased land values, banking and other monopoly profits, to society. Unemployment will cease in the sense of citizens being no longer excluded from access to land, except on paying rent to land's appropriators; and in the sense of being no longer excluded from access to society's savings, which are now misdirected by the banks to politicians and to the 'job-grabbing' owners of appreciating property. Unemployment will cease also in the sense that there will be no unemployment benefits or assistance, paid conditional on the citizen doing no work. The citizen's national dividend will be paid unconditionally and will be uninfluenced by income from other sources, including employment.

It does not follow from the above that employment will increase. It probably will; though it may not. Citizens in receipt of a national dividend, when given the choice of increasing their incomes by working or saving more, may choose to work and/or save more. Alternatively, they may choose to work and/or save less. Giving people the option of increasing their incomes by working more implies terminating unemployment; for unemployment means denying people the opportunity to secure even a moderate income by working. The critically important policy objective is the abolition of unemployment so that people should have the option of increasing a basic income by working. How people exercise that option is irrelevant, at least from a national policy viewpoint. Providing employment, or job creation, is an irrational policy objective.

Decolonizing Northern Ireland

Chapter 6 sought to make clear the deep-seated, intractable division between the Protestant majority of British descent, and the Catholic Irish minority in Northern Ireland. The Catholic Irish minority are one of two outstanding groups of descendants of agriculturists whose land and sovereignty were appropriated in the process of capitalist colonization. The other group are the Bantu peoples of South Africa. All the other descendants of all the other food producers have by now regained their lands and their sovereignty. Clearly, the world-wide and centuries-old process of decolonization will not cease while the Catholic decendants of the Irish agriculturists of Northern Ireland occupy a position inferior to that of the Protestant descendants of the British settlers.

The Protestant majority in Northern Ireland for their part are, together with the Boers of South Africa, the only survivors of five similar groups of metropolitan settlers who colonized and farmed lands that had been previously held by agriculturists. The descendants of the others, in Algeria, Kenya and Rhodesia, fought long, desperate and bloody rearguard wars of resistance against the Third World decolonizing process. Clearly the Northern Ireland Protestants will resist decolonizing just as fiercely; and, given the relative sizes of the two peoples, they will resist more successfully than the settlers of Algeria, Kenya or Rhodesia.

There is no hope of reconciling the conflict of interests between Protestants and Catholics in Northern Ireland, given the existing social order. The changes that have been proposed would not attempt to reconcile a conflict that history and world-wide experience have shown to be irreconcilable. Instead, by changing the social order, by transforming undevelopment into development and by making it possible for all the Irish to get a livelihood in Ireland, the proposals, if implemented, would make the conflict between Catholic and Protestant irrelevant. That, like the conflict between brown and white in Algeria and the conflict between black and white in Kenya, Rhodesia and South Africa, is a struggle for livelihoods in which Protestant privilege in Ireland and white privilege in Africa has conferred substantial advantage on the settlers while putting the indigenes under serious disability. A social order that makes it possible for all Irish people to get a livelihood in Ireland would make both Protestant privilege and Catholic disability equally meaningless. Protestant and Catholic differences in Ireland would sink into the oblivion where the relics of a thousand other past conflicts are now forgotten.

Conclusion

This work has been concerned with the failure of half the Irish to secure a livelihood in Ireland during the past 160 years or so, since the emergence of factory capitalism in England. It has been argued here that that failure is part of the much larger phenomenon of undevelopment that affects half the world's population. Undevelopment is defined as a condition where more people are worse off than formerly; or fewer people are as well off as formerly. The latter is the Irish case, where fewer people get a livelihood now than at any time in the last 250 years.

Capitalist colonialism is an experience that is common and peculiar to all the countries, including Ireland, that are undeveloping now. Countries that have been capitalist colonized, undevelop; countries that have not been capitalist colonized, develop. Continuing undevelopment is perceived to be the enduring heritage of an historical experience that involved the superimposition, out of context, of the institutions and technology of the West's individualistic, capitalist culture on indigenous, non-individualistic, non-capitalist cultures. The undevelopment of every one of the 138 or so former capitalist colonies, which embrace literally a world of differences, persists, although some of them have been politically independent for 160 years.

There are special features of Irish undevelopment, which derive from the country being geographically and racially part of the West though historically part of the Third World. This membership of both worlds is reflected in Ireland having now the highest population growth rate in the West and having the highest income per head among the former capitalist colonies. Another feature of the Irish scene that is traceable to the dual membership of the Western and Third Worlds is the fact that, per person or relative to GNP, Ireland has the highest and most rapidly growing incidence of public indebtedness, domestic and foreign, in the world.

The combination of rapid population growth, high and rapidly growing public indebtedness, and high incomes is new. It was made possible, or was caused by, external circumstances beyond the country's control. The combination is unsustainable. It will end when foreign creditors withold the credit upon which the country is now so absolutely dependent. A crisis, comparable in intensity to that of the period 1820 to 1850, will rapidly develop when government can no longer contribute, from borrowed funds, the one-fifth or more of national income it has regularly done in recent years. That forthcoming crisis cannot be relieved by mass emigration, as in the nineteenth century. There is now no metropolitan army of occupation to contain it. The crisis will be the more intense in that the population is now immeasurably wealthier and more literate. The progress of the crisis will be expedited, though it will by no means be caused, by the presence in Ireland of a large number of Catholics who are already disaffected from the Northern Ireland state.

The absence of any precedent for transforming undevelopment into development among the former capitalist colonies makes it highly unlikely that Ireland can avert the coming crisis. There is, moreover, an aspect of the Irish scene that makes action capable of averting a crisis peculiarly unlikely: the emigration of the less contented half of six Irish generations has left a 'fat cat' society peculiarly unwilling and/or unable to act radically.

The highly deterministic character of all that has been written here is recognized. The environment within which people struggled determined the outcome of those struggles. That was the case in the evolution over millenia of individualistic capitalism in Central Western Europe. That is the case with the rapidly developing revolutionary situation in Ireland now. However, this is by no means to deny the tremendous contribution that groups of individuals have made on occasion towards shaping the environment within which they lived and struggled. No more than a handful of Greeks at Thermopylae, Marathon and again at Salamis, barred the way to the hordes from the east and gained for Europe a thousand years' respite, during which the Ancient Mediterranean civilization flourished and produced a literacy, thought and technology that contributed enormously, and possibly even critically, to the less precocious development of individualism in Central Western Europe (Appendix A). Again, much more recently, the West's ability to save itself from the barbarism threatened by Hitler depended upon the efforts of a few individuals; and, at a critical period in 1940, on a very few individuals indeed. Daily now, the preservation of the planet from nuclear holocaust depends on the decisions of a handful of persons. Recognition of the extent to which ecological, historical and social circumstances affect man's actions by no means involves 'robbing man of the right to make his own history.. [rather] ... it merely defines the conditions within which he is free to act.'[16]

Study of the past helps in understanding the forces that have influenced man's behaviour, shaped the consequences of his actions and, to that extent, affected the environment within which he existed. Study of that past makes clear that the sequence of events is not random, but orderly and subject to laws that are, however, enormously complex. Study of the past makes clear that what happens, happens as the consequence of earlier action; and that what happens now, influences what will happen in the future. Man cannot escape the consequences of the past; but neither can he avoid shaping the future. His success in shaping that future in accordance with his needs depends on his understanding of the forces involved. For, as with natural forces, social forces can be dominated only by observing and understanding them. The teguments of Irish society are about to be sundered. That is the inescapable consequence of the conduct of affairs by that half of the Irish people who remained in Ireland during the past 60 years. How events develop subsequently will depend on decisions taken during the course of the coming crisis, just as the crisis itself is the consequence of the decisions — of commission or omission — of the past decades. If precedent is to be the guide, then the experience of a hundred and more former capitalist colonies, where populations grow rapidly, where governments' credit is exhausted, and where the incomes of the masses decline, is unambiguous. Government of the state will fall into the hands of a military clique, purporting to save the nation's soul according to the values of right or left wing political extremism.

But man, though the product of social forces, has the capacity to understand those forces and therefore, at critical times in critical ways, to influence them. The remaining years of this century will be such a time in Ireland. One way in which its people could direct this former capitalist colony away from the chaos that embroils or threatens all the other former capitalist colonies has been delineated here.

Appendix A

Individualistic Capitalism: Its Nature and the Timing and Location of its Emergence

A Neolithic Revolution

Fossils of distinctively human type date back at least two million years. Not until 10,000 years ago did any member of the species reach Ireland.[1] Meanwhile the species had evolved through the aeons and around the same time that hunter-gatherers first arrived in Ireland the first civilization was being established in Mesopotamia. As the first people reached Ireland, the first farmers, from the 'Fertile Crescent' at the foot of the Taurus and Zagros mountains, were moving out on to the well-watered alluvium of modern Iraq to establish there the first cities and to invent the first alphabeth in order to count their wealth.

The progression from hunter-gatherer to food producer had been almost infinitely slow. But somewhere, sometime — most likely in the Fertile Crescent around 12,000 years ago — the critical steps were taken. Some individual gatherer of the wild wheat or barley that was collected every year, but was reproduced from seed that escaped the gatherer's clutch, took the epoch-making step of consigning some of the harvested seed back to the earth in the hope that it would yield manifold a year later. Hunters in the same Middle Eastern location corraled wild sheep and goats, to be drawn on and slaughtered as required. Occasionally the wild, corraled animals bred and probably reproduced before they were slaughtered. Some day, some hunter took another epoch-making step by choosing not to slaughter a young ewe or a young goat, but to breed it instead in the hope of getting a lamb or a kid from it later. By planting harvested seed and by breeding a mature female instead of consuming them, probably the most important people in history established that by foregoing a little consumption now and by using the savings productively, future wealth and future consumption could be greatly increased. In that case, the increase was the difference between the food that could be gathered and hunted and the food that could be produced.

The epoch-making steps, of first planting grain that had already been harvested and of breeding rather than slaughtering and consuming a mature female animal, were taken after aeons of evolution, at a specially felicitous time in a specially favoured location. The last Ice Age had passed; average temperatures had risen; and with a much extended area of ocean, rainfall had also increased. More heat and rainfall meant better growth and more abundant food, while the higher temperatures also reduced the need for food to maintain body temperatures.

The Fertile Crescent of the Middle East, as well as enjoying a salubrious climate that was neither too hot, as in the fetid tropics, nor too cold as further north, also had a wide range of natural conditions that included level valley land, sloping foothills and mountain streams and rivers. These varied and generally favourable ecological conditions attracted a range of potentially useful plants and animals that was wider than existed anywhere else. The plants that were indigenous to the region included wild barley and wheat; the indigenous fauna included wild cattle, sheep, goats and pigs.[2]

It is important to emphasize the favourable circumstances under which man made the most momentous step in human achievement, from hunter-gatherer to food producer. The circumstances illustrate the importance of favourable conditions for further progress; they serve to refute the dangerously misleading view that 'pressure of population' — that is, the existence of numbers of hungry people — is the main stimulus to achievement.[3] As the Irish experience, especially in the first half of the nineteenth century — and an almost infinite number of similar experiences — demonstrate: misery, hunger and degradation beget nothing but more misery, hunger and degradation, and finally extinction.

Food production, embracing both livestock and crop husbandry, moved from the foothills of the Taurus and Zagros mountains on to the plain of Iraq, through which flowed the twin rivers, Euphrates and Tigris. There, with oxen and water-buffaloes to pull the implements with which they cultivated the deep, fertile alluvium that was watered by the two rivers and warmed by a sun that was almost overhead in the summer, the Sumerians were the first to escape the tyranny of life: the compulsion on all to secure the nourishment necessary to sustain life. Riverine cultivators, on warm, watered, alluvial soils, with simple techniques of cultivation, could produce enough to maintain and reproduce themselves and to yield a surplus that was sufficient to maintain and reproduce as many, or more, others. That surplus was used to build the first cities, the first civilization, on the plain between the two rivers, in Mesopotamia some 8 — 10,000 years ago. That, as noted, was around the same time as the first hunter-gatherers reached Ireland, which in evolutionary terms had only recently been freed from the ice that, in the last Ice Age, covered the island north of a line from Wexford to Dingle, and wiped out all vegetable and animal life underneath.

The ideas and sometimes the seeds and artefacts of Sumeria spread to other riverine locations. First to Egypt, then to the Indus valley. Rice cultivation commenced in Thailand perhaps 6,000 years ago.[4] The earliest cultivators in China were those of the Yellow River Valley some 5,000 years ago.

The ending of the Ice Age and the melting of the polar ice-caps ameliorated the climate which in turn triggered off the neolithic revolution, i.e. the switch from hunting and gathering to food production; the planting of harvested seed and the breeding instead of slaughtering of captured, mature female animals. It also raised the world's water level by some 200 feet, and in the process drowned the land bridges that had joined Asia to America and Australia. Without these land bridges, it was impossible to carry a chief part of the neolithic revolution from the Old to the New World. The domesticated cattle, sheep, goats, pigs and horses of the Old World did not reach America until 500 years ago and did not reach Australia until the eighteenth century.

Neither did any of the seeds of the cultivars used in the Old World reach America in pre-Columbian times. This raises the issue of whether pre-Columbian crop-growing in America, mainly confined in the absence of domesticated livestock to a narrow strip of land in the high Andes/Rockies mountains, between the tropics of Cancer and Capricorn, was a spontaneous, local phenomenon. Against the hypothesis that the commencement of crop-growing in America, some 4 — 5,000 years ago, was due to the influence of the neolithic revolution of the Old World is raised the objection: if the idea, why not the seed? A possible explanation for the absence of the seed is that pre-Columbian migrants from the Old to the New World, either blown accidently across the ocean or following in boats along the traditional northern route that had become the Bering Straits, would have exhausted all their food supplies, including seed, long before they reached a territory where the seed would not merely germinate, but would also reproduce. That is to say, the idea of crop-growing was probably a more durable traveller than the seeds. Or, 'man is a biosocial species, and with the dispersion of human groups, not only genes move about but also basic know-how and ideas critical to the emergence of new cultural phases'.[5] Once the idea of crop-growing reached a favourable environment, it was possible there to discover suitable local cultivars like maize, potatoes, squashes, tobacco, etc. This topic is comprehensively treated by Bender.[6]

Pastoralism and Lactose Tolerance

The three great civilizations of Sumeria, Egypt and the Indus valley developed in river valleys that were surrounded by desert. The less extensive but no less ancient civilization of the Jordan valley was bounded too, on the east, by desert. But it was not possible to confine the neolithic revolution to the river valleys; the desert also was influenced. It is unclear, and immaterial for present purposes,how the revolution spread: whether it was elements of the riverine population who migrated to the desert, taking with them as much of the new food production technology as could survive in the desert; or whether it was hunting-gatherering desert denizens who learned by observing the cultivators and borrowed from them as much of their technology as could work outside the river valleys. An example of the latter process was observed in recent centuries. The hunting-gathering Khoikhoi of the savannah of Southern Africa acquired cattle from the Bantu cultivators, who were still percolating southwards through the African bush. With these and with sheep which they had acquired earlier from a different source, the predominantly hunting-gathering Khoikhoi were able to resist further encroachment by the Bantu cultivators from the north. They continued to do so until taken in the rear by other cultivators landing from the sea in the seventeenth century.[7]

Livestock husbandry, that part of the neolithic revolution which could survive outside the river valleys and oases of the Middle East, spread into neighbouring lands. It spread northwards beyond the Caucasus, where it was too cold for crop-growing. It spread out into the desert that lay eastwards and leewards of the Lebanese mountains where, except on the banks of the Euphrates and Tigris rivers and in oases, it was too dry to grow crops. The neolithic revolution spread southwest of the Nile Valley into the Sahel, which stretches across Africa from the Nile to the Atlantic and which again was too dry to support crop-growing.

The northern Eurasian pastoralists (who included both the Indo-European groups and the Mongols), the Bedouin pastoralists of the Middle East and the Nilo-Hamites of the Sahel all effected an important genetic change that greatly adapted them to their non-crop-growing environments. All three groups of pastoralists acquired the genetic mutation of lactose tolerance.

It is characteristic of the order Mammalia that while mother's milk is essential in infancy, later, due to enzymatic change in the digestive system, milk becomes less digestible, causes nausea and, in some cases, induces vomiting and diarrhoea. This clinical condition, which appears to be common to all members of the order Mammalia, is referred to as lactose malabsorption.[8] It is presumably a device of nature to expedite weaning and to ensure that mothers, having fulfilled the essential role of feeding their offspring in infancy, are then set free to re-engage in their primary function of reproduction.

Mutations occur which are lactose tolerant, perhaps in one per cent of populations that are normally lactose malabsorbent. These mutants have the capacity to drink milk and to gain nourishment from it beyond infancy. That capacity, in a situation where people have domesticated ruminants but could not grow crops, conferred major advantages.

The use of domesticated ruminants solely for meat provides little more nutrition for the husbandmen than the same grazing area might yield to hunters. This is illustrated, for example, by observation of the nutrition obtained from hunting reindeer in Greenland.[9] The persistence of hunting rather than husbandry among the Lapps of northern Europe also suggests that the latter form of exploitation has no overwhelming advantages for a predominantly lactose malabsorbent people, as the Lapps are. Likewise in Southern Africa, the survival in the same area of both the Khoikhoi and the Sen, the latter of whom are purely hunter-gatherers but both of whom are lactose malabsorbent, supports the point that the use of domesticated ruminants for meat yields little if any more nutrition than hunting from a given grazing area.[10]

The acquisition of lactose tolerance and the ability to drink the milk of domesticated ruminants transforms this situation. The advantage of lactose tolerance under these conditions may be illustrated as follows. Very roughly: the same pastoral resources will, in a year, produce 400 gallons of milk (the yield from a mediocre cow) or 250 lbs liveweight gain from a bullock.

The milk, which weighs roughly 10 lbs per gallon and has about 12% dry matter content gives 400 x 10 x 0.12 = 480 lbs of digestible dry matter. The bullock liveweight gain will convert into carcass at around 55 lbs carcass per 100 lbs liveweight. The carcass has about 70% meat and fat (the balance being inedible bone), of which the dry matter content is about 50%. The bullock liveweight gain gives therefore 250 x 0.55 x 0.70 x 0.5 = 48 lbs (approx) of digestible dry matter.

Thus the acquisition, through natural selection under these crop-less circumstances, of the ability to consume milk from other species beyond infancy and, indeed, as in the case of the Tutsi in Rwanda, to live on an almost exclusively milk diet,[11] made it possible for more people, and therefore more efficient and powerful people, to live on given pastoral resources.

The acquisition of lactose tolerance by cropgrowers, by contrast, would have been an evolutionary handicap rather than advantage. It would have resulted in the cropgrowers' limited pastoral resources being diverted to milk production rather than to draught services, with consequent reduction in total food output. Something similar to this is occurring in Southeast Asia now, where bovines are being diverted from traditional draught services to supplying beef to the expanding, relatively wealthy urban population.[12] Indians acquired lactose tolerance as a result of sexual intercourse over the millenia with invading pastoralists from northern Eurasia. The potentially dire consequences of India's being transformed into a beef and milk producing rangeland were, however, avoided by apotheosising the cow and tabooing beef consumption.[13]

Pastoralist Incursions

The acquisition of lactose tolerance, which made it possible for more pastoralists, and therefore more efficient pastoralists, to subsist on given pastoral resources, shifted the balance of power away from the riverine cropgrowers towards the pastoralists. Perhaps the most important theme of all subsequent history has been the efforts of the pastoralists to move in from the desert of the Middle East and the semi-desert of the Sahel, and from the cold, northern steppes, to secure a place — or perhaps to recover a place given up by their migrating forebears — in the better watered, warmer, crop-growing regions. The Nilo Hamites of the African Sahel have been least successful in moving to better land. The bedouins of the Middle East have had limited success. But the migrating northern, Eurasian pastoralists have been the dominant force in world history during the past five millenia.

The Africans. The Nilo-Hamite pastoralists of the Sahel were limited on the west by the Atlantic ocean. Expansion northwards was blocked by the desertification of the parklands that were once the Sahara Desert.* The narrow route down the Nile was easily blocked to the pastoralists by forts, the maintenance and manning of which were a primary defence charge on the crop-growing Egyptians.[14]

Expansion eastwards was blocked by the Ethiopian massif, wherein dwelt a people who have ever been more Asian than African. The Ethiopians embraced Asia Minor monotheism, in the form of Christianity, centuries before any other part of subSaharan Africa accepted Islamic monotheism. The Ethiopians can grow only cereals on their plateau and not the tubers and bananas of lower land, frost-free Africa. To grow these cereals, the Ethiopians have perforce had to use their cattle for draught, which no other subSaharan African people have done. Understandably, because they use their cattle for draught, the Ethiopians have not milked them and so are

---

*Some, at least, of the moisture from the pre-desert parkland streams has been retained as groundwater, which Colonel Gadaffi speaks about raising to make the Libyan desert bloom.

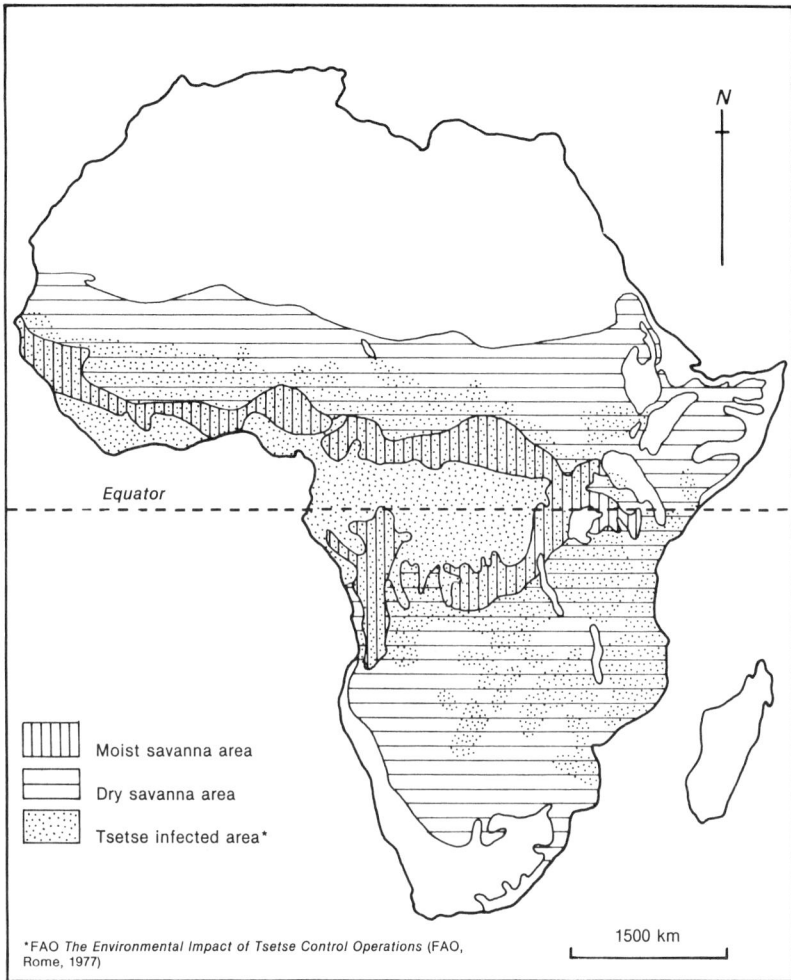

⬛ (vertical lines)	Moist savanna area
⬛ (horizontal lines)	Dry savanna area
⬛ (dotted)	Tsetse infected area*

*FAO *The Environmental Impact of Tsetse Control Operations* (FAO, Rome, 1977)

1500 km

almost entirely lactose malabsorbent*.[15] Neither have they used their cattle as bridewealth to acquire wives, as is the norm everywhere else in subSaharan Africa. Instead women in Ethiopia, as generally in Eurasia, have paid dowries on becoming married.[16]

*The dumping of the EEC's embarrassing surplus of skimmed milk powder as 'food aid' to relieve famine in Ethiopia probably hastened the end for many starving Ethiopians, who were too hungry to reject food that they would not normally touch; and who were too weak to survive the digestive disorders caused by milk and its products in the systems of lactose malabsorbent people.

159

The spread of Nilo-Hamitic influences was almost as constrained southwards as it was to the west, north and east. The African rainforest and the lighter bush and scrub of the east African plateau, south of the Sahel, stretched from the Atlantic to the Pacific. All of this was infested with the trypanosomiasis-bearing tsetse fly (see map). Because cattle, like the other domesticated ruminants, are not indigenous to Africa but were introduced there from Eurasia, perhaps 4 or 5,000 years ago,[17] they do not share the natural immunity of the indigenous species and quickly die from trypanosomiasis. The spread of pastoral influences in Africa, south of the Sahel, therefore was not achieved by the pastoral, lactose tolerant Nilo-Hamites. Instead that influence was spread southwards by the very different Bantu races, who are primarily cropgrowers and have only acquired a limited degree of lactose tolerance within comparatively recent times.[18]

The Bantus, originating in the present day Cameroons, found themselves some 2,000 years ago possessed of three important assets. They had by then acquired the art of iron making from the Middle East; high yielding yams and bananas from Southeast Asia; and cattle from the Nilo-Hamites of the Sahel. Drawing on this combination of resources, they penetrated, in the remarkably short time of some 1,500 years, the whole of subSahelian Africa as far as the savannah lands south of the Limpopo river and west of the Drakensberg mountains.[19] With iron they cleared the forest and on the cleared land they grew yams and bananas. The clearing of forest for crop-growing also removed the trypanosomiasis-bearing tsetse fly. Cattle were then able to follow the crops and in this way percolated through the east African tsetse fly belt. The Bantus, who did not use their cattle for draught and who had acquired only a limited degree of lactose tolerance so that they could not get the fullest nutritional value from their cattle, were unable to wrest the south-western savannah of Africa from the indigenous, predominantly hunting-gathering Khoikhoi. That was done, as noted above, by a pastoral people arriving by sea who, being fully lactose tolerant and using their cattle for draught, were better adapted to the South African savannah than the indigenous hunter-gatherers or the Bantus encroaching from the north.

The innumerable taboos and restrictions pertaining to the milking of cows and the consumption of cow's milk among the Bantu races seem to be a further consequence of their relatively recent introduction to this food (which was also virtually unknown in Ireland up to about 2,500 years ago; Chapter 2). Thus among the Gogo, and typical of a host of similar constraints on the use of milk by Bantus that have been noted by ethnographers: 'Milk is drunk fresh, but mostly by children...cattle are milked by married women who are the heads of the houses to which they are allocated.'[20] Or: 'Cows' milk is drunk fresh or eaten with millet porridge [by the Nuer]...the whey is drunk by women and boys. The milk of sheep and goats is used only by children.'[21]

The limited lactose tolerance of the Bantu Nguni and Tswana of South Africa is attested, apart from the clinical evidence, by their omission to milk their goats, even though these are their most numerous stock and are regularly milked by all true pastoralists (see Table A.1). The South African Bantu peoples also prefer sour milk to fresh milk, because the acid in the former makes it more digestible for lactose malabsorbent people. There is also etymological evidence for the comparative novelty of cows' milk among the Bantu races. 'It is a fact of the greatest historical interest that proto-Bantu, before its dispersal from the cradleland, was already quite clearly a language of food producers. Among domestic animals it included words for dog, goat, pig, chicken and probably also a word for cow, although there were no special words for cows' milk or for the art of milking.'[22]

The bedouins. The predominantly sheep-and goat-herding pastoralists of the Middle East were more diffused and thinly spread on the sparse pastures of the region than were the predominantly cattle-keeping pastoralists to the north and south (see Table A.1). With their sheep, they were less mobile than the cattle-keepers, and so could less easily mass to influence the course of history. Normally they offered little threat to the cropgrowers on the oases and on the rivers of the region.* It took the fanaticism induced in a primitive, unlettered people by a monotheism that derived from the sophisticated Judaic and Christian monotheisms of Asia Minor to weld these scattered, impotent, poor and unsophisticated shepherds and goatherds into an effective force. Even then their effectiveness was dependent on the void left by the collapse of Rome and the Ancient Mediterranean society. In that moment of history, when the word of Allah was revealed to the primitive bedouin of the Middle East and when the Mediterranean world was in turmoil, Islam swept to dominance. Though control did not long remain with the bedouin, Islam, which originated among the pastoralists of the arid lands of the Middle East, has remained a dominant world force. Its adherents control much of the tropics and semi-tropics from Morocco in the west to the Philippines in the east.

*Though Judaic monotheism appears to have been part of the defensive mechanism of the lactose malabsorbent Israelites who sought to preserve their identity by isolating themselves on the windward, rainfed western side of the Lebanese mountains from the bedouin pastoralists of the surrounding Middle Eastern desert. Being lactose malabsorbent it is unlikely that the tribes of Abraham were ever the shepherds that tradition would have it. Like the peoples of Mesopotamia and Egypt they probably descended directly from hunter-gatherers.

The Northern Pastoralists

The northern pastoralists have been the most successful in moving in from the wilds. This was in no small measure because of their success in domesticating the horse, which was indigenous to the Eurasian steppes and which greatly increased the mobility of the Golden Hordes.* These northern pastoralists have been the dominant influence in world history ever since, 5,000 or so years ago, the Hittites swept in from the steppes. Four distinct flows of northern pastoralists from off the Eurasian steppes are noted: in east, in central and in southwest Asia; and into Europe.

East Asia. Pastoral influence was largely negative in character in East Asia, where they provoked an instinctive resistance by the riverine crop-growing peoples of the region. The Great Wall of China, possibly man's single greatest structure, part of it built 3,000 years ago and stretching 4,000 miles from its origin on the Yellow River into the heart of Asia, is a palpable, enduring monument to the resistance of the civilized cropgrowers to the barbaric pastoralists.[23] Time after time in the long course of Chinese history, at periods of exceptional leadership among the barbarians, or when dynasties were in decline in China, and especially when both of these coincided, the pastoralists broke through, plundered and devastated the ricefields of China. But once the accumulated wealth of the cropgrowers was dissipated and their complex hydraulic systems were broken down, all that remained was famine, for the invading pastoralists no less than for the indigenous cropgrowers. The pastoralists perforce withdrew back to the more extensive northern grazing lands; and the people of China set about repairing the dykes, filling the breaches in the Great Wall, tilling their ricefields, accumulating wealth, and waiting for the next onslaught.

The most complete and enduring of these pastoral invasions and conquests of China was by the Mongols in the thirteenth century. China then was incorporated into a much more extensive Mongolian pastoralists' empire that, at its zenith in the fourteenth century, was the most extensive that the world has ever seen, stretching from modern Vietnam on the South China Sea, in a great arc westwards, to modern Yugoslavia on the Adriatic

The Times Atlas of World History has surely got it wrong in stating that the domestication of the horse made pastoralism possible in the Eurasian steppes (p. 60). Only in America, where there is no indigenous pastoral tradition, are horses relied upon principally for herding stock. In the Old World, where pastoralism has been practiced for millenia, stock for the most part are either led by the pastoralists, or are controlled by collie dogs that have been guarding and working domesticated ruminants from the beginning. Rather then: successful adaptation by the northern pastoralists, including especially their acquisition of lactose tolerance, enabled them to domesticate the wild horses that were indigenous to the northern steppes; and by doing so, enabled them further to develop their capability.

Sea. Not until the end of the fourteenth century did China manage to drive out the barbarians and establish the Ming dynasty.

Even then, at the height of their influence in East Asia, the pastoralists never subdued Japan. Two invasions were attempted, in 1274 and 1281, but both were repulsed. The second was destroyed in part by an unexpected storm — a heaven-sent storm, or 'Kami-Kaze' in the Japanese view. Japan in this respect, had the best of both worlds. It had, like the other societies of the Old World, the benefit of domesticated ruminants for its crop-growing; and like the New World, but unlike any other extensive area of the Old World, it was spared invasion and conquest by marauding pastoralists. That immunity from pastoral invasion would seem to account in large measure for modern Japan's remarkable sense of national identity and exclusiveness.

Chinese crop-growing and Eurasian pastoralism were elements so alien to one another that synthesis was impossible. Time after time, China rejected the foreign pastoral influence. Even when, as happened also in the case of South Africa (see above), that influence came by a devious sea route, China resisted invasion and indoctrination from the outside. Though invaded, it was never conquered and colonized by the West. Chinese governments, however ineffectually, continued to govern at all times. More recently, China mobilized its resources under the foreign flag of Marxist-Leninism, and under the leadership of Mao Tse Tsung cast off western influences. But more recently still, in a manner entirely consistent with the millenia-old resistance of the riverine cropgrowers to the barbarous pastoralists from the north, the Chinese appear to have discarded the intellectual imperialism of Marxist-Leninism together with the tutelage of its Russian proponents who are the ancient, northern barbarians in modern guise (see, for example, the Peking *Peoples' Daily,* as reported in the *Irish Times,* 10/12/84).

An Indian synthesis. No mass break-through to the south was possible by the pastoralists in Central Asia. Penetration instead occurred by the pastoralists percolating through the passes in the great central Asian mountain massif. The pastoralists came mainly through the Hindu Kush and roundabout through Afghanistan.

With cultivation more diffuse — 49% of India's surface is cropped compared to 11% of China's[24] — and crop yields lower — Indian yields are less than half those of China[25] — centralized political power has always been weaker in India. Maharajahs have contested with maharajahs, rajahs with rajahs. India has rarely been ruled by the all-powerful, all-centralising rulers of the more typical riverine societies of China or Egypt. In the absence of powerful central rule, India has rarely been able to mount an effective defence against invasion, especially by the pastoralists. There was no centralized Indian state to maintain a string of forts, as Egypt did on the Upper Nile; nor a great defensive wall, as the Chinese emperors did. India instead has forever played the role its cartographical outline suggests: a net into which the flotsam and jetsam of Eurasia flowed, was held and merged, to create a unique Indian culture.

The alien pastoral influences from the northern steppes within that net, acted on, and reacted with, the indigenous crop-growing culture in a manner that was altogether different from the transient, traumatic interactions of pastoralism and crop-growing in China. Out of the interaction of the alien pastoral and the indigenous crop-growing cultures two distinctively Indian societal adaptations evolved. These adaptations continue to be dominant influences in Indian society in the atomic age, when India has acquired the capacity to make atomic bombs and when its prime minister is a former pilot of jet airliners. The first of these most durable and powerful adaptations was caste which, though originally colour-based, was more durable than a colour-bar inasmuch as the progeny of a couple from different castes do not acquire the caste of the upper caste partner. The institution of caste thus enabled the minority of paler-skinned pastoral invaders, who comprised the upper caste, to have a range of economic, social and sexual relationships with the indigenous, wealth-producing cropgrowers without becoming absorbed into, and losing their privileged status to, the mass of indigenes.[26]

The second major societal adaptation was the apotheosis of the cow. The exercise of the conqueror's power of access to the women of the invaded territory meant the implantation and spread of the genetic characteristic of lactose tolerance in crop-growing India. The incidence of lactose tolerance, which the invaders brought with them from the Eurasian steppes, now spreads from a peak of almost 100% tolerance in North-West India to virtually 100% lactose malabsorbtion in East Bengal and in Kerala in South India.[27]

Lactose tolerant, milk-consuming stockowners breed their stock as frequently as possible in order to induce lactation and milk production. Lactose malabsorbent people, on the other hand, breed their stock, which they use as draught animals, only in order to secure replacements, in the same way as in the pre-tractor West farmers bred their working mares about once in ten years on average to secure replacement horses.[28] If female bovines are bred regularly to induce lactation, as Indian cows and female buffaloes are, they are unavailable for draught purposes, as Indian female bovines — unlike those of East Asia — are.

Moreover, all the cows of lactose tolerant, milk-consuming pastoralists who graze their animals communally are of the *Bos indicus* type. Cows of this type lactate only in the presence of their live calves. The failure of *Bos indicus* cows to let down their milk, except when they are stimulated by the presence of their live calves, is presumably a consequence of natural selection. Lactose tolerant pastoralists existing at a subsistence level would have been irresistibly tempted to draw all the milk they could from their stock. Strains of animals that let down their milk freely would have become extinct under these circumstances and only those strains that witheld their milk for their offspring would have survived. Throughout Asia and Africa, lactose tolerant people therefore not merely breed their animals as frequently as possible; but, willy-nilly, they divert much of the milk to keeping the progeny alive as long as the dams lactate, as part of the price of inducing them to do so. The progeny of the invading, lactose tolerant pastoralists and of the indigenous, lactose malabsorbent Indian cropgrowers, therefore, got from their cows not only milk which, for the most part being lactose tolerant, they relished, but calves which perforce were reared through the normal six to nine months of their dams' lactation. It would not have been surprising if, under the circumstances, India's pastoral resources were, like those of northern Eurasia, diverted into milk and beef production for a small pastoral population. Something of this sort occurred in Africa, where cattle are used exclusively for milk and meat and where, on almost eight times as much land, only a little more than half as many people are supported, at a generally lower level of nutrition, as on the sub-continent of India, Pakistan and Bangladesh.

The apotheosis of the cow, which appears to have occurred no more than 2,000 years ago,[29] prevented India from being transformed into a sparsely populated cattle walk, its people leading a crude and barbarous existence. Presumably whatever sect first tabooed beef-eating found itself with an abundant supply of young male cattle, which had to be reared to induce their *Bos indicus* dams to lactate and which provided draught power to cultivate India's relatively extensive croplands; and with the resultant crops, they were able to support a more numerous, and therefore on average also a more efficient, population. More populous and efficient, non-beef-eating, cropgrowing sects would in time have forced out people who continued to use India's limited pastoral resources for milk and beef production and, as a result, failed to grow sufficient crops. The overwhelming advantage in food output, secured among a lactose tolerant people with *Bos indicus* cattle, of apotheosising cattle would seem to account for the continued centrality of cow-worship today in India where, side by side with atomic power, satellite broadcasting and a jet-flying prime minister, cow slaughter is prohibited by laws which it is now proposed to reinforce and entrench by constitutional amendment*.

*The diversion of Indian resources for the production of livestock products for the few instead of food grains for the many, which was averted in the past by the apotheosis of the cow and the tabooing of beef consumption, is now occurring in large measure as a result of the dumping of EEC dairy surpluses as food aid in India (see Appendix C).

Middle Eastern destruction. Further west, the horse-mounted, Indo-European pastoralists flowed with little hindrance through the gaps between the Southwest Asian chain of inland seas: the Azov, the Caspian and the Black seas. They were attracted mainly by the wealth of crop-growing Mesopotamia. Mesopotamia, though the cradle of civilization, was peculiarly vulnerable to the power realized by the acquisition of lactose tolerance by the pastoralists of the Eurasian steppes. The vital water supply of the Mesopotamian plain was more precarious than that of any other major riverine culture. It depended, in the first instance, on moisture from the Atlantic carried over the whole length of the Mediterranean before the prevailing west winds deposited it as rain and snow on the Taurus mountains of Anatolia. Even the timing and the amount of water-flow into Mesopotamia depended on the Spring thaw in the mountains. If that were late or incomplete the rivers too flowed late or inadequately.

The twin rivers, Euphrates and Tigris, flowing slowly through the broad Iraq plain, deposited their silt on the way. Many cities grew along the banks of the rivers and in the area between them. Centralized government came slowly and was incomplete, by contrast with nearby Egypt, where the more regularly flowing Nile deposited its greater wealth in a narrower, more fertile strip.[30] The larger Egyptian surplus provided the means to support a more powerful state which, because of its narrower bounds, could in any case be more easily ruled and defended. Government in the Middle East was therefore even less able than in India to defend the crop-growing territory against successive pastoral invasions; and these, in order to reach their Mesopotamian quarry, had not to surmount or circumvent any natural barrier at all comparable to the Himalayan mountains.[31]

Moreover, Mesopotamia, as well as being less protected against invading pastoralists, was more vulnerable to the havoc they created. The rivers, as they meandered through the plain depositing silt, in many places caused the river bed, confined by flood banks, to rise above the surrounding land. Mesopotamian civilization was, therefore, peculiarly dependent on the maintenance of these banks. Once they were breached by the invaders, or through neglect by harrassed and war-torn cropgrowers, the basis of the world's oldest civilization was destroyed. Unsurprisingly therefore, following invasion by the Indo-European pastoralists, many of the oldest cities in the world sank back into the Mesopotamian alluvium from which they had arisen, acquiring in time a covering of herbage on which the bedouin sheep, goats and camels grazed. Many of these most ancient cities have been rescued from oblivion by recent archaeological excavations, and many continue to be so rescued.[32] The entire region, which was once the most densely populated part of the world, retrogressed for millenia. It contained, 2,000 years ago, when already the most severe damage had been done by the invading pastoralists, 12% of the world's population. By 1,800 AD its share of the world's population had declined to 1.5%.[33]

The indigenous Semitic peoples of the Middle East, both the lactose malabsorbent cropgrowers of Mesopotamia, Israel and the oases and the lactose tolerant bedouin shepherds and goatherds of the deserts, have continued to occupy the lower, more arid lands that were too hot and too dry for permanent occupation by the cattle-owning, Indo-European pastoralists from the steppes. These latter, over the long term, have remained in the cooler, better watered uplands of Anatolia and Iran, though from time to time extending their imperial sway over the Semitic lowlanders. The age-old struggle persists with the Indo-European, lactose tolerant, pastoralist Persians now (1986) at war with the Semitic, lactose malabsorbent, cropgrowing Iraqis, and having the avowed aim also of wiping out the Jews of Israel, the other major lactose malabsorbent cropgrowers of the Middle East. The unceasing conflict between lactose tolerant Indo-European pastoralists and predominantly lactose malabsorbent Semitic cropgrowers has caused the Middle East to retrogress for millenia. The region is now widely recognized as one of the most dangerous flashpoints for an atomic conflagration.

The Pastoralists and the Mediterranean

The modern world is one created and wholly dominated by the Indo-European pastoralists who, leaving the Asian steppes, moved into Europe. These pastoralists laid the foundations for their future success on the steppes. First, they had acquired there lactose tolerance, which enabled more of them to survive on given pastoral resources. Second, they had domesticated the horse, which was to play a dominant military and economic role until superceded by the internal combustion engine in recent decades. Third, they had learned about, and had become expert in, metallurgy.

Demand for metals first emerged in the cities of Mesopotamia and Egypt. Ironically, the deep alluvium on which these cities and their civilization rested buried the bedrock in which metals lay.* Of necessity, they imported their metals. Most of these came from the north and the barbarians, in supplying the metal demand of the ancient civilizations, became skilled metallurgists:

> Copper and tin shaped the penetration of Europe...because these commodities were needed and were only available in [the advanced civilizations of] the near east in small quantities. Europe was the major primary producer of the ancient metallurgical world and also a major

---

*The alluvium also denied anchorage to trees so that these richest parts of the ancient world had to import all their tree product requirements, including timber, charcoal, olive oil and wine.

manufacturer... [the European peoples'] importance in history was to be that they would provide the stocks which would receive the impress of civilization later. At least in their metallurgy, the ancient Europeans serviced other civilizations' needs.[34]

First they worked copper ores. Then they added tin to the copper to make the much stronger bronze. But this required ores from usually distant deposits to be brought together. The break-through that made the Indo-European pastoralists invincible was the discovery of iron smelting, apparently 'south of the Caucasus by the legendary tribe of Chalybes in the 15 century B.C.'[35]

Two distinct streams of Indo-European pastoralists flowed off the Eurasian steppes into Europe. One moved south-westwards towards the Mediterranean sea. The other moved westwards, eventually to reach the Atlantic coast of Ireland.

The pastoralists migrating from the Eurasian steppes to the Mediterranean littoral adjusted the character of their stock to the environment. They changed from the cattle-dominant stock of the Russian steppes to the sheep- and goat-dominant stock of the Mediterranean basin (see Table A.1). The shepherds and goatherds who debouched on the Mediterranean shore encountered there a distinctive type of cropgrower. These people grew, on pockets of naturally rich, volcanic soils, rain-fed crops that were nevertheless much poorer than those grown on the river-fed alluvium of nearby Egypt and Mesopotamia. This was mainly because the Mediterranean rainfall occurs principally in winter, when it is least beneficial, while the heat of summer parches the rainless soil.*

To eke out a subsistence the indigenous Phoenician cropgrowers of the Mediterranean basin engaged in trade by sea with the rich cropgrowers of Egypt, through the Nile delta; and with those of Mesopotamia, through the headwaters of the Euphrates, which rose close to the Lebanese coast. The Phoenicians were able to exchange for the grain that grew abundantly in Egypt and Mesopotamia the tree products that grew well on the stony soils, in the hot and arid Mediterranean summers. These included timber itself, wine and olive oil.

A synthesis occurred between the vanguard of the Indo-European shepherds, arriving perhaps 5,000 years ago on the Mediterranean shore, and the sea-going, trading Phoenicians, who already occupied and grew crops on favoured sites on that shore. There are two surviving phenomena, one philological and the other physiological, that are evidence of that synthesis. The philological evidence is that in the Greek language, while

---

*This contrasted with the situation in Japan on a similar latitude to that of the Mediterranean but where the rainfall, brought by the north east monsoon, occurs mainly in the summer and gives rise to a combination of heat and moisture that is very conducive to high yields.

most roots are of Indo-European origin, those pertaining to the sea and to commerce are mainly of Phoenician origin, indicating a blend between the indigenous seafarers and traders and the newcomer pastoralists.[36] The physiological evidence is the predominance of lactose malabsorption among those Mediterranean peoples on the southernmost extremes of the northern littoral and especially those in the islands, from Sicily to Crete. Lactose tolerance becomes increasingly dominant further from the shore.[37] These phenomena indicate the survival of a strong Phoenician influence close to the Mediterranean shore, which was the origin and principal location of the Ancient Mediterranean culture.

The ecology of individualism. The conjunction of Indo-European shepherds and Phoenician cropgrowers on the northern Mediterranean shore offered interesting possibilities. This was especially the case with adaptable peoples as — almost by definition — were pastoralists who had migrated from the central Eurasian steppes to the Mediterranean sea and as were the sea-going traders who tapped the alluvial wealth of Egypt and Mesopotamia.

The Mediterranean littoral contained limitless arable land. 'Arable land' is defined as land which, when cultivated with the existing technology, gives to the cultivator a return, Y, which is greater than the seed (s) required to plant it; plus the grazing that it would afford if not cultivated (g); plus the energy expended by the cultivator (e). That is, land is arable if Y is greater than ($>$) s + g + e.

Three grades of arable land are identified:

$$s + g + e < Y_1 < s + g + M$$
$$s + g + M < Y_2 < s + g + R$$
$$s + g + R < Y_3$$

Y_1, Y_2 and Y_3 signify in every case the gross output per cropgrower using the available cultivating technology. M is the amount of nutrition required to maintain a cultivator. R is the amount of nutrition required to maintain and to reproduce a cultivator. R is approximately equal to three times M ($R \simeq 3M$). This is because about one-third of most populations are 'productive'; the others are too young or are too ill or weak to work; or they are pregnant or are nursing infants. Thus the Irish workforce of 1.2 million is approximately one-third of the total population of 3.4 millions.

Riverine land in the tropics and sub-tropics typically gave cultivators a return, Y_3. That return in Sumeria, Egypt, the Indus valley and in the Yellow River valley in China supported and produced more than enough people to cultivate all the land in the confined river valleys. One half or more of all the people supported and reproduced by the produce from these fertile, well-watered, warm lands were surplus, in the sense of having no land to cultivate. Thus, 'Egyptian peasants of the third millenium may have been able to produce three times as much as their own domestic needs.'[38]

At the margin of cultivation in every case was desert or, in China, mountain. The surplus populations of these riverine societies were used mainly for great public works of construction: hydraulic works of drainage and irrigation to extend the cultivated area; defence works, like the Great Wall of China or the forts of the Upper Nile; or monuments to rulers who invariably held absolute power, like the pyramids and royal tombs of Egypt.[39]

A grain of cereal planted in the warm, watered alluvium of Ptolemaic Egypt yielded ten in the resulting crop.[40] Contemporaneously in the environs of Rome, a cereal grain planted yielded a harvest of four.[41] Some centuries later in France, when a grain was planted, two were harvested.[42] As a given quantity of seed sows approximately the same area of land, which must then be weeded, tended and harvested, these rates of return to seed in the past suggest that, with the same technology, ancient Egyptian, Roman and French cultivators produced in the ratios of 10 : 4 : 2. If, in every case, seed is deducted (to repay the seed used to grow the crop or to provide for the following crop), then the net return to the cultivators was in the proportions of 9 : 3 : 1.

'Certainly not less, and perhaps more than half' the Egyptian cultivator's output was appropriated by the Pharaonic state in taxes and used to support the population who were not required as cultivators.[43] The half of the crop left to the cultivator was sufficient normally for his maintenance and reproduction. It is deduced from this that Y_e', or the return net of seed to the Egyptian cultivator, who may be taken as a typical riverine cultivator, was about 2R; or $Y_e' \approx 2R$.

The return net of seed to the Roman cultivator, Y_r', which may be taken as typical of the return to cultivators on the Mediterranean littoral, was, as seen above, about one-third of that to the Egyptian cultivator; or $Y_r' \approx 2R/3 = 2M$.

Given, as appears to have been the case, that the return net of seed to cultivators in the Ancient Mediterranean with the prevailing, predominantly hoe agriculture, though greater than the amount needed for maintenance, was less than the amount needed to reproduce the cultivator, a crop-based civilization could not be sustained from its own resources. It required supplementation. The adaptable progeny of the Phoenician crop-growing, seagoing traders and the early Indo-European shepherds secured that supplementation by capturing later, 'barbarian', immigrants and forcing them to cultivate favoured patches of land on the northern Mediterranean littoral. There the enslaved shepherds produced 2M, of which 1M was pre-empted to sustain the slave in a life of 'work, food and punishment', and the other M was appropriated by the slave's owner. Added to the 2M that the slaveowner produced himself, there was sufficient (2M + 1M = R) for the slaveowner's maintenance and reproduction.

There was limitless available arable land on the Mediterranean littoral where the return to the cultivator, though less than R (so that the population could not reproduce from its own resources, populate the region and pre-empt the arable land, as the populations of Egypt, India and China did) was greater than M; and where, therefore, slavery was profitable. The wheat-based Roman empire, at its peak, had two million square miles of territory and its 50 million inhabitants, with the available technology, could not have cultivated one-tenth of that.[44]

The limitless availability of arable land in the Mediterranean basin opened possibilities that did not exist either in the riverine crop-growing valleys that were the centres of civilization or on the pastoral steppes and savannahs. The availability of arable land made it possible for the individual to contribute to wealth production. Wealth production in the riverine valleys and on the pastoral steppes and savannahs depended entirely on the amount of land available. The surplus people in the river valleys were powerless to add to the crop output which was determined absolutely by the amount of land available. Likewise on the pastoral steppes and savannahs: the amount of grass that grew, and therefore the amount and productivity of the stock carried on it, was determined exclusively by nature; by the weather and the quality of the land. *Individual* pastoralists were powerless to influence output. A similar situation applied in the case of hunter-gatherers. The wealth that riverine cropgrowers, pastoralists and hunter-gatherers consumed and that was necessary for their maintenance and reproduction, therefore, came from a common social product, to which the individual was powerless to contribute. The individual's dependence on society was, in this way, absolute.

Individuals who had arable land available, as in the Ancient Mediterranean, could apply themselves to that land in order to produce wealth. The Ancient Mediterranean slaveowners were not only able to produce sufficient wealth to maintain and to reproduce themselves (as shown above) but by their presence they were able to add to the well-being and security of their fellow slaveowners. This was because the more numerous slaveowners were, the greater was the division of labour and consequently, under conditions where land was effectively limitless, the more productive was the individual slaveowner. Also, the more numerous the slaveowners were, the more secure they were behind their defensive city walls. As the city, *polis,* or *civis* expanded to contain an expanding population, the length of the wall to be defended ($2\pi r$) expanded more slowly than the area (πr^2), and therefore more slowly than the population to be defended and available to man the walls. That situation, where the individual by his presence contributed to the well-being of his fellows, contrasted sharply with the case of hunter-gatherers, riverine cropgrowers and pastoralists. In all of those cases, the consumption by individuals of a share of a total product that was determined entirely by the amount and quality of land available and to which the individual was powerless to contribute, reduced *pro tanto* the amount and size of the share available to his fellows.

These very different and very distinctive economic relationships between the individual and society in the Ancient Mediterranean were reflected in very distinctive institutions. Foremost of these was the rule of law. Law, a more or less explicit corpus, determined relations between individuals and society. It incorporated the views of citizens as to what those relations should be; and it was amendable from time to time in an orderly fashion. Law freed man from the tyrannies of anarchy, despotism and unchanging custom.

The rule of law was an expression of the unique politico-economic relationship that existed between the individual and society where land did not limit production; and where the individual's production sustained himself and simultaneously enhanced the productivity and security of his fellows. The individual hunter-gatherer, the individual on the communally grazed pastures and in the over-crowded riverine valleys, was powerless to add to production; but by his presence, he reduced the amount available to all the other members of society. His economic insignificance was mirrored by his political insignificance. In Egypt, 'the Pharaoh, son of Ra, [was] a god upon earth whose words laid down the law.'[45] In Persia, 'all the subjects, without exception, up to the highest dignitories, including ministers and generals, were considered to be the slaves (bandaka) of the king.'[46] In the Ottoman empire, 'subjects, especially non-Moslems, were in reality what they were in name, Raya (Arabic:ra'ayah, herd) a human flock to be shepherded, milked and fleeced.'[47] China was unified, centralized and ruled 'by the universal pre-eminence of the Son of Heaven...the whole system of administration was monolithic.'[48] The neighbouring Japanese 'ideally saw the feudal bond as committing the inferior to absolute obedience and loyalty and granting the superior unlimited authority.'[49] The Inca in Peru was divine, like the Egyptian pharaoh.[50] And so on.

The principal concern of law has ever been the protection of the property that has been the economic basis of law-governed societies. 'Of property, the first, the most necessary kind, the best and most manageable, is man.'[51] Ancient Mediterranean civilization depended on the surplus that the slave produced over and above his necessary maintenance. To procure that surplus it was essential that the slaveowner should have secure and exclusive property in the slave's output. All the power of society was directed towards that purpose, which was correctly deemed to be essential for society's survival. When rulers infringed the property of individual citizens, those infringements were perceived as aberrations and their perpetrators as tyrants rather than rulers.

The rule of law and property, which was protected by law, were perhaps the most tangible manifestations of the distinctive economic relationship between the individual and society that emerged in the Ancient

Mediterranean, and that is here hypothesized to have resulted from the combination, under particular ecological circumstances, of Indo-European pastoralism and Phoenician crop-growing. On a possibly more fundamental, though less explicit, level than the rule of law and the institution of property, the relationship that evolved between the individual and society in the Ancient Mediterranean found expression in a concern with the individual that was new and that is frequently referred to as humanism. The Greeks perceived and gave expression in philosophy, mathematics, history, medicine, sculpture, architecture, drama and literature, to this new and over-riding importance of the individual. Nothing perhaps proclaims so magnificently the glory of the individual, as perceived by the Greeks, as the Parthenon of Athens. By contrast, the giant pyramids of Egypt, which are typical of similar structures in most major riverine societies, while encompassing a degree of skilled design and implementation are, above all, the products of massed human effort mobilized to generate brute force for the glorification of society as personified in the carcasses of its dead pharaohs. The elevation of the individual vis-a-vis society which occurred in the Ancient Mediterranean, was institutionalized by law and made economically possible by law-created and law-protected property, is here referred to as individualism.

Available arable land, while a necessary, was not a sufficient condition for individualism. There were other locations with available arable land where individualism did not spontaneously emerge. The eastern and southern shores of the Mediterranean were probably naturally more productive than the northern shore, with its lower temperatures in the winter especially. But they were too vulnerable to outside intervention to allow the same flowering of individualism, law and property as occurred on the northern littoral. The eastern Mediterranean lay between the headwaters of the Euphrates and Tigris rivers, on the one hand, and the delta of the Nile, on the other; and for millenia it has been dominated by the forces located on these great river systems. Likewise, North Africa has always been accessible to the military power of Egypt, one of the great powers of the ancient world. The Bosphorus and the Mediterranean, on the other hand, protected the northern Mediterranean littoral against invasion by the land-based forces of the great, despotic empires of the east. When the despots put to sea, the individualistic, law -governed, slave-owning Greeks, operating in their favourite milieu, trounced the Persians in the naval battle of Salamis.

SubSaharan Africa also had unlimited arable land. But the interaction between the Nilo-Hamitic pastoralists and the cropgrowers of the region did not result in any flowering of individualism like that of the Ancient Mediterranean. Two factors that may have contributed to this different result are noted here. First, the Nilo-Hamites were and are predominantly cattlekeepers and goatherders (see Table A.1). That combination of stocking was, and is, dictated by the ecology of African grazing lands. There the limitation on stocking is access to water during the killing droughts of the African continent. Stock graze bare the land surrounding the waterholes and are forced, as drought progresses, to move ever further from these holes to reach grazing before they die of starvation. There they graze and move back to drink. Cattle, which are more mobile, can effect this shift between water and grazing better than sheep, their competing grazing species. Goats, as well as being browsers and therefore not competing with cattle for grazing, are also highly mobile and thus fit well into the system. As keepers of cattle and goats the Nilo-Hamites were much more mobile, and therefore had greater power to mass and to overcome the resistance of cropgrowers, than had the Mediterranean shepherds.

Second, while the Indo-European shepherds interacted with the indigenous Phoenician cropgrowers against a maritime background in which the Phoenicians were at home but the pastoralists were 'at sea', in subSaharan Africa there was no sea to which the cropgrowers could escape from the massed pastoralists.

These considerations would have accounted for the pastoral-dominant outcome of the interaction between pastoralism and crop-growing in subSaharan Africa, compared to the crop-urban-dominant outcome in the Ancient Mediterranean. It is noteworthy, however, that throughout

Table A.1
Composition of Grazing Stock by Region

	Sheep and Goats per 100 Cattle	Goats per 100 Cattle
World	126	41
Africa[a]	156	120
Middle East[b]	564	39
Mediterranean[c]	338	29
C.W. Europe[d]	61	3
USSR	130	4

Note: a) Africa exclusive of Morocco, Algeria, Tunisia, Libya, Egypt and South Africa.
b) Afghan, Iran, Iraq, Jordan, Saudi Arabia, Yemen, Syria, Turkey.
c) Morocco, Algeria, Tunisia, Libya, Egypt, Israel, Lebanon, Greece, Albania, Yugoslavia, Italy, Spain.
d) Austria, Belgium, Luxemburg, Czechoslovakia, Denmark, France, Germany (East and West), Ireland, Netherlands, Switzerland, United Kingdom.
Source: FAO Production Yearbook, 1979.

subSaharan Africa, where arable land has also been virtually limitless, an inchoate form of slavery has been practiced to profit from the situation where $Y_2 > s + g + M$. That slavery is 'bridewealth'; or the use of livestock to purchase women to provide sexual services and to grow sufficient crops to maintain themselves and to contribute to the maintenance of their husband-owners.

The dynamics of slavery. Ancient Mediterranean individualism ascribed to the individual a significance that was incomparably greater than that possessed in hunting-gathering, riverine crop-growing and pastoral societies. That significance, however, only attached to certain individuals: to citizens and, to a less extent, to the citizens' allies. It was not accorded to barbarians or foreigners who were deemed suitable material for enslavement. Nor did it attach to slaves who, as the property of individual citizens, had the legal status of 'things that talk', 'property with a soul.'[52] The Ancient Mediterranean slaves had, in law and in practice, a status and living conditions inferior to those of hunter-gatherers, riverine cropgrowers or pastoralists. These, if in no other way, were better off than the slaves in that they were left with sufficient not merely to maintain but to reproduce themselves, whereas the slaves, for whom life was a matter of 'work, food and punishment', had sufficient food for their maintenance only. For the citizens of the Ancient Mediterranean to realise themselves as no others had previously done, it was necessary that they should trample on and dehumanise, to an unprecedented degree, those who were not citizens, who were 'lesser breeds without the law'.

The basic law of survival in an Ancient Mediterranean society that was essentially parasitical, in that it could not reproduce its labour supply, was 'enslave or be enslaved'. As the slave workforce was worn out, it could be replaced profitably only by conquest and by fresh enslavement. Those who succeeded attained to 'the glory that was Greece'; those who failed, risked being enslaved,to become 'things that talked'.This gave to Ancient Mediterranean society a distinctive dynamic. All earlier hunter-gathering, riverine crop-growing and pastoralist societies, the well-being of which depended on the land they held, had proceeded in cycles. Given unchanged land resources, there were scarcely any perceptible differences between similar positions on succeeding cycles. A phase of poor game would be followed by one of more abundant game when the hunter-gatherers would eat better, have lower mortality rates and would increase in numbers. Their added numbers would contribute to a fall in game stocks, with poorer hunting, lower nutrition, higher mortality, and declining population. After innumerable similar cycles, the Stone Age hunter-gatherers of Papua New Guinea now lead a life that is not perceptibly different from that suggested by the archaeological remains of other hunter-gathering societies that existed tens of thousands of years ago.

Likewise Egypt, China and the civilizations of pre-Columbian America had their rises and declines, but up to modern times remained unchanged in all essential respects from what they had been millenia earlier. Cook makes this point:

> Ancient Egyptian civilization remained more or less uniform for two and a half millenium....The Hyksos invaded, took over and finally were expelled....Egypt was a prize colony of the Roman Empire, but Rome did little to change the Egyptians.....It was not until the Arab invaders of 639 AD that the turning point arrived.[53]

Toynbee makes the same point: 'The Sumerian, Akhadian and Egyptian civilizations had accomplished most of their great creative achievements in all fields of human activity before the close of the third millenium BC.'[54] Thereafter, he suggests, there were just repeated cycles. Lambert erroneously attributes this homeostasis to the proliferation of parasitic worms in warm, moist environments, 'which stagnated the cradles of civilization.'[55] The Baseri, far away from a 'warm, moist environment', graze the parched lands of south Persia and lead there a life that is very little different from that of their forebears of 4,000 years ago.[56] And so it goes.

The rule of 'enslave or be enslaved' forced the Ancient Mediterranean polities into unceasing conflict. The logic of the conflict led to geographical expansion as first Athens and later Rome became dominant and sought further afield fresh conquests and new captives to enslave in order to replenish an ever-wasting and non-reproducing labour supply. Geographical expansion was necessarily accompanied by political concentration. In a slave-based economy returns to labour tended towards the level needed to maintain slaves, which was below the level at which citizens could reproduce themselves. From a basically equal starting position,[57] the fortunes of war and peace would have caused some citizens to lose their slaves. Slaveless citizens could not reproduce themselves, except by borrowing from slaveowners. These conditions of production caused, within cities, an unavoidable polarization between slaveless and slave-owning citizens; and between cities, the conditions of production caused the rise to dominance of a single city. Thus as the Roman imperium spread, power within Rome became ever more concentrated into the hands of an ever smaller oligarchy.

The Persian plateau on the east, the Sahara desert on the south, and the Atlantic ocean on the west, forced Rome to expand northwards to secure the labour replenishments on which Ancient Mediterranean society depended. The further northwards the empire spread the less favourable growth conditions became and the lower yields fell. As observed above, the returns net of seed to crop-growing in Egypt, Rome and France were in the proportions of 9 : 3 : 1. If the Roman cultivator could produce 2M, one of which maintained a slave cultivator and the other being the slaveowner's profit, with a similar technology the cultivator in France produced only 2M/3, or insufficient to maintain a slave.

The Ancient Mediterranean, for all its brilliant achievements in the arts, sciences and humanities, made little economic or technological progress.[58] That was unsurprising. Scope for attainment in the Ancient Mediterranean was principally in military matters and politics. Production in field, factory, shop or office was servile, to be performed by slaves who had no interest in increasing their productivity.

Once the Roman *limes* extended to Hadrian's Wall in Britain and to the line of the Rhine and Danube on mainland Europe, where $Y < s + g + M$, existing conquests could be held only at a loss, which would be aggravated by further conquests in territory even less favourable for crop-growing. The limits of Ancient Mediterranean expansion had been reached; and with expansion ended so also ended the replenishment with captives of the Ancient Mediterranean's wasting labour supply.

The limits of territorial expansion were reached almost at the same time as the ultimate concentration of political power within the empire. The last years of the Roman Republic were marked by acute instability as a tiny oligarchy struggled for power, steeping the empire in ruinous civil wars.[59] Rome and the Ancient Mediterranean were rescued from unceasing civil war only by concentrating all power into the hands of the Divine Augustus and his successors. Thus, contemporaneously with the cutting off of the supply of slave labour on which the Ancient Mediterranean depended economically, the rule of law was replaced by a despotism no different from that of riverine crop-growing or pastoral societies. The empire nevertheless survived for a few more centuries, sustained by the momentum of its ancient vigour, until finally, drained demographically, economically, militarily and politically, it lay defenceless and exposed to the northern barbarians when these crossed the frozen Rhine on the last night of the year 406 AD.

The Pastoralists and Central Western Europe

Both the rise and the decline of the Ancient Mediterranean were inherent in a glorious, but fatally flawed, precocious individualism that was essentially parasitical. Further north in Europe the Indo-European pastoralists created a different individualism that was non-parasitical. It developed more slowly and hesitantly; but it has been more durable and, in the long run, more glorious and productive.

The pastoralists who moved into Central Western Europe had important basic similarities with those who debouched on to the Mediterranean shore. Both groups were lactose tolerant, Indo-Europeans who originated from the same Asian steppes. Moving off the steppes, both found available arable land, one lot on the Mediterranean littoral, the other when the Central Western European forest was cleared. Both groups of pastoralists acquired from the sedentary cropgrowers of the Middle East the art of growing crops and the cereal species to grow. Both had acquired a knowledge of metallurgy, probably in large measure as a result of trading in ores and metals with the wealthy Mesopotamian and Egyptian civilizations. Learning to smelt iron was particularly important to the northern pastoralists who moved from the steppe into the Central Western European forest, because abundant, inexpensive, hard-wearing iron implements were needed to clear the forest and to cultivate the hard ground underneath.* Finally, both groups of pastoralists encountered conditions that allowed a large measure of freedom from external influences to adapt to local conditions. The Mediterranean sea and the Bosphorus held at bay the riverine despots of the Middle East and Egypt and permitted a synthesis of Phoenician crop-growing and Indo-European pastoralism to evolve according to its own genius. The forest, through which the Indo-Europeans percolated further north, excluded more effectively than the Great Wall of China did the Golden Hordes that dominated the steppes and imposed a gregarious conformity on their denizens.

There were three major differences in the off-steppe conditions encountered by the two groups of pastoralists. Sparse summer rainfall and vegetation required the Mediterranean littoral to be grazed mainly by sheep. The heavier rainfall to the north gave a stronger growth of pasture that was more suitable for cattle. Moreover, the deciduous forest of Central Western Europe was unsuited for sheep, the wool of which would become entangled in briars and other forest undergrowth (see Table A.1). Secondly, the productivity under crop of the northern land was less than that of the warmer Mediterranean littoral. The productivity of the land was: $s + g + e < Y_1 < s + g + M$.

Finally, the pastoralists in Central Western Europe encountered different precursors from the Phoenician sea-going cropgrowers whom the shepherds met in the Mediterranean basin. The precursors of the pastoralists in Central Western Europe were the neolithic, lactose malabsorbent farmers who built such structures as Ireland's Newgrange burial mound.[61] The more efficient, lactose tolerant, metal using Indo-Europeans left little trace — apart from archeological — of these earlier agriculturists. The Basques

---

*There was later, around the time of Christ, a similar concurrence of cattle, crops (high-yielding yams and bananas from Southeast Asia) and iron-smelting in the Cameroons in central tropical Africa. Little more than a millenium later the Bantu people, who combined these attributes, had spread their influence through most of subSahelian Africa with an astonishing rapidity that is testified to by the basic similarity of the Bantu languages, which are spoken throughout most of subSahelian Africa.[60]

Forests in Medieval Europe

Main areas of forest

Forested areas whose boundaries and density are uncertain

.... Limits of investigation

From: G. Duby *The Early Growth of the European Economy* (London, Weidenfeld & Nicolson)

of northern Spain appear to be a surviving pocket of these earlier European farming people. The Lapps may be another. The hunting-gathering Lapps resided in the northern tundra, where they had followed the reindeer as these retreated before the deciduous forest that had spread over Central Western Europe after the last Ice Age. There was a limited interaction between the Indo-European pastoralists and the Lapps, sufficient perhaps to account for the difference between the way the reindeer are husbanded in northern Eurasia and the way the closely related caribou are hunted by the eskimos of North America.[62] No synthesis between pastoralism and crop-growing occurred in Central Western Europe as there did on the Mediterranean littoral and in India. Central Western European society and culture are a result of a unique, organic evolution by pastoralists, who were Indo-European, as they moved from the steppes into the forest.

The first critical problem that the purely pastoral Indo-Europeans must have encountered when they entered the forest of Central Western Europe was to keep their cattle alive during the long, hard winters. The solutions available to other stockowners either did not apply, or applied only to a very limited extent, in the northern forest. Migration or transhumance, which was the normal practice of pastoralists for coping with dormant seasons or prolonged drought, was not practicable through the forest. A limited transhumance, or 'boolying' in Irish, has of course been traditional in Europe; but this provided no general answer to the problem. Neither was it practicable to leave animals to live off their accumulated fat during the dormant season, as is widely done in more southern and warmer climates. While cattle can survive through dry seasons for months and even years on minimal fodder in warm climates, a month of Central Western Europe's cold, damp, winter weather would be fatal for most cattle without ample winter fodder.

The feeding of the preserved leaves of trees, particularly elm trees, was one approach to the critical problem of winter fodder. The destruction of elm trees by this use of their leaves for winter fodder, which is recorded in pollen counts at different archaeological levels, is an important clue for prehistorians in tracing man's progress through Central Western Europe.[63] Preserving elm leaves was a very inadequate answer to the central problem of keeping alive, during long hard winters, the cattle on which the Indo-European pastoralists were absolutely dependent. A more adequate solution was to use straw and other by-products of crops as winter fodder. Crop-growing, therefore, was a condition of survival for the Indo-European pastoralists once they entered the forest of Central Western Europe. But though the land of Central Western Europe, when cleared of trees by the pastoralists, was arable, its yields were poor. With riverine or Ancient Mediterranean technology, the yield per person was insufficient for the cultivator's maintenance, i.e. $s + g + e < Y < s + g + M$. Slaves could not be used to grow crops, mainly because the product of slave-grown crops in Central Western Europe would have been insufficient to maintain, let alone reproduce, the slaves. The answer for the cattle-keeping pastoralists, forced to grow crops to provide winter fodder for their cattle, was to use cattle intensively for this purpose.

Neither the growing of crops, nor the cereal crops that the pastoralists grew, was new. Nor was the use of cattle as draught animals to grow crops new. Nor again was the use of straw and cereal by-products as dormant season fodder new.* What was new was the scale on which the pastoralists of Central Western Europe used their cattle to grow crops. In a location where the net return for the seed planted was only one-third as much as on the Mediterranean littoral and only one-ninth as much as in Egypt, the only way to grow the crops that were essential for the survival of cattle was to use large numbers of cattle to cultivate extensive areas of cleared land to grow sufficient low-yielding crops to fodder the cattle through the winter and to feed the cropgrowers through most of the year.

It was necessary, in order to secure a given amount of grain, to sow nine times as much seed in Central Western Europe as in Egypt; or three times as much as on the Mediterranean littoral. It was also necessary to plough, till, plant, weed and harvest nine times as much land for the reception of that seed in Central Western Europe as in Egypt and three times as much as on the Mediterranean littoral. To secure a given crop output then, vastly more seed, more cultivating livestock and more fodder to support those livestock in winter were needed. The same applied with implements to cultivate and weed the land, carts to gather the sparse harvest, and larger, sturdier barns to shelter the bigger volume of straw but equal volume of grain, against the longer and more severe central European winters. The Indo-European pastoralists, in the forest of Central Western Europe, did not use any resource that had not been used before to do anything that had not been done before. But they were forced by circumstances — circumstances that also made these things possible for them — to use these resources in ways and in combinations that had not been used before. It was a question of proportions. The pastoralists who entered the Central Western European forest some 5,000 years ago, in order to secure a given output had to use vastly more resources that had been saved from consumption than other producers. That is to say, they had to use far more capital. This greatly increased capital/output ratio was capitalist production.

Capitalist Production

The misconception that commerce and a market-oriented economy are a *sine qua non* of capitalism and are the 'engines of growth' is common to

*The cropgrowers of east Asia have for millenia relied, and continue to rely, mainly on rice straw and rice bran as feed during the dormant season for their bovines, which they use principally for cultivating.

Marxists and non-Marxists. Capitalism, for Marx, was the production of goods — or commodities — for the market:

> The *original* formation of capital does not, as is often supposed, proceed by the *accumulation* of food, tools, raw materials or in short, of the *objective* conditions of labour detached from the soil and already fused with human labour...Its *original formation* occurs simply because the historic process of the dissolution of the old mode of production, allows value, existing in the form of *monetary wealth to buy* the objective conditions of labour on one hand, to exchange the *living* labour of the new workers for money, on the other. What separates them out is a historic process, a process of dissolution, and it is *this* which enables money to turn into capital.[64]

For Marx, capitalist production commences when labour that is hired for wages is used to produce goods for sale:

> In the infancy of capitalist production, things often happened as in the infancy of medieval towns, where the question, which of the escaped serfs should be master and which servant, was in great part decided by the earlier or later date of their flight. The snail's pace of this method corresponded in no way with the commercial requirements of the new-world market that the great discoveries of the end of the fifteenth century created. But the middle ages had handed down two distinct forms of capital, which mature in the most different economic social formations, and which, before the era of the capitalist mode of production, are considered as capital *quand même* — usurer's capital and merchant's capital.
>
> The money capital formed by means of usury and commerce was prevented from turning into industrial capital, in the country by the feudal constitution, in the towns by the guild organisation. These fetters vanished with the dissolution of feudal society, with the expropriation and partial eviction of the country population.[65]

A recently stated typical non-Marxist view is:

> The prospect of change depended on the rise of a market economy. In the ancient societies, there was a certain amount of trade but under primitive conditions of transport, it was confined to luxury goods, goods of small bulk and high value.[66]

Although for millenia capital-based, virtually all production in Central Western Europe, until well into the eighteenth century, was for home consumption. 75% of the working population were farmers, producing the food, etc. that they themselves mainly consumed; or exchanging a small portion of it for the goods and services provided by the 25% of the workforce who were not farmers.[67] Even today the world continues to need to have almost half its workforce in agriculture.[68] Yet China and Egypt several thousand years earlier, were by contrast able to grow on their warm, watered, alluvial soils, with less than half their labour forces, sufficient food in normal years to support their entire populations. For example, 'Egyptian peasants of the third millenium BC may have been able to produce three times as much as their own domestic needs.'[69] The existence of currencies in these countries centuries — if not millenia — earlier than in Central Western Europe testifies to the existence of developed markets where a large volume of agricultural produce was exchanged for non-agricultural goods and services; including especially those services provided by despotic states. The existence of organized markets in riverine societies millenia ago did not make them capitalist and dynamic; neither did the virtual absence of markets until recent centuries prevent the economy of Central Western Europe from being capitalist.

The new, capitalist form of production practised by the Indo-European pastoralists in the forests of Central Western Europe substituted capital — seed, cattle, winter-fodder and implements — for the warm, moist alluvium of the tropical and sub-tropical valleys, to make it possible to grow crops on cool, dry upland. It was essential for the cropgrowers of Central Western Europe, unlike those of the tropics and sub-tropics, to avoid low-lying valley land where, in a higher latitude, the cold, wet soils rotted crops. On the better drained upland of the cooler, northern latitude, the soil was warmer and more congenial for growing the cereals — wheat and barley — that were first domesticated in the Middle East. There was a virtually limitless extent of that upland in the great plains of Central Western Europe. Production was limited only by the need to clear the land of forest and to stock and equip it with seed, cattle, implements, etc. This was a fundamentally different form of production, with fundamentally different limitations and possibilities.

With the exception of the Ancient Mediterranean, all previous production had been limited exclusively by land. That was the case with hunter-gatherers too, who could not extract from a region more than nature provided there. It was the case with the riverine cropgrowers, whose cultivations spread to the edge of the drained and irrigated valley, but could go further. The drained and irrigated area was, from time to time, extended by socially undertaken hydraulic works, but always within limits determined topographically; and the surplus population quickly spread into the new land and produced there a still larger surplus population.

The grass growth of the steppes and savannahs was a natural product, like the quarry of the hunter-gatherers. It depended solely on the extent and quality of land available. The amount of stock that could be carried and the produce of that stock depended on the fodder available *in situ* during the dormant season; and on the stock's ability to survive on that fodder. Any attempt to keep more stock was subject to this purely natural constraint.

Production in the Ancient Mediterranean was not constrained by land. There the limit on production was labour to cultivate the limitlessly available land which, with the technology practised, yielded more than enough for subsistence, but less than sufficient for reproduction. A brilliant, humanist culture was possible as long as the labour supply could be replenished by conquest and subsequent enslavement. But that expedient was exhausted when conquest was extended to the margin at which, with the slave technology practised, production dropped below the producer's maintenance requirements. The subsequent failure of the labour supply coupled with, and aggravated by, internal conflicts caused the decline and fall of the Roman empire.

The circumstances confronting the Indo-European pastoralists who, 4 — 5,000 years ago, moved from the steppes of Asia into the Central Western European forest made it both possible and necessary for them to adopt capitalist production. In doing so they exploited more fully their cattle stocks than any other people. Hidden away in the forest, they used their cattle for draught, which Africans do not. The African cattleowner has always had to hold his cattle in the open to avoid the tsetse fly which is fatal to cattle, which are not indigenous to Africa. Cattle held in the open have always been a prey to raiding, which made that activity, or defending against it, the primary activity of African males. Forced to defend their own, or to raid their neighbours' cattle, African males were primarily warriors who produced little food and never harnessed cattle for that purpose. Food production was instead left to the non-warrior women who, with hoes on Africa's limitless, warmer soil and growing yams and bananas, could produce a maintenance and more. The men used their cattle as 'bridewealth' to buy the women for their sexual and crop-growing services.

The Indo-European pastoralists were, of course, lactose tolerant. They drank the milk of their cattle, unlike the riverine cropgrowers of Egypt, Sumeria and east Asia.

Unlike the only other lactose tolerant people who used their cattle for draught, the Indians, the Europeans did not have to taboo beef consumption. This was because Central Western Europe, unlike India, never was in danger of becoming a sparsely populated cattle-walk. Cattle could, and do, survive the dormant season on little or no nutrition in India's warm climate, so there was no compulsion on India's Aryan invaders to grow crops to supply winter fodder for their stock. As explained already, it was otherwise in Central Western Europe where, if pastoralists were to retain their cattle for milk production, they had no option but to use them for draught to grow the crops that yielded, as a by-product, essential winter fodder. The pre-Colombian American farmers, of course, had no cattle.

The ecology of capitalism. Capital constrained production in Central Western Europe. Ignoring transfers, saving is the only source of capital. Production therefore, uniquely in Central Western Europe, depended on the ability and willingness of people 'to defer gratification' or to save and to invest what they saved in expanding production. The forest of Central

Western Europe provided a milieu in which, for the first time ever, the essential requirements for that investment existed. When cleared, it provided arable land. It did not harbour the tsetse fly and was therefore safe for cattle. It provided shelter and a measure of security for those who wished to save and to invest. The individual in the forest escaped from the tyrannical gregariousness of the steppes and savannahs, where all were bound to a common, customary, impotent existence. He was safe from pursuit within the forest, where only individuals could percolate between the trees. No Golden Hordes or Pharaoh, Inca, Maharajah or Emperor, with their massed troops supported by a large riverine surplus, could follow him. And the northern forest land, where two grains were harvested for one sown, was too sparse in quality and too great in extent to yield a surplus to support local tyrants.

People for the first time ever, 4 or 5 thousand years ago, found in the forest of Central Western Europe the opportunity, by their own efforts and not through enslaving others, to escape from the tyrannies of want, ignorance, custom and of arbitrary, absolute government. People, by saving and by investing those savings, could expand production without effective limit. It was an opportunity that occurred after, and as a result of, aeons of human evolution. That evolution had resulted in an Indo-European people who were lactose tolerant and able to derive maximum nourishment from their pastoral resources; who had learned the skills of metal-working, largely through commercial intercourse with the earlier Middle Eastern civilizations; and who had got not merely the idea, but the seeds, for cropgrowing from the same source.

There was more than an opportunity to save and invest in the Central Western European forest: there was a necessity to do so. For as capital made production possible there, production was impossible without capital. This was particularly so over time as the sparse game of the temperate forest was increasingly preserved for rulers, and its hunting became poaching, which was frequently a capital crime. The capital-less in Central Western Europe were in even worse circumstances than the slaves of the Ancient Mediterranean. The latter were assured of a maintenance as long as they could labour, and by their labour produce more than a maintenance; the former, by their labour alone, produced less than a maintenance, and though not enslaved, were free only to starve. The elevation of some, which was secured by saving and investing, was therefore accompanied by an even more brutal degradation and destruction of others, who failed to save and invest, than occurred in the Ancient Mediterranean. The opening of the prospect of realizing man's potential, for the slaveowner of the Ancient Mediterranean and for the capitalowner of Central Western Europe, was necessarily and unavoidably accompanied by the debasement, in the one case of the slave and, in the other case, of those without capital. That debasement would have been as pointless as it was unknown among the hunter-gatherers, riverine cropgrowers or pastoralists. That debasement, leading to extinction, was most brutal in Central Western Europe.

The margin between production and the requirements for subsistence must have been pathetically narrow for the pastoralists as they moved from the Asian steppe into Central Western Europe. Those who secured a margin survived and possibly prospered; those who did not secure a margin disappeared. But like the slave-based production of the Ancient Mediterranean, capital-based production in Central Western Europe had its distinctive dynamic, which was very different from the cycles of hunting-gathering, riverine crop-growing and pastoral economies which resulted in long term stasis. Capital, in a situation where land and people were effectively limitless, was subject to increasing returns. That is, in any particular situation, the more capital there was the more productive that capital tended to be. Thus, ten oxen yoked to a single massive plough did more than ten times as much work as one ox pulling a small plough; and they did it better, because they ploughed deeper, bringing up fresher soil and burying weeds and thrash deeper. The produce of two ten-oxen teams in a district was more than twice as valuable as that of a single ten-oxen team; because only a slightly longer, broader, higher barn was needed to shelter the produce of both teams; and only a slightly larger mill, but the same miller, would have been required to mill it.

There were, in addition to these scale economies, other benefits from capital accumulation which may be called external economies. The more capital that was acumulated in a district, the more people there were who could find support there. The more like-minded, capital-using people there were in a district, the more secure they were against marauders who could still penetrate the forest. And apart from being better able to share the services of specialists like millers, wheelwrights and blacksmiths, because man is a social animal and because *proximus hominis primus homo,* people gained solace, comfort and culture as well as productivity and security from the larger communities that saving and capital formation made possible.

One external economy was particularly important and illustrates well the new dynamic brought into human affairs by saving and capital formation. The unique and critical need for winter fodder for cattle that has been stressed above had three consequences — apart from compelling pastoralists to grow crops — which greatly facilitated and expedited further capital accumulation. First, the inherent scarcity of winter fodder necessitated choice in its allocation. Cattle/fodder owners were forced to decide every autumn to which of their cattle they should allocate the limited fodder, which was insufficient to carry through the winter all the cattle that survived easily during the growing season. Inevitably they chose to retain the animals that produced the most draught power, milk or meat, and they slaughtered and consumed the balance. In doing this they introduced an element of selection that no other pastoral people exercised. Livestock on communal pastures elsewhere survived on the residual grazing left in the dormant season; and the criterion of their survival was their natural fitness and not their productivity. Purposeful selection of the animals retained to share the scarce winter fodder led, over time, to the evolution in Central Western Europe of cattle that worked, milked and fattened better than any other cattle.

The second important consequence of winter foddering was the emergence, uniquely among lactose tolerant cattlekeepers, of cattle with the *Bos taurus* characteristic of milk let-down in the absence of the cow's live calf. As cattle were selected for their milking and other qualities rather than naturally selected by their ability to survive, the dominant *Bos indicus* characteristic of refusing to let down milk in the absence of the cow's live calf regressed. This made possible the selection at birth of the calves required to maintain or expand the milking and working herds, and the slaughter of the balance. That in turn avoided the sort of waste that occurs in India now, where 20 million calves are reared annually as a necessary condition of inducing their dams to milk and in the process consuming a substantial proportion of the little milk produced by cows selected by the survival of the fittest. In the second year of their lives — when cattle are most valuable in the West — ten million of these young cattle, which are surplus to replacement requirements, of necessity perish.[70]

The third indirect benefit that followed from the need to winter feed cattle was perhaps the most important. Competition for grazing occurs during the season of scarcity. Fodder for the amount of stock able to survive the dormant season bottleneck is normally superabundant, with no competition for it in the growing season. There is a regular seasonal cycle of famine followed by feast. It is in the dormant season that strife occurs between and within pastoral groups, when the destruction of one pastoralist's livestock leaves more scarce grazing for the surviving stock. The need to supply fodder conserved by the stockowners to maintain cattle through the winter and the virtual absence of winter grazing in Central Western Europe removed from there the normal dormant season conflict between stockowners for grazing. In doing so, it helped to enhance the social significance of, and the social concern for, the capital of individuals, including their cattle which in sustaining the owners of capital enriched and strengthened society too.

The dynamics of capitalism. Uniquely in Central Western Europe within the past 5,000 years, capital became the key to production. Production in all other societies was determined by the fixed amount of land or slaves available. But neither the amount nor the productivity of capital was inherently limited. On the contrary: both had an inherent tendency to increase. This was firstly because as the stock of capital increased output increased and, from the larger output, it was easier to save in order to increase further the capital stock. Secondly, as the capital stock increased, without land or labour being limiting, scale and external economies raised capital's productivity. There was and is, therefore, no inherent constraint on the quantity or productivity of capital, short of the satisfaction of human needs and the realization of man's nature by freeing it from want.

Myriads of people in tiny 'islands of population' in the 'sea of forest' that was Central Western Europe[71] had the opportunity to save and to invest. Some succeeded; many failed. Those who failed were lost to posterity. Those who succeeded, who acquired capital and used it productively, survived. The islands of population that they inhabited expanded, coalesced and developed into large communities. Those core areas which occupied a fertile location, or one that was easily defended and secure, or that was well placed to tap surrounding trade, where government was less depredatory and less bellicose — where, in a word, all-important capital could be most easily accumulated and get the highest and most secure return — these areas tended to emerge dominant during the course of the millenia of conflict that distinguished Central Western Europe from the monolithic governments of Egypt, of the Eurasian steppes, of China and, to a less extent, of India. As recently as 800 years ago there were a thousand petty statelets in Central Western Europe. Most of these have disappeared and are survived by a little more than a score, which adapted best to the changes in circumstances brought about by the accumulation of capital and all that flowed from that accumulation.[72]

The transformation of Indo-European pastoralists into capital-based cropgrowers who created a great civilization was unique and it was organic. All the other great civilizations were founded by lactose malabsorbent peoples, whose ancestry presumably hunted and gathered on, or near, the sites of those civilizations prior to the domestication of crops and livestock; although in two cases there were important pastoralist inputs. India's civilization originated in the Indus valley, which was brought into cultivation by lactose malabsorbent cropgrowers and was destroyed by invading Aryan pastoralists. Subsequently the crop-growing and pastoralist elements merged to create a distinctively Indian culture. The Ancient Mediterranean culture was also the result of a synthesis between Indo-European shepherds and Phoenician crop-growing, seagoing merchants. But the culture of Central Western Europe is the only case where pastoralists, by a process of organic change or social evolution in response to a particular environment, were transformed into cropgrowers who supported a major civilization.

The society of Central Western Europe, originating on sparsely yielding land cleared from the forest, was initially diffuse and rural, unlike other crop-growing societies which were concentrated into rich river valleys in the tropics and subtropics; or in the Ancient Mediterranean, centred on cities. But whereas the cities of the Ancient Mediterranean regressed into the rural villas of the late Roman empire, the originally sparse fields of Central Western Europe eventually supported great cities where most of the population now dwells. The pastoralists coming from the steppes were governed, as pastoralists still are, by custom. Law, on the other hand, was a key feature of Ancient Mediterranean society from the start. But whereas that law regressed to the will of a divine Caesar, Central Western European custom evolved into a corpus of law much more full and complete than that of the Ancient Mediterranean. Most of the pastoralists who entered the forests of Central Western Europe took to crop-growing — they had no option if they were to survive; only a minority continued as warriors and these in time became an encastled elite. That was in contrast to the universal warrior status of African males. The concentration of European hierarchal society on food production contrasted also with the Ancient Mediterranean situation where the individual was cultivator, slaveowner, citizen and warrior in a society that was basically democratic.[73] But while Ancient Mediterranean democracy regressed into absolute imperial authority, the hierarchal society of Central Western Europe has evolved in time into democracy as real as anything that has existed outside Solon's Athens.

A Network of Tensions

The unique, organic evolution of Central Western European society and culture was supported and sustained by a remarkable network of social tensions. Consideration of major elements of that network can contribute to an understanding of the character of individualistic capitalism as it evolved over the millenia in Central Western Europe.

Consumption and investment. The first and most critical of these social tensions and one peculiar to Central Western Europe was that between consumption and investment, between gratification now and deferred gratification. The pastoralist in the Central Western European forest was confronted by this choice at every stage: to rear a calf or drink the milk (other pastoralists, with *Bos indicus* type cows, had no such choice); to use scarce winter fodder to support a young animal that would be productive some seasons later, or to support a cow that would give milk in the spring (other pastoralists had no problem of fodder allocation); to use half his crop for seed, or to consume it (the Egyptian peasant needed only one-tenth of his crop for seed). The Central Western European was, at all stages, confronted, as others were not, with the opportunity to increase his consumption; but he was also continuously offered the opportunity to invest, as others were not.

If he reared additional animals, there was always adequate summer grazing and the animal's survival in winter did not, as elsewhere, depend on a finite amount of socially controlled, dormant season grazing, but on the fodder that the stockowner conserved. If a Central Western European farmer decided to save more of his crop and use it to plant more land, he had limitless land available. Bringing it in to production depended on his investment in it. Whichever the choice, the individual, sheltered and hidden in the forest of Central Western Europe, had freedom to make it. The gregarious pastoralists of the steppes or savannahs had no such freedom; nor did the cropgrowers dominated by powerful riverine states.

Cabin and castle. The second major tension in this evolving society was that between cabin and castle. Early European society was essentially defensive. The forest sheltered its denizens and made it possible for most of them to produce, rather than to fight to defend their own or to raid their neighbours livestock. The soil's poverty also precluded the maintenance of a large military class, like the *samurai* on Japan's volcanic valley soils, watered by summer rain (Appendix C). But as the forest was cleared and production was expanded there was greater need of, and means for, defence. The clearances made movement and attack easier. The crops provided the means to provision strong points capable of holding out for protracted periods against attack. Central Western Europe's distinctive, castle-based defensive system reflected the character of its economy. Its crops were too sparse and widespread to permit of their being gathered, together with their growers, into walled cities. And even if they could be so gathered to sustain the population during a siege it would have been altogether impracticable to gather in, and similarly to defend, the livestock on which Central Western European crop-growing was more dependent than any other. Defence in Central Western Europe entailed leaving the producers and their capital exposed to attack, and relying instead on the effect of retaliatory action by the military elite within the castle as the main deterrent. This entailed the emergence within society of classes that had conflicting interests but that were mutually dependent.

The cabin-dwellers depended on the castle-dwellers for their defence. They also depended on them to maintain internal law and order, which included refraining from using their superior military power to make excessive exactions. The military elite in the castles, for their part, depended on the cabin-dwellers to grow the crops without which they could not exist in the castles. While their power over the cabin-dwellers may have been absolute in the short run, in the longer run it was tightly circumscribed. First, given Central Western Europe's narrow margin between output and the producers' subsistence needs, excessive exactions quickly undermined production and created a desert around the castle in which it too perished. Thereafter, given the great extent of Central Western Europe's 'sea of forest', it was always possible, in the final analysis, for the capitalist producers to shift, to escape the depredations of local tyrants as they had escaped those of the pastoral hordes and the riverine despots by moving from the steppes into the forest. As Georges Duby put it: 'No man could exploit the workers excessively without seeing their productivity fall, or forcing them to take flight in a world where there was plenty of room for emigrants.'[74]

There existed therefore in Central Western Europe a unique division of political-military power in the castle and of economic power in the cabin. No such division of power existed anywhere else. It did not occur in riverine cropgrowing society or in pastoral society, where the total product accrued to society and where the individual, therefore, was totally dependent on society for his existence. Nor did any similar division of power exist in Ancient Mediterranean society, at least prior to its regressing; citizens shared alike in the economy, defence and politics of their cities. That unique division of power between castle and cabin which occurred in Central Western Europe, is referred to as feudalism. The term correctly implies mutually dependent relationships.

Castle and king. Capital accumulation was accompanied by specialization and the growth of markets. The lords of some castles, which were located in more fertile areas or were strategically better placed, or who themselves were more forceful — lords who, for whatever reason, had better access to markets — achieved dominance over others who drew less on the market. Specialization applied pre-eminently to the martial arts, and for rulers able to acquire on the market the increasingly specialist men and materials of war it 'meant the possibility of eliminating first the tumultous and anarchic feudal levies, which were also ineffectual, as the French defeats at Crecy, Agincourt and Poitiers show so clearly.'[75] These rulers became *primus inter pares.*

With time, with further capital formation, growth of the market and specialization, and with increasingly preferential access to the market, these dominant lords or kings secured a measure of sovereignty. 'States began to emerge about 900 AD; supposedly there were still 1,000 polities in the fourteenth century....by 1900 there were 25. What is noteworthy is that the core area is clearly traceable in many of the survivors. A large and fertile heart remained an advantage if one were to swallow rather than be swallowed up. Many lesser core-areas had disappeared in the raising of the average size of state.'[76]

Kings, who were the forerunners of the modern state, became eventually a critical element in the network of tensions that sustained Central Western Europe as the tribal pastoralism of the steppes was metamorphised into a capital-based, crop-growing agriculture. Kings had interests that were different from those of the castle and the cabin. They had a common interest with the lords in maintaining the political supremacy of a military,

191

aristocratic elite that protected property and, in return, took from the property owners a privileged share of the product. But they shared with the property owners a common interest in maximizing output and in minimizing the share of that output sequestered by the lords; for the less the lords took, the more there was available for the monarchs; and the less the lords got, the less able were they to compete in military and political power with the monarch — the fewer 'over-mighty subjects' there were.

Monarchic power in Central Western Europe also contained its own internal balance. The 1,000 or so petty states that emerged in early medieval Europe have been reduced over time to some 25. But the gradual consolidation of states has heightened rather than diminished the limitation of state sovereignty to specific, geographical boundaries beyond which lay similar political entities that incorporated a similar sovereignty. Central Western Europe never experienced the emergence of a monolithic political power that exercised an absolute authority, not only over those subjects close to the throne, but over all persons within the system's purview. The Chinese emperors, typically, ruled the whole of the 'middle kingdom', leaving the outlying regions to the barbarians. The separate, competing existence of other sovereign monarchs was an integral element of European sovereignty and of the network of tensions that sustained Central Western Europe's dynamic.

Geography helps to explain the persistence in Central Western Europe of numerous monarchs and the competition between them that was a factor in preventing the emergence of a single, powerful ruler who might have curbed the individualism, thrift and enterprise of subjects. The area's natural poverty did not yield the rich surplus of riverine states to support powerful rulers. The poverty of rulers meant that they were unable to exercise the centralizing role of riverine despots; nor could they move freely over the forested terrain as pastoral rulers did over the steppes and savannahs to dominate their exposed subjects. As a consequence political power remained decentralized, with many centres of power and the power held at any centre modest.

Feudalism, real and false. There were striking and informative parallels between the situation in feudal Europe and in contemporary Japan. Both societies, located respectively at the western and eastern extremities of the Eurasian land mass, were fragmented into innumerable tiny polities. Within these, the peoples were dichotomized into a mass of peasants and a castle-dwelling military elite. The military elites in both cases drew for their support on the peasants' produce and provided a measure of defence, of a mainly deterrent nature, for the peasant producers. That, however, is as far as the parallel runs. The differences were fundamental.

The term 'feudal' is frequently, though very incorrectly, applied to social conditions that are backward and unjust, but that lack the interdependence that was the essential feature of relationships between cabin and castle in Central Western Europe. 'Feudal' is especially applied to Japan in the 1,000 years or so prior to the Tokugawan Shogunate, which commenced in the sixteenth century.[77] This usage is incorrect and misleading. It fails to distinguish between the essentially mutual interdependence of cabin and castle in capitalist Central Western Europe and the absolute dependence of the individual on society, as represented by the *daimyos* or lords, in riverine cropgrowing Japan. Japan's narrow valleys and plains, with their alluvial or volcanic soils well watered by the summer monsoon, supported many more people than were needed to cultivate the soil. Labour's marginal product was zero: all the output accrued to land, sufficient only being left with the cultivators for their maintenance and reproduction. If one lord's or *daimyo's* peasants failed for any reason to reproduce themselves there was an abundance of population to flow in from surrounding, over-populated territories.

The existence in Central Western Europe and in Japan of a multiplicity of frequently warring statelets had different geographical causes as well as different social consequences. The fragmentation of political power in Europe was, as already argued, due principally to natural poverty. The fragmentation of political power in Japan was due to its archipelagaic topography. This, first, protected Japan from conquest by the neighbouring continental powers. Second, it divided the country into four principal islands, none of which could easily dominate the others. Finally, the islands in turn were fragmented by mountains into numerous small, isolated valleys and plains. None of these was sufficiently extensive to generate the wealth that would have been necessary to establish effective, enduring rule over the whole country, fragmented as that was into numerous petty polities, each of which drew power from its own large, local surplus. In Central Western Europe the fragmentation of political power increased the dependence of the castle on the cabin and reinforced the network of tensions that sustained the transformation of pastoralism into capitalism. In Japan it led to a thousand years of bloody civil war which held the country in long term stasis and which ended only as a result of western intervention. The Portuguese introduced cannons which, in Japan, as previously in Central Western Europe, were used to demolish castles and to establish the centralizing power of the Tokugawan Shogunate.[78]

Material and spiritual. A final element to be noted in the network of tensions that sustained the transformation of Indo-European pastoralism into European capitalism was that between north and south, between material and spiritual, between consumption here and consumption hereafter. The major role of the Church of Rome in post Roman Empire Europe reflected an almost universal phenomenon: the intellectual dependence of culturally less developed societies on the religious ideas of the civilised, crop-growing societies of lower latitudes. The monotheistic Judaism of the crop-growing Israelites evolved into Christianity, which first became the religion of the depressed classes of the decadent Roman empire and later became the religion of the unlettered pastoralists of Central Western Europe. Islam was another offshoot of monotheistic Judaism which satisfied the religious needs of the pastoralists of the Middle East, and of Africa as far as the equatorial forest and bush. The Hindu religious concepts that evolved from India's rich, crop-growing society satisfied the intellectual needs of the invading Aryan pastoralists as well as those of the peoples of Southeast Asia. Buddhism, another Indian religious creation, gained the adherence of the Tibetan and Mongolian pastoralists. Adoption of Christianity by the pastoralists of Central Western Europe was part of a general pattern of intellectual dominance of primitive peoples by the more advanced concepts of the civilized cropgrowers of the lower latitudes.

The prestige and residual authority of Rome reinforced the intellectual attractions of Christianity for unlettered northern peasants and for the military elite that they supported. The Church also had a monopoly of literacy further to secure its position in a barbaric age. There was, in any case, no overweening temporal power to curb the Church; the Caesars had gone down with Rome, and there was nowhere in Central Western Europe the great economic surplus that maintained in absolute power the Pharaoh in Egypt, the Inca in Peru, the Emperor in China and the Maharajah in India. There was, in Central Western Europe, both an intellectual and a political vacuum for the Church to fill. Not only did both the peasants and military elite accept the religious ideas of the Ancient Mediterranean, but they accepted, to a unique extent, a hierarchal organization of religion that left a substantial degree of control continuing to be exercised from *Roma aeterna,* the capital of the fallen empire.

The Church of Rome inherited much of the Ancient Mediterranean's preoccupation with law, its humanism, its concern for the individual, and much of the universalism of Rome, capital of a polyglot empire. But the Church's law was the law of *civitatis Dei*; it was the will of God for man's conduct on earth, which would secure for him eternal salvation in heaven. The Church's concern for the individual was as a creature of God possessing an eternal soul, which it was the Church's mission to guide towards eternal heavenly bliss. The Church, like the authority of imperial Rome, over-rode local interests in fulfilling a paramount mission. That mission was to secure the *pax Romana* in imperial times; and it was to establish God's order under the Church in post-Roman Europe. The Church recognized no superior authority as intervening between it and its followers, for whom it had the responsibility of preaching and demonstrating the path to salvation.

The Church contributed to securing a balance between the political power of the castle and the economic power of the cabin. It did so by emphasising the hierarchal character of society, with each layer subordinate and owing allegiance to the one above it. The peasant was subordinate to the lord, the lord to the king, the king to the emperor, and the emperor to God, the origin of all power and authority. This emphasis on hierarchy implied the exercise of authority in conformity with the will of God, the source of authority. The Church claimed to be the arbiter of God's will and it enforced that claim by excommunicating those who were deemed to have acted contrary to the will of God, as interpreted by the Church. The very real and cogent restraint that was thus imposed on temporal powers by the medieval Church may be gauged from incidents like the Penitence of Canossa in 1077 AD, when the Holy Roman Emperor, Henry IV, did public penance and yielded politically to Pope Gregory VII in order to be readmitted to membership of the Church; or the public penance of King Henry II of England in 1174 AD at the tomb of Thomas à Beckett in atonement for the archbishop's murder by the king's knights because of his defence of the Church's position against the crown's encroachments. It was not until the sixteenth century that west European monarchs found it safe to defy the collateral power of the Church of Rome. Henry VIII was the first English king to succeed in defying openly the claims of Rome to be able to make and to unmake kings and emperors (see Chapter 3).

The Church, while tempering the power of lords and kings, simultaneously preached the obligation of subjects to submit to an authority that derived from God, even when that authority was harsh. By curbing lords' power and by enjoining obedience on subjects the Church contributed to a more orderly and less violent society. It was a society in which the power of rulers, already curbed by economic and topographical considerations, was further restrained by religious sanctions; and in which religious sanctions also enjoined the ruled to submit without the use of force. The Church thus helped to prevent Europe from slipping into the unceasing, ubiquitous, internecine conflict that characterized pastoralist Africa.

The insistence on hierarchal order created conditions favourable to the rule of law and therefore favourable to property. The Church, more directly, favoured property by preaching that as property is essential for human well-being it must have been ordained by God and is therefore divinely sanctioned. Infringements on 'the sacred rights of property', either by lords and kings through excessive taxes or other exactions or by subjects by robbery or theft, were therefore equally immoral. Moreover the Church of Rome, long before the emergence of a 'Protestant ethic', preached the virtues of abstinence, of restricting current consumption in order to store up blessings for the future. There was a close consonance between what the medieval Church taught as the will of God and what the peasants strove for: to defer gratification now in order to save assets that would make possible greater future output. The conviction that in saving one was storing up blessings, not only in this but also in a future life, must have increased the incentive to desperately poor people to save and to alleviate their poverty in the future, on earth as in heaven.

The Church too powerfully influenced demographic practice. Human birth rates have normally been biologically determined. Women generally have had as many births as possible under their physical condition, as determined by such factors as age, nutritional level, suckling other infants, and so on. Attempts to reduce birth rates below their biological level, by continence, *coitus interruptus,* or induced abortion have been abnormal. Two main reasons can be identified for people not generally taking action to curb birth rates. The first is that, within the perception of any society in the past, population growth cannot have appeared to be a problem. Biologically determined birth rates were normally accompanied by equal death rates, giving rise generally to stable populations. The world's population grew at rather less than 0.1% annually up to 200 years ago. That was about one-thirtieth the rate of population growth in several poor countries now. The population growth rate was about one-sixtieth the current birth rate. People were much less aware of the imperceptible, long term growth of population than they were of the frequent catastrophic declines of population that were associated with epidemics, famines or wars. Understandably therefore, for most of human history, concern has been with depopulation rather than overpopulation.

A second major reason people were not generally concerned to limit birth rates was the generally subsistence standard of living. Poor people, preoccupied with the needs and insecurity of the present, have little opportunity for forethought; or to contemplate the future and to make provision for it. Poor people, in modern jargon, discount the future heavily. The virtually imperceptible and highly problematic future difficulties associated with a present action that may result in a birth cannot normally have had any influence on that action.

Birth rates, therefore, have normally been biologically determined and have been uninfluenced by poor peoples' concern about imperceptible, questionably undesirable consequences in a distant and largely irrelevant future. It is noteworthy therefore that western Europe alone appears traditionally to have had birth rates significantly below the biological limit. These lower birth rates were important for Europe's subsequent economic development. They were secured by institutional constraints; and the Church played an important part in imposing and maintaining those constraints.

People's virility, productivity and fertility have normally been closely correlated. This was, and is, clearly so in hunting-gathering societies. Pastoral societies have traditionally made provision for members, on approaching adulthood, to acquire some of the clan's or sept's livestock so that they might have the means essential for a more-or-less independent social subsistence. Young people, with a hoe and a bucket of seed in riverine crop-growing societies, could pay as much tax as older people and so could acquire land, forcing out older people whose productive powers had waned. Access to capital was the condition of production in post-Roman western Europe. The individual without capital was less productive than anywhere else.

Young people in medieval Central Western Europe, where society was structured and deeply concerned to protect property rights, did not have customary rights to a portion of the family stock, as young people had in less structured, pastoral societies elsewhere. Crop yields were so low that the cultivator without capital got less than maintenance. Growth of population had reduced the product per person secured from hunting and gathering to a precarious supplement to a diet procured overwhelmingly from crop-growing, with hunting and fishing being increasingly reserved as a sport for the aristocracy. Young people in Central Western Europe, to acquire even the rudimentary independent economic existence that made marriage possible, were absolutely dependent on capital, either their own or that of their employers. Normally they had to wait to inherit, or to acquire by gift, the capital that their parents held with an absoluteness that reflected society's recognition of the economically vital role that capital played. The young people of Central Western Europe were as dependent for their existence on the society's property owners — who were mainly their parents — as were traditional pastoralists dependent on the tribe, or riverine cropgrowers on the absolute ruler, or the Ancient Mediterranean slaves on the slaveowners. Absolute dependence on capital implied that people could not marry until they acquired capital by saving, gift or inheritance; or until a prospective employer had done so. The result was the well known west European phenomenon of delayed marriages and a higher incidence of people who never married, which caused birth rates to be lower.[79] Lower birth rates were matched by lower death rates. This meant that people on average lived longer, that there was a smaller proportion of dependent people, and that society was therefore more productive.

The medieval Church, by its anathema on extra-marital sex, reinforced by religious sanctions the sex mores of an increasingly property-oriented society. The Church, as well as buttressing the powerful economic constraints on the birth rate, reduced the anguish caused by those constraints. It did so by making a virtue of necessity and by preaching the blessings in a future life of a celibacy that was in any case hardly avoidable in this one; and it offered, in its monasteries and nunneries, an honourable and secure life for that large section of the population who, while still virile, were unable to secure the economic basis for a married life of the style to which they were accustomed.[80]

The Church in the Dark Ages thus, in a variety of ways, eased the transition from tribal pastoralism to feudal, capital-based crop-growing. The principal contribution is seen as curbing the power of an encastled military elite who might otherwise have exercised a more arbitrary and retarding power over the productive population in their defenceless cabins. The Church simultaneously enjoined obedience on the people and in that way made it possible for society to operate with minimal use of force, the arbitrary exercise of which is incompatible with the formation of the capital on which the Central Western European crop-growing economy was entirely dependent. The Church, by preaching abstinence, encouraged saving; and by preaching celibacy, encouraged a lower birth rate, hence a lower death rate and a more productive population structure. In these ways, it contributed importantly to the unique, organic transformation of Indo-European pastoralism into Central Western European capitalist crop-growing.

Did the Church make the transformation possible? Or was it the organic transformation which occurred in Europe that made possible the medieval Church? This, of course, is the old issue of the extent to which the institutions created by society in turn shape society. The view taken here is that, given the environmental conditions of the place and time, the current of human advancement was virtually irresistible. Anything caught up in the flow of events would have been swept along, adding to the momentum, unless it was of truly momentous scale, when it might have dammed the flow and turned it back upon itself, as has been the case with all societies other than Central Western Europe's. A temperate climate, extensive forests growing on arable land, lactose tolerant pastoralists who were skilled in metallurgy and knew about crop-growing, were conditions that provided scope for man's search for fulfilment, to raise himself above an animal-like level of maintenance and reproduction. The social forces let loose were unlikely to be easily contained. The medieval Church did not contain them. Rather, by channelling those forces in favourable directions, it gave impetus to them. The Church, in doing so, secured a place for itself in European and world history.

Appendix B

Patterns of Capitalist Colonialism

The central theme of this book is that the persistent undevelopment of countries that contain almost half of the world's population is the result of contact, through capitalist colonialism, between two fundamentally different cultural categories. The distinctive natures of these separate cultural categories have been discussed in Appendix A. The present examination is concerned to understand the manner of the cultural contact that occurred, through the process of capitalist colonialism. That understanding is sought by pursuing eight separate, revealing threads through the vast, tangled skein of capitalist colonialism. These threads are: (1) motivation; (2) sequence and timing; (3) manner of interaction; (4) land appropriation; (5) race and ascendancy; (6) the nature and role of property; (7) socio-economic consequences of colonialism; and (8) the ending of colonialism.

Motivation

The spread of European influences westward and southward over a broader world was in response to motives that were different from those that had given rise to all earlier colonial expansions. Athens and Rome expanded in order to secure the slaves that were necessary to sustain their economies. Other empires were an expression of society's omnipotence, as personified in their despotic rulers, and of their insistence on bringing all those within range into subservience. Such was the case with the Egyptian Pharaohs who brooked no competing power on the Nile below the cataracts. Such too was the case with the Chinese emperors, who sought to rule the whole of the 'middle kingdom'; and with the Incas, who were extending their sway over the hunter-gatherers in the Chilean Altiplano when Pizarro arrived. Genghis Khan was in the same tradition when he fought and plotted to establish the Mongol empire in a great arc from the South China sea to the Adriatic sea.

The motivation for European colonialism was much more complex. That complexity reflected the whole network of tensions that sustained the organic transformation of tribal pastoralism into individualistic capitalism over millenia in the forest of Central Western Europe. It included the special need of European monarchs for plunder to enable them to exercise their kingly roles, without trenching on that property which was the basis of the European economy and which it was the primary function of kings and feudal lords to protect. Securing revenue, especially in the form of the precious metals, was an over-riding preoccupation of Renaissance rulers. These revenues had become critically important in the later stages of feudalism, as the pace of economic and technological change accelerated. The market-place alone could supply the skilled, disciplined men and the increasingly sophisticated equipment needed to survive as a political entity in the later stages of feudalism. The absolute monarchies which emerged at this stage were based on access, through money, to the market. As Louis XIV declared, and confirmed for himself, 'after all, it is the last louie d'or which must win'.[1] But an access to markets that was secured by taxing capital threatened to drive out the footloose capital that was the basis of European wealth; or to precipitate revolt by Europe's individualistic property owners:

> If one leaves aside religious movements, it is striking that most of the rebellions in European states from the fourteenth to the seventeeth, and even eighteenth century, were tax revolts...the importance of fiscal rebellions has not been understood, and this despite the impressive number of tax revolts, several hundred in France under the single ministry of Richelieu.[2]

The sovereigns of Castile and Aragon were singularly successful in acquiring the specie that gave them access to the increasingly important market, without simultaneously antagonising property by taxing it. They secured these resources by conquering the non-pastoral, unwarlike Aztecs and Incas and plundering from them the great wealth of Mexico and Peru. The English Tudor dynasty achieved much the same objective by confiscating the valuable Church lands (Chapter 3). But whereas the Spaniards conquered and held Mexico and Peru with a handful of *conquistadores,* the Tudors, in securing their western flank in the new maritime age, lost, in the bogs and woods of Ireland, most of the wealth they had plundered from the Church.[3] The result in Spain was an autocratic state that stifled development for centuries; and in England, an impoverished monarchy that was quickly forced to come to terms with the contemporary world's most powerful group of property owners — England's landed proprietors. The outcome of that clash was the first modern, progressive, property owners' state (Chapter 3).

It was typical of the complex character of Europe's evolved society that, after plunder, perhaps the salvation of souls was the next most powerful motivating force of European colonialism. The major role of spiritualism in European culture has already been considered (Appendix A). It is not surprising therefore that the cross and the bible went hand in hand with the sword and the gun in the frequently bloody spread of European culture. For example, great store was placed by the Spanish *conquistadores* in converting the Inca, Atahuolpa, to Christianity so that, when stripped of his power and of the millions of pounds worth of Inca gold and silver and then garrotted, his soul should go to the Christians' heaven. This concern of westerners with the salvation of souls continues, in the post-colonial era, to be a major factor in inculcating western culture in non-western situations.

After specie and souls, the next major concern of European colonialism was profit. Profit initially was made by procuring for Central Western Europe the exotic products of the lower latitudes and the refined manufactured goods of the great riverine societies, especially Indian textiles and Chinese porcelain. As capital was accumulated, output expanded in Central Western Europe, while other economies moved in unchanging cycles (Appendix A). The value of European goods inescapably declined in terms of non-European goods, and the potential profit from a trade between Central Western Europe and the settled areas of the non-European world increased.

The manner in which slavery became profitable once more in the western economy was a particularly revealing and important aspect of the deterioration of the terms of trade between European temperate zone products and exotic tropical and semi-tropical products. Slavery was unprofitable at all times in Central Western Europe, where capital limited output and where hoe-based cultivators produced less than their maintenance needs (Appendix A). However, once the value of tropical products, grown by hoe-cultivating slaves in the Caribbean islands, exceeded the cost of the temperate foods required for their maintenance, plus shipping costs, slavery became profitable for Europeans again. The most important part of colonial trade in the seventeenth, eighteenth and well into the nineteenth centuries, was in slaves, in provisions for slaves and in slave-grown produce.

The decline in the significance of slavery in the European colonial system owed as little to humanitarian reasons as its decline in the Ancient Mediterranean did to the rise of Christianity. The decline in both cases was dictated by economic considerations. Slavery disappeared in Europe because the Ancient Mediterranean could no longer get slave replacements; and it never was a feature of Central Western Europe because slaves could not maintain themselves there. Slavery in the European colonial system began to decline with Britain's ban in 1809 on the slave trade. By then the mercantile age, with its preoccupation with preserving small and vulnerable domestic metropolitan markets by excluding competing, temperate zone goods and importing only non-competing tropical products, had given way to the era of factory capitalism. Then the key to success became scale of production, to be secured especially by free trade. The metropolitan powers, at that stage, could trade freely with the great economies of the east, knowing there was nothing any longer to fear from the cottage industries of India and China. In the era of factory capitalism, once the low cost, rice-fed labour of the east was thus integrated into the European colonial system, there was neither need for, nor profit in, kidnapping Africans for enslavement in the West Indies, where they laboured on relatively infertile soil and were fed on temperate zone foods that became relatively expensive from the mid-eighteenth century onwards.[4] The rise and fall of slavery thus mirrored the shift in the preoccupation of the metropolitan economies from the procurement of complementing tropical products, in the earlier mercantile phase of colonialism, to procuring markets in the later phase of free trade, factory capitalist colonialism.

A fourth important motivation for the spread of European individualistic capitalism may be noted. This applied especially to England, where land had been appropriated for grazing. It was the age old Central Western European settler drive of moving into the wilderness to escape the exactions or regulations of established society. That could best be done in those extensive areas of the world where, until well into the eighteenth century, the land was occupied by hunter-gatherers. These regions, like Central Western Europe's forest wastes in the past, offered little prospect of profit and were therefore of little interest to Europe's monarchs, traders or investors. They were left to European settlers. 'Until the end of the eighteenth century, European authorities regarded all these outposts in much the same bleak light. They entered them, if at all, with extreme reluctance and for the purpose of advancing their interests in quite different parts of the world.'[5]

Strategic considerations provided the fifth, and last to be considered here, of the motivations for the spread of European colonialism. As Denoon observed, European authorities entered certain unpromising regions 'with extreme reluctance and for the purpose of advancing their interests in quite different parts of the world'. That was the strategic motivation. An important case was the Spanish control of the cone of South America (modern Chile and Argentina) where, apart from scattered groups of agriculturists on the river Paraguay, the population were hunter-gatherers who offered no prospect of profit. Spain deemed that control of this unprofitable region was strategically essential for the security of its rich Peruvian empire.[6] The need for a staging post on the long voyage to and from the East Indies was the Dutch motivation, in the seventeenth century, for colonizing the Cape of Good Hope, which was then populated by the hunting-gathering Khoikhoi. Securing the route to its Indian empire motivated the British in the nineteenth century to extend their influence from the Cape province far northwards into Africa and also to secure control of the Suez Canal and of Egypt.

Sequence and Timing

The sequence and the timing are the second of the illuminating threads woven into the pattern of European colonialism. These were determined by the resources and needs of the metropolises, which were changing at an ever faster rate as capitalist growth accelerated.

The Atlantic basin, and more particularly the western hemisphere, was the principal sphere of European colonial activity during the first quarter millenium of its existence, from around 1500 to around 1750, or the commencement of the industrial revolution. European resources, during that earlier period, were inadequate to intervene to much effect east of the Cape of Good Hope:

> The previous experience of the Portugese, the Dutch and the British had shown that Europeans were not yet in a position to enforce their claims even against minor rulers. The Dutch came up against the Raja of Trevencore in 1739 and the battle ended in disaster for the Netherlanders...In the trading period, 1610-1758, Europe influenced Asia but little.[7]

Marshall articulated the contrast being made here between the Atlantic basin and Asia:

> In the early centuries of overseas expansion, Europeans trading in Asia were in a very different situation to those in the western hemisphere. Rather than creating their own economic systems, they had to adapt themselves to complex and sophisticated economies which had been flourishing for centuries and into which Europeans were unable to introduce major changes before the nineteenth century. In America Europeans brought their own capital and labour to develop mines, ranches and plantations.[8]

It was not until the late eighteenth century that European resources grew great enough and powerful enough to do more than establish entrepots and forts east of the Cape of Good Hope.

It was not until a century later still that the metropolitan European powers, hungry for markets and laden with capital, were tempted to colonize Africa generally. Africa had little, apart from slaves, to attract profit-seeking colonists, and what wealth it had, it guarded with the militancy that had prevented cattleowners from using their animals to grow crops and to produce wealth (Appendix A): 'Africa was the bottom of the imperialist barrel.'[9]

Interaction with the Indigenes

A third revealing thread which gets to the core of European colonialism is the manner in which the colonists interacted with the indigenes. These were mainly, or exclusively, hunter-gatherers in America north of the Rio Grande; in Africa from the Cape of Good Hope eastwards to the Drakensberg mountains and northwards to the Limpopo river; and in Australia and New Zealand. There the colonists, mainly from land-hungry Britain, moved in and virtually exterminated the native peoples, who thereafter effectively ceased to influence events in these settler colonies. This was the pattern of behaviour established since man became a food producer. Wherever the food producers wanted land they took it and exterminated the indigenous hunter-gatherers. The process continues now in South America and Southeast Asia, where the 'tribalists' are pushed out to make way for the agriculturists.

The settlers appropriated what land they needed and, like the earlier European peasants who had moved into the forest wilderness of Central Western Europe, they were left very much to their own devices by the established authorities; the feudal lords of ancient Europe and the metropolitan governments in the age of European colonialism.

The pattern of colonial interaction with farming indigenes was different. Where there were farmers and where therefore there was the prospect of metropolitan profit, a colonial regime was established and sustained by the metropolitan powers. That pre-eminently was the case in the Americas south of the Rio Grande, where the Messo-American agriculturists had tapped the rich mineral wealth of the Andes mountains and their Central American extension. This generalization holds true for the southern cone of Latin America where, apart from those on the Paraguay river, there were no farmers:

> From first to last, the Spanish dominions in the Americas were controlled with the object of providing an income for the leading institution of Spain, the Crown of Castile...The first development of productive and commercial activities in what is now Argentina was connected with the mining industry of what was then the Viceroyalty of Peru.[10]

That pattern of behaviour also held true in the case of of India and in most of Africa. Denoon also makes this point:

Exceptions could be cited, but in general nomadic people (i.e. predominantly hunter-gatherers) have been lucky to survive the shock of European settlement, whereas the complete annihilation of settled communities has rarely been adopted and even more rarely accomplished. A general explanation...would place more emphasis on the circumstances of the conquered community, in particular the greater capacity of agricultural communities, with their denser populations, to defend themselves and *the relative ease with which agricultural societies can be 'squeezed' after conquest to provide labour, or commodities, or tribute.*[11] (Italics added).

The term 'capitalist colonies' is used here to refer to those situations where the indigenous societies were agricultural, to 'be "squeezed" after conquest, to provide labour, or commodities, or tribute'. It is used particularly to distinguish these situations from the 'settler colonies', where the indigenes were hunter-gatherers and 'were lucky to survive the shock of European settlement', where the land was appropriated and settled by migrating Europeans, especially British, and where there was little prospect of profit for metropolitan interests.

Land Appropriation

The practice in relation to land appropriation is the fourth of those revealing threads to be considered here in the pattern of European colonialism. Land was not normally appropriated from indigenous agriculturists. In Asia and in most of Africa, where the indigenes were agriculturists, the colonials were content to secure the pinnacles of power, so to speak, and to leave the overseeing and operation of land to the indigenes. When in these cases land was appropriated and planted by Europeans, it normally represented only a small proportion of the area concerned. 'Even by the 1970s, only about one-fifth of the total area of Peninsular Malaysia has been alienated.'[12] Of the land that had been alienated for crop-growing in this most intensively colonized country, most had gone to local, non-European people.

The appropriation of land by the Spanish *conquistadores* from the agriculturists of Latin America was, therefore, a practice that was not normally followed in subsequent capitalist colonies. The special circumstances of Latin America help to explain the disparity. As noted already, unlike the farmers of the Old World, the indigenes of Latin America had not integrated domesticated ruminants into their farming, apart from the limited case of llanas and alpacas in the Andean highlands. That appears to account for the remarkable docility of the Latin American agriculturists and the ease of their conquest. Conquest and subjugation through the *encomienda* system entailed the granting of land, together with its inhabitants, to the *conquistadores* and their successors. People, as much as land, were assigned by the Spanish colonial power to the grantees. The purpose of the grants was to mobilize the land and people of the empire to tear the precious metals from the Andean mountains to sustain the decaying Spanish monarchy. The exceptional combination of a docile Indian people and the mineral wealth of the Andes, made it advantageous for the colonial power to enforce the expropriation of the land of Latin America from its agricultural indigenes. These, however, were left in effective possession, while passing the land's surplus over to the creole landed proprietors.

In addition to (1) the appropriation of land by settler colonists from hunter-gatherers; (2) the general practice of leaving the ownership and operation of land to indigenous agriculturists to be "squeezed" .. to provide labour, or commodities, or tribute'; and (3) the exceptional appropriation of land, together with its agricultural indigenes, in Latin America, there was a fourth procedure. That procedure, which was followed in five separate instances, was the appropriation of land from indigenous agriculturists and its subsequent operation by settler farmers from the metropolises. This was the same procedure as that of the first noted above, except that the indigenes were agriculturists rather than hunter-gatherers; and they were not exterminated. Under this procedure, the settler agriculturists from the metropolises usually employed the dispossessed indigenous farmers and their offspring as paid labourers.

Four of the five cases in this pattern of land appropriation occurred in Africa. In chronological order, the first of these four African cases was in the eastern parts of the Cape Province of South Africa: in Natal and the Transvaal where the Boer farmers, following the Great Trek through the savannahs occupied by the mainly hunter-gathering Khoikhoi, appropriated land that had been farmed by Bantu peoples. The second occurred in Algeria, following the conquest of that territory in the 1830s, when French *colons* appropriated and operated the land of the indigenous Arabs and Berbers. The third in sequence was Rhodesia/Zimbabwe, seized by the British South African Company in the 1890s. The last was the White Highlands of Kenya, which occurred mainly between 1903 and 1911, and again in the years immediately after the First World War. The fifth, and only non-African, case of this form of colonial land appropriation was chronologically the first and occurred in Ireland. There, under the Plantation of Ulster (1603-25), settlers from Scotland and northern England moved in to operate the land of six Irish counties from which the indigenous Irish agriculturists had been cleared.

Special circumstances accounted for these five exceptional cases. The South African case was only one of two situations where metropolitan settlers, on land appropriated from hunter-gatherers, came into contact with indigenous agriculturists. The other was on the Rio Grande in North

America, south of which was the territory of the Aztecs and other Messo-American agriculturists.

Military adventurism had become much more dangerous and less feasible in nationalist, post-revolutionary and post-Congress of Vienna Europe. The glory that the lacklustre, bourgeois king, Louis Philippe, badly lacked had therefore to be sought outside Europe. The North African Maghrib, the closest non-European territory, though occupied by Arab and Berber agriculturists, promised to fit the bill safely, easily and profitably.[13]

The drive into the lightly wooded,largely tsetse-free Rhodesian plateau by the British South African Company in the 1890s fitted into the broader British colonial strategy of dominating the route to India. That strategy was perceived as involving control of east Africa 'from the Cape to Suez', the two strategic points that dominated the route. The drive northwards in the 1890s was fed by the wealth of the gold from Johannesburg and of the diamonds from Kimberley; and by the megalomania of Cecil Rhodes, who had cornered a large part of that wealth:

> The south to north drive of the British prevailed not because of its superior rationality but because they carried bigger guns and because an eccentric idealist multi-millionaire was at hand to give it a forward push at a critical time — a time when common sense personified by Goschen, Salisbury's Chancellor of the Exchequer, was unwilling to find a mere two thousand pounds for its incidental expenses.[14]

The clearance of the Maasai pastoralists to make way for British settlers on Kenya's equatorial plateau was one of the final gestures of European colonialism. Initially it formed part of British strategy to contain German colonial expansion in East Africa, which threatened communications with the Indian empire. Later it appeared to be an easy and inexpensive way of rewarding officers from a victorious army, especially as the colonial power had now the authority to resettle the displaced pastoralists in neighbouring Tanganyika which, as a result of the First World War, passed from German to British control.

The Plantation of Ulster, as well as being the earliest case of settler metropolitan farmers replacing indigenous farmers, was also the only non-African one. The particular circumstances that obtained in this case were, first, the need to secure firmly the Gaelic, tribal bastion of Ulster, which had most successfully resisted the earlier Norman penetration and which had fought most stubbornly against the Tudor conquest. Second, there was the possibility, even in the early seventeenth century, of getting substantial numbers of Scotch and English farmers, who were squeezed by the encroaching 'sheep [which] do eat up men', to transfer across the narrow straits from Dumfries in Scotland to Down in Ulster. There was, finally, the consideration that a relatively easily, but firmly planted Ulster would make more secure the metropolisis's control over the whole island.

Racial Ascendancy

The role and character of the garrison, or ascendancy, classes that existed in all capitalist colonies is the fifth aspect of European colonialism to be considered. This class was established and maintained by the metropolitan powers, the superior interests of which the garrison class served. The class members acted as the metropolis's agents in the colonies. Such were the creoles of Latin America, who were persons of European origin but born in the colonies. They were, in many cases, the descendants of the *conquistadores* and the proprietors, through the *encomienda* system, of the lands and people of the region. Such too were the proprietors, managers and agents of the West Indies' plantations, who depended absolutely on the metropolitan European countries for markets for their tropical produce, food for their slave labour, and force to control the slaves. For slavery in the West Indies was very different from slavery in the Ancient Mediterranean or in *ante-bellum* North America. In the latter cases, it was a supplementary source of labour and the slave population did not normally exceed the free population. The slave population of the West Indies, producing wealth for distant capitalists in Europe, outnumbered the local free population of the West Indies by as much as ten to one.[15] Slavery on that scale, which maximized metropolitan profits by minimizing costly, white supervisory labour was only possible by the application of metropolitan force.

The maharajahs, rajas and — especially after the Mutiny of 1857 — the collectors of land taxes, or zamindars, were the local auxiliaries of the British troops, civil servants and business people in India. It was these who garnered the great wealth of the subcontinent for metropolitan profit.

The creoles of Latin America, the slaveowners and drivers of the West Indies, the colonial administration and senior management in South and Southeast Asia and in the African colonies were all distinguished from the indigenes by their white, Caucasian skins. The colour difference facilitated control of many by few. Thus purchased African slaves were more attractive than felons from Europe, though these were delivered free, to West Indian plantation owners. 'The Irish in particular were a serious nuisance to the authorities. As early as 1644, well before the influx of Irish transported on the instruction of Cromwell began, an act was passed [by the Council of the Barbados] "for the prohibition of landing Irish persons...and such others as are of the Romish religion".'[16] Irish and other transported white labourers regarded as liberators hostile European forces when these attacked the island colonies. The white convict labourers made common cause with the invaders in assaulting the garrison. Understandably, therefore, the Council of Barbados in 1690 decreed: 'We desire no Irish Rebels may be sent us, for we want no labourers of that Colour to work for us; but men in whom we may confide to strengthen us'.[17]

Ireland was exceptional in being the only European capitalist colony where the colonizers and the colonized were of the same Caucasian race. Religion played in Ireland the role of race in the other capitalist colonies: that of distinguishing the garrison from the garrisoned (Chapter 4).

Property

The quintessentially European institution of property was the nexus that bound the colonial garrison, ascendancy classes to the metropolitan interests which they served. Metropolitan Spain enforced the titles of the creoles to the land and peoples of Latin America. France, England, the Netherlands and Denmark secured the property of their nationals — their agents — in the lands and slaves of the West Indies. In riverine India, where rulers had exercized absolute power, there could as a result be no concept of law or of property which depends on law. 'The Asian condition was summed up...as "property is insecure". In this one phrase the whole history of Asia is contained.'[18] The English raj brought the rule of law and conferred secure titles to land on its agents, the maharajahs, rajas and zamindars. Lord Cornwallis, the eighteenth century Governor General, was 'on dubious grounds when he insisted upon seeing the zamindar, the Bengal tax-farmer, as a landowner in the English sense. This represented a total misunderstanding of the Indian system of land tenure...But Cornwallis, in a laudable attempt to regularize the tax system, fastened the "Permanent Settlement" upon Bengal in 1793.'[19] From the newly created proprietors of India's land the English raj collected taxes which initially amounted to a third of the gross produce, though that proportion declined over time.[20] These land taxes were for long the principal source of revenue for the administration of Britain's Indian empire. The most important product, and one of the most enduring, of that administration was 'the imposing and truly magnificent legal structure, under which the 483 million people of India, Pakistan and Burma have lived during the past one hundred years [and which] has changed the basis of society in a manner which few people realize.'[21] Law and property, both inextricably mixed, were the major part of the West's heritage to India.

Property was in capital in Central Western Europe, with the significant exception of England (see Appendix A; Chapter 3). Throughout those colonies where the indigenes were agriculturists — and therefore were not exterminated — property was created by the colonials in land. These ex-colonies now comprise the Third World. Where the land was superabundant (in Latin America) property in the land's occupants was also created through the *encomienda* system. This vast expansion of property in land in the colonies was a very different process from the unique and spontaneous, though hesitant, evolutionary emergence of property in English land under the Tudors (Chapter 4). In time the latter was to put the 'great' into Great Britain; the former has been an insurmountable barrier to progress.

The metropolitan powers conferred on their local agents, and sustained for them, titles to the lands of those colonies that had agricultural indigenes and from which, therefore, there was a prospect of metropolitan profit. This applied also to the southern cone of Spain's Latin American empire which, though populated almost entirely by hunter-gatherers who could not be 'squeezed', was a jealously guarded outpost of the immensely wealthy Peruvian territory.[22] That metropolitan-maintained military presence made possible in due course the extension of property in the hunter-gatherer land of Latin America's southern cone. By the mid-nineteenth century, 'as a result of the distribution of vast tracts of public land by Rivadavia (to secure collateral for a British loan) and Rosa (to reward his supporters) the large private *estancia* had become an established feature of the country.'[23]

There was no prospect of metropolitan profit in the other settler colonies where the indigenes were hunter-gatherers. These territories were America north of the Rio Grande; South Africa eastwards to the Drakensberg mountains and northwards to the Limpopo river; and Australia and New Zealand. Without prospect of metropolitan profit, there was minimal metropolitan intervention with the settlers, who followed the millenia old Central Western European practice of moving, with their 'penny capitals', into the wilderness, there to hack out a new life for themselves. Metropolitan intervention in the affairs of the settler colonies was characterized, as Edmund Burke observed, 'by an easy and salutary neglect,'[24] which was in sharp contrast to the rigorous control exercized, for example, by Spain over its mineral-rich Peruvian domain.

Princely grants of land were made in colonial North America. But without an effective army of occupation, for which the settlers were unwilling and probably unable to pay, and from which England, the colonial power, could expect no commensurate return, the land grants were worth little more than the paper on which they were written. Effective occupation was the only generally recognized title to North American land, as it had been to land in Central Western Europe.[25]

The South African Boers, chafing under metropolitan control in the Cape, escaped from that control by trekking eastwards and northwards with their ox-wagons and the rest of their 'penny capitals' to the semi-arid areas now known as the Karoo, the Orange Free State and the Transvaal. The agricultural Bantu races, moving southwards, had not occupied these regions, which were too arid to support a Bantu agriculture that was of relatively recent origin and had only partly exploited its pastoral potential (Appendix A). The Bantus of southern Africa were lactose malabsorbent and so could not get full nourishment from their milking animals.[26] Thus, they do not drink the milk of goats, as true pastoralists do, even though goats are the animals most suited to the region and are their most numerous stock (Appendix A). Like all subSaharan Africans they did not use their cattle for draught. They were thus less well adapted to farm the savannahs of southern Africa than the lactose tolerant Boers, who did use their cattle for draught (Appendix A). 'A strong Boer [in the Orange Free State] will have thirty, forty or perhaps fifty acres of cultivated land around his house — including his garden.'[27] Trekking eastwards and northwards from the Cape, the Boers, like the North American settlers, appropriated and occupied the land that had previously been inhabited by the predominantly hunting-gathering Khoikhoi. As traditionally in Central Western Europe and as contemporaneously in North America, effective occupation was the basis of titles to this land.

In Western Australia there was the well known case of Thomas Peel, second cousin of Robert Peel, the English prime minister, who organized and financed settlement in the new colony of Swan River. The expectation was that, on arrival in Australia, the settlers would operate and pay rent for land that the entrepreneur had previously been granted. The rent would constitute a return on the cost of transporting the settlers from England. 'He landed 300 settlers, and spent altogether £50,000 but in a very little time his stock had wasted away, and most of his settlers had left him.'[28] Subsequent efforts to colonize Australia by financing emigration through land sales, as advocated by Wakefield and the Colonisation Society, were also undermined by the ease with which the need to purchase land was avoided by moving beyond the limits of officially settled locations.[29] Without metropolitan intervention to create and to enforce property titles, land in the settler colonies remained, as in Central Western Europe, free or virtually free. That relatively easy access to and abundance of land in Central Western Europe and in the settler colonies persists and is manifested now by such phenomena as the USA's 'land bank' and the EEC's policy of land retirement.[30]

The European institution of property in the settler colonies, free from outside intervention and on a *tabula rasa,* acquired there an essentially Central Western European character. Spontaneously evolved property in the settler colonies, as in Europe, took the forms of property in people (slavery) and in things (capital). Property in the capitalist colonies, by contrast, has been predominantly in land, with little property in capital or — apart from Latin America and the Caribbean — in slaves. People generally in capitalist colonies have been free; often they have been free to starve.

Consequences of Colonialism

Yet another revealing thread in the history of European colonization were its socio-economic consequences. Everywhere, as with all successful colonizations, the interests of the colonized indigenes were subordinated to those of the colonists. The same thing had happened when the agriculturists spread and appropriated territory that had previously been held by hunter-gatherers, so that, of the original population of these 10,000 years ago, which is estimated to have been around ten millions, only 250,000 now survive.[31] It happened in Ireland when the farming *Tuatha de Danann* of megalithic times exterminated the hunter-gatherers who had occupied the island some thousands of years earlier. It happened again when the lactose tolerant Celts arrived some millenia later and in turn exterminated the *Tuatha de Danann*.

The indigenous hunter-gatherers of the settler colonies were virtually exterminated, as they continue to be in South America, Africa and in Asia when the agriculturists want their land. The same principle of subordination to the superior interests of the colonists obtained in the capitalist colonies, where the indigenes were agriculturists, though the consequences in practice varied according to circumstances.

The population of Latin America, which had been one of the world's largest concentrations of people when Columbus arrived there, was almost obliterated during the following two centuries as the Spanish metropolitan power mobilized the empire's manpower to tear silver and gold from the Andean mountains. When the gold and silver and the Spanish monarchy were all exhausted, the colonized people were suffered to survive and to compete against the colonists' cattle for access to the appropriated lands, as peasants did in Tudor England when, following the enclosures, 'sheep [did] eat up men'.

Once the price of tropical produce rose sufficiently in terms of temperate zone produce slavery became profitable again, as it had been in the Ancient Mediterranean. It was reintroduced by profit-seeking Europeans in the Caribbean. As in the Ancient Mediterranean, the Caribbean slaves did not reproduce themselves, but were replaced by the fresh captives of the slave traders who plagued Africa for centuries. But the conquest of India and the tapping of its vast, inexpensive, rice-fed labour from the late eighteenth century onwards made slavery less profitable and gave rise to interests in the metropolises that were hostile to the old Caribbean planter interest. The new interests based on the Indian empire succeeded more effectively than a belated humanitarianism, in 1809, in outlawing the slave trade that for centuries had plundered Africa of its population and had shipped millions of them to the Americas.[32] However, notwithstanding competition in tropical and semi-tropical produce from India and notwithstanding the cutting off of replacement slaves, Caribbean and American slavery continued to be profitable. Only now the profits were reduced by the need to give the slaves sufficiently more than 'work, food and punishment' to enable them to reproduce. This they did in the Caribbean, but more especially in the USA, where the *ante-bellum* slave population grew, without the benefit of immigration, at the then phenomenal rate of 2% annually.[33] Because it was part of the world capitalist system, Caribbean and American slavery, unlike Ancient Mediterranean slavery, could afford to reproduce its slaves. In doing so it refuted the misconception propagated by Weber, among others, that slaves are incapable of reproducing themselves.[34]

India's vastness, wealth and distance constituted a greater challenge than the Atlantic basin to early colonists. Its wealth of tropical produce and of finely worked manufactures was coveted by Europeans. Yet their own crude economy, built in the difficult northern forest, had little to offer in exchange, apart from the specie plundered from Latin America. Mercantile Europeans were the more reluctant to see their gold and silver flow to India in that some of the goods acquired there, particularly textiles, competed with their own emerging industry. This dilemma of early European colonialism had naturally suggested its own solution to an enterprising people, who were no more moral or amoral than others:

> The Directors (of the English East India Company) were advised by some ingenious people to conquer the territories, or plant colonies in the country, in order to avoid sending them so much bullion, but this idea was then regarded as 'altogether impracticable in respect of a long voyage, the diseases to which our people are liable in those hot regions, and the Power, Force and Policy of most Indian nations'. Of course that was in 1709 when Auranzeb ruled at the head of a united empire.[35]

The relationship between the metropolitan power, Britain, and India changed during the following eighteenth century. Firstly, Britain acquired the military capacity to conquer India. Once political control was secured, it was possible to order the economic affairs of the populous sub-continent almost as thoroughly as the affairs of the Caribbean islands, which effectively were large, slave-operated plantations. Anglo-Indian relationships were further changed by the fact that Britain's economic power grew *pari passu* with its military capacity. Britain's textile industry, now organized on factory lines, no longer feared competition from India's older, traditional, highly skilled craft industry. By the time that Britain was militarily strong enough to seize India, Britain's economy was strong enough no longer to be motivated primarily by considerations of seizing bullion or avoiding the payment of it. With the progress of the industrial revolution, India had become for Britain primarily a source of raw materials and a market for manufactured goods.

The one constant feature of the relationship between the colonies and the metropolitan powers was that the former were held so that they might serve the interests of the latter. In the early mercantile colonial period, those metropolitian interests were served, as noted already, by procuring from the colonies specie and tropical produce; and simultaneously, by excluding the temperate produce of the North American colonies, which would have competed with the metropolises and would have drained specie. The progress of the industrial revolution changed the needs of the metropolises and particularly those of Britain, the economically most advanced country. The protection of meagre profits by excluding competing products was no longer a primary concern. Procuring raw materials and markets had now become the main concern and, in the age of factory capitalism, these were best secured by free and unfettered trade with the colonies. William Gladstone, who was no imperialist and who never spent a shilling of public funds without a good return, understood this point clearly when he observed that while 'the passing of unwise and bad laws in foreign countries may greatly restrict and hamper the extension of your trade...with respect to a colony you have no such danger.'[36]

Free, unfettered trade between a capitalist colony and the metropolitan power could have only one outcome. Starting in the age of factory capitalism, as all such trade did, from the position where the metropolitan power had already established a comparative advantage in manufactured production, free trade emphasized the colony's dependence on primary production. Products made in factories located in metropolitan countries replaced those made by traditional craft and cottage industry in the colonies. Under nineteenth century free trade conditions and according to the principle of comparative advantage, the colonies concentrated on primary production, which was subject to decreasing returns; and the metropolises concentrated on manufacturing, which was subject to increasing returns. This was the 'so-called *pacte colonial,* the exchange of colonial primary produce for metropolitan manufactures and services.'[37] South and Southeast Asia ended the nineteenth century with smaller proportions of their workforces engaged in manufacturing and larger proportions in agriculture than at the beginning of the century. 'The proportion of the Indian population engaged in agriculture rose and that engaged in industry and commerce fell.'[38] The same was true of Latin America where, at this time, 'exports were developed at the expense of subsistence economic activities'.[39]

The demographic consequences of colonialism were, as noted, variable. Generally in the earlier mercantile phase, colonialism resulted in depopulation. That was the case in Latin America; in the Caribbean, where the slave population was worked too hard and fed too little to reproduce itself; and in Africa where slave-raiding exacerbated the depopulating effects of traditional cattle-raiding. At all times, up to the nineteenth century, European colonialism, as with all earlier colonizing, resulted in the extermination of indigenous hunter-gatherers. The last of the indigenes of Tasmania perished in 1876 and the last battle of extermination of the North American Indians was fought at Wounded Knee in 1890.

In contrast to the overall demographic experiences of the colonies, which varied considerably over the colonial period, there was an element in all colonial populations that at almost all times, in all colonies, expanded and prospered. That was the bourgeoisie. Property, or the concern of society to secure and defend the rights of individuals, even against society, to the exclusive enjoyment of specific resources, is an essentially European institution. Its spread and growth outside Europe accurately reflected the spread and penetration of European influence. The bourgeois property owners floated upwards on the expanding pool of property in the colonies. Such were the men and women of substance in Colonial America who, together with their property, the British Redcoats protected against indigenous Red Indians, against Spanish and French raiders, and against the local, colonial riff-raff. Such too were the creoles of Latin America, locally born persons of Spanish origin who, though never admitted to the highest colonial offices, which were reserved for Spanish-born persons, were heirs to the land and its occupants. It was this colonial bourgeois class that maintained the West Indian lobby, one of the most powerful of its kind, at the Westminster parliament throughout the eighteenth century. Property in India's rich land, created first by the 'Permanent Settlement' of 1793 and vested originally in the maharajahs and rajahs, increased and spread over time under the British raj and was shared by a broadening mass of indigenous proprietors of large and small properties. These properties ranged in value from the exclusive right of princes to the revenues of populous territories down to a tenant's right in a patch of ground.

The elite that emerged under capitalist colonialism in impoverished Africa was based more on educational advantage than on property in material goods. That educational advantage was secured in some cases as a result of position, like being the sons of chiefs; or as a result of exceptional talent; or because of such fortuitous circumstances as early contact with missionaries.[40] Whatever the cause, the educational advantage, once secured, created in Africa an elite as powerful and as thrusting as the property-based elites of other capitalist colonies.

However, property did play a role too in colonial Africa. Under colonial influence the ill-defined, collective, tribal titles to cattle became much more individualized and absolute. One consequence of that has been the increased polarization of rural Africa into those with cattle and those without.[41] Another has been the increased incentive and resources available to cattleowners to expand their herds, thus contributing to the overgrazing and deterioration of communal pastures.[42] A third probable consequence of applying European property concepts to African cattle stocks and the resultant concentration of ownership of those stocks has been an increase in polygamy as wealthier men have been able to pay more cattle to acquire more wives.[43]

The impact of colonialism on the peoples of the metropolises was scarcely less far-reaching than that on the colonial indigenes. Europe's increased wealth from plunder, trade and production overseas made possible greatly increased capital formation. Contact with a broader world helped to relax and often to dissolve some of the constraints that bound the ancient culture that had emerged so slowly from Europe's forest; and it not only permitted but required that culture to continue to evolve, though more rapidly. Colonialism did not cause the growth of European capitalism. Rather that growth, deeply rooted in the ecological, technological and historical conditions of Central Western Europe, caused colonialism. But like so many other factors in the complex European scene, colonialism accelerated capitalism's growth and was capitalism's most powerful propellant.

The process was not, however, sudden. The first quarter millenium of European colonialism was, in a sense, a gestation period — or perhaps more appropriately, a period of digestion. It took a quarter millenium, from the great voyages of discovery at the end of the fifteenth century until the mid-eighteenth century, for the new wealth and the new influences introduced by colonialism to dissolve and to relax sufficiently the accretions of millenia of European history; to permit the birth of a radically changed production system and all that that entailed in political, social and intellectual adjustment.

The reign of George III, from 1760 to 1820, may be regarded as the era of the English industrial revolution. It was a period during which the economic, political and social changes initiated by the Black Death of the 1340s and the appropriation of land for private profit (Chapter 3) finally culminated in an unprecedented burst of technological change, investment and expanding output. The reign was a transitional period, between the preceding mercantile age of cottage and craft industry and the succeeding liberal, free trade age of factory capitalism. The protection of meagre profits, by trading as far as possible only in complementary products like tropical goods, was of paramount importance in the earlier, mercantile age. The expansion of markets became of paramount importance in the later age of factory capitalism. That new age was marked by a miracle of economic growth that was contributed to in large measure by the great, good and unrepeatable fortune of it being possible almost to double the world's farmed area within a century. A large extension of the farmed area was possible in Russia because of the earlier subjugation of the Golden Hordes by Russian forces using western military technology: 'At the outset of the nineteenth century, the sown area in New Russia was estimated to have been 800,000 desiations, and in four Volga provinces one million desiations. In the 1860s, these figures had risen to six million and 4.6 million desiations respectively.'[44] In North America, in the pampas of Argentina, in South Africa and in Australia and New Zealand the farmed area was extended simply by exterminating or driving out the indigenous hunter-gatherers.

Land in lower latitudes, warmer and therefore inherently more productive, was brought into production with minimal capital, by the

Table A.2

World's Farming Area: Distinguishing between regions farmed in 1800 and those brought into farming since then.

		Million Hectares
Total area of world's crops and pastures:		4,540
Of which in:		
Americas (North + South):	1,169	
USSR:	607	
Oceania:	507	
South Africa:	96	
Sub Total:		2,379
(Brought into production mainly during nineteenth century)		
Balance, being land in production pre-1800		2,161

Source: FAO Production Yearbook, 1981, Vol. 35.

application in these settler colonies of the livestock and draught animal agriculture that had evolved in Central Western Europe. The result was an explosion in food production. This occurred at a time when public hygiene and medical science were still rudimentary so that, notwithstanding improved nutritional levels, death rates were only slowly brought down from traditionally high levels.[45] The result was that the population of Europe (exclusive of Russia), North America and Oceania increased by less than 1% annually during the nineteenth century, the period of its most rapid growth.[46] This was much less than the rate of expansion of the food supply available to it.

Economic growth, and especially the explosion of food production, enabled the masses of Central Western Europe and of the European settlements in the New World to secure what no masses anywhere had ever previously secured: living standards substantially above the subsistence level. The price of wheat in Britain declined by two-thirds while the general price level dropped by half between the opening and closing years of the nineteenth century. Average real incomes in Britain increased fourfold over the same period.[47] The masses of Central Western Europe and of European settlements in the New World were no longer exclusively preoccupied with the immediate problems of subsistence. The peoples of these areas were able to do what no proletariat mass had previously done: they could contemplate the future. In doing so they could perceive and consider the matter of propertyless proletariat having numerous children.* In increasing numbers, for the first time ever, they opted to restrict, by artificial control, birth rates that had previously been determined biologically. These declined generally from the mid-nineteenth century onwards.[48] With birth rates increasingly determined rationally rather than biologically, it has been possible for the peoples of Central Western Europe and of their overseas settlements to attain ever improving living standards and to aspire to a want-free status.

The Ending of European Colonialism

Its ending is the final aspect of European colonialism that needs to be considered here. That ending had begun almost before colonization was half done. England's North American colonies gained their independence in 1767, a little over 250 years after Europe's discovery of America, and 200 years before the general winding up of capitalist colonialism in the Old World. The ending of European colonialism had three basically similar characteristics that were common to all the colonies, whether settler colonies like America north of the Rio Grande or capitalist colonies like Latin America and the rest of the Third World. First, the bourgeois middle class, or elites, which had been created by metropolitan rule, was in all cases the element that led the challenge to that rule. They did so when their strength had grown sufficient to make them confident of their ability to maintain their position both internally and externally without metropolitan support; and when, at the same time, that strength and their self-confidence caused them to chafe against metropolitan control and tutelage.

Property in the European colonies generated the same sort of tensions as property did in Central Western Europe (Appendix A). The tension, in Central Western Europe, was between cabin and castle; in the colonies, it was between the property owners and elites, on the one hand, and the metropolitan powers on the other. The latter created and protected the status of the former, who acted as the local agents of metropolitan interests. This conflict between economic and political power, which was common to Central Western Europe and its colonies, did not, as has been seen, exist in the early days of the other individualistic society, the Ancient

---

*Europe's pre-industrial 'penny capitalists' also had incomes sufficiently above the subsistence level to allow them to contemplate the future. That future included the free labour of their children with the family capital, on which the children were more dependent than the coolie was on the riverine despot, or the slave on the slaveowner. Their free, lifelong labour made children no disadvantage to the 'penny capitalists' (Appendix A). The proletariat had no such prospect of gain from their children.

Mediterranean. Nor did the conflict exist in other non-individualistic societies, where all power lay with society and the individual was powerless (Appendix A). This conflict between economic and military/political power was first reconciled in England by the erstwhile feudal lords, turned landed proprietors, who captured the English state (Chapter 3). It was reconciled in mainland Europe when the French Revolution captured political power for the bourgeoisie. Where England had its civil war and France had its revolution to resolve the conflict between economic and political power, the colonies had their independence movements which sometimes became wars.

Europe's revolutions involved change in the social order necessitated by capitalism's essentially organic growth. A time came when the property owners grew sufficiently powerful to challenge, and to wrest political control from, the warriors. In Russia too organic change required change in the social order, with the Communist Party and the dictatorship of the proletariat replacing autocratic tsarist rule and the commissars replacing the nobles with their serfs. The colonial independence movements, by contrast, were concerned to conserve, and to remove the impediments to the further development of, a social order originally established in the colonies by the metropolitan powers. Independence movements were not generally protests against the established social order, but against what were perceived by the elites of that order as continued, unwarranted intervention by the metropolitan powers; which denied them the full potential benefits of the social order. Insofar as there was mass discontent, that discontent was deflected away from the social order and directed against the metropolitan power. The metropolitan power, rather than the social order it had established and protected in its early, vulnerable years, was perceived as the source of social evils. National independence rather than social reform was seen as the means to rectify the evils. Popular, mass independence movements, which sought to remove the curbs placed by the metropolitan powers on their bourgeois agents in the colonies, evolved in this way.

The second important characteristic that is common to all cases of the termination of European colonialism was the emergence within the metropolis of a strong opposition group that favoured the ceceding colonists viv-a-vis the metropolitan establishment. The third important characteristic that can be identified in all successful colonial independence movements is the existence of another party: one or more other metropolitan power that favoured the independence of a rival metropolisis's colony.

England's North American colonies were the first of the European colonies to secure independence. There the burghers who, with a modicum of English protection against hostile indigenes and their own lawless elements, and against the threat of French or Spanish attack from abroad, had acquired sufficient substance by the mid-eighteenth century to give them confidence in their own ability to protect themselves against internal and external attack. That self-confidence engendered impatience with continuing metropolitan tutelage which increasingly was perceived as infringing the rights of the property that the colonists had amassed. That impatience was succinctly expressed by the aphorism: 'no taxation without representation'.

The protest of the American colonists was heard sympathetically by the English Whigs. The Whigs were in the tradition of those elements of English society who had been foremost in opposing, in 1641 and again in 1688, the divine right of kings to rule; and in asserting instead the sacred rights of property. They continued to be highly suspicious of any exercise of the royal prerogative, or the exercise of arbitrary administrative government, especially when directed against property or its proprietors. The English Whig position in support of the American revolution and in opposition to the Tory government's attempts at its suppresion was perhaps best articulated by Edmund Burke, especially in his classic speech on the American revolution.[49]

The American revolutionaries, struggling against metropolitan English infringements on American rights — and especially property rights, by taxation without representation — were also supported by France. English and French rivalry had dominated the European and colonial scenes for a century. France, therefore, readily availed of the rebellion of the American colonists to strike at the traditional enemy.

The Central and South American colonies rebelled against their Spanish masters in a manner similar to that of the North American colonies. In the first phase of Spanish colonial rule in America, lasting for about 150 years:

> The ruling class was composed of men directly connected with Spain, integrated in the apparatus of the State and in key positions of control of the productive system that yielded the surplus transferred to the mother country. In the second phase the landowning class, having little connection with the mother country and strictly local horizons of interest, became increasingly important.[50]

After three centuries of colonial rule these creole *haciendados,* the locally born descendants of the *conquistadores,* were confident enough of their ability to maintain, without metropolitan support, their privileged position against the local masses. It was 'under the auspices of the creole elites in the more outlying regions' that the Spanish South American countries secured their independence.[51] Meanwhile and quite typically:

> The great mass of the colonial population, the mestizos and the Indians, paid little heed to the dramatic events transpiring across the seas and in their homelands....The great majority of the creoles, less educated and far more provincial (than the leaders) were disinclined towards any move that might upset the social order. They sided with the independence leaders because Spain had been overrun and because

of their class interest in displacing Spaniards who ruled in America.[52]

The success of the Latin American independence movement depended critically on the overthrow of the Bourbon monarchy in Spain by the invading armies of Napoleonic France and its replacement by a radical party that supported the rebellious colonists. Finally, Britain, the premier colonial power, then at war with France and occupied Europe, gave to the Latin American revolutionaries aid similar to that given by the French to their own North American rebel colonists 50 years earlier.

The Congress Party was representative of the 'western type middle class [that] in India came only with British rule'.[53] Congress grew more critical of, and hostile to, that colonial rule as the mass of Indian property expanded and as, by various reforms initiated by the British raj, its base broadened from the original small clique of maharajahs, rajahs and zamindars, to include the owners of burgeoning industrial and commercial capital; to include peasants who, under a liberal rule, had acquired various interests, including tenant rights in the land, which had not existed before the British;[54] and persons with tenure of more or less permanent official and semi-official employment. The Indian nationalist movement, *swadishi*, had earlier on been encouraged by the example of the Irish separatist movement. 'In the 1870s too India found entirely new champions in the Irish nationalists. ...By 1886 Dufferin was complaining to Lord Kimberley, the Secretary of State for India, that ''all the arts of Irish agitation had come to India''.'[55] Nationalism in both countries was founded on the simultaneous emergence to dominance of local bourgeoisie.

There was in Britain, by the time the issue of Indian independence came to a head, increasing antipathy to colonialism. That centred on the ascendant Labour Party and was best articulated by Strachey. Its British opponents, following Lenin's interpretation, perceived in imperialism:

> ...an undeniable connection between (i) the existence of highly developed capitalist societies creating surpluses, which their distribution of income made it difficult for them to invest profitably at home; (ii) a high rate of foreign investment, and (iii) the acquisition of much of the habitable globe by those societies as their colonies.[56]

Colonialism was an alternative to domestic income redistribution and to domestic investment. Decolonization was, therefore, a milestone on the road to a more equitable metropolitan society for which colonies would be unnecessary.

The foreign influence that was relevant in India's case and in the case of Asia generally was Japan and the USA:

> From the time of the first World War, the incipient nationalist movements in the non-European world profited substantially from the rivalries among the colonial powers, and the sudden collapse of the European empires after 1947 was to a large extent a consequence

of external pressures and of the impact of world politics. In Asia, neither Britain nor France nor the Dutch ever recovered from the blows inflicted by Japan between 1941 and 1945, while in Africa and the Middle East they were checked and forced into retreat by pressure from the USA.[57]

Russia, in a manner that was reminiscent of the fourteenth century Mongolian penetration through China as far as the South China Sea (Appendix A), acted as the external influence in Indo-China. One consequence of Russo-Chinese intervention in Vietnam was the quite exceptional concern of that country's independence movement to change the social order as well as to secure political independence. Reminiscent too of the millenia old conflict between the northern pastoral barbarians and the civilized Chinese cropgrowers has been the recent reassertion of Chinese independence from Russian influence, which has cut off the Vietnamese clients from their Russian patrons, in much the same way as Vietnam dropped out of the Mongolian empire in the fifteenth century.

The termination of European colonialism adhered to the same pattern in Africa. Educational advantage rather than property, as already noted, was the material basis of African nationalism, which culminated in independence. Better educated Africans found their advancement to higher positions in the colonial administration blocked by the established network, which reserved senior positions for expatriate, white officials, possibly of inferior quality. The:

> ...new elites and strata — wealthy, cash crop farmers, businessmen and managers, workers and intelligentsia — none of which had pre-colonial roots...formed political associations and parties and constituted the driving force...behind the movement for independence and national integration after independence.[58]

Virtually all parties in metropolitan Europe were, in the 1950s, disillusioned with colonialism. There was little opposition to African independence in a Europe that was, in any case, experiencing full employment and unprecedented prosperity. In some countries, like the Belgian Congo, there was precipitous haste to discard the responsibilities of colonialism, and chaos filled the resulting void. The principal foreign influence in the decolonization of Africa, along with the USA, was Russia. Russia, in Africa as in Vietnam, offered the possibility of a new social order to the independent colonies, as well as military and economic support to achieve independence. But the continental Russian power was less committed to securing change in the social order in Africa than it was in Indo-China, with which, through its quondam ally China, it had land contact.

Appendix C

The Capitalist Colonial Heritage: A Model of Undevelopment

Individualism out of Context

The significance of the individual has at all times been the distinctive characteristic of European culture. Referred to here as 'individualism' this was grounded on very peculiar ecological, technological and historical circumstances that have been treated of at length in Appendix A. Central to individualism has been the rule of law. This defines the relationship between individuals and society in a society where individuals are economically and politically significant. Law also creates and protects property which, again in a distinctive manner, has always been the basis of European production. However, the significance of the individual, the law that defined the individual's relationship to society, and the property that law created and protected have not been absolute, or immutable. These values, concepts and institutions evolved in Europe and adapted to changing circumstances and to the changing social requirements that were of the essence of 'the European miracle'.

The significance of the individual in the Ancient Mediterranean was based on slavery, which deprived slaves of every element of humanity and made them 'things that talk'. The slaveowner, but not the slave, had significance in the Ancient Mediterranean. Law defined the relationship between the citizen slaveowner and the city; and law created and protected the citizen's property in his/her slave, on whose labour the entire economy depended. In Central Western Europe, where capital, not slaves, was the basis of production, only those with capital had significance. The propertyless could not even justify their existence by labour, as the Mediterranean slaves did.

Like them, the propertyless of Central Western Europe were more dehumanized than the masses elsewhere; than the Egyptian fellahin labouring on the pyramids, or the Chinese coolie building the Great Wall, or any other masses in history. The dichotomy between the favoured individuals within the law and the masses outside the law is again distinctive and peculiar to European culture. It is the basis of the class war, which Marxists correctly perceive as an enduring dynamic in western society. But Marxists incorrectly generalize to the world scene where, outside Europe and the European settler colonies, individualism did not exist: and therefore, neither did the dichotomy between those protected by the law and those against whom the law was a protection.

Individualism, law and property were aspects of European culture that evolved and adapted over millenia in a specific European environment, in response to local needs and circumstances. Part of those circumstances were pressures and influences from outside, including for example, the Persian invasion of Greece in the fifth century BC; and the Ottoman assault on Vienna in the sixteenth century AD. But European society remained free to adapt to these and to other pressures, and its character was determined by such adaptation (Appendix A). Likewise, Europeans in the settler colonies of North America, South Africa and Oceania, built in those colonies societies that were similar to Central Western European society and that necessarily adapted to local circumstances in the absence of major intervention by the metropolitan powers (Appendix B).

Russia, Japan, Taiwan and Korea borrowed eclectically from western culture. Something similar happened, and continues in China. Western culture was established on the islands of Hong Kong and Singapore, where the handful of natives had less impact than the hunting-gathering aboriginees had on the development of the settler colonies, and western culture bloomed there (Appendix B).

Matters were very different in the capitalist colonies. There western culture was superimposed on indigenous, non-western, non-individualistic, non-capitalist cultures. That western culture was superimposed in order to secure benefit for the metropolitan powers and without reference to the needs or circumstances of the colonized. The superimposed western culture rooted and grew, under the protection and guidance, and for the profit, of the colonial power. The contrast between the spontaneously evolving culture of Central Western Europe, necessarily adjusting to the needs and pressures of the society from which it emanated, and the rigidity of that culture when superimposed in a capitalist colony and maintained there by force of metropolitan arms, is epitomized by the contrast between the sensitive evolution of property in land in England and the insensitive application of the same institution in nineteenth century Ireland. In the one case, a social institution evolved in response to the unique challenges and opportunities confronting society (Chapter 3). In the other case, an alien, superimposed, social institution was sustained by a metropolitan power, unresponsive to changing needs and circumstances; and the society on which it had been superimposed was destroyed by being forced to make all the adjustment called for by changing exogenous conditions (Chapter 4).

It was plausible 40 years ago to ascribe the defects of Irish society to the aftermath of '800 years of English rule', which was perceived as commencing with the Norman invasion. It is less convincing to do so now, when English rule has been terminated in Ireland for 60 years. It is equally facile to ascribe the undevelopment of former capitalist colonies to the colonial experience in the case of Latin America, where colonial rule ended over 160 years ago, which is about half as long as the duration of that rule. The plausibility of attributing to the metropolitan powers responsibility for the undevelopment of former capitalist colonies is further weakened by India's persistent undevelopment 40 years after independence; and by the universal undevelopment of Black Africa, although parts of it have now been independent for almost as long as they were capitalist colonies.

Neither does it carry any weight to ascribe the ubiquitous undevelopment of former capitalist colonies to acts of colonial spoliation or deprivation which, in any case, were relatively few. The causation was less direct and more subtle. Capitalist colonialism injected elements of its culture, out of context, into the non-individualistic, non-capitalist cultures of the colonies. There those elements of Central Western European culture have taken root and in doing so have precluded the development, even over a period as long as 160 years in Latin America, of antibodies that would neutralize the foreign elements, or bring them into harmony with the social requirements of the former capitalist colonies.

Independence was gained for all former European colonies by those elements in the colonies who had gained most from colonialism. Independence came when these local elites deemed their position to be sufficiently secure to survive without metropolitan support; and when they were strong enough to challenge a metropolitan tutelage that was increasingly perceived as an infringement on the rights that the support and tutelage had originally created, and had safeguarded at an early stage. 'We hold these truths to be self-evident,' declared the founding fathers of the United States of America, 'that all men are created equal, that they are endowed by the Creator with certain inalienable rights, that among these are Life, Liberty and the pursuit of happiness.' The colonial freedom fighters, on securing independence, have in all cases been concerned to preserve and to enhance those individual rights which were introduced by the European colonists, even though the context is very different from the Central Western European context where the rights originated. That preoccupation with the preservation, out of context, of individual rights is expressed in the concept of 'basic needs', a recent one of those 'meteorites of fashion' that Samuel Johnson saw 'rise and fall'. The concept of 'basic needs' is the belief that individuals, by their very existence, have a right to those things that are essential for their existence; and that that right is not qualified by the capacity of society to meet those needs.[1]

The elevation of the individual outside a western context is the invariable, persistent consequence of capitalist colonialism. Two aspects of this are particularly germane to the no less persistent undevelopment of all former capitalist colonies. These are, first, the individual's right to property; and, second, the individual's right to a longer life than that of traditional societies, where death rates of necessity, over the long run, equated with birth rates, which latter were biologically determined.

Property

Property in the settler colonies was in capital and, in the USA, in people (slaves) also (Appendix B). The 'inalienable right [to] Life, Liberty and the pursuit of happiness' of the colonists who were within the law included the right to enslave negro people, who were deemed to be outside it. The North American colonists exercised their independence to preserve their property in slaves for decades after it had been abolished in the British empire.

Property in the capitalist colonies was overwhelmingly in land. The preservation, enhancement and occasional broadening through 'land reform' of those rights in land have been, everywhere in the former capitalist colonies, a prime political concern and a prime economic objective.

The creole governments of Latin America, 160 years after independence, continue to preserve the property rights in the region's land created through the *encomienda* system of the *conquistadores*. The peonage that was part of that system was retained in Bolivia, until at least 1953.[2] The unchanging character of Latin America's social structure has been commented on by Morse, among others: 'Thus the social and spiritual structure of the past is preserved under new forms...its political and legislative forms and its international status change.'[3] 40 years after independence the property rights that were created in India by the British raj also persist. They are indeed more deeply and firmly entrenched now than when the British first imposed them because the process of extending those rights has been continued by the Indians. India's landowning class is vastly larger than when created by the British through the Permanent Settlement of 1793. It needs to be if it is not to be overwhelmed by the still larger growth that has occurred in the landless class that was simultaneously created by the Permanent Settlement. The total population of south Asia, comprising India, Bangladesh and Pakistan, was then around 130 millions.[4] In 1971 India's population alone was 548 millions, of whom 78 millions were farmers and 47 million were landless agricultural workers. India's total population had increased by 129% between 1901 and 1971; the population of farmers increased by 39% and the population of landless agricultural workers increased by 152%.[5]

The ill defined, diffuse titles to livestock on communally grazed African pastures have been transformed, by the application and enforcement of western concepts of property in cattle.[6] Grazing stock have now become the absolute property of specific owners whose rights are sometimes registered with the state, as in Botswana and in KwaZulu in South Africa; and are invariably protected with the overwhelming power of the western type states of the former capitalist colonies.

Property in land, including livestock on communally grazed land — by far the most important form of property in the former capitalist colonies — differs fundamentally from property in people (slaves) or in products that have not been consumed (capital) which were the predominant forms of property in Europe and in the former European settler colonies. The supply of slaves and more so of capital was elastic; and one citizen's property enhanced the capacity of his fellow citizens to acquire more property (Appendix A). The reverse applies to land. The supply of land is fixed, as is also the stock-carrying capacity of communally grazed land. Therefore, the appropriation of land by some excludes others. The more firmly some citizens are confirmed in their titles to land or to stock on communally grazed pastures, the more firmly are others excluded from access to that land and to those stock. The security of tenure of a few is contingent on the firmness of exclusion of the many. The paradox of the concern of the newly independent USA to preserve and to enhance the rights of its citizens to enslave and to deprive others of all rights has been well recognized. But there has been no recognition of the equally paradoxical, but more pressing and enduring concern of all former capitalist colonies — supported and encouraged by western 'development experts' — to strengthen the security of tenure of some in land, which by corollary, denies access to land to others no less firmly.

Enhanced Life Expectancy

The rule of law and the enhanced life expectancy that it conferred applied in the Ancient Mediterranean to citizens. Slaves were outside the law and, *de facto* as well as *de jure,* did not have the right to reproduce themselves. The capital-less of Central Western Europe likewise did not reproduce; the men could not maintain themselves and the women could not dower themselves (Appendix A). It became generally possible for individuals without direct access to capital, in Central Western Europe, to marry only with the coming of the industrial revolution. Laslett observes: 'a high proportion of ordinary Englishmen, the peasants, the craftsmen, the labourers and the paupers, in the time of Elizabeth, or Anne, or of the first three Georges, got married in their late twenties, and even in their early thirties.'[7] Wrigley makes a similar point: 'Indeed women in Elizabethan England married two or three years later on average than they do in England today.'[8] England, in this respect, conformed to a general pattern of late marriages in Europe.[9]

The industrial revolution brought mines, factories, the building of railways, sewers and so forth, and provided employment for millions of capital-less people. Employment gave them the minimal economic and social independence to marry. The industrial revolution made it possible for Europeans, for the first time, to have the biological birth rates that have been normal in non-European societies. Increased knowledge of the principles of hygiene and of medical science simultaneously reduced death rates. The combined effect was the rapid population growth of Europe and of the settler colonies in the nineteenth century. The industrial revolution also triggered off for these populations a period of rapid, sustained economic growth, such as was never previously, or subsequently, experienced by people at their income level. Output increased more rapidly than population and, with increasing incomes, people exercised forethought and practiced artificial birth control (Appendix B). The ultimate effect of these different influences has been the reduction of annual death rates in the West to ten per 1,000, or less, and an increasing tendency for artifically controlled birth rates to fall below that level.

The early mercantile phase of European colonialism was a period when the masses in the capitalist colonies, like the slaves of the Ancient Mediterranean and the capital-less of Central Western Europe, generally did not reproduce themselves. Most of Latin America's large population was wiped out; and the slave population of the Caribbean was maintained only by imports of kidnapped persons from Africa, the sparse population of which was further depleted as a result. Ireland's population was likewise reduced under the early Stuarts, to make possible the large expansion in cattle and sheep exports to England that occurred then (Chapter 4). Cromwell further exhausted Ireland's population by shipping Irish people to work on West Indian estates. Petty, in 1687, proposed the virtual extinction of the Irish, leaving only sufficient on the island to tend flocks and herds producing for the English market.[10]

The non-reproduction of the colonial masses ended with factory capitalism. Metropolitan profits were then extracted less crudely from capitalist colonies and the metropolises extended their control over the large rice-fed populations of Asia. The extension of the West's rule of law, coupled with the application of the elementary principles of public hygiene and disease control, effected a sufficient reduction in death rates, which, like birth rates, had been around 40 per 1,000 per annum, to allow the populations of the capitalist colonies and of the former capitalist colonies of Latin America to increase annually by around five per 1,000 during the nineteenth century. That rate of population growth accelerated somewhat in the twentieth century up to the years of the Second World War, when most of the capitalist colonies of the Caribbean, Africa and Asia became independent. Thus, quite typically in the Indian continent: 'The estimated 100 million population in Akbar's India (1605) and 130 million in 1800, had become 200 million in the first census in 1872. In 1941 the Census gave a population of all India of 387 million.'[11] Western influence, at very little direct cost, enhanced the life expectancy of the peoples of the capitalist colonies.

The governments of former capitalist colonies have been almost as concerned to preserve and to raise their peoples' life expectancy as they have been to preserve and to enrich property rights. The enhancement of life expectancy is extremely cost effective. A drain to carry away stagnant water may cost only a few pounds to dig, but may save thousands of people from dying with malaria. Modern drugs, discovered and developed in the West, where annual deaths and births are around ten per 1,000 population, can save the lives of people and their animals in the Third World for a few pence per treatment. The need of the people of the former capitalist colonies for these hygiene measures and drugs, which make the difference between life and death for themselves, their families and livestock, grows as pressure of population, of people and their livestock, depresses nutritional levels. The clamour for medicine is as strident as it is irresistible, especially as the direct cost involved is so slight. Understandably, therefore, death rates have continued to be reduced in the former capitalist colonies and their peoples' expectancy of life has been increased.

However, the circumstances in which the individual's life expectancy was lengthened in the West were very different from those of the former capitalist colonies. The enhancement of life expectancy was generally qualified in the West: it was limited to those 'within the law'. It was gradual. The increase in life expectancy was barely perceptible for millenia; then it accelerated slowly for the first century or so of the industrial revolution, before plateauing off in more recent decades. It was accompanied, and largely made possible, by rising incomes, which also led to reduced birth rates. The result has been that, as western people have increased their life expectancy, they have also reduced their reproduction rate to less than a quarter of its biological limit.

The enhancement of life expectancy in the former capitalist colonies has been far more dramatic. It commenced with the era of factory capitalism, no more than 160 years ago. It has applied quite unselectively; western type law and order and disease control, of their nature, protect the poor and their livestock scarcely less effectively than they protect the wealthy and their livestock. The enhancement of life expectancy has led to rapid population growth but without a commensurate growth in output, so that people have become poorer and less nourished (Chapter 1).

Demographic Transition

Reservations about the social implications of benefiting individuals by prolonging their lives and the lives of their immediate relatives, without a concomitant reduction in birth rates, are stilled by theories of 'demographic transition'. Social scientists, drawing on the West's experience, predict that, after a lag, Third World birth rates will decline and come roughly into line with greatly reduced death rates.[12] But in making these predictions, social scientists overlook the altogether exceptional and inherently unrepeatable circumstances that made it possible for people in the West to experience rising living standards in the nineteenth century, at the same time as their populations were growing most rapidly. The situation is fundamentally different in the Third World now. Population is growing far more rapidly than it ever did in the West; and living standards for the masses, which were low, have been declining and continue to do so.

Theories of 'demographic transition' are propounded and popularized by social scientists who are based in the West, or in western cultural enclaves within the Third World; and who, in conformity with that culture are normally permanently, pensionably and lucratively employed and are frequently childless. In a word, social scientists are part of a very different culture from that of the Third World about which they theorize. Nevertheless, and reflecting the many individual interests that benefit from death rate reductions, their improbable theories succeed in allaying concern about the social implications of a persistent, substantial reduction of death rates below birth rates.

It is an improbable fabrication of permanently, pensionably and lucratively employed, frequently childless, western oriented, social scientists that under conditions of low and declining subsistence levels, people have children in order to secure the future benefits of rising and secure incomes. The deduction from that premise that, as poor people observe more of their children surviving they need not breed as many in order to achieve a given future level of income and security is no less improbable.[13] The essence of a subsistence existence is that people are so preoccupied with the struggle to meet immediate needs, that they cannot afford thought for the future. People under these circumstance, which have been the condition of most peoples at most times, reproduce for the most part biologically, like birds and bees.

This is not to deny the effect that various social mores and customs, such as the emphasis on virginity prior to marriage, may have had on birth rates. It is highly questionable, however, that these social attitudes owed anything to a concern over excessive population. Given the almost imperceptible long term rate of population growth of around 4% per century, excess population was unlikely to have been a major social concern until quite recent times. Instead, given the not infrequent decimations of populations by disease, by drought-induced famine, by war, etc. it is understandable that, in former times, societies were more concerned to 'increase and multiply and inherit the earth'.That continued to be the case in parts of Africa until quite recent times. 'The rivalry between chiefs was primarily for men, cattle and women. Until 1938 every chief and every village sought to attract men and increase its fighting strength; and in some areas the dominating desire to increase in size, to attract a following, was still conspicuous in 1955.'[14]

It is typical of the western-centred social sciences that they perceive the question as: why do undeveloping Third World countries have biologically normal birth rates of around 50 per 1,000 per annum? Rather than as: why do developing, western countries have abnormally low birth rates of around ten per 1,000 per annum? The answer is clear when the question is phrased in the second way: better off people have low birth rates because they are able to contemplate the future; and, in doing so, they perceive the present discounted cost of having children as being sufficiently great to warrant artificial birth control.

There is little in the Third World situation now to suggest an early, major departure from established biological birth rates. Urbanization, especially when accompanied by higher living standards, does reduce birth rates; but the mass of the Third World's population is, and will for long continue to be, rural.[15]

The Paradox of Property

The preservation of property rights and the enhancement of life expectancy, the two principal heritages of western individualism, have the effect, in the former capitalist colonies, of each supporting and reinforcing the other. Together they are the cause of the pathology of the undevelopment of the former capitalist colonies. Property in land results in its unproductive use in the former capitalist colonies and reduces the resources available to support the masses. Impoverished, malnourished people, devoid of forethought and therefore tending to reproduce themselves at biological rates, increase in numbers because of western-originating, highly cost effective methods of reducing death rates. The coexistence of expanding masses of increasingly impoverished people and of a privileged minority of landowners reinforces, through the paradox of property, those tendencies that cause land in the former capitalist colonies to be used ineffectively.

The paradox of property is that the more valuable it becomes relative to general income levels, the less efficiently it is used. This is for various reasons that are explained and illustrated below. The slaves/capital that were / is the main form of property and the basis of the economies of Europe and of the settler colonies, were/is in elastic supply. Their value could never increase disproportionately to general incomes. As already noted: in the capitalist West, the tendency has been for income levels to rise relative to the value of capital. Property, under these circumstances, has been used efficiently and productively. Because land is in fixed supply, its value increases absolutely with population growth. When, as in the former capitalist colonies, population growth causes, and is caused by, worsening poverty, the value of land relative to general incomes is raised both because land values rise and incomes fall.

The end result is that the status of the individual in the former capitalist colonies, where land has always been limiting and the individual has been dependent on society (Appendix A), is further eroded; and land is used still less efficiently. The imposition on these societies of the key elements of western, individualistic capitalist culture, debases and undermines the status of the individual in these former capitalist colonies. It does so in a manner that is reminiscent of the absolute debasement of slaves in the Ancient Mediterannean and of the capital-less in Central Western Europe before the industrial revolution. The manner in which peoples' lives are devalued and land is used inefficiently is considered next for different categories of former capitalist colonies.

The Latin American Case

The appropriation of land as property dichotomizes society into landed and landless. The landless can never, by their own efforts, acquire land, as the slaveless could acquire slaves (by conquest); or as the capital-less can acquire capital (by saving). The landless have access to land, and therefore to life, on the conditions set by the landed. The mitigating circumstances of that ordering of affairs in England, where alone property in land evolved spontaneously, have been noted (Chapters 3 and 4). The logical consequences of dichotomizing society into the landed few and the landless many, in a post-capitalist-colonial setting where there is no metropolitan controlled army of occupation, can be most clearly observed in Latin America. The ability of the few, in the post colonial era, to exclude the many depends on the military force acquired in trade from the metropolises. Within the former colonies, power in turn resides unstably with those who command the military forces. Control of the military, and therefore power, shifts unpredictably from military clique to military clique. Bolivia is the extreme case of this instability, having experienced 189 such unconstitutional shifts in power during its 160 years of independence.[16]*

Agricultural investment by *latifundistos* is discouraged by chronic political

---

*Russian autocratic power was similarly based on the exchange of crude primary products for more sophisticated, western products (Appendix A). The myth of the divinity of the tsars, and more recently of the communist party, has conferred a

instability and the confiscation or destruction of exposed and liquid agricultural assets like cattle, which is probable at every change of rule. With the mass of the people denied access to land, except on the conditions of the landed, and with the landed unwilling to invest because of chronic political instability, agricultural production lags. Simultaneously, because of the reduction of death rates population grows. The more population grows, the greater is the gap between the needs of the increasing population and the capacity of a poorly ordered agriculture to meet those needs. Quite typically of Latin America: 'By 1900 ... the condition of the great majority of Mexicans had sunk below what it had been at any time during the colonial period.'[17] Political tension and instability are exacerbated. The dichotomy of society and the reduction in death rates, combined, initiate a cycle of undevelopment: of inefficient land use, of low and declining incomes for the expanding mass of population, heightened political tension, less investment and less output. There is a chronic tendency in Latin America for agricultural output to tend towards zero while prices tend towards infinity.[18]

The Latin American situation is represented by Figure A1.

Figure A1
The Latin American Case

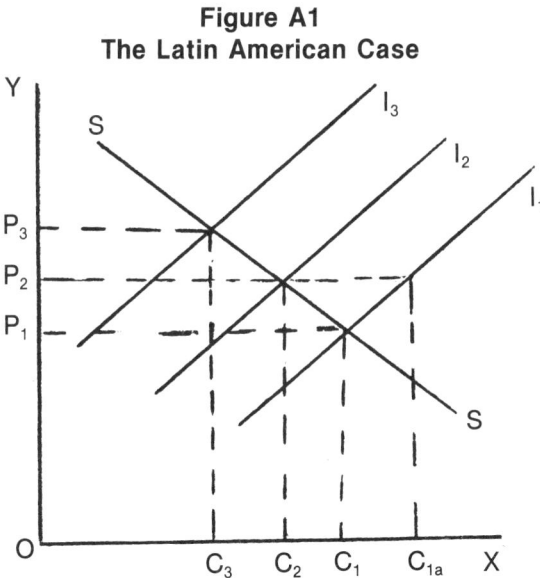

degree of stability on Russia — except during the interregnum between the death of one tsar or communist party secretary general and the emergence of a successor — not enjoyed by Latin America. Latin Americans, despite their notorious spiritual superstitiousness, appear to be more sceptical than Russians about their leaders' infallibility, whether it derives by grace from God or by the scientific study of Marxist-Leninist dialectical materialism.

Agricultural prices are shown on the OY axis and quantities of capital used in agriculture are shown on the OX axis. As agricultural prices rise, the amount of capital used tends to increase, as shown by the positive slope of I_1. Thus a rise in agricultural prices from P_1 to P_2, other things being equal, would cause an increase in the amount of capital used from C_1 to C_{1a}, which additional capital should raise agricultural output. But food price increases in Latin America heighten political instability in a politically unstable region, and that makes landowners less willing to supply capital. This is illustrated by a shift in the capital supply curve from I_1 to I_2 as a result of the heightened political instability associated with an increase in food prices from P_1 to P_2. It is possible, as is shown here, that the upward shift in the capital supply curve, caused by the heightened political tension, will result in less capital being used (C_2), even though agricultural prices have risen. Such a reduction in the amount of capital employed would cause agricultural output to decline further, driving food prices up further, to P_3. The still greater political instability associated with food prices at P_3 would cause a further shift to the left of the capital supply curve, to I_3, reducing further the amount of capital employed and causing output to fall again. The long run tendency is towards accentuated political instability, reduced investment, and — despite rising prices — declining agricultural output. The long run agricultural supply curve tends to be backward sloping, as SS, with output tending to decline as prices rise.

The Indian (Irish) Case

'Reforma agraria' has for several years been the most popular catchphrase of Latin American countries. It means, under the most favourable circumstances, some broadening of the base of land ownership, moving Latin America some part of the way towards the condition of a broad participation in land ownership which has obtained in the former capitalist colonies of the Old World. But agricultural production has failed also in those countries of the Old World, though for different reasons.

The broad mass of property rights established in India under the British raj and extended during the post colonial years (Appendix B) has been a politically stabilising influence in India. The size and heterogeneity of the subcontinent's large population has also militated against the sort of sudden, violent political change that is characteristic of Latin American countries (as in the past it precluded a united defence against pastoral intrusion). Relative political stability combined with the rapid growth of a poor population has caused land values to rise while the incomes of the landless majority have declined.[19]

Increased relative land values imply greater agricultural profitability and therefore greater incentives to expand agricultural output. Higher land values also, however, influence the ownership and possession of land. When land is free all who can use it can acquire land; and they have neither the means nor the incentive to retain free land if they cannot operate it. Land that is valuable can be acquired only by the wealthy. Because land is valuable and because, *ipso facto,* its owners are wealthy, even if they cannot make use of it they have the resources to retain it, either because of inertia or in anticipation of further increases in land values.

The higher agricultural prices rise, the lower fall the real incomes of the landless, who must buy their food from the landed. Under conditions of political stability as in India, the higher agricultural prices rise, the higher land values also rise. High agricultural prices therefore both raise land values and depress the incomes of the landless. The higher land values rise, the greater are the incentive and the resources that the landed have to retain land and to acquire more of it. The higher land prices rise and the lower the incomes of the landless fall, the less likelihood is there that landless, or nearly landless, persons can get possession of land. High agricultural prices, in these circumstances, have two contradictory effects. First, they are an incentive to landowners to increase output. Second, they change the pattern of landownership, concentrating it increasingly into the possession of the wealthy and making it more difficult for the poor and the landless, who can make best use of it, to acquire land. The ownership effect of higher agricultural prices may well offset the incentive effect, causing higher agricultural prices to depress agricultural output.

Figure A2
The Indian (Irish) Case

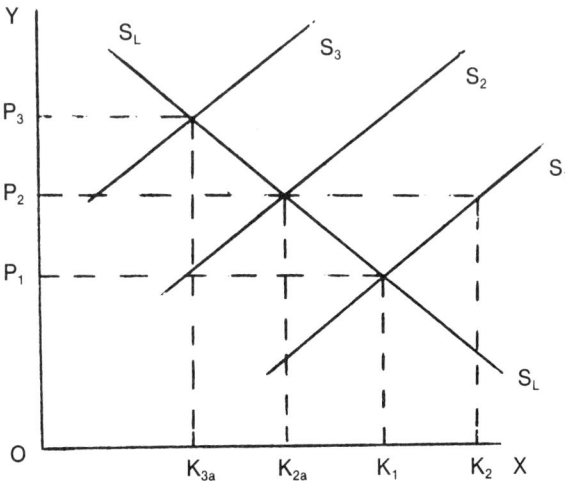

The situation in relation to agriculture in countries like India and Ireland, where land prices are high relative to incomes, is illustrated in Figure A2. S_1 represents a normal supply curve, showing agricultural output (measured on the OX axis) increasing as agricultural prices (measured on the OY axis) rise. At an initial price level, P_1, output is K_1. If prices rise to P_2 (as a result, say, of population growth in India) if other things remain equal, output would increase to K_2. But other things do not remain equal in the former capitalist colonies. As agricultural prices rise, land values rise, landowners become better off and the landless become worse off. Possession of land becomes increasingly concentrated into the hands of the oldest, the wealthiest, those with most land, and those who are therefore least competent to use it. Because of this deterioration of the pattern of land ownership the agricultural supply curve moves upwards, to S_2. Here successive agricultural price rises are shown as causing upward shifts of the agricultural supply curve, from S_1 to S_2 to S_3, which result in decreasing agricultural output, K_{2a} and K_{3a}, as prices rise to P_2 and P_3. S_L S_L tends to be the long run supply curve for Indian (Irish) agriculture.

The African Case

The combination of western concepts of property and of western disease control also depresses agricultural output in Africa. In cattle dependent Botswana, 75% of the cattle now belong to 15% of the people, while 45% own no cattle.[20] In East Africa, 'one of the features of many of the subsistence cultivator tribes is the great difference in cattle wealth, with often a few people owning large numbers while many people have only a few stock or none at all ...It is estimated that 80% of the cattle are owned by 20% of the people of the Duruna and Giriana tribes in Kenya.'[21] The writer observed in 1983, from inspection of cattle dip-tank records in Kwa Zulu, in South Africa, a similar phenomenon. About half the cattle were owned by 10% of households; the other half were owned by 40% of households; and half the households owned none. Ownership of cattle was traditionally much more evenly spread in Africa where weak, indigenous political structures precluded sharp distinctions in the amount of wealth held. 'In this connection, ownership of stock must be clearly distinguished from the exercise of certain rights against them. There is a basic "stock-owning unit" in each tribe — the "house" in Jieland and the "nuclear family" in Turkanaland — within which, subject to the privileges of seniority, rights are largely communal and egalitarian, and administered by the head of the unit.'[22]

Powerful individual African rulers, like the Zulu, Shaka, did of course exist and usually held very large herds and flocks.[23] But rulers of this sort were exceptional in Africa[24] and where they did exist, their cattle, like the demesnes of European feudal lords, were a public resource that helped to defray the cost of government.

Concentration of property rights in cattle, which are defended in post-colonial Africa by strong, western-type states, increases both the incentive and the resources to expand cattle stocks. Because African cattleowners are no longer required by custom and social pressures to share the produce of their cattle they have a greater incentive to increase that produce; and because they can now save their surplus, instead of sharing it with their neighbours, they can use these savings to acquire more stock. Western veterinary science has curbed the great animal epidemics like rinderpest that traditionally swept through Africa and decimated cattle stocks. Kwa Zulu veterinary services endeavour each week to dip all cattle in the territory against tick-borne diseases. This, which must be one of the most rigorous veterinary regimes in the world, largely accounts for the survival of large numbers of cattle and goats through several recent drought years, though producing virtually nothing on land growing little but thornbush. At the other end of Africa: 'The amassing of large herds has caused serious problems. Now that the Baggara have access to veterinary techniques and modern husbandry, the herds are no longer being reduced as they were by disease and the land is becoming severly overgrazed.'[25] Except in the rain forest, where cattle do not penetrate, similar conditions obtain throughout Africa.[26] The problem is aggravated by a warm climate and the absence of the cold, wet winters that curb cattle stocks effectively in higher latitudes. Cattle survive for months — if not years — in Africa under grazing conditions that, in Europe, would kill off cattle within weeks.

The suppression of cattle raiding is another important aspect of the enforcement, by western-type states, of western concepts of property in cattle. Reference was made above (Appendix A) to the distinctive character of African cattle keeping. Because of trypanosomiasis, cattle have had to be kept in the open. But unlike the Eurasian steppes, where for lack of shelter cattle were also kept in the open, land in subSaharan Africa is generally arable and African cattle-keeping, unlike northern Asian cattle-keeping, has usually been associated with cropgrowing. African cattlekeepers have, therefore, been less mobile and less gregarious than the Eurasian 'Golden Hordes'. African society, as a result, has been characterized by extreme political fragmentation, as evident, for example, by the presence there of 'some 3,000 languages and dialects'.[27] This implied, in a continent with an estimated 120 million people in 1900[28] that each language was spoken, on average, by 40,000 people. The virtually continuous warfare, involving principally defending and raiding cattle, which resulted from these conditions must have been a major curb on cattle stocks in traditional Africa. That curb on cattle stocks has been removed by western-type states that seek to suppress cattle-raiding and to secure for individuals their titles to cattle.

These western influences, which are both institutional and technological, have made possible the persistent, chronic overstocking of communally grazed land, which was not possible in the past. Overstocking in turn causes the deterioration of pastures, the spread of thornbush and desertification.[29] Acute breakdown and widespread famine and drought occur where the resource endowment is weak, as in the Sahel. There, thousands starved to death and millions of livestock perished in the early 1970s; and there is an imminent prospect of the same recurring in the 1980s.[30] Elsewhere in Africa the breakdown is less dramatic, but it affects very many more people. It is perhaps best reflected by the decline during the 1970s of 9% in food output per person in Africa, from a base that was already lower than in any other continent.[31]

A somewhat similar pastoral phenomenon exists in India. Western originating veterinary science has made it possible to crowd 18% of the world's cattle on to a small, communally grazed part of the 3% of the world's land that is in India. A western-created Indian elite generates a strong demand for milk, which India's disrupted traditional cattle keeping cannot supply. The result is that the price of milk in terms of wages is nearly 50 times greater, and in terms of wheat is twice as great, as in the West.[32] That, in turn, has made it profitable for Indian landowners to divert land from growing food crops for the masses to growing fodder for cows producing milk for the elite.[33]

Figure A3
Overstocking Communal Grazing

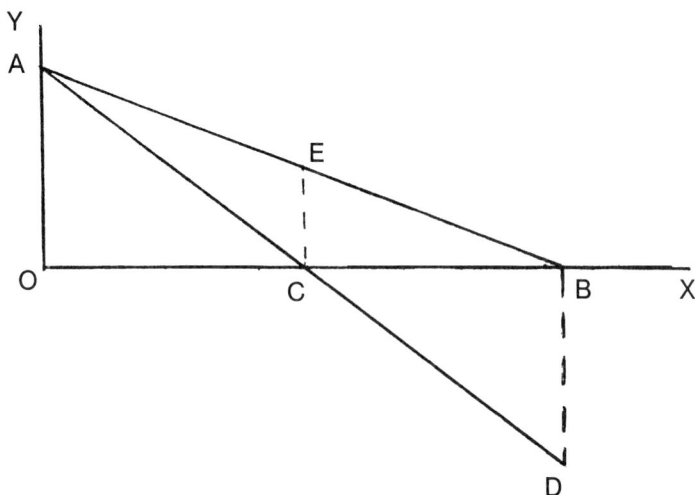

Two thirds of the world's agricultural area is grazing land and about half of that is in Africa and Asia where it is communally grazed.[34] Figure A3 illustrates how the impact of western culture disrupts this traditional way of using one-third of the world's agricultural land. (It is assumed, for simplicity of exposition here, that there are no labour or other costs of keeping livestock). OY measures the return, in terms of meat, milk, blood etc. from adding increasing numbers of stock, as measured along OX, to a finite grazing area. The line AB shows how average output per unit of stock changes as stock numbers are increased from zero up to OB stock. At OB stocking level, land is so overgrazed that nothing is got from it. All of the reduced herbage produced by overstocked land goes simply to maintain and to reproduce the stock, which yield neither milk nor meat for their owners, but do fulfill the traditional role of money and of symbols for them. Conditions like this were observed in Kwa Zulu in 1983.[35]

AD represents the impact of individual stock units on total output. It is the marginal product curve, corresponding to the average product curve, AB. This shows that the OCth animal adds nothing to total output, though at OC stocking average output per head of stock is CE.

Livestock in the West are normally grazed in severalty; each individual's stock occupies a specific area of grazing exclusively. OC is the normal stocking level under those conditions, with animals on average having an output CE. Adding more stock would, as CD indicates, reduce total output. But, under the conditions of communal grazing that are normal in Africa and Asia (and that obtained in pre-Tudor Ireland; see Chapter 2), at a stocking level OC, individuals could gain CE by adding stock. It would be largely immaterial to them that their gain of CE would be at the cost of those who already had the OC stock on the land. If stock-keeping costs are zero as assumed, stockowners, under conditions of communal grazing, cannot be satisfied until the stocking level reaches OB, when CB overstocking has reduced output by CBD to zero.

Traditional pre-colonial societies in Africa, Asia and Ireland, strove to increase stocking levels to OB. They were continuously twarted in doing so by stock-raiding and disease, the incidence of which tended to become increasingly severe at stocking levels in excess of OC, when total output was being reduced by overstocking and when nutritional levels for stock and stockowners declined. Western technology and institutions have greatly weakened and largely neutralized these traditional, crude though effective, balancing mechanisms. Western influences, out of context, have utterly disrupted a finely balanced, traditional farming system, allowing stock numbers to increase towards OB, causing output to decline towards zero, and giving rise to widespread, irreversible soil deterioration and making mega-famine imminent.

The Equatorial Rainforest Case

There are extensive areas of the world where land remains unappropriated, a 'sea of forest' as in Central Western Europe in the past. These are the great equatorial rainforests of South America, Africa and Southeast Asia. Their agricultural use presents special problems arising from the severe leaching of nutrients from the soil by continuous, heavy tropical rains and from the rapid breakdown of exposed soils by the combination of high rainfall and high temperatures. Effectively, only tree crops or irrigated rice can be grown on a sustained basis in the rainforest tropics.[36]

Western medical science, by the control of malaria and numerous other diseases particularly associated with the rainforest tropics, has achieved a greater demographic transformation in these regions perhaps than anywhere else. Thus, the population of indigenous Malays, which was around half a million in the mid-nineteenth century, had increased ten times a century later.[37] In tropical Africa, where labour was so scarce a century ago that indentured workers were brought in from India and Java, there is now chronic unemployment.

This rapid, western induced population growth in the rainforest tropics precludes the same sort of expansion in output that occurred in Central Western Europe and in the European settled territories, in both of which areas land was also freely available. Sustained, rapid population growth depresses incomes. In Ghana, real wages declined by 25% between 1960 and 1970.[38] In southwest Perak state, one of the longest settled and most fertile parts of peninsular Malaya, it was observed in 1975 that 'it is likely that smallholder real incomes in the study area are substantially lower now than they were seven years ago.'[39] Low and declining incomes compel the inhabitants of the tropics to direct their resources towards activities that generate an immediate return in order to support their larger numbers of surviving children. Because their resources are limited, including especially their ability as increasingly malnourished people to work, the people of the tropics are forced to neglect the slower maturing, longer lasting tree crops that are most suitable for tropical agriculture. Smallholder rubber production declines in southwest Perak.[40] Ghana cocoa production, a smallholder enterprise, declined from an average annual production of 454,000 tons in 1961/2 — 1965/6 to 259,000 tons in 1978/9 — 1980/81.[41]

As the supply of labour in the tropics increases and its cost decreases, the stock of capital to employ that labour also decreases. The same western influence that causes a rapid increase in the labour supply cause simultaneously a decrease in the effective demand on small farms for that labour, so that less of it is employed even at lower real wages. This is illustrated by Figure A4.

AB represents the return to increasing quantities of labour applied to given tree crop resources in the tropics. I_1 represents these returns dis-

Figure A4
The Decline of Wages and Employment

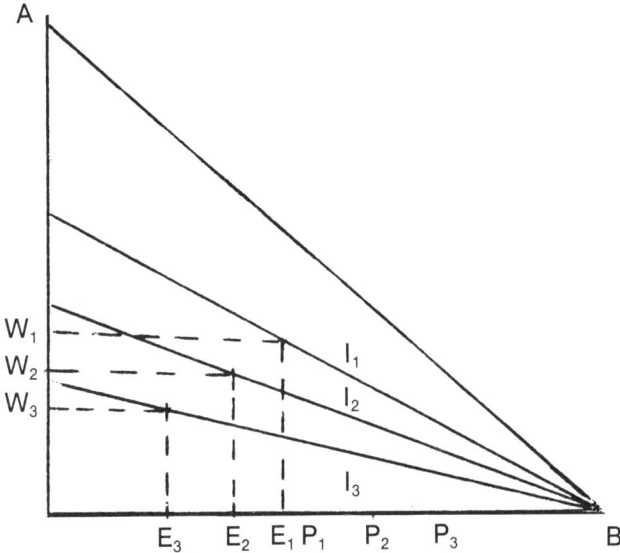

counted to the time of application of the labour, for example to plant the trees, at a time discount rate r_1. This time discount rate, r_1, is associated with income/wages of W_1. At these income/wage and time discount rates, E_1 labour is employed on family farms ($\cong P_1$ labour available on family farms). This is a normal, full employment situation in traditional, pre-colonial society. Western influences cause population to increase rapidly to P_2, which causes income/wages to decline to W_2. The time discount rate increases to r_2 and the present discounted return to labour on family farms declines to I_2. Even at the lower income/wage rate, less labour is employed, E_2. There is now $E_2 P_2$ unemployment or underemployment. With further increase in population to P_3, reduction in income/wages to W_3, increase in the discount rate to r_3, decline in the present discounted return to labour to I_3, employment drops to E_3 and unemployment/underemployment increases to $E_3 P_3$. There is, as is widespread in family farm areas in the Third World, a large and rapidly increasing supply of family labour, of which less and less is employed.[42]

Coping with Undevelopment

The palpable undevelopment of the former capitalist colonies invites

241

intervention by their governments and, increasingly, by outside agencies. Much reliance is placed on education and extension to appraise farmers of unexploited opportunities for the profitable expansion of output.[43] This emphasis on the developmental powers of education is normally placed by persons who have had little practical experience of the conditions they speak and write about; people, that is, who have never made a living by growing crops or raising livestock under the conditions that obtain in undeveloping former capitalist colonies. But they are usually persons who have themselves received more than the average complement of formal education, who are often purveyors of educational services, and who might therefore, be suspected of bias in favour of the efficacy of formal education. There is, of course, a close positive correlation between education and income but, as in many such cases, it is difficult to distinguish between cause and effect. Are people wealthy because they have much formal education? Or have they much formal education because they, or their parents, are wealthy? Indubitably, as people grow wealthy, they demand and are able to pay for more education. Very many skills and occupations associated with high income economies require considerable formal education. It can scarcely be questioned that it expedites development. What can and needs to be questioned is whether formal education can generate development. Or even whether it is necessary for development. For, after all, Central Western Europe developed for millenia with no mass formal education. What is beyond question is that extensive formal education has not prevented the undevelopment that is the concern of this work.

The proponents of formal education do not appear to realize that, in a Latin American situation, attempts to expand agricultural output invite confiscation of the necessary investment at the next *coup d'etat*; that the systematically selected landowners of Ireland and India are more interested in security, leisure and other benefits than in cash income from higher output; that for the individual African (or Indian) to reduce his cattle numbers, while benefiting his neighbours who use the same communal grazing, would harm him; and that for the impoverished Southeast Asian or Ghanaian smallholder, the problem is not the best variety of rubber or cocoa to plant, but how to survive for the five to seven years between clearing land to plant a tree and getting a return from that tree. Expenditure of effort and resources on formal education in these circumstances will almost certainly be wasteful. Worse: it may be harmful. This is not because the advice given is usually illconceived and likely to cause loss if implemented; for most farmers are empiricists who are guided by what they see works rather than by precept. Rather it is because expenditure on formal education and extension inculcates a sense of accomplishment. Much effort on educational and extension services by governments and international agencies implies that these bodies are not 'just standing there'; they are doing something. In reality, less harm would be done if they stood there, did nothing and cogitated on how the pursuit of individual interests, out of a western context, undevelops the Third World. Formal education and extension services do nothing at all to impede the pursuit of these socially destructive individual interests.

Meanwhile, the boundless arrogance of these intellectual imperialists who presume to advise its farmers about their business is one more affliction on the Third World. Few of these advisors have ever raised a crop or an animal in their lives; fewer still have made a living by doing so; and none of them has depended for a living by growing crops or raising livestock as an indigene in a former capitalist colony, which all those whom they advise must do or perish.

The high mortality of the virtually valueless and therefore neglected calves of Latin America invites the UN's Food and Agriculture Organization and various donor countries to intervene by providing veterinary services and medicines. They succeed only in further depressing the value of young stock and making them still less worth tending.[44] The emaciated condition of cattle on the overstocked communal grazing of Africa and India creates an insatiable demand for veterinary services and medicines to keep the animals alive; which succeeds only in causing worse overstocking, greater emaciation and still greater need of, and profit for, veterinarians and drug companies.[45]

Capital is injected into agriculture and into the other sectors of the economies of the former colonies by governments and by international agencies like the World Bank and the various regional development banks. The results almost invariably are similar to those secured in Kenya where, in the case of World Bank sponsored projects, 'investments financed by loans on private ranches are having to be refinanced by government grants in order to avert the ranches' "financial collapse".'[46] Or as in Ireland in the early 1970s, the World Bank lent money to Irish farmers to increase their cattle breeding stocks at a time when these were already excessive in relation to cattle fattening capacity, and so contributed importantly to the major, disruptive cattle crisis in Ireland in the mid-1970s.[47]

More generally, the injection of credit by governments and by international agencies like the World Bank leads to the sort of situation depicted in Table 1.2 above. The cost of servicing debt increases more rapidly than GNP; competitiveness is reduced; balance of payments deficits increase; and dependence on further borrowing, internally and more critically externally, increases. Borrowing countries become enmeshed in a web of foreign indebtedness, which preempts any buoyancy in their export earnings. The professional injectors of capital — the banks and the international lending agencies, including the World Bank and the various regional development banks — meanwhile profit by assuring a gullible public that the capital will generate a flow of wealth to service the borrowing. In fact, the debts can only be serviced by further borrowing or by taxation.

The various extension, credit, marketing, land reform, and land development projects and programmes, which are aimed at expanding agricultural production, cost more than they are worth. They absorb more resources than they generate. Because of that, they further impoverish the societies that practice them; and because of that further impoverishment, they tend to depress agricultural output in the various ways indicated already above. Not merely do these measures generate a false sense that 'everything possible is being done' to expand primary production; they are positively detrimental to increased output.

Industrialization: Property in land, which becomes more valuable as the landless masses of the former capitalist colonies become more numerous and poorer, causes land to be used inefficiently and unproductively. Understandably, most former capitalist colonies, discouraged by failure to expand agriculture sufficiently rapidly at least to prevent the deterioration of already low nutritional levels, have attempted to develop their economice on the basis of manufacturing industry. Following the List argument[48] of producing first for a protected home market and then, with a secure domestic base, expanding into export markets, they believed they could attain the scale necessary to make their manufacturing industry, using low cost Third World labour, competitive with metropolitan industry.

Several Latin American countries set about industrializing in the 1930s, behind protective tariff walls.[49] They did so partly because of List-type arguments and partly because of the collapse of world trade, especially in the primary commodities that the region exported. What Latin America attempted in the 1930s, the more recently independent capitalist colonies of Asia and the Caribbean attempted in the 1950s and 1960s. India in particular has attempted to develop through industrialization.

These attempts by the former capitalist colonies to by-pass agriculture and to develop on the basis of protected manufacturing industry were departures from the precedents set by metropolitan and settler colonial economic development. Industrialization invariably occurred in the metropolises and in the settler colonies either following, or hand-in-hand with, agricultural growth. Both sectors were closely interdependent, with agriculture providing for industry raw materials, food for industrial workers, occasionally export earnings to buy necessary imports, and a market for industry's products. This close interdependence of agriculture and industry was also manifested in the more recent and highly successful economic development of Japan (see below). Despite these precedents, to assert that industrialization is impossible without agricultural development would smack of dogmatism. There are, after all, the cases of Hong Kong and Singapore, which are heavily industrialized, are indubitably developing (as defined in Chapter 1) without agriculture. It would not appear inconceivable that India, for example, which has been able to split the atom, should also be able to master modern technology and commercial practice sufficiently to develop manufacturing exports to enable it to pay for all the food that its own lagging agriculture is unable to produce for its expanding population.

It has to be remembered in this connection, however, that Hong Kong and Singapore, as well as having no agriculture, are also free of the heritage of capitalist colonialism (Chapter 1); and it is that heritage which, it has been argued here, causes the former capitalist colonies to undevelop. The failure of India and of all the former capitalist colonies to escape from that heritage powerfully suggests that though they may acquire the technology necessary for modern manufacturing, they are unlikely to acquire the commercial skills, the organisation and the financial resources that would allow them to market manufactured products on world markets, in sufficient quantity, at sufficiently high prices, to enable them to buy the food that their own lagging agriculture cannot produce for their ill fed, expanding populations.

The record of industrialization in the former capitalist colonies supports the view that it is not an alternative to agricultural expansion as a means of securing economic development. The limitations of industrialization based on protection were experienced by the former colonies of Latin America in the 1950s, some twenty years after initiating protected industrialization. The protected industries never succeeded in exporting adequately to pay for the raw materials and capital goods that they required. The Latin American economies continued to be restricted by their ability to import, with now their protected manufacturing industries suffering from the lack of imported plant, spare parts, raw materials and fuel. These restrictions have been relaxed, to some extent, by foreign borrowing, which has brought the region and its financial relations with the metropolises full circle to the position prior to the economic collapse of the 1930s. An important element of that global economic collapse was the growing indebtedness of Latin America and the failure of the region to meet its international financial commitments when its export earnings declined.[50]

The countries of Asia and Africa, which were colonized and became independent later than Latin America, also industrialized later. The protected industrialization of these countries, which aimed at 'import substitution', occurred in the 1950s and 1960s. As in the case of Latin American protected industrialization, the African and Asian countries have experienced the inadequacies of the policy some twenty years after its initiation. Throughout the former capitalist colonies of Africa and Asia — especially those of Africa — there are factories operating well below capacity, or idle, for want of imported parts, raw materials or fuel; or for want of local demand from an impoverished population; or because of the inability to export competitively. Tanzania's metal fabricating industries are a case in point. Although accorded the highest priority by government as a strategic sector to which preference is given in allocating foreign exchange, the industries operate at about a quarter capacity because of the want of imported raw materials, which Tanzania has not the foreign exchange to buy for them.[51] Industrialization has not been found, in any former capitalist colony, to be an alternative route to economic development which might avoid the need to shed the heritage of capitalist colonialism; to mobilize land resources effectively and to secure a right balance between people and the resources to meet peoples' needs.

Development aid: All these and many similar efforts to alleviate the symptoms of the structural defects in the economies of the former capitalist colonies absorb considerable resources. Some of these resources come from favourable trading arrangements with the developing metropolitan countries, which aim to raise prices of primary products in the former capitalist colonies. Higher agricultural prices have the long run structural consequences already mentioned. It is also observed, in this connection, that low, and not high, agricultural prices have invariably been the condition under which economic development has been initiated in Europe, North America, Oceania and Japan. These wealthy countries, which are developing, adopted policies of raising agricultural prices and farmers' incomes only when their agriculture had ceased to be economically critically important, as agriculture continues to be for the poor, undeveloping, former capitalist colonies.

Other resources come to the undeveloping Third World as aid from the West. Official development assistance increased from an annual average of US $1.9 billion in 1950-55 to US $15.5 billion in 1975-78.[52] The equivalent amount for 1980 was US $33.5 billion, with an additional US $55.5 billion of credit.[53]

Aiding the Third World caters for a western need for emotional expression that grows with the continued decline of birth rates and with the increasing number of western one-child and no-child families. Aiding the Third World's starving is a surrogate for the emotional traumas of numerous family births, sicknesses and deaths which have been the normal experience of all peoples in the past, but which western people now rarely experience. Another manifestation of the same increasing need for emotional expression is the growth in the number of domestic pets and expenditure on them. Expenditure on animal pets by UK households increased from £200 million in 1972 to £962 million in 1982. This was much more rapid than the growth of GNP and more rapid than the growth of official aid to the Third World. The latter increased from £218 million to £859 million between 1970 and 1980.[54]

The Third World's demand for food and medical aid is insatiable, like its demand for veterinary services. The west, at minimal cost, can dramatically reduce mortalities, especially during crises. The persons saved by a few penceworth of food or drugs supplied in a crisis by the West remain, after the crisis, like the surplus animals on communal grazing, part of the burden of the Third World's excess population. Typically in the non-individualistic, non-western Third World, their maintenance needs exceed what they can contribute to production (Appendix A), and the excess of what they consume over what they can produce while they live reduces the amount that would have been available to others had they died in the crisis. Many years ago, Sir Louis Mallet, a Permanent Under Secretary in Britain's pre-independence Indian Office, referring to the relief of famine in India, wrote of the British public 'hugging itself at Indian expense in a cheap and selfish philantrophy'.[55] Only the scale and not the character of western aid to the Third World has changed since television has brought the misery of the Third World into the sitting rooms of the West. The West now indulges in orgies of 'cheap and selfish philantrophy' at the expense of famine-stricken Ethiopians and others. The latter day counterpart of the missionaries plea to 'save a black baby's soul for five shillings' is the UNICEF advertisement: 'Africa's drug problem. Every year at least 700,000 African children die for lack of life-saving drugs. It is as big a killer as lack of food.... These deaths can easily be prevented. £5 is enough to protect one child for life'.[56] A formidable Third World aid establishment now exists to stimulate and channel the flow of aid; and frequently to profit from that flow.

Not infrequently, western 'aid' to the Third World serves covert donor interests while harming those who are supposed to benefit in the Third World. This is especially the case with food aid, of which the EEC's support for India's 'Operation Flood' is a good example.

Operation Flood is an Indian government sponsored programme to 'flood' Indian cities with the milk that its milk-drinking, largely vegetarian population cherishes and for which it pays, relative to incomes, almost fifty times as much as the West.[57] The EEC delivers large quantities from its butter and skimmed milk powder surplus 'mountains' free to India, where these are reconstituted into milk and sold in the cities by the Indian Dairy Corporation (IDC). The proceeds of these sales enables the IDC to pay a higher price for more milk in India's villages, which it processes and delivers, up to 500 kilometres, to 'flood' the cities.

The shipment of hundreds of thousands of tons of EEC surplus butter and skimmed milk powder to India has benefitted powerful interests. Without those shipments, the 'mountains' of dairy surpluses would be higher. There would have been more pressure to dump more of the surpluses abroad and, as a result, there would have been more agitation by British and German consumers about Russians getting EEC dairy products at a small fraction of their cost in the EEC; and there would have been more complaints and threats of reprisals from the USA and New Zealand about the dumping of more EEC dairy surpluses on their export markets.

Without the Operation Flood outlet the EEC's 'super-levy' to discourage milk production, which Ireland vetoed, would have come sooner and it would have applied more severely. Thanks to Operation Flood the cost of dairy surplus disposal appears in the books of the EEC and of the member countries, including Ireland, not as a subsidy to agriculture, about which voters have become increasingly critical; but as aid to the Third World, about which voters are much more enthusiastic. Ireland's share of the EEC's dairy surpluses supplied to Operation Flood, in this way, accounts for almost a tenth of what is returned as Irish government 'development aid'.[58]

The EEC's participation in Operation Flood avoids the principal criticism that has been made against food aid to poor countries. This is that, by lowering the price of food in the recipient country, it depresses food production there and makes the recipient perpetually dependent on the donor country. Operation Flood, on the contrary, while, as noted, reducing the price of milk to consumers in the cities, raises its price to producers in the villages.

EEC participation in Operation Flood has other major advantages. The sale of hundreds of millions of dollars worth of EEC dairy surpluses in India[59] as well as making possible higher prices for village milk producers, provides funds for the employment by the IDC of a large and, by Indian standards, very highly paid staff. And Operation Flood works. Visiting monarchs and princes, presidents and prime ministers can see model milk collecting centres in the villages; and, in turn, can be seen doing so, via the world's media, by their constituents in the donor countries. This is a singular improvement on the more usual story of food aid's disappearance into the great black holes of Third World corruption and chaos.

The disadvantages of Operation Flood are less obvious and they affect less powerful and less articulate interests. The vast majority of India's poor live in the villages, and the vast majority of these rural poor are without cows or land. The EEC's participation in Operation Flood raises for these, who are among the world's poorest, the price of the milk which is effectively their only source of animal protein.

Most Indian cowkeepers are poor, landless persons who, apart from whatever scavenging is to be got in a country that has 18% of the world's bovines and 16% of the world's population crowded on to its 2% of the world's land, must rely on fodder bought from those who own land. Under the circumstances, that fodder understandably is expensive, with a ton of straw — the poorest of fodders and virtually worthless in the West — typically costing the equivalent of half the annual income of an average Indian.[60] A higher milk price in the villages reinforces all those factors already operating to cause the country's gross overstocking with cattle. A higher price for milk thus forces the landless cowkeepers to pay even more to the landed for the fodder, without which even Indian cows cannot survive, in order to maintain a given milk output.

Finally, the EEC-financed Operation Flood, by raising the price of milk in Indian villages, makes it more profitable than it would already be for

248

Indian landowners to use their land for milk production. Thanks in part to Operation Flood, the price of milk relative to the price of grain is almost twice as high in India as it is in the West. In the West it pays to feed large quantities of grain to cows. So the EEC supported Operation Flood makes it still more profitable for Indian landowners to use their grain and their grain-producing resources for fodder for cows producing milk for the relatively wealthy urban middle class, who alone can afford to buy it. This, in part, accounts for the fact that India's masses have now less grain per person to consume than formerly.[61] The EEC, in giving 'food aid' to India, while placating and rewarding powerful, wealthy interests both in Europe and India, exacerbates the grinding, hopeless poverty of the subcontinent's teeming, inarticulate, impotent masses.[62]

Marxism. Palpable economic failure in the former capitalist colonies normally precludes western, liberal, democratic political evolution. Political power, which is almost invariably based on control of the army and police,* oscillates between oligarchies of the right, representative of property owners, and those of the left who hold that property is incompatible with social well-being. The latter draw intellectual inspiration from a western source: the nineteenth century European political economist, Karl Marx, whose analysis, of whatever validity for his own time and place, is singularly inappropriate to the undeveloping Third World in the final decades of the twentieth century. Groups in the Third World look to Russia as a model and as a source of encouragement and material assistance. In doing so, they overlook the differences that make the Russian model as inappropriate as the metropolitan model to the conditions of the former capitalist colonies. They overlook the enormous wealth of natural resources relative to population that Russia has. The USSR, with 6% of the world's population, has 12% of its pastures, 16% of its cropland, 22% of its forests and 17% of its landsurface.[63] These resources have been developed over the ages by commercial and cultural contact with the West. Proponents of the Russian model overlook the essential continuity of modern, communist Russia with the thousand-year-old tsarist Russia, autocratic rule by the tsars having been replaced by the dictatorship of the communist party. They overlook the fact that Russia was never a capitalist colony in which western individualism and especially the western institution of property were never established (Appendix A).

---

*India is exceptional because its great size and heterogeneity makes a military takeover difficult (Appendix A). Ireland is also exceptional for the reasons given in Chapters 5 and 6.

Uncolonized East Asia

The rice-growing countries of East Asia, which are China, Japan, Korea and Taiwan, were never colonized (Chapter 1). Because of that, they provide by contrast useful insights into the experiences and performances of other non-western, non-individualistic, non-capitalist countries which, however, have been capitalist colonies.

Free of the heritage of capitalist colonialism the countries of East Asia have been able to appraise western technology and culture more objectively. They have been able to do so free from the biases and preconceptions of the former capitalist colonies. These derive, in large measure, from the powerful individualistic interests established in the former capitalist colonies. They owe much also to continued intellectual imperialism. East Asia, without this handicap, did not accept the principle of comparative advantage which has been the basis of western, international economic relationships since the time of David Ricardo; though, it may be noted, it was not so in the earlier mercantile period (Appendix B). Free trade, in accordance with the principle of comparative advantage in the age of factory capitalism, has resulted in the realisation by the metropolitan, industrialized countries of the economies of scale associated with manufacturing. In the capitalist colonies, where land has always been limiting, free trade has resulted in specialization in primary production which is subject to decreasing returns. That specialization has enhanced the value of the landed property created by the metropolitan powers while specialization on primary production, subject to decreasing returns, has accentuated the impoverishment of the masses whom property made landless. Free trade has thus been a key factor in the undevelopment of the former capitalist colonies (see Appendix B).

Japan occupies the same latitude as the Mediterranean. But whereas the Mediterranean gets its rainfall in the winter, when it is least beneficial, Japan, thanks to the northeast monsoon, gets its rainfall in the summer when it is most beneficial. Crop-growing in the Ancient Mediterranean was founded, necessarily on slavery (Appendix A); but Japan's crop-growing is riverine. Japan's rich, volcanic soil, well watered in the warm summers, supported more people than were necessary for its cultivation. There was, as a result, no place for individualism in Japan (Appendix A).

> Throughout Japanese history, up to the present, individualism has never prospered, and, as a result, a strong advocacy of liberalism has been virtually non-existent...In spite of her economic success in the postwar era, the prospects of individualism and liberalism blossoming and maturing in Japan are still extremely remote.[64]

Japan differed from most riverine societies which tended, as in China, Egypt or Peru, to be monolithic. The archipelegaic, mountainous topography favoured fragmentation:

> There is only one relatively extensive plain in Japan, the Kanti Plain

around Tokyo, which stretches a mere 120 miles in the longest dimension. Otherwise the habitable portions of Japan consist of small sea coast flood plains, relatively narrow river valleys, and a few basins in the mountains. The division of the country into many small units of terrain has been conductive to local separatism... [Apart from Tokyo, Osaka and Kyoto] the rest of Japan was dotted with castle towns which ranged up to 100,000 in population and were the seats of roughly 265 semi-autonomous feudal lords.[65]

Japan's feudal lords, or *daimyos,* resembled Europe's feudal lords in-as-much as they were numerous, each exercised political power within a small territory, and warring with neighbouring lords was continuous. They differed fundamentally from Europe's feudal lords whose relationship with their capital-owning peasants was symbiotic, contractual and legal (Appendix A).

In Japan, the Chinese system had placed less emphasis on law and more on morality — that is, on the subordination of law to the moral sense of the ruler, since his right to rule was theoretically based on his superior wisdom and morality. Hence the lord-vassal relationship was seen as one of unlimited and absolute loyalty on the part of the vassal, not one of legal contract between the two. There was thus no room for the development of the concept of political rights, as happened in Europe.[66]

Japan's *daimyos,* with a power that they derived from the local, riverine surplus and that they exercised against the mainly nominal emperor, differed even more fundamentally from England's landed gentry. The latter held titles 'in fee simple' from the crown, adhering to feudal forms while departing radically from feudal content. The titles were nothing apart from the underlying state power to enforce them, and hence the critical importance of the seventeenth century's struggle by the newly created social class of English landed proprietors to capture the state (Chapter 3). Japan, by contrast, had never been colonized by the West and so did not have superimposed on it European concepts of property. Each of Japan's *daimyos* was sovereign, or tried to be so, and unlike European feudal lords, had no countervailing obligations. In so far as sovereigns could be said to have a class interest, that class interest was to curb the power of any emperor who might challenge their local sovereignty.

Neither the Chinese nor the Mongolians from mainland Asia succeeded in invading Japan. Japan was the only considerable crop-growing society of the Old World of Eurasia and Africa that did not have contact with those pastoralists whose diffusion, from their original homes in the Eurasian steppes and the semi-arid lands of the Middle East and of Sahelian Africa, has been a dominant influence in human affairs during the past four or five millenia (Appendix A). But these pastoral influences reached Japan eventually by an indirect route. They arrived in Japan via the Portugese and other European traders and would-be colonizers. The Tokugawan

Shogunate, having acquired control of Japan by the use of western military technology, proceeded in 1618 to force the West out of Japan. They then, for 240 years of traditional Japanese isolation, exercised an uneasy sovereignty over the fissiparous local lords. That isolation was shattered in 1853 when Commodore Perry and the US navy sailed into Tokyo bay and dragged Japan once more into the comity of nations.

Following the Meiji restoration Japan set about creating a modern society, largely with a view to acquiring the strength to 'expel the barbarians' who had followed Perry and had secured extra-territorial status for themselves.[67] There was no place in a modern society for the *daimyos* who, with the appropriated surplus of Japan's productive soil, had exercised their local sovereignty. They became the rentiers of the new Japanese state, which then itself proceeded to appropriate the agricultural surplus which the *daimyos* had previously taken:

> The annual land tax...was paid in rice and it usually amounted to between forty and fifty per cent of the total yield of the paddy fields...The land tax remained for many years the only important source of revenue, and in 1879-80 it accounted for four-fifths of the whole tax revenue.[68]

Thus the surplus, which traditionally had been used for the most part to support the warring samurai caste who had kept Japan in continuous civil war for a thousand years, provided most of the revenue for Japanese governments until well into the twentieth century.[69]

The absence from Japan of the property/land-owning class that was created in every capitalist colony had the following important effects:

1. There was in Japan no powerful group to press for maximizing agricultural prices, especially through an export trade, unlike the situation in India and in other capitalist colonies. The annuities of the *daimyos* were fixed and independent of agricultural revenue, except to the extent that the lower food prices were the higher was the real value of the annuities. The peasants were too poor and too weak to exercise any influence on agricultural price policy; and in any case, any benefits from higher agricultural prices would have been appropriated by higher land taxes. Only the central exchequer could have benefited from higher agricultural prices, because these would have made possible still higher land taxes.*

---

*It is a paradox of economics that high agricultural prices are least likely to occur when they are most likely to be beneficial and least likely to do harm. In Japan, where land taxes would have appropriated the surplus from higher agricultural prices for social purposes and would thus have prevented them from causing agriculture to become inefficient there was no powerful interest concerned to secure higher agricultural prices.

Because of the absence of a powerful group pressing for higher agricultural prices, neither was there a 'free trade' lobby pressing the case for comparative advantage in foreign trade. Comparative advantage between metropolises and colonies implies, in accordance with the *pacte colonial,* that the former focus on manufacturing, where economies of scale obtain, and the latter focus on primary production, where declining returns obtain but land values rise. Japan instead, unlike the capitalist colonies, concentrated on exporting manufactured goods as the metropolises did. These included peasant grown silk which, though requiring mulberry leaves, which are grown on land that is otherwise useless for agriculture, for feeding the pupae from which the silk is spun, is so labour intensive and so land-extensive as to warrant being classed as a manufactured product.

2. Japan had an efficient agriculture. Heavy land taxes forced farmers to be efficient or to make way for those who were. An efficient Japanese agriculture caused agricultural and food output more than to double with output per head increasing by around 20% in the 50 years from the 1880s to the 1930s.[70] This contrasts sharply with Ireland's stagnating agricultural output between the 1840s and now; and the static or declining output of food per person in much of the Third World (Chapter 1).

3. The Japanese government, with most of its revenue obtained from land taxes, did not have to tax labour or capital heavily. This avoided raising costs to Japanese manufacturing industry, which would have impaired its ability to fight its way into export markets.

4. The absorption by government, through land taxes, of the agricultural surplus and the direction of that surplus towards industrial capital formation, forced surplus labour out of agriculture while simultaneously opening opportunities for it in non-agricultural employment, including silk production.

These profound structural consequences of the absence of a landed class in modern Japan placed the country firmly on the path to development. Once established on that path, Japan did all those things that are most frequently recommended for making agriculture productive and thereby stimulating general economic development. It provided agricultural extension services; it undertook agricultural research; and it encouraged the formation of agricultural cooperatives. These and other things were possible for a rapidly developing Japan. They may have facilitated development; or they may have hindered it. But contrary to the views of a host of undiscerning foreign observers and possibly contrary to the views also of most Japanese, these activities were the effect, and not the cause, of development. Development was made possible, first, by appropriating the agricultural surplus through land taxes for development purposes; and second, by drawing eclectically on western technology. These things were possible because Japan had not been capitalist colonized.

Once set on the development path Japan has developed as consistently as the 138 former capitalist colonies have undeveloped. Devastating wartime defeat in Japan, as in Germany, merely expedited growth by obliterating many remnants of the old order. Not even the MacArthur 'land reforms', which imposed property in land on Japan, could impede progress: for with land declining in value relative to a rapidly growing GNP, in accordance with the paradox of property, it continued to be efficiently used despite these 'reforms'.

China's reaction to western culture, like its reaction through the ages to foreign influences, has been more ambivalent and less decisive and zenophobic than Japan's. However, the dictatorship of China's communist party is not fundamentally different from the absolute rule that has been practised by Chinese emperors for millenia. Mao Tse Tung's 'Great Leap Forward' accorded with tradition in originating with the Eurasian influence of Marxist-Leninism, and in resulting in the same sort of havoc to China's complex riverine economy as other invasions from the barbarous north had occasioned frequently in the past. But after the trauma of this intrusion had passed, China once again, collected itself together and drove out the alien influences in a way no former capitalist colony has ever done.

Having once more reasserted its political and intellectual independence China has begun to address the problems of the age in accordance with its native genius.[71] Neither of the two interests established by the West in their former capitalist colonies is being permitted to undevelop China. Titles to land — originally created by the metropolitan powers and still protected by the western-type states of the former capitalist colonies — in China are dependent on compulsory crop deliveries. These land taxes ensure the efficient operation of land and, by increasing the supply of food while reducing the value of land, prevent the emergence of the paradox of property.

The People's Republic of China, freed alike from western Marxist-Leninism and from western liberal preconceptions, recognizes the inescapable social need to match the higher expectancy of life, which modern technology makes easy and inexpensive, with birth rates reduced well below their biological norm. The individual's right to a higher life expectancy, which is unconditional in the former capitalist colonies — a 'basic need' — has been made conditional on reducing birth rates in the People's Republic of China. Through such measures as the one-child family programme, China reduced its annual population growth from 2.1% in 1950 to 1.2% in 1970: or to less than half the average rate of population growth in the Third World. It plans to stop, by the end of this century, the growth of a population that already exceeds 1000 million people. It plans thereafter to reduce its population, by continued low birth rates, to about 700 millions within 100 years.[72]

The prospects for China, in so far as it is unencumbered by the heritage of capitalist colonialism which elevates individual rights outside their western metropolitan context, but instead makes the individual's possession of land conditional on its being efficiently used and makes the individual's expectation of a long life conditional on his or her restraining procreation, are brighter than the prospects for the undeveloping former capitalist colonies. None of these has escaped its heritage.

Epilogue: On Population Stabilization

Chapters 7 and 8 of this work specify a course of action that is designed to rid Ireland of its heritage of capitalist colonialism. Elements of that course of action, which is designed to secure the more productive and equitable use of resources, have relevance to the other former capitalist colonies. However, Irish capitalist colonialism differs in one fundamental respect from the heritage of capitalist colonialism elsewhere: the population made surplus in Ireland has, in the past, emigrated. While that has created its own problems (Chapter 5), it has also resulted in Ireland's residual population having incomes that are higher than the incomes of two-thirds of the world's population. Elsewhere the surplus population has not emigrated; it has remained to generate more and worse poverty. Given Ireland's relatively high incomes, the necessary and sufficient condition for development is getting factor prices right (Chapter 7). That, together with the suggested elimination of Childrens' Allowances after a specified early date ought to reduce Irish birth rates and eliminate the excess of births over deaths in Ireland which, reflecting its relatively high incomes, is far less than in other former capitalist colonies. Rectifying the structural economic defects that are everywhere the heritage of capitalist colonialism would, in other former capitalist colonies, raise incomes, reduce death rates and possibly accelerate population growth. Given the low incomes and the high population growths of these countries, any improvement in their productive capacity would be likely to be quickly offset by increased calls from an expanded population on that capacity. Attempting to develop other former capitalist colonies is like trying to fill a sieve with water. It is necessary first to place a bottom in the sieve. Even radical attempts to develop former capitalist colonies, other than Ireland, will fail if unaccompanied by purposeful, specific measures to bring birth rates into line with much reduced death rates.

The People's Republic of China has demonstrated one way of doing so. But China does not have a capitalist colonial heritage, a major element of which is that the rights of individuals to reduced death rates is unqualified; a part of 'basic needs'. It is unrealistic to expect these societies to strip their members of this right, which was implanted by capitalist colonialism.

Any such attempt, as in India in the 1970s, would be likely to precipitate a major crisis, like the haemorrhage caused by the excision of a cancerous growth which will in any case be fatal. It is therefore necessary to buy back (instead of taking back, as in the People's Republic of China and as was unsuccessfully attempted under Mrs Gandhi in India in the early 1970s) the right of individuals to have birth rates approaching the biological limit while simultaneously having death rates greatly reduced by centralized, western-type states and by western originating public hygiene and medical science.

The cost of having children when discounted to the time of conception at 'reasonable' rates of time discount is sufficiently high for most people with relatively high incomes to make them wish to avoid pregnancy. But these costs, when discounted at the extremely high rates of time discount that are normal among poor, malnourished, hopeless people, are derisory. It makes little sense to hungry people, who are unsure of their next day's existence, to take steps to avoid costs in a distant future which, while of concern to better off people, is of no concern to them. If, however, payment were made to poor, fecund women *not* to be pregnant, then they would have the incentive that they do not have now to remain non-pregnant. If the payments were withdrawn when the women became pregnant, there would be a deterrent to pregnancy that does not now exist.

Women in the fecund age group, 15-45 years, wishing to qualify for non-pregnancy payments would take a pregnancy test, say every six months. If proven non-pregnant, they would receive a dated certificate, valid for six months, to that effect. The certificate would entitle them to receive, at a local post office or its equivalent, weekly payments. Women wishing to continue to receive non-pregnancy payments would undertake further pregnancy tests as desired. The poorer the women, and therefore the more likely they are now to have biologically determined birth rates, the more eager they are likely to be to earn non-pregnancy payments of any given level. The higher the level of the non-pregnancy payments, the more women who will try harder to avoid pregnancy and the more sharply birth rates will fall.

Western aid, which now greatly harms the masses of the Third World, would be beneficial if it were used to provide incentives to women to remain non-pregnant. Western aid is harmful now, because the concepts that inform it have different implications in the West, where the aid originates, from the implications that it has in the Third World, where the aid is applied. Western aid forwards those individual interests which have been the powerhouse of progress in the West (Appendix A); but which everywhere in the Third World have been socially destructive. The only form of western aid that can assist the Third World is aid that deters people from pursuing socially destructive, western-implanted, self-interest. This aid might be in the form of subsidies to governments pro rata to the taxes they levy on land, which would deter incompetent persons from retaining possession of it; or subsidies pro rata to taxes on livestock, which would deter stockowners from overstocking communal grazing land. Western aid would be *most* effective if paid to deter fecund women in the Third World from becoming pregnant.

Western official aid to the Third World has been averaging about US$ 15.5 billion annually in recent years.[73] Western loans to the Third World increased by US$ 400 billion between 1972 and 1982.[74] The annual flow of western official aid and of credits to the Third World has, therefore, been some US$ 60 billion in recent years. It was US$ 88.95 billion in 1980.[75] That flow of resources exceeds US$ 200 per annum for each fecund woman in the Third World, these accounting for some 20% of the total Third World population of some 1.8 billion people. Average GNP per person in the Third World is around US$ 660 (Chapter 1), so the amount of aid and credit flows to the Third World is substantial relative to Third World incomes. Focusing more narrowly on poorer women, whose fertility tends to be highest, there were in 1978 an estimated 256 million fecund women with average incomes of less than US$ 300.[76] The annual flow of official aid and of credit from the West to the Third World would make it possible to pay these women over two-thirds of their present incomes for remaining non-pregnant. (The equivalent amount in Ireland would be some £200 per month.) If, as a result of the proposed payments, birth rates in the Third World were reduced from an average of around 40 per thousand per annum to around 20 per thousand or less, then, even allowing for the decline in death rates that would result from higher incomes and improved nutritional levels, populations would quickly stablize and would then decline, especially in the poorest countries where population growth is now fastest.

The stabilization or reduction of Third World populations, secured by paying women not to become pregnant, would bring more benefit to more poor people than anything else. The women who would receive the payments are the world's poorest and weakest and would be made immediately better off. The most money would be received by the poorest women who suffer most. Resources that are now pre-empted in poor societies for rearing and supporting the rapid growth of populations that are economically excessive would be freed for physical capital formation. Capital formation per person would increase because populations would be smaller and the amount available for physical capital formation would be larger. Poor countries and poor people would secure quick relief from the inefficiency, iniquity and corruption that are the inescapable consequence of the rapid growth of poor populations and the degradation of individuals implicit in that situation.

The benefit of using western aid and credit to pay Third World women not to have children is the excess of what the children would consume at virtually all stages of their lives over what they could produce in economies where labour does not limit output (Appendix A). The value of that excess of lifetime consumption over lifetime production is substantial when discounted to the present at the low time rates of time discount of the aid and credit donors. That present value is many times greater than when discounted at the astronomical interest rates that are normal among the world's poor (and among poor Irish housewives who borrow from moneylenders[77]). No other major development aid project would yield a benefit nearly as great in relation to its cost to so many of the world's poorest as the use of western funds to make it attractive for Third World women to avoid pregnancy.

Notes

Ireland in Crisis

1. Ireland here, in a pre-1922 context, refers to the whole island. After 1922, it normally refers to the 26 Counties that seceded from the United Kingdom of Great Britain and Ireland to form an independent state. The 26 Counties and the Republic are synonyms for Ireland in this sense. The Six Counties that remained within the UK after 1922 are referred to as Northern Ireland.

2. *World Bank Atlas* (Washington DC, World Bank, 1978) p.6. However, more than a quarter of the world's population have average incomes higher than the Irish. Countries with higher incomes now, but not 60 years ago, include Japan, Italy, Spain, Poland and the USSR. There are eight more countries with incomes that are between 80 and 100% of Irish incomes: Greece, Venezuela, Bulgaria, Hungary, Puerto Rico, Hong Kong, and Trinidad and Tobago. Allowing for differences in climate associated with Ireland's higher latitude, US $80 in any of these countries is likely to be deemed by most people as preferable to US $100 in Ireland.

3. Based on the following estimates:

	1953	1982
National income (£m.)	437	9036
Population ('000s)	2961	3481
Consumer price index	100	945

4. World Bank *Development Report* (Washington DC, World Bank, 1980) pp.112-57.

5. W. MacArthur 'Medical history of the Great Famine' in R.D. Edwards and T.D. Williams (eds) *The Great Famine: Studies in Irish History, 1845-52* (Dublin, Brown and Nolan, 1956).

6. *Statistical Abstract of Ireland 1936* (hereinafter *Statistical Abstract*) p.4; *Statistical Abstract, 1980,* p.20.

7. *Statistical Abstract 1980* p.20.

8. R. Crotty 'Modernisation and land reform: real or cosmetic, the Irish case'. *Journal of Peasant Studies*, Vol. 11. No.1 (1983) pp.101-16.

9. C. Clark *Population Growth and Land Use* (London, Macmillan, 1977) p.64. The populations of Britain and Ireland changed as follows over a period of 150 years:

	Population in Thousands	
	1821	1971
Ireland (26 Counties)	4422	2978
Ireland (Northern)	1380	1536
England	11261	46019
Scotland	2093	5229
Wales	717	2731

Source: *Census of Population of Great Britain 1821;* UK *Annual Abstract of Statistics 1984;* Ireland *Statistical Abstract 1980.* The closest parallel in historic times to Ireland's failure for 160 years to provide a livelihood for half its people is, perhaps, the collapse of Mexico's population from 25.2 millions at the Spanish conquest in 1519, to 1.1 million in 1605 (M. Gongora *Studies in the Colonial History of Spanish America* (Cambridge, University Press, 1975) pp.140-1.

10. *Irish Times* 12.11.1984.

11. *See* Table 1.2. There is an almost perfect correlation ($r^2 = 0.91$) between columns 6 and 7 of Table 1.2. Irish producers add the cost of servicing debt to prices which, under free trade conditions, depresses exports and/or increases imports.

12. T.K. Whitaker *Interests* (Dublin, Institute of Administration, 1984) p.101.

13. *Budget 1984* p.107; *Central Bank Annual Report 1984* p.15.

14. *Statistical Abstract 1936* p.4; *Statistical Abstract 1980* p.20. A more normal marriage rate is that in Britain where, in the 1970s, it was about eight per 1000 *(UK Annual Abstract of Statistics 1981* p.31).

15. *Statistical Abstract 1980* p.20.

16. United Nations *Demographic Yearbook 1979* (New York, United Nations, 1979) p.170; *Statistical Abstract 1936* p.6; *Statistical Abstract 1980* p.20.

17. The clearest and most comprehensive evidence of the continued deprivation of Northern Ireland Catholics is contained in the *Census of Population 1971 Religion Tables, Northern Ireland* (Belfast, HMSO, 1975). This shows a strong, consistent bias in favour of the non-Catholic population, who have a disproportionately large share of all jobs and of the better jobs; and a similarly strong, consistent bias against Catholics, of whom a disproportionately large number are unemployed or are in the poorest paid and least attractive employment. Sectarian violence in Northern Ireland is firmly grounded on the use of political power to secure a livelihood for Protestants on preferential terms, by denying Catholics their fair share of opportunities.

18. R. Crotty *Irish Agricultural Production: Its Volume and Structure* (Cork, University Press, 1966) pp.164-5.

19. Ireland's population was as large in the 1730's as it is now (Crotty, 1983, *op.cit.*).

20. Based on the distribution of Indian incomes by deciles. *See* World Bank *Development Report 1981* (Washington DC, World Bank, 1981) p.182.

21. T.G. Weiss and A. Jenning *More for the Least? Prospects for the Poorest Countries in the Eighties* (Lexington, Lexington Books, 1983) p.5.

22. *Ibid.* p.15.

23. R.M. Sundrum *Development Economics: a Framework for Analysis and Policy* (Chichester, Wiley, 1983) p.245.

24. Weiss and Jenning *op.cit.* p.15.

25. S. Jain *Size Distribution of Income: A Compilation of Data* (Washington DC, World Bank, 1975).

26. Weiss and Jenning *op.cit.* p.13.

27. *Ibid.* p.15.

28. *Irish Times* 23.11.1982.

29. M. Godet and O. Ruyssen *The Old World and the New Technologies* (Brussels, EEC, 1982).

30. J. Simmons 'Education for development reconsidered' in M.P. Todaro (ed) *The Struggle for Economic Development* (London, Longman, 1983).
31. D.W. Fryer and J.C. Jackson *Indonesia* (London, E. Benn, 1977) p.58.
32. *The Ecologist* December, 1980.
33. C.M. Cipolla *The Economic History of World Population* (Harmondsworth, Penguin, 1965) p.105.
34. G. Barraclough *An Introduction to Contemporary History* (Harmondsworth, Penguin, 1966) p.231, quoting K.G. Myrdal *An International Economy: Problems and Prospects* (New York, Harper and Brothers, 1956).
35. K.G. Myrdal, *Asian Drama: an Inquiry into the Poverty of Nations* (London, Allen Lane, 1968).
36. N. Atkinson *Irish Education: a History of Educational Institutions* (Dublin, Allen Figgis, 1969) p.83.
37. Myrdal *op.cit.* p.677.
38. Mahatir bin Mohamed *The Malay Dilemma* (Singapore, Asia Pacific Press, 1970) pp.16-31.
39. R.D.C. Black 'The progress of industrialization, 1850-1920' in T.W. Moody and J.C. Beckett (eds) *Ulster Since 1800: a Social Survey* (London, British Broadcasting Corporation, 1955) p.59.
40. Food and Agriculture Organisation (FAO) *Production Yearbook, 1975* (Rome, FAO, 1975).
41. World Bank, 1978, *op. cit.*
42. A.R. Brown and C.D. Forde *African Systems of Kinship and Marriage* (London, International African Institute, 1950) p.v.
43. A. Toynbee *Mankind and Mother Earth* (Oxford, University Press, 1976) p.569. Except, it might be thought, in Ireland which also occupies a position in two worlds: geographically it is part of the West, but historically it is part of the capitalist colonized Third World. Relative to its population, its literary contributions have been no less remarkable than Russia's.
44. Liu Zheng *et al, China's Population: Problems and Prospects* (Beijing, New World Press, 1981) p.6. The Middle East fits least well into the development/undevelopment dichotomy suggested here. The region, in recent centuries, was part of the Turkish Ottoman empire, which was not a capitalist society; though, like Russia, it interacted with capitalist Europe. Following the dismemberment of the Ottoman empire after the First World War, the countries of the Middle East came under British and French colonial rule for some decades. Now Saudi Arabia, Bahrein, the United Arab Emirates and Kuwait are indubitably developing, in the sense of having more people better off than formerly. Iraq, Syria, Iran and possibly Jordan are undeveloping in as much as these countries now have more people experiencing poverty than formerly. Their undevelopment is hardly attributable to capitalist colonialism, as these countries were only briefly colonized by Britain and France between the First and Second World Wars. Development, on the other hand, has been thrust upon the region by the fortuitous presence there of major oil resources relative to the region's population. The Middle Eastern situation is further complicated by the colonization of the region for several centuries by Ottoman Turkey which, to repeat, was similar to Russia in being powerfully influenced by Central Western Europe, without being individualistic and capitalist (P.K.

261

Hitti *The Near East in History: A 5,000 Year Story* (Princeton, D. Van Nostrand Company, 1961) p.330. The matter requires more thought.

The Evolution of Individualistic Capitalism: Regional Variations
1. E.L. Jones *The European Miracle* (Cambridge, University Press, 1981).
2. R. Crotty 'Review of E.L. Jones *The European Miracle*' in *Irish Journal of Agricultural Economics and Rural Sociology,* Vol.9, No.2, 1983, pp.193-5.
3. Jones *op.cit.* p.15.
4. M. Bloch *French Rural History: an Essay on its Basic Characteristics.* Translated by J. Sondheimer. (London, Routledge, 1966) p.274.
5. *See* J.L. Bolton *The Medieval English Economy, 1150-1500* (London, Dent, 1980) pp.175-7 for Italian financing of the English crown and of the wool trade. *See* J.M. Thompson *Lectures in Foreign History* (Oxford, Blackwell, 1956) pp.26-8, for Italy as a source of plunder.
6. Jones *op.cit.* p.47.
7. P. Farb *Man's Rise to Civilization* (London, Paladin, 1971) pp.39-40, treats of the very different cultures of the Lapp-like Chucki of Siberia and the Eskimos of Alaska.
8. *See* F.D. Logan *The Vikings in History* (London, Hutchinson, 1983) map p.13.
9. J. Blum *Land and Peasant in Russia from the Ninth to the Nineteenth Century* (Princeton, University Press, 1972) p.23.
10. Blum *op.cit.* p.21; N.V. Riasonovsky *A History of Russia* (Oxford, University Press, 1977) p.51.
11. Blum *op.cit.* p.128.
12. Russia approached nearest to establishing the rule of law, property and individualism in the decades following its defeat in the Crimean War by the western powers. Defeat made clear how dangerously an autocratic Russia lagged, economically and technologically, behind the West. To safeguard itself against the threat inherent in that situation, Russia had no option but to modernize.

    Modernization meant, above all, capital formation. The need for vast amounts of capital, from domestic and foreign sources attenuated the autocratic power of the tsarist state. To adapt and to survive, this state was forced to recognize the rights of those with savings and who were willing to provide the essential capital. Reforms included the emancipation of Russia's serfs, who had always been held in bondage at the will of the autocratic tsars. This contrasted with the situation in Central Western Europe where monarchs sought, from an early date, to eliminate serfdom together with 'coign and livery' as part of a protracted campaign to tame their 'over-mighty subjects'. Reform included also the introduction, if not of parliamentary government, of parliamentary representation.

    These reforms, however, were insufficient to spare Russia from ignominious defeat by Japan in 1904 and from massive and much more costly losses in the First World War. The hesitantly reforming tsarist state was toppled and Russia reverted to its traditional autocracy. The main difference is that since 1917 that autocracy, which is incompatible with the rule of law and with property and individualism, has been exercised by the self-elected and self-prepetuating communist party.

13. G.F. Mitchell *The Irish Landscape* (London, Collins, 1976) p.98.
14. *Ibid.* p. 162.
15. M. Herity and S. Eogan *Ireland in Prehistory* (London, Routledge and Keegan Paul, 1977) p.222.
16. Herity and Eogan *op. cit.* p.128; L.H. van Wijngaarden-Bakker 'The animal remains from the beaker settlement at Newgrange, County Meath. First report.' *Proceedings of the Royal Irish Academy* Vol. 74, Section C (1974) pp.313-83. *See also* Appendix A on lactose tolerance.
17. Mitchell *op. cit.* pp. 115, 136-7.
18. *Ibid.* pp.105-13.
19. E. McCracken *The Irish Woods since Tudor Times* (Newton Abbot, David and Charles, 1971) p.33.
20. *See* Appendix A. The advantage of grass over trees in Ireland's insular climate is still testified to now by the country's relatively small area of woodland, after more than 50 years of sustained government effort at afforestation. Land that can grow virtually nothing in continental Europe, grows grass in Ireland; so the opportunity cost of putting it under grass is greater in Ireland. More importantly, once planted in trees, the cost of suppressing competing grass growth is much greater in Ireland than in continental Europe. These considerations, rather than the frequently assumed prejudices of Irish farmers, account for the fact that only 5% of Irish land is forested, compared to 33% in Europe as a whole. On the other hand, 64% of Irish land is pasture as compared to 18% of European land. Food and Agriculture Organisation *Production Yearbook 1979* (Rome, FAO, 1979) pp.52-61.
21. The fact that Irish cereal yields are 37% higher than the European average confirms rather than refutes this point (FAO *op.cit.* p.94). The difficulty of growing crops in Ireland is such that they can be grown profitably only under specially favourable circumstances, where high yields compensate for the greater difficulty. Ireland has only 7% of its farmland under cereals compared to 31% for Europe as a whole (FAO *op.cit.*) pp.52-3.
22. A.T. Lucas 'Cattle in ancient and medieval Irish society' *O'Connell School Union Record, 1937-58* (Dublin, O'Connell School, 1958). European cattle generally are of the *Bos taurus* type, which lactate without the presence of the dam's live calf. *See* Appendix A.
23. Lucas *op.cit.* The Gaelic *creagh,* when successful, yielded its participants loot in cattle and probably also in women, to sustain a polygamous society. The term, pronounced 'crack', continues to be used colloquially in Ireland with reference to jollification and celebration, as in the ballad: 'The crack was good in Cricklewood'.
24. M. McCurtain *Tudor and Stuart Ireland* (Dublin, Gill and Macmillan, 1972) p.117.
25. C. Litton Falkiner (ed) 'The itinerary of Fynes Moryson' in *Illustration of Irish History and Topography mainly of the Seventeenth Century* (London, Longman Green, 1904) pp.230, 321.
26. J.M. Roberts, *The Hutchinson History of the World* (Harmondsworth, Penguin, 1976) p.46.
27. Mitchell *op. cit.* p.161.
28. M. Dolley *Anglo-Norman Ireland* (Dublin, Gill and Macmillan, 1972) pp.148-89.

29. K. Hughes 'Introduction' in A.A. Otway-Ruthvan *A History of Medieval Ireland* (Cambridge, University Press, 1968) p.9.
30. Quoted by B. Bradshaw *The Irish Constitutional Revolution of the Sixteenth Century* (Cambridge, University Press, 1979) p.28.
31. *Ibid.*

The Evolution of English Capitalism
1. G. Rickman *The Corn Supply of Ancient Rome* (Oxford University Press, 1979) p.83.
2. J.Z. Titow *English Rural Society, 1200-1350* (London, Allen and Unwin, 1969) p.72.
3. J.M. Roberts *The Hutchinson History of the World* (Harmondsworth, Penguin, 1976) p.46.
4. Titow *op.cit.* p.53.
5. R. Crotty *Cattle, Economics and Development* (Slough, CAB, 1980) p.23.
6. R.B. Smith *Land and Politics in the England of Henry VIII* (Oxford University Press, 1970) p.44.
7. On twelve monastic estates in 1536-39 the average rents per acre were: on cropland, 8 pence; on pasture 11 pence; and on meadow 24 pence. (Smith *op.cit.* p.278).
8. M.J. Tucker *The Life of Thomas Howard* (The Hague, Mouton & Co. 1964) p.37; G. Carter *Outlines of English History: Dates, Facts, Events, People* (London, Ward Lock, 1984) p.181.
9. G.R. Elton *England Under the Tudors* (London, Methuen, 1955) p.232.
10. L. Stone *The Causes of the English Revolution 1529-1642* (London, Routledge and Keegan Paul, 1972) p.154.
11. T.B. Macauley *The Works of Lord Macaulay: Essays and Biographies* (London, Longman Green, 1898) Vol. 11, pp.190-1.
12. Smith *op.cit.* p.49.
13. E.H.P. Brown and S.V. Hopkins 'Seven centuries of the prices of consumables' in E.M. Carus-Wilson (ed) *Essays in Economic History* Vol. 2. (London, Arnold, 1962).
14. B.H.S. van Bath *The Agrarian History of Western Europe, AD 500-1850* (London, Arnold, 1963) pp.80-1; P. Laslett 'Introduction: the numerical study of society' in E.A. Wrigley (ed) *An Introduction to English Historical Demography* (London, Weidenfeld and Nicolson, 1966) p.6; E.A. Wrigley *Population in History* (London, Weidenfeld and Nicolson, 1969) p.13.
15. Based on particulars of vine establishment costs in South Africa now, supplied by Professor A. Kassier, Department of Agricultural Economics, University of Stellenbosch, South Africa, March, 1983.
16. B. Moore *The Social Origins of Dictatorship and Democracy* (Harmondsworth, Penguin, 1967) pp.46-8.
17. I. Wallerstein *The Modern World System: Mercantilism and the Consolidation of the European World Economy 1600-1750* (London, Academic Press, 1980) p.85.

Irish Capitalist Colonialism
1. J.H. Parry *The Discovery of the Sea* (London, Weidenfeld and Nicolson, 1975) p.17.

2. D. Denoon *Settler Capitalism* (Oxford, University Press, 1983) p.27.
3. D.B. Quinn and K.W. Nicholls 'Ireland in 1534' in T.W. Moody *et al.* (eds) *A New History of Ireland* (Oxford, Clarendon Press, 1976) Vol. III p.36.
4. R. Elphick *Kraal and Castle: Khoikhoi and the Founding of White South Africa* (Yale, University Press, 1977).
5. Denoon *op.cit.* p.27.
6. W. Petty 'A treatise on Ireland' in C.H. Hull (ed) *Economic Writings of Sir William Fetty* Vol. 2 (Cambridge, University Press, 1899).
7. L.M. Cullen *The Emergence of Modern Ireland* (London, Batsford Academic, 1981) p.11.
8. See, for example, the list of subscribers to the Virginian and Irish companies in T.K. Rabb *Enterprise and Empire: Merchant and Gentry Investment in the Expansion of England, 1575-1630* (Cambridge, Mass. University Press, 1967) pp.233-410.
9. C.M. Andrews *The Colonial Period of American History* (Yale, University Press, 1967) Vol. 2, p.197; Vol.3.
10. G. de Beaumont *Ireland: Social, Political and Religious*. Translated and edited by W.C. Taylor (London, Richard Bartley, 1839) pp.282-3.
11. M. McCurtain *Tudor and Stuart Ireland* (Dublin, Gill and Macmillan, 1972) p.127, quoting a report from the Irish Privy Council to James I in 1608.
12. S.J. Connolly *Priests and People in Pre-Famine Ireland 1780-1845* (Dublin, Gill and Macmillan, 1982) p.75.
13. Another was that between the Muslim religion of the Ottoman rulers and the Christianity of many of their Balkan subjects.
14. J.H. Hutton *Caste in India: Its Nature, Function and Origins* (Oxford, University Press, 1963) p.149.
15. L. Meir *Primitive Government* (Harmondsworth, Penguin, 1962) p.135; D.W. Philippson *The Later Prehistory of Southern Africa* (London, Heinemann Educational, 1977) p.16.
16. W.F. Butler 'The policy of surrender and regrant' *Journal of The Royal Society of Antiquaries of Ireland* Vol.XLIII (1913) p.48-57.
17. Quinn and Nicholls *op.cit.* p.36.
18. D.V. Glass and D.E.C. Eversley (eds) *Population in History* (London, Arnold, 1965); E.H.P. Brown and S.V. Hopkins 'Seven centuries of the price of consumables' in E.M. Carus-Wilson (ed) *Essays in Economic History* Vol.2 (London, Arnold, 1962).
19. D. Woodward 'The Anglo-Irish livestock trade in the seventeenth century' *Irish Historical Studies* Vol. 18 (1973) pp.489-523.
20. E. Strauss *Sir William Petty: Portrait of a Genius* (London, Bodley Head, 1951) p.226.
21. These proposals, in so far as they related to cattle numbers and to the people required to tend them, were strikingly and ironically similar to those made three centuries later by the Irish state's economic planners in the *Second Programme for Economic Expansion* (Dublin, Stationery Office, 1962).
22. C.A. Edie 'The Irish cattle Bills' *Transactions of the American Philosophical Society* Vol. 60, Part 2, 1970.
23. A. Clark 'The Irish economy 1600-1660' in T.W. Moody *et al.* eds *A New History of Ireland* Vol. III (Oxford, University Press, 1976) pp.246, 249.

24. The city states of the Ancient Mediterranean were also property owners' states. They existed to defend the citizens' right to property in slaves; and the city states were, in turn, sustained by that property (Appendix A).
25. Quoted by Edie, *op.cit.*
26. *See* the *Second Programme for Economic Expansion* 1962.
27. B.H.S. van Bath *The Agrarian History of Western Europe, AD 500-1850* (London, Arnold, 1963) pp.326-7; P.J. Cain and A.G. Hopkins 'The political economy of British expansion overseas, 1750-1914' *Economic History Review* XXXIII (1980) pp.463-90.
28. R.B. Sheridan *Sugar and Slavery: an Economic History of the British West Indies* (Barbados, Caribbean University Press, 1974) p.313.
29. E. Williams *From Columbus to Castro: the History of the Caribbean, 1492-1969* (London, Andre Deutch, 1970) p.162.
30. R. Pares *Yankees and Creoles* (London, Longmans Green and Co. 1956) p.86.
31. Based on the growth in the value of exports which is taken as a proxy for GDP growth. Irish exports increased more than twelvefold in value between 1668 and 1811 (G. O'Brien *The Economic History of Ireland in the Seventeenth Century* (London, Maunsel, 1919) p.170; E. Wakefield *An Account of Ireland, Statistical and Political* (London, Longman, Hurst, Rees, Orme and Browne, 1812) pp.46-57. Exports from Britain, which was almost certainly the most rapidly growing European economy, increased less than tenfold in value between 1697 and 1811 (B.R. Mitchell and P. Deane *British Historical Statistics* (Cambridge, University Press, 1962) pp.279-82.
32. Strauss *op.cit.* p.11, quoting Petty; M.G. Mulhall *Mulhall's Dictionary of Statistics* (London, Routledge and Sons, 1909) p.341.
33. R. Crotty 'Modernisation and land reform' *The Journal of Peasant Studies* Vol. 11, No. 1 (1983) pp.101-16.
34. *See* Crotty *op.cit.* where the interplay of these forces is considered in greater detail.
35. R. Crotty *Cattle, Economics and Development* (Slough, CAB, 1980) p.32.
36. *Minutes of evidence taken before the Select Committee of the House of Lords appointed to enquire into the state of Ireland, more particularly with reference to the circumstances which have led to disturbances in that part of the United Kingdom.* British Parliamentary Paper (BPP) 1825 (181) IX.
37. *Evidence taken before Her Majesty's commissioners of inquiry into the state of the law and practice in respect to the occupation of land in Ireland.* Part 1. BPP 1845 (606) XIX p.41.
38. Output per hectare of wheat and sugarbeet in Ireland in 1980 averaged £628; and per hectare of grassland, £282. (This assumes that four hectares of 'other land' is the equivalent of one hectare of grassland). (*Statistical Abstract 1980,* pp.64-5, 89). These figures make no allowance for the value of crop products used to feed livestock, which enhances the value of grassland production; nor for the much greater extent by which the EEC's Common Agricultural Policy raises cattle and milk prices than it does wheat and sugarbeet prices.
39. R. Crotty *Irish Agricultural Production: Its Volume and Structure* (Cork, University Press, 1966) p.277; *Agricultural Returns of Great Britain* BPP 1890/91 (C.6524) XCI, pp.78-9.
40. *Census for Ireland 1841* BPP 1843 (459) XXIV; *Ditto, 1871*; BPP 1876 (C.1377).

41. *Statistical Abstract 1936* pp.6-7.
42. *Census of Ireland 1871. General Report* BPP 1876 (C. 1377) LXXXI.
43. Irish Free State, Department of Industry and Commerce *Census of Population 1926, Vol. II Occupations* (Dublin, Stationery Office, 1928).
44. Crotty, 1966 *op.cit.* pp.68-80.
45. J.H. Hexter *Reappraisals in History* (London, University of Chicago Press, 1979) p.109.
46. Crotty, 1966 *op.cit.* p.18.
47. *Ibid.* Chapter 2.
48. *Ibid.* p.276; Irish Free State, Department of Industry and Commerce *Trade and Shipping Statistics for December* (Dublin, Stationery Office, 1927).
49. L. Stone *The Crisis of the Aristocracy, 1558-1641* (Oxford, Clarendon Press, 1966) pp.166-70.
50. *Ibid.* p.177.
51. See the following subsection for three others.
52. R. Orsingher *Banks of the World* (New York, Walker and Co., 1967).
53. J. Lee *The Modernisation of Ireland* (Dublin, Gill and Macmillan, 1973) p.16.
54. P. Lynch and J. Vaizey *Guinness's Brewery in the Irish Economy, 1759-1876* (Cambridge, University Press, 1960).
55. Evasion of the malt duty in Ireland was a matter of special concern to the Commissioners of Inquiry into the Excise Establishment (1833). Illicit malting of grain was made easy mainly because the excise's principal preoccupation was to curb illicit distilling and shebeens, which were regarded as hotbeds of sedition, and most of its resources were directed to that task *(Tenth Report of the Commissioners of Inquiry into the Excise Establishment; Malt Duty, Ireland.* BPP 1934 (11) XXV). An English malster, Mr. Stead, gave evidence to the Commissioners as follows: 'Do you send any [malt] to Ireland now?' 'Prior to the time of the certificate scheme being abandoned I sent a great deal to Ireland, but since that period I have not sent a bushel; and I understand that there is not now a tenth part of the malt duty paid in Ireland . . . I think that it will become of great consequence, for the Irish porter comes over in very large quantities from Ireland into England, without being subject to the duty of malt; it is, therefore, cutting into the English porter from Liverpool and Manchester – nay, even it comes into London in large quantities and increasing daily. Mr. Bass, the eminent brewer at Burton, tells me that it is selling next door to him at Burton cheaper than he can make it . . . I have heard of a very eminent Dublin brewer, was very conscientious in his mode of dealing, and who would not purchase during the certificate time uncertified malt; he had to pay in consequence a high price for malt with a certificate, there being at the time two distinct articles, certificated and uncertificated malt, sold in Dublin market. The moment the certificate ceased he immediately said: "I have no such feeling now it comes to me in open market; and I buy what I can get and give market price".' *Fifteenth Report of the Commissioners of Inquiry into the Excise Establishment; Malt. Appendix No. 61.* BPP 1835 (17) XXXI.
56. BPP 1856 (155) LV through 1860 (242) LXIII. *Return of the number of persons in each of the general collections in the United Kingdom licensed as brewers, victuallers, to sell beer to be, and* not *to be drunk on the premises.*
57. *Report of the Commission of Inland Revenue on the Duties under their*

management for the years 1856 to 1869 inclusive with some retrospective history. Vol. II. BPP 1870 (C82.1) XX.

58. J.E. Vaizey *The Brewing Industry 1886-1951: an Economic Study* (London, Sir Isaac Pitman & Sons, 1958) p.6.

59. R.D.C. Black 'The progress of industrialization, 1850-1920' in T.W. Moody and J.C. Beckett (eds) *Ulster Since 1800* (London, BBC, 1955) p.59.

60. W.A. Maguire *The Downshire Estates in Ireland* (Oxford, Clarendon Press, 1972). The tenant right on the part of the Downshire estates located in Ulster was worth £12 per acre (p.143). In the South, 'at Edenderry . . . most of the inhabitants of the estate had the status of cottiers and never acquired tenant right.' (p.145).

61. Crotty, 1983, *op.cit.*

62. The 'yarn counties' were Meath, Westmeath, Longford, Tipperary and the five Connaught counties (C. Gill *The Rise of the Irish Linen Industry* (Oxford, University Press, 1925) p.38. The poverty of Connaught's soil hampered the emergence of the grazier class and dampened the polarization of rural society into coolies and graziers, which occurred principally in Leinster and east Munster. The less proletarianisation of Connaught and the consequent better preservation there, during the reign of George III, of a more traditional farm family structure accounted for Connaught's (and Kerry's) persistence of flax-growing after it had declined elsewhere in the 26 Counties. But Connaught's rack-rented smallholders, lacking the protection of the Ulster Custom, did not have the capital to process yarn into cloth and were forced instead to sell it to the Ulster weavers. Thus, the rack-renting of Catholic Connaught contributed importantly to the industrialization of Protestant Ulster.

63. In a population that fell from 8.2 millions in 1841 to 4.4 millions in 1911, the number of male and female clerics increased from 7,191 to 19,016 *(Census for Ireland 1841* BPP 1843 (459) XXIV; *Census of Ireland 1911. General Report* BPP (Cd. 6663) XVIII.

64. The estimated expenditure on Catholic churches and ancillary structures during the period of most acute economic crisis, 1817 to 1847, was £4 millions (E. Larkin 'Economic growth, capital investment and the Roman Catholic church in nineteenth century Ireland' *American Historical Review* Vol. 72 No. 3, 1967, pp.852-84). A farmworker's wage at the time, when he could get employment, was around three shillings a week (D. Bleakley 'Industrial conditions in the nineteenth century' in T.W. Moody and J.C. Beckett, 1957 *op.cit.* p.123). 'No less than twenty-four cathedrals and over 3,000 substantial churches were erected in the century following Catholic Emancipation' (T.P. Kennedy 'Church building' in P.J. Corish (ed) *A History of Irish Catholicism* Vol. 5 (Dublin, Gill and Macmillan, 1970) p.8.

65. The following numbers of theological students and marriages per 1,000 population were recorded in recent censuses:

	Theological Students	Marriages
1951	1.38	5.5
1956	1.73	5.4
1961	1.45	5.7
1971	0.72	6.5

Census of Population of Ireland 1961, Vol. 3; *Ditto 1966,* Vol. 4; *Ditto 1971,* Vol. 4.

66. The Irish continue to spend an exceptionally high proportion of their incomes on alcohol; but because these are low and the cost of alcohol is high, per caput consumption is no longer high (B.M. Walsh and D. Walsh 'Economic aspects of alcohol consumption in the Republic of Ireland' *Economic and Social Review* Vol. 2 No. 1, 1970). Ireland has an exceptionally large number of persons in mental hospitals (D. Walsh 'Hospitalized psychiatric morbidity in the Republic of Ireland' *British Journal of Psychiatry Vol.* 114, 1968, pp.11-4).

67. *Census for Ireland 1841* BPP 1843 (459) XXIV; *Census of Population of England and Wales. Occupation Abstract* BPP 1845 (606) XIX; *Census of Ireland 1911. General Report* BPP 1912/13 (Cd. 6663) XVIII; *Census of England and Wales 1911. Occupations and Industries* BPP 1913 (Cd. 7018) LXXVIII.

68. G.C. Bolton *The Passing of the Irish Act of Union* (Oxford, University Press, 1966) p.2.

69. Crotty, 1983 *op.cit.*

70. Bolton *op.cit.* p.216-22.

71. Crotty, 1983 *op.cit.*

72. An otherwise very similar situation, but without metropolitan-controlled force and Ireland's ease of emigration, has given rise to chronic political instability and continuing revolution in Latin America since independence 160 years ago.

73. Parnell was one of an amorphous collection of persons who, from the Great Famine of the 1840's until independence in 1922, dominated the Irish political scene. They included the Welshman's son, Thomas Davis; the Anglo-American-Irish Protestant, Parnell; Pearse, the son of an English monumental sculptor; de Valera, born in America of a Spanish father; and Desmond Fitzgerald, the father of the present (1986) taoiseach. This assorted collection of persons shared a common antipathy to England which, in an age of rampant nationalism, probably reflected their own uncertain status; and a large measure of indifference to the social order maintained by England in Ireland. In an Ireland bled by emigration of indigenous radicalism, their strident nationalism won for them roles of political prominence which they would have been most unlikely to have attained in a society less crippled and warped by emigration.

74. Balfour's policy. *See,* for example, E. Strauss *Sir William Petty* (London, Bodley Head, 1954) p.201.

75. *Returns relating to imperial revenue (collection and expenditure) (Great Britain and Ireland) for the year ending 31 March, 1902.* BPP 1902 (285) LV. *Ditto. for the year ending 31 March, 1914* BPP 1914 (387) L.

76. A.E. Murray *A History of the Commercial and Financial Relations between England and Ireland from the Period of the Restoration* (London, King, 1907) p.393.

77. F.S.L. Lyons *Ireland Since the Famine* (London, Weidenfeld and Nicolson, 1971) p.263.

78. G. Dangerfield *The Damnable Question: a Study in Anglo-Irish Relations* (London, Constable, 1977) pp.53-4.

79. T.W. Moody 'The Irish university question of the nineteenth century' *History* Vol.XLIII (1958).

80. R. Crotty *The Cattle Crisis and the Small Farmer* (Mullingar, National Land League, 1974) p.14.

81. Quoted by Dangerfield *op.cit.* p.133.
82. *Ibid.* pp.251, 292-300.
83. E.L. Jones *The European Miracle* (Cambridge, University Press, 1981) p.106.
84. *See,* for example, E. Weber *A Modern History of Europe* (New York, Newton & Co., 1971) p.190; N.V. Riasonovsky *A History of Russia* (Oxford, University Press, 1984) pp.281-3; and J. Topolski 'Polish economic decline' in P. Earle (ed) *Essays in European Economic History* (Oxford, Clarendon Press, 1974).
85. A. Toynbee *Mankind and Mother Earth* (Oxford, University Press, 1976) p.569.

Ireland: A Case of Capitalist Colonial Undevelopment (Part 1)
1. R. Crotty *Irish Agricultural Production* (Cork, University Press, 1966) p.18.
2. *See* T. Balogh 'The mechanism of neo-imperialism' *Bulletin of the Institute of Economics and Statistics, University of Oxford* Vol. 24 No. 3, 1962, pp.331-46; M.E. Chamberlain *Britain and India* (Newton Abbot, David and Charles, 1974) p.114; C. Furtado *Economic Development of Latin Amercia* (London, Cambridge University Press, 1970) p.30.
3. Quoted by E. Norman *A History of Modern Ireland* (Harmondsworth, Penguin, 1971) p.11.
4. K. Marx and F. Engels *Correspondence 1846-1895* (London, Martin Lawrence, 1934) p.94.
5. Ireland *Reports of the Commission on Emigration and Other Population Problems* (Dublin, Stationery Office, 1956) p.64.
6. S.J. Connolly *Priests and People in Pre-Famine Ireland* (Dublin, Gill and Macmillan, 1982) pp.175-218.
7. R. Crotty *Cattle, Economics and Development* (Slough, CAB, 1980) pp.21-2. *See also* Appendix A.
8. Crotty, 1966 *op.cit.* p.354; *Irish Statistical Bulletin,* September 1982.
9. There was a similar, though less pronounced, withdrawal of the minimal socio-economic independence necessary for marriage in 'merrie' Tudor England. Coincidental with the diversion of land to sheep-grazing, England's population, which had been growing more rapidly than the rest of western Europe's (B.H.S. van Bath *The Agrarian History of Western Europe* (London, Arnold, 1963) pp.80-1, began to grow less rapidly. 'A high proportion of ordinary Englishmen, the peasants and craftsmen, the labourers and the paupers, in the time of Elizabeth, or Anne, or of the first three Georges, got married in their late twenties and even in their early thirties' (P. Laslett 'Introduction' in E.A. Wrigley *An Introduction to English Historical Demography* (London, Weidenfeld and Nicolson, 1966) p.6. Also E.A. Wrigley *Population and History* (London, Weidenfeld and Nicolson, 1969) p.13. Not until the industrial revolution of the nineteenth century did the mass of English people become as well bedded and fed as they had been in pre-Tudor England, before land was diverted from supporting people to grazing sheep for profit.
10. Banking Commission, 1926, *Reports* (Stationery Office, 1926).
11. *Guardian* 9.1.1979. Cromwell sold Irish land bonds in London for as little as one old penny an acre to finance the reconquest of Ireland in the 1650s (K.S. Botteigheimar *English Money and Irish Land* (Oxford, University Press, 1971) pp.142-63. The most substantial and enduring consequence of that reconquest

has been the subsequent millionfold increase in Irish land values.

12. G.A. Duncan 'The social income of the Irish Free State' *Journal of the Statistical and Social Inquiry Society of Ireland* Vol. XVI (1939/40); *National Income and Expenditure* 1981 p.15.

13. *See,* for example, Crotty, 1980 *op. cit.* pp.100-1.

14. *See,* for example, World Bank *Development Report* (Washington DC, World Bank, 1981) p.56.

15. Crotty, 1966 *op. cit.* pp.126-9.

16. *National Income and Expenditure* 1981; private communication, Revenue Commissioners, 2.3.1984.

The proposal of the Labour Party, which, with the dominant Fine Gael party, comprise the present (1986) government, to tax farmland has come late in the day. The proposal to tax land on holdings of 80 'adjusted acres' and over, at a rate of £10 per 'adjusted' acre, will yield a derisory amount, if implemented. Not least of the difficulties of implementation will be defining and establishing in practice what an 'adjusted' acre is. Neither equity nor efficiency will be served by the proposed tax which seems rather to aim at placating urban PAYE voters without antagonising the predominantly small farmers (i.e. less than 80 'adjusted' acres) in the rural constituencies of several Labour Party Dáil members.

17. *Budget 1984* p.110.

18. Crotty, 1966 *op. cit.* p.163; *National Income and Expenditure,* various years; B.R. Mitchell and H.G. Jones *Second Abstract of British Historical Statistics* (Cambridge, University Press, 1971) pp.151-3; UK *Annual Abstract of Statistics,* various years.

19. *Statistical Abstract 1980* p.20.

20. *Statistical Abstract 1980* p.24.

21. *National Income and Expenditure,* 1981, pp.14-15.

22. Even when emigrants' remittances were recorded in the balance of payments, their value relative to GNP was also very small. They are no longer recorded separately.

23. Crotty, 1966 *op. cit.* Chapter 9.

24. *Ibid.* p.162.

25. D. McAleese *Effective Tariffs and the Structure of Industrial Protection in Ireland* (Dublin, Economic and Social Research Institute, 1971).

26. *Twelfth Report of the Commissioners of Customs and Excise for the year ending 31 March, 1921* BPP 1921 (Cmd. 1435)X. *Forty second ditto. for the year ending 31 March, 1951* BPP 1951-2 (Cmd. 8449)X.

27. *Statistical Abstract 1951.*

28. Crotty, 1966 *op. cit.* p.155.

29. Other long established patterns were also reversed during this period of unaccustomed political pressure in Ireland, which lasted from around 1930 to 1935. The workforce in agriculture and *in toto* increased; tillage expanded; and cattle prices declined relative to other agricultural prices. Old patterns, however, were quickly re-established with the recovery in the world's economy from 1936 onwards and with the recommencement of Irish net emigration.

30. C. Furtado *Economic Development of Latin America* (London, Cambridge University Press, 1970) pp.82-92.

31. R.M. Sundrum *Development Economics: a Framework for Analysis and Policy* (Chichester, Wiley, 1983) p.235.
32. P. Chaudhuri 'India: objectives, achievements and constraints' in P. Chaudhuri (ed) *Aspects of Indian Economic Development* (London, Allen and Unwin, 1971) pp.81-4.
33. *See,* for example, R. Ehrenberg *Capital and Finance in the Age of the Renaissance* (New York, Augustus M. Kelly, 1963).
34. 'The first spark [setting off the French Revolution] was the Government's declaration of bankruptcy following the American War', G. Rude *Revolutionary Europe 1983-1815* (London, Collins, 1967) p.76.
35. UK *Annual Abstract of Statistics* 1953, pp.239, 265; *Ditto.* 1984, pp.249, 271; *Statistical Abstract of the USA 1985*, pp.117, 224; *Ditto.* 1981, pp.264-420 (Washington DC, U.S. Bureau of Census),
36. H.S. Ferns *The Argentine Republic 1516-1971* (Newton Abbot, David and Charles, 1973) p.117.
37. D.E. Worcester and W.G. Schaeffer *The Growth and Culture of Latin America* Vol. 2 (London, Oxford University Press, 1971) p.167.
38. Crotty, 1966 *op.cit.* Chapter 4.
39. T.K. Whitaker, *Interests* (Dublin, Institute of Public Administration, 1983) p.89
40. S. Griffith-Jones *Transnational Finance and Latin American National Development* (Brighton, Institute of Development Studies, 1982) p.12.
41. *Ibid.* p.13.
42. *See,* for example, K.A. Chrystal *Controversies in Macroeconomics* (Deddington, Philip Allan, 1983).
43. Whitaker *op.cit.* p.101.
44. Coolies, by contrast, are self-employed persons who grow crops with virtually no capital on land that they do not own.
45. *See,* for example, C. Mulvey *The Economic Analysis of Trade Unions* (Oxford, M. Robertson, 1978), especially chapters 9, 10 and 11.
46. The situation is strikingly similar to that in rural Ireland in the nineteenth century. There, as noted above (Chapter 4), greatly accelerated capital formation was in the form of labour-replacing cattle and sheep. The situation in the metropolises now, however, is very different in that though the capital replaces labour, it also greatly increases output, whereas the nineteenth century replacement of labour by cattle and sheep reduced output while increasing profits. Much Irish capital formation, however, retains its nineteenth century character in that it replaces labour, increases profits, but does not increase output. This is illustrated by the Smurfit case below, Chapter 6.
47. There is 'in the USA a ragbag of well over 100 federal programs that have been enacted to help the poor', M. Friedmand and R. Friedman *Free to Choose* (London, Secker and Warburg, 1980) p.108; in the UK there are '60 ways to get cash help' from the state (UK Department of Health and Social Security *Which Benefit? 60 Ways to Get Cash Help* 1980). *See* M. Rose *Reworking The Work Ethic* (London, Batsford, 1985). for the fundamental reappraisal that is now occurring concerning that core element of western, individualistic capitalism, 'the work ethic'.
48. K. Walsh *Strikes in Europe and the United States: Measurement and Incidence* (London, Francis Pinter, 1983) p.158.

49. *Ibid.* p.213.
50. Based on the following data for 1981:

	United Kingdom	Ireland
GNP @ factor cost, own currency, £m.	214,922	9,032
Population, thousands	55,773	3,443
£stg.1=IR£1.198		

   Source: UK *Annual Abstract of Statistics 1984,* pp.6, 249; *National Income and Expenditure 1981, p.13; Central Bank Annual Report* 1984, Appendix p.24.
51. *National Income and Expenditure* 1981, pp.15, 33.
52. P. Humphreys *Public Service Employment: an Examination of Strategies: Ireland and the Other European Countries* (Dublin, Institute of Public Administration, 1983) p.88.
53. J. Meenan *The Irish Economy Since 1922* (Liverpool, University Press, 1970) Appendix 1; B. Chubb *The Government and Politics of Ireland* (Harlow, Longman Group, 1982) p.101; Institute of Public Administration *Administration Yearbook and Diary 1981, 1982* and *1983.*

Ireland: A Case of Capitalist Colonial Undevelopment (Part 2)

1. *See* J. Meenan *The Irish Economy Since 1922* (Liverpool, University Press, 1970) p.258, where he cites J.A. Costello, head of the coalition government, on this point.
2. The intellectual void clearly did not stifle Ireland's literary creativity any more than tsarist autocracy stifled Russia's (above, Chapter 4). But it is remarkable that almost all of Ireland's literary greats felt compelled to escape the Irish ambience in order to realise their potential.
3. T.K. Whitaker *Interests* (Dublin, Institute of Public Administration, 1983).
4. G.M.D. Fitzgerald 'Economic Planning in Ireland' A Ph.D. thesis, National University of Ireland, 1968.
5. Telesis Report *A Review of Industrial Policy* (Dublin, National Economic and Social Council, 1982) p.160. Hereinafter *Telesis Report.*
6. For a comprehensive statement of the incentives provided, see *Telesis Report* pp.157-61. *See also* Bank of Ireland memoranda 'Fixed Interest Section 84 Facility with Bullet Repayment' and 'Equipment Leasing' (n.d.).
7. W.W. Rostow, *The Stages of Economic Growth: a Non-Communist Manifesto* (Cambridge, University Press, 1960).
8. J. McKeon 'Economic appraisal of industrial projects in Ireland' *Journal of the Statistical and Social Inquiry Society of Ireland* Vol. XXIV, Part II, 1980, pp.119-43.
9. D. McAleese *Effective Tariffs and the Structure of Industrial Protection in Ireland* (Dublin, ESRI, 1971), p.50.
10. R. Crotty *Irish Agricultural Production* (Cork, University Press, 1966) pp.164, 192-211.
11. K.A. Chrystal *Controversies in Macroeconomics* (Deddington, Philip Allan, 1983).

12. C. Toibin 'Fear in the valley' *Magill Magazine* Vol. 6 No. 9, 1983, pp.26-38; *Sunday Tribune,* 11.8.1985.
13. R. Graham *The Aluminium Industry and the Third World* (London, Zed Press, 1982) p.79.
14. *Fortune* 19.8.1985.
15. *World Bank Atlas 1978* (Washington DC, World Bank, 1978).
16. G. Fitzgerald 'A just equilibrium'. Text of an address in the General Debate at the United Nations General Assembly, 25.9.1974. (Dublin, Department of Foreign Affairs).
17. *See,* for example, C. Jones, 1977 *The £200,000 job: A Study of Government Intervention in Aluminium Smelting* (London, Centre for Policy Studies, 1977) for the concessions won from the UK government by the aluminium companies.
18. *Telesis Report* pp.127, 184.
19. Aughinish Alumina Company, personal communication, 29.6.1984.
20. *Irish Times,* 2.4.1985.
21. Crotty *op.cit.* Chapter 8; *Statistical Abstract 1978* p.88; CSO *Agricultural Output 1983* July, 1984; CSO *Estimated Output, Input and Income in Agriculture 1980-1984 New Series* July, 1985.
22. CSO *Household Budget Survey* 1984, pp.88-97.
23. The average price, fob, paid by non-EEC importers of Irish cattle in 1984 was £654, of which they got a rebate of £302 from the EEC. Similar arrangements applied to beef. (C.S.O., private communication, 11.9.1985).
24. McKeon *op.cit.*
25. *Sunday Press* 22.7.1984.
26. Commission of the European Communities *Bulletin of Energy Prices* No. 1 (Brussels, EEC, 1984).
27. *Statistical Abstract 1980,* pp.130-1.
28. F.E. Banks *Bauxite and Aluminium: an Introduction to the Economics of Non-fuel Minerals* (Lexington, Lexington Books, 1979) pp.58-9.
29. *Statistical Abstract* 1980 pp.130-1.
30. R. Crotty *Cattle, Economics and Development* (Slough, CAB, 1980) p.181.
31. *Telesis Report* p.111.
32. *Ibid.* p.188.
33. Ireland *Economic Review and Outlook 1984* (Dublin, Stationery Office, 1984) p.41.
34. *Irish Times* 8.2.1985.
35. Industrial Development Authority, Private Communication, 1984.
36. *Census of Ireland, 1871, General Report,* BPP 1876 [c.1377] LXXX1; *Census of Ireland, 1911. General Report* BPP 1912-13 (Cd.6663) XVIII. *See also* Chapter 4.
37. P. Humphreys *Public Service Employment* (Dublin, Institute of Public Administration, 1983) pp.14, 88; Ireland *Building on Reality: 1985-1987* (Dublin, Stationery Office, 1984) p.26.
38. Public service employment was 31% of non-agricultural employment in 1970-74 (Humphreys *op.cit.* pp.14, 88). Applying the same proportion to non-agricultural employment in 1951 gives, for that year, 224, 230 in employment that is now classed as 'public service'.
39. R. Crotty *The Cattle Crisis and the Small Farmer* (Mullingar, National Land League, 1974) and Central Bank *Annual Report 1984.*

40. For cost of debt service, *see* CSO *Estimated Output, Input and Income in Agriculture 1980-1984 New Series.*
41. Crotty, 1974 *op.cit.* p.29.
42. Taking the triennial period 1971-2-3 as the base (=100), net agricultural output in 1981-2-3 averaged 85.2 *(Statistical Abstract 1978;* CSO *Agricultural Output, 1983).*
43. *See* note 23 above.
44. Crotty, 1966 *op.cit.* p.161.
45. For Ireland *see:* R.K. Carty *Electoral Politics in Ireland: Party and Parish Pump* (Dingle, Brandon, 1983); for India see N.K. Nicholson 'Factionalism and public policy in India' in F.P. Belloni and D.C. Beller (eds) *Faction Politics: Political Parties and Factionalism in Comparative Perspective* (Oxford, University Press, 1978); for Renaissance Italy *see* E. Whelpton *A Concise History of Italy* (London, Robert Hale, 1964) pp.58-68. For Africa *see* for example, C. Gertzel *The Dynamics of the One Party State in Zambia* (Manchester, University Press, 1984) and the many index references.
46. *Irish Times* 26.10.1983.
47. T. Paine *Rights of Man* (Harmondsworth, Penguin, 1969) p.228; *see also* P.A. Brunt *Social Conflict in the Roman Republic* (London, Chatto and Windus, 1971).
48. *Statistical Abstract* 1980, p.48.
49. J. Joyce *Portrait of the Artist as a Young Man* (London, Jonathan Cape, 1968) pp.208, 250.

A Radical Alternative

1. *Telesis Report* 1982.
2. The employer's contribution to Pay Related Social Insurance for a single person earning £12.750 per annum is 12.5%. If the employer wishes to pay his employee an additional £100 in gross salary, he must also pay £12.5 additional PRSI, so that the total cost to the employer of the rise is £112.50. The employee's marginal tax rate, in 1985, was 65%. So, of the £100 salary increase, PAYE takes £65. Additionally, the employee must pay another £7.50 in PRSI. The employee therefore receives a net £27.50, out of what has cost the employer £112.50. Thus, to put an additional £1 into an employee's pocket has cost the employer £4.08.
3. K.S. Boteigheimer *English Money and Irish Land* (Oxford, University Press, 1971) pp.142-63.
4. *See,* for example, United Nations *Manual of Land Tax Administration* (New York, UN, 1968); A. Woolery (ed) *The Art of Valuation* (Lexington, Lexington Books, 1978); American Institute of Real Estate Appraisers *The Appraisal of Real Estate* (Chicago, AIREA, 1973).
5. Central Bank, *Annual Report 1984* Appendix pp.17-19.
6. These, which are generally accepted as the cheapest form of public transport, are found in many cities, including Port-of-Spain, Lima, Istanbul, Teheran and Belfast. *See* T. Bendixson *Instead of Cars* (London, Temple Smith, 1974) pp.192-8.
7. *See,* for example, J.E. Meade *The Intelligent Radical's Guide to Economic Policy* (London, Allen and Unwin, 1975) pp.49-50, 118-9.

8. *See* B. Chiplin and B. Sturgess *Economics of Advertising* (London, Holt, Rinewart and Winston with the Advertising Association, 1981) pp.135-6.
9. *See,* for example, Kristensen *Land Valuation and Land Value Taxation in Denmark* (London, International Committee for the Taxation of Land Values, 1964).
10. *Evening Press* 13.6.1984.
11. Central Bank *Report 1984* Appendix p.13.
12. *Ibid.* Appendix pp.13, 17, 19.
13. The reported purchase price of a public bar in Ranelagh, Dublin, was £750,000 *(Sunday Tribune* 22.9.1985). *See Irish Times* 27.6.1985 for report of the fraudulent issue of taxi licence.
14. *National Income and Expenditure 1981* p.9.
15. There were 2.2 million persons on the voters' register in April, 1980 *(Statistical Abstract* 1980 p.51). From the original proposal in an individualistic, capitalist context, by C.H. Douglas in Canada *Economic Democracy* (Sudbury, Bloomfield Books, 1920) to the Young Fine Gael memorandum 'Basic Income System' (December 1984) there has been a wide and increasing awareness of the inadequacies, in present times, of the old, capitalist precept, 'thou shalt earn thine bread by the sweat of thine brow'. *See,* for example, M. Rose 1985 *Re-working the Work Ethic* (London, Batsford, 1985) for the sort of fundamental reappraisal that is occurring in the metropolises. That precept never obtained, in pre-colonial times, in the capitalist colonies. It has never operated to the benefit of those societies, either during the capitalist colonial era or in the era of post-capitalist colonial independence.
16. Ireland, Department of Social Welfare *Rates of Payment for the Department of Social Welfare for July 1985; Rates of PRSI Contribution for 6 April, 1985; Rates of Pay for Health Boards for July 1985.* (Dublin, Stationery Office, 1985).
17. Ireland's high living standards imply that an excessively high birth rate is a problem of a lower order of importance than in other former capitalist colonies, where the excess of birth over death rates is much greater. Relatively high Irish incomes mean that the future is less heavily discounted, more forethought is exercised, and the birth rate is lower than in other former capitalist colonies. Because of the prior need to stabilise population, there is no prospect in other former capitalist colonies of securing development without first acting to reduce birth rates.
18. J. Margach *The Abuse of Power* (London, W.H. Allen, 1978) p.38.

Other Issues Briefly Considered
1. T. Paine *Rights of Man* (Harmondsworth, Penguin, 1969) pp.63-4.
2. *See,* for example, M. Moffitt *The World's Money* (London, Michael Joseph, 1983). *See also* statement by Belasario Betancur, president of the Cartagena's Debtor Conference, as quoted by A. Kaletsky *The Costs of Default* (New York, Priority Press) p.63.
3. Central Bank *Report 1985* Appendix pp.86-7.
4. *Ibid.*
5. *Ibid.*
6. *See,* for example, D. Seers *Development Options: The Strengths and Weaknesses of Dependency Theories* (Brighton, Institute of Development Studies, 1981).

7. S. Griffith-Jones *Transnational Finance and Latin American National Development* (Brighton, Institute of Development Studies, 1982) p.22.
8. J.M. Keynes *The Economic Consequences of the Peace* (New York, Harcourt, Brace and Howe, 1920).
9. Moffitt *op.cit.* p.229. Kaletsky *op.cit.* is the most recent and the best discussion on the costs and benefits of repudiating internationally held public debt. Kaletsky, in reviewing the international politics of default, concludes that there are circumstances where defaulting would have net benefits for a debtor country (p.20). The net benefits of defaulting would be much greater in Ireland where total public debt, including that which is held domestically and abroad (as well as the latter part alone) is much greater relative to GNP than anywhere else. The net benefits would be particularly great if, as is envisaged here, repudiation were part of an overall strategy of transforming capitalist colonial undevelopment into development.
10. State expenditure, at current prices, has increased 7.39 times on police, prisons and army compared to a 4.88 times increase in GNP at current prices between 1974 and 1984 *(Statistical Abstract* 1980 pp.278, 286-7; *Estimates for the Public Services* 1984; *Central Bank Report* 1985, p.6).
11. Sir Louis Mallet, as quoted by M.E. Chamberlain *Britain and India* (Newton Abbot, David and Charles, 1974) p.123.
12. T.K. Whitaker *Interests* (Dublin, IPA, 1983) p.101.
13. *Telesis Report* 1982, p.111.
14. There is no better illustration of Ireland's intellectual barreness than the recent Economic and Social Research Institute report *Employment and Unemployment Policy for Ireland* (ESRI, 1984). Having failed to recognise the inability of the Irish socio-economic order for 160 years to provide for half its people; the imminent exhaustion of the state's ability to borrow; the implications of that exhaustion of credit for employment; and the permanent decline that has occurred in the overseas demand for Irish labour – the report offers, as the ESRI's remedy for relieving unemployment, the banal suggestions of job-sharing and the state-financed expansion of service industries.
15. Securing a sustainable, long run balance between death rates that have been reduced by modern technology and traditional birth rates that approached the biological limit is another essential condition for reintegrating into society the landless, jobless masses. Securing that balance should not be difficult in Ireland, where incomes are higher than in other former capitalist colonies.
16. F.W. Walbank *The Awful Revolution* (Liverpool, University Press 1969) p.110.

Individualistic Capitalism: Its Nature and the Timing and Location of Its Emergence

1. M. Herity, G. Eogan *Ireland in Prehistory* (London, Routledge and Keegan Paul, 1977) p.3.
2. S. Piggott *Ancient Europe from the Beginning of Agriculture to Classical Antiquity* (Edinburgh, University Press, 1965) pp.37-8.
3. *See,* for example, C. Clark *Population Growth and Land Use* (London, Macmillan, 1977) and E. Boserup *The Conditions of Agricultural Growth* (London, Allen & Unwin, 1965).

4. G. Clark *World Prehistory in New Perspective* (Cambridge, University Press, 1977).
5. *Ibid.*
6. B. Bender *Farming in Prehistory: from Hunter Gatherer to Food Producer* (London, John Baker, 1975).
7. R. Elphick *Kraal and Castle: Khoikhoi and the Founding of White South Africa* (Yale, University Press, 1977).
8. F.J. Simoons 'The geographic hypothesis and lactose malabsorption: a weighing of the evidence' *American Journal of Digestive Diseases* Vol. 23, 1978, pp.963-80.
9. D.A. Sturdy 'The Exploitation Patterns of a Modern Reindeer Economy in West Greenland' in E.S. Higgs (ed) *Papers in Economic Prehistory* (London, Cambridge University Press).
10. Elphick *op. cit.*
11. J. Middleton (ed) *Peoples of Africa* (London, Marshall Cavendish Books, 1978) pp.180-3.
12. L. Wajananawatch 'An inquiry into the feasibility of increasing the contribution of bovines to Thailand's economy' (Unpublished M.Sc. thesis, University of Dublin, 1983-4).
13. R. Crotty *Cattle, Economics and Development* (Slough, CAB, 1980) p.166.
14. P.K. Hitti *The Near East in History: a 5,000 Year Story* (Princeton, D. Van Nostrand Co., 1961) p.14.
15. Simoons *op.cit.*
16. D.N. Levine *Wax and Gold: Tradition and Innovation in Ethiopian Culture* (Chicago, University Press, 1965) pp.103-4.
17. J.D. Clark *The Prehistory of Africa* (London, Thames and Hudson, 1970) p.204.
18. Simoons *op.cit.*
19. J.D. Clark *op.cit.* p.216; R. Oliver 'The problem of the Bantu expansion' *Journal of African History* Vol. VII, 1966; R. Oliver and B.M. Fagan *Africa in the Iron Age* (Cambridge, University Press, 1975) p.203.
20. P. Rigby *Cattle and Kinship Among the Gogo* (Ithace, Cornell University Press, 1969) p.45.
21. B.A.L. Cranstons 'Animal husbandry: the evidence from ethnography' in P.J. Ucko and G.W. Dimbleby (eds) *The Domestication of Plants and Animals* (London, Duckworth, 1969) p.21.
22. Oliver and Fagan *op.cit.* p.30.
23. R. Lattimore *Inner Asian Frontiers of China* (Irvington-on-Hudson, Capital Publishing Co., 1951) pp.440-3.
24. FAO *Production Yearbook 1979* (Rome, FAO, 1979) pp.45-52.
25. Crotty *op.cit.* p.165.
26. J.H. Hutton *Caste in India: Its Nature, Function and Origins* (Oxford, University Press, 1963).
27. Simoons *op.cit.*
28. Wajananawatch *op.cit.*
29. M. Lal 'Cow cult in India' in A.B. Shah (ed) *Cow Slaughter: Horns of a Dilemma* (Bombay, Lalvani Publishing House, 1967).
30. Hitti *op.cit.* p.14.
31. H. Frankfort *The Birth of Civilization in the Near East* (London, Wiliams and Norgate, 1951) p.75.

32. G. Daniel *A Hundred and Fifty Years of Archaeology* (London, Duckworth, 1975) pp.190-227.
33. C. Clark *op.cit.* p.64.
34. J.M. Roberts *The Hutchinson History of the World* (Harmondsworth, Penguin 1976) pp.183-5.
35. J.D. Bernal *Science in History Vol. 1. The Emergence of Science* (Harmondsworth, Penguin, 1969) p.147.
36. O. Murray *Early Greece* (Brighton, Harvester, 1980) p.80.
37. Simoons *op.cit.*
38. Oliver *op.cit.* p.64.
39. K. Wittfogel *Oriental Despotism: a Comparative Study of Total Power* (New Haven, Yale University Press, 1959).
40. A.H.M. Jones *The Later Roman Empire, 284-602 AD: a Social and Administrative Survey* Vol. 2 (Oxford, University Press, 1964) p.767.
41. R. Duncan-Jones *The Economy of the Roman Empire: Quantitative Studies* (Cambridge, University Press, 1982) p.49.
42. B.H.S. van Bath *The Agrarian History of Western Europe, AD 500-1850* (London, Arnold, 1963) p.18; G. Duby *The Early Growth of the European Economy: Warriors and Peasants from the Seventh to the Twelfth Century.* Translated by H.B. Clark. (London, Weidenfeld and Nicolson, 1974) p.28.
43. M.I. Rostovtzeff *The Social and Economic History of the Hellenistic World* (Oxford, Clarendon Press, 1953) pp.272-80.
44. Duncan-Jones *op.cit.* p.3; M.I. Finley *Aspects of Antiquity* (Harmondsworth, Penguin, 1968).
45. R. de Vaux *Ancient Israel: Its Life and Institutions.* Translated by J. McHugh. (London, Darton, Longman and Todd, 1961) p.145.
46. M.A. Cook (ed) *Studies in the Economic History of the Middle East* (Oxford, University Press, 1970) p.78.
47. Hitti *op.cit.* pp.340-1.
48. R. Dawson *The Chinese Experience* (London, Weidenfeld and Nicolson, 1978) pp.12, 43.
49. E.O. Resichauer *The Japanese* (London, Harvard University Press, 1977) p.237.
50. C.A. Burland *Peru Under the Incas* (London, Evan Brothers, 1967) p.41.
51. M.I. Finley 'Was Greek civilization based on slavery?' in M.I. Finley (ed) *Slavery in Classical Antiquity: Views and Controversies* (Cambridge, Heffer, 1960) p.54.
52. M.I. Finley *Slavery and Modern Ideology* (London, Chatto and Windus, 1980) p.73.
53. Cook *op.cit.* pp.35-6.
54. A. Toynbee *Mankind and Mother Earth* (Oxford, University Press, 1976) p.119.
55. E.D. Lambert 'The role of climate in the economic development of nations' *Land Economics* Vol.47, 1971, pp.334-44.
56. F. Barth *Nomads of South Persia: the Baseri Tribe of the Khamseh Confederacy* (Oslo, University Press, 1975).
57. A.H.M. Jones *Athenian Democracy* (Oxford, Blackwell, 1960) pp.99-133.
58. A.H.M. Jones, 1964 *op.cit.* p.138; Finley, 1980 *op.cit.* p.109.
59. P.A. Brunt *Social Conflicts in the Roman Republic* (London, Chatto and Windus, 1971).

60. Oliver *op.cit.*
61. Herity and Eogan *op.cit.*
62. P. Farb *Man's Rise to Civilization* (London, Paladin, 1971) pp.39-60.
63. *See,* for example, S. Piggott 'Prehistory' in J. Thirsk (ed) *The Agrarian History of England and Wales* Vol. 1 Part 1 (Cambridge, University Press, 1981) p.29.
64. K. Marx *Pre-capitalist Economic Formation.* Translated by E. Hobsbawn. (London, Lawrence and Wishart, 1964) p.110.
65. *Ibid.* pp. 702-3.
66. R.M. Sundrum *Development Economics* (Chichester, Wiley, 1983) p.51.
67. C.M. Cipolla *Before the Industrial Revolution European Society and Economy 1000-1700.* (London, Methuen, 1976) p.75.
68. FAO *Production Yearbook 1981* (FAO, Rome, 1981) p.61.
69. Oliver *op.cit.* p.37.
70. Crotty *op.cit.* pp.168-70.
71. E.L. Jones *The European Miracle* (Cambridge, University Press, 1981) p.106.
72. *Ibid.*
73. A.H.M. Jones, 1960 *op.cit.* pp.99-133.
74. Duby *op.cit.* p.178; also pp.183, 224.
75. G. Ardant 'Financial policy and economic infrastructure of modern states and nations' in C. Tilly (ed) *The Formation of the National States in Western Europe* (Princeton, University Press, 1975) p.104.
76. E.L. Jones *op.cit.* p.106.
77. *See,* for example, M. Morishima *Why Has Japan 'Succeeded'?* (Cambridge, University Press, 1982) p.45; E.O. Reischauer *The Japanese* (London, Harvard University Press, 1977) p.57; and Appendix C.
78. Morishima *op.cit.* pp.57, 64.
79. J. Hajnal 'European marriage patterns in perspective' in D.V. Glass and D.E.C. Eversley (eds) *Population in History: Essays in Historical Demography* (London, Arnold, 1965) pp.101-43.
80. Crotty *op.cit.* p.22.

Patterns of Capitalist Colonialism

1. E.L. Jones *The Miracle of Europe* (Cambridge, University Press, 1981) pp.132-3.
2. G. Ardant 'Financial policy and economic infrastructure of modern states and nations' in C. Tilly (ed) *The Formation of the National States in Western Europe* (Princeton, University Press, 1975) p.194.
3. L.M. Cullen *The Emergence of Modern Ireland* (London, Batsford Academic, 1981) p.11.
4. B.H.S. van Bath *The Agrarian History of Western Europe AD 500-1850* (London, Arnold, 1983) p.326-7.
5. D. Denoon *Settler Capitalism: the Dynamics of Dependent Development in the Southern Hemisphere* (Oxford, University Press, 1983) p.25.
6. T. Halperin-Donghi *Politics, Economy and Society in Argentina in the Revolutionary Period* (Cambridge, University Press, 1972) p.26.
7. K.M. Pannikar *Asia and Western Dominance* (London, Allan and Unwin, 1959) pp.74, 315; *see also* M.E. Chamberlain *Britain and India* (Newton Abbot, David and Charles, 1974) p.23.

8. P.J. Marshall *East Indian Fortunes: the British in Bengal in the Eighteenth Century* (Oxford, University Press, 1976) p.33.
9. J. Gallagher and R. Robinson 'The imperialism of free trade' *Economic History Review,* second series, Vol. 6 No. 1, 1958, pp.1-15.
10. H.S. Fern *The Argentine Republic 1516-1971* (Newton Abbot, David and Charles, 1971) p.12.
11. Denoon *op.cit.* p.12.
12. C. Barlow *The Natural Rubber Industry: Its Development, Technology and Economy in Malaysia* (Kuala Lumpur, Oxford University Press, 1978) p.201.
13. A. Nasr *A History of the Maghrib* (London, Cambridge University Press, 1971).
14. R.J. Hammond *Portugal and Africa, 1815-1910* (Stanford, University Press, 1966) pp.131-2.
15. N. Deerr *The History of Sugar* (London, Chapman and Hall, 1949-50) Vol. 1 p.379; A. Burns *A History of the British West Indies* (London, Dent, 1965) pp.216-7; R.W. Fogel and S.L. Engerman *Time on the Cross* (Boston, Mass., Little and Brown, 1974) Vol. 1 p.21.
16. J. Sheppard *'The Redlegs' of Barbados* (Millwood, N.Y., KTO Press, 1977) p.34.
17. *Ibid.* p.35.
18. Jones *op.cit.* p.165.
19. Chamberlain *op.cit.* pp.66-7.
20. *Ibid.* p.125; P. Spear *The Oxford History of Modern India 1740-1975* (Oxford. University Press, 1975) p.196.
21. Pannikar *op.cit.* p.324.
22. J.R. Scobie *Argentina: a City and a Nation* (New York, Oxford University Press, 1971) Chapter 2; Halperin-Donghi *op.cit.* Chapters 1 and 2; Ferns *op.cit.* Chapter 1; A.J. Bauer, *Chilean Rural Society from the Spanish Conquest to 1930* (Cambridge, University Press, 1975) p.3.
23. G. Pendle *Argentina* (London, Oxford University Press, 1963) p.40.
24. E. Burke *Speeches and Letters on American Affairs* (London, Dent, 1908) p.89.
25. C.M. Andrews *The Colonial Period of American History* (Yale, University Press, 1936) Vol. 2, p.197; also Vol. 3.
26. F.J. Simoons 'The geographic hypothesis and lactose malabsorption' *American Journal of Digestive Diseases* Vol. 23, 1978, pp.963-80.
27. Denoon *op.cit.* p.65 citing A. Trollope *South Africa* (London, 1878).
28. R.C. Mills *The Colonization of Australia 1829-42* (London, Sidgwick and Jackson, 1915) pp.63-4.
29. *Ibid.* pp.205-17.
30. USA Department of Agriculture, Economic Research Service *Major Uses of Land in the USA* (Washington DC, USDA, 1969); European Communities Commission *Memorandum on the Reform of Agriculture in the EEC* (Brussels, EEC, 1968).
31. C.S. Coon *The Hunting People* (London, Cape, 1971) p.i.
32. E.P. Le Veen 'A quantitative analysis of the impact of British suppression policies on the volume of the nineteenth century Atlantic slave trave' in S.L. Engerman and E.D. Genovese (eds) *Race and Slavery in the Western Hemisphere: Quantitative Studies* (Princeton, University Press, 1975).
33. USA Department of Commerce *Historical Statistics of the United States:*

Colonial Times to 1957 (Washington DC, US Department of Commerce, 1960) p.9.
34. M. Weber *The Theory of Social Organisation*. Translated by A.M. Henderson and T. Parsons (London, Collier Macmillan, 1964) p.276.
35. P.J. Thomas *Mercantilism and East Indian Trade* (London, P.S. King & Son, 1926) p.10.
36. Quoted by A.W.L. Shaw (ed) *Great Britain and the Colonies, 1915-1865* (London, Methuen, 1970) p.22.
37. T. Balogh 'The mechanism of neo-imperialism: the economic impact of monetary and commercial institutions in Africa' *Bulletin of the Institute of Economics and Statistics, University of Oxford* Vol. 24 No. 3, 1962, pp.331-46.
38. Chamberlain *op.cit.* p.114.
39. C. Furtado *Economic Development of Latin America* (London, Cambridge University Press, 1970) p.30.
40. A.D. Smith *State and Nation in the Third World* (Brighton, Wheatsheaf, 1983).
41. *See,* for example, J.R. Peperdy 'Rangeland' in W.T.W. Morgan (ed) *East Africa* (London, Longman, 1972) p.170.
42. R. Crotty *Cattle, Economics and Development* pp.128-9.
43. M. Wilson *For Men and Elders* (London, International African Institute, 1977) pp.116-7.
44. N.V. Riasonovsky *A History of Russia* (Oxford, University Press, 1977) p.331.
45. C.M. Cipolla *The Economic History of World Population* (Harmondsworth, Penguin, 1965) p.8.
46. C. Clark *Population Growth and Land Use* (London, Macmillan, 1977) p.108.
47. Based on (a) an increase in national income from £232 millions in 1801 to £1,643 millions in 1901; (2) a drop in the general price index from 167 in 1800-4 to 80 in 1896-1900 (base 1865/85 = 100); and (3) an increase in population from 10.7 to 36.7 millions. Source: B.R. Mitchell and P. Deane *British Historical Statistics* (Cambridge, University Press, 1962).
48. A.M. Carr-Saunders *World Population: Past Growth and Present Trends* (Oxford, University Press, 1936) pp.61-8.
49. Burke *op.cit.*
50. Furtado *op.cit.* pp.17-8.
51. R.M. Morse 'The heritage of Latin America' in L. Hartz (ed) *The Founding of New Societies* (New York, Harcourt, Brace and World, 1964) p.160.
52. D.E. Worcester and W.G. Schaeffer *The Growth and Culture of Latin America* (London, Oxford University Press, 1971) Vol. 1 pp.387-9.
53. Chamberlain *op.cit.* p.111.
54. R.E. Frykenberg *Land Control and Social Structure in Indian History* (Madison, University of Wisconsin Press, 1969) p.xvi.
55. Chamberlain *op.cit.* p.171.
56. J. Strachey *The End of Empire* (London, Victor Gollancz, 1959) p.124.
57. G. Barraclough *An Introduction to Contemporary History* (Harmondsworth, Penguin, 1966) p.154.
58. A.D. Smith *op.cit.* pp.74-5. *See also* Barraclough *op.cit.* pp.154-60.

The Capitalist Colonial Heritage: A Model of Undevelopment

1. In an extensive literature on 'basic needs' *see* for example P. Streeten and S.J. Burki *First Things First: Meeting Basic Human Needs in the Developing Countries* (Oxford, University Press, 1981).
2. H.S. Klein *Parties and Political Change in Bolivia 1880-1952* (Cambridge, University Press, 1969) pp.160-7, 403-4.
3. R.M. Morse 'The heritage of Latin America' in L. Hartz (ed) *The Founding of New Societies* (New York, Harcourt, Brace and World, 1964) pp.161-2.
4. P. Spear *The Oxford History of Modern India* (London, Oxford University Press, 1975) p.197.
5. India *Census of Population 1971. General Report* (New Delhi, Registrar General and Census Commissioners, 1975) pp.xxvii-xxxii.
6. R. Crotty *Cattle, Economics and Development* (Slough, CAB, 1980) Chapter 9.
7. P. Laslett 'Introduction' in E.A. Wrigley (ed) *An Introduction to English Historical Demography* (London, Weidenfeld and Nicolson, 1966) p.6.
8. E.A. Wrigley *Population and History* (London, Weidenfeld and Nicolson, 1969) p.13.
9. J. Hajnal 'European marriage patterns in perspective' in D.V. Glass and D.E.C. Eversley (eds) *Population in History* (London, Arnold, 1965) pp.101-43.
10. R. Crotty *Irish Agricultural Production* (Cork, University Press, 1966) pp.13-4.
11. Spear *op.cit.* p.197.
12. For a review of current thought on the subject, *see* R.H. Cassen 'Population and development: a survey' in P. Streeten and R. Jolly (eds) *Recent Issues in World Development: a Collection of Survey Articles* (Oxford, Pergamon, 1981).
13. *Ibid.* pp.4-10.
14. M. Wilson *For Men and Elders* (London, International African Institute, 1977) p.68.
15. United Nations, Department of International Economic and Social Affairs *Population Studies No. 79 World Population Trends and Policies 1981 Monitoring Report* Vol. 1. (New York, UN, 1982).
16. *Guardian* 27.4.1981.
17. D.E. Worcester and W.G. Schaeffer *The Growth and Culture of Latin America* (London, Oxford University Press, 1982) Vol. 1, p.228.
18. Crotty, 1980 *op.cit.* p.101.
19. *See*, for example, M.P. Pandey *Land Records and the Agrarian Situation in Bihar* (Calcutta, Debesh Duta, 1980) p.15; J. Lindauer and S. Singh *Land Taxation and Indian Economic Development* (New Delhi, Kalyani Publications, 1979) pp.138-9.
20. Crotty, 1980 *op.cit.* p.138.
21. J.R. Peperdy 'Rangelands' in W.T.W. Morgan (ed) *East Africa* (London, Longman, 1972) p.170.
22. P.H. Gulliver *The Family Herds: a Study of Two Pastoral Tribes in East Africa* (London, Rutledge, 1955) p.247.
23. E.A. Ritter *Shaka Zulu; The Rise of the Zulu Empire* (London, Allen Lane, 1976).
24. G. Bennett 'Tribalism in politics' in P.H. Gulliver (ed) *Tradition and Transition in East Africa* (London, Routledge and Keegan Paul, 1969).
25. J. Middleton (ed) *Peoples of Africa* (London, Cavendish Books, 1978) p.37.

26. Crotty, 1980 *op.cit.* Chapter 9.
27. Middleton *op.cit.* p.8.
28. C. Clark *Population Growth and Land Use* (London, Macmillan, 1977) p.108.
29. N.M. Tainton *Veld and Pasture Management in South Africa* (Pietermaritzburgh, Shuter and Shooter Ltd. in association with University of Natal Press, 1981).
30. A. Grainger *How People Make Deserts: How They Can Stop* (London, Earthscan, 1982).
31. FAO *Production Yearbook 1981* (Rome, FAO, 1981) p.79.
32. Crotty, 1980 *op.cit.* p.174.
33. R. Crotty 'Operation Flood: another view' *The Illustrated Weekly of India* 19.2.1984.
34. FAO *op.cit.* pp.45-55.
35. R. Crotty, *Report of a study of communal grazing in Kwa Zulu* (Mimeograph, University of Kwa Zulu, 1983).
36. *See Financial Times* 12.4.1979 for an account of an attempt to farm extensively otherwise in the Amazonian basin.
37. J. Kennedy *A History of Malaya AD 1400-1950* (London, Macmillan, 1970) p.188; Malaya, Department of Statistics *Population Census 1956. Final Report* (Kuala Lumpur, Government Printers, 1960).
38. F. Avorkliyah 'Development of non-traditional exports in Ghana: the case for natural rubber' (M.Sc. thesis, unpublished, University of Dublin, 1983).
39. A. Crotty 'The problems of smallholder agriculture in Southwest Perak state, Malaysia' (B.A. dissertation, unpublished, University of Dublin, 1978) p.27.
40. *Ibid.* Appendix Table 5.
41. FAO *Production Yearbook 1966; Ditto 1981* (Rome, FAO, 1966, 1981).
42. *See,* for example, A. Crotty *op.cit.*
43. *See,* for example, R.E. Evenson and Y. Kislev *Agricultural Research and Productivity* (New Haven, Yale University Press, 1975); J. Simmons 'Education for development reconsidered' in M.P. Todaro (ed) *The Struggle for Economic Development* (London, Longman, 1983); R.M. Sundrum *Development Economics* (Chichester, Wiley, 1983) Chapter 8.
44. R. Crotty, 1980 *op.cit.* Chapter 8.
45. *Ibid.* p.129.
46. S. Sandford, *Management of Pastoral Development in the Third World* (Chichester, Wiley, 1983).
47. R. Crotty *The Cattle Crisis and the Small Farmer* (Mullingar, National Land League, 1974) pp.27-30.
48. G. List *The National System of Political Economy.* Translated by S.S. Lloyd. (London, Longman and Co., 1885).
49. C. Furtado *Economic Development of Latin America* (London, Cambridge University Press) pp.82-92.
50. M. Moffitt *The World's Money: International Banking from Bretton Woods to the Brink of Insolvency* (London, Michael Joseph, 1983) pp.94-6.
51. M. Nkuba 'A pre-feasibility study for the manufacture of machined auto-components in Tanzania' (M.Sc. thesis, unpublished, University of Dublin, 1984/5).
52. Sundrum *op.cit.* p.307.

53. J.P. Lewis *Development Cooperation 1981 Review* (Paris, OECD, 1981).
54. UK Department of Employment *Family Expenditure Survey 1972; Ditto 1982;* UK Central Statistics Office *Annual Abstract of Statistics 1972; Ditto 1984.* (London, HMSO).
55. M.E. Chamberlain *Britain and India* (London, Methuen, 1976) p.123.
56. *Daily telegrpah* 24.6.1985.
57. Crotty, 1980 *op.cit.* p.174.
58. Ireland, Department of Foreign Affairs *Assistance to Developing Countries: Report for the Year 1984* (Dublin, Stationery Office, 1985).
59. Crotty, 1980 *op.cit.* p.181.
60. *Ibid.* p.178.
61. C.M. Cipolla *The Economic History of World Population* (Harmondsworth, Penguin, 1965) p.105.
62. *See also* S. George *Operation Flood* (New Delhi, Oxford University Press, 1985).
63. FAO 1981 *op.cit.*
64. M. Morishima *Why Has Japan 'Succeeded'?* (Cambridge, University Press, 1982) pp.18-19.
65. E.O. Reischauer *The Japanese* (London, Harvard University Press, 1977) pp.8-25.
66. *Ibid.* p.57.
67. *Ibid.* p.80.
68. G.C. Allen *A Short Economic History of Modern Japan* (London, Allen and Unwin, 1972) pp.15, 42.
69. T. Smith *The Agrarian Origins of Modern Japan* (Stanford, University Press, 1959) p.211.
70. Allen *op.cit.* pp.194-201.
71. *People's Daily* Peking, as reported in *Irish Times* 10.2.1984.
72. Liu Zheng *et al. China's Population: Problems and Prospects* (Beijing, New World Press, 1981) pp.6-31.
73. Sundrum *op.cit.* p.307.
74. Moffitt *op.cit.* p.102.
75. T.W. Schultz 'A critique of US foreign aid' in K.C. Nobe and R.K. Sampath *Issues in Third World Development* (Epping, Bowker Publishing Co. 1984).
76. M. Godet and O. Ruyssen *The Old World and the New Technologies* EEC series 'European Perspectives' (Brussels, EEC, 1982).
77. Radio Telefis Eireann *Today Tonight* Programme on moneylending, 3 and 4 December, 1985.

Index

Italics indicate Chapter, Section or Sub-Section on topic.